MILTON STUDIES
53

Laura L. Knoppers
Pennsylvania State University
EDITOR

EDITORIAL BOARD

Sharon Achinstein
University of Oxford

Thomas N. Corns
Bangor University, Wales

Mario A. Di Cesare
University of North Carolina, Asheville

Karen L. Edwards
University of Exeter

Stephen M. Fallon
University of Notre Dame

Stanley Fish
Florida International University

Estelle Haan
Queen's University, Belfast

Maggie Kilgour
McGill University

Paul J. Klemp
University of Wisconsin, Oshkosh

Barbara Kiefer Lewalski
Harvard University

David Loewenstein
University of Wisconsin, Madison

Catherine Gimelli Martin
University of Memphis

Stella Revard
Southern Illinois University

John Rogers
Yale University

Jason P. Rosenblatt
Georgetown University

Elizabeth Sauer
Brock University

Nigel Smith
Princeton University

Paul Stevens
University of Toronto

James D. Simmonds
FOUNDING EDITOR, 1967–1991

Albert C. Labriola
EDITOR, 1992–2009

❧ MILTON STUDIES ❧

Volume 53

Edited by Laura L. Knoppers

DUQUESNE UNIVERSITY PRESS
PITTSBURGH, PENNSYLVANIA

Milton Studies is published annually by Duquesne University Press as a forum for Milton scholarship and criticism. Essays submitted for publication may focus on any aspect of John Milton's life and writing, including biography; literary history; Milton's work in its literary, intellectual, political, or cultural contexts; Milton's influence on or relationship to other writers; or the history of critical response to his work.

Manuscripts should conform to *The Chicago Manual of Style* and be approximately 8,000–12,000 words in length. Authors should include a written statement that the manuscript is being submitted exclusively to *Milton Studies*. We encourage electronic submissions in Microsoft Word format, sent to llk6@psu.edu, followed by one hard copy (printout) of the essay sent by regular mail to Laura L. Knoppers, Editor, *Milton Studies*, Department of English, Burrowes Building, The Pennsylvania State University, University Park, PA 16802.

Milton Studies does not review books.

Within the United States, *Milton Studies* may be ordered from the Duquesne University Press, c/o CUP Services, 750 Cascadilla Street, Box 6525, Ithaca, N.Y., 14851-6525. Toll free (800) 666-2211.

Copyright © 2012 Duquesne University Press
All rights reserved

Published in the United States of America by
DUQUESNE UNIVERSITY PRESS
600 Forbes Avenue
Pittsburgh, Pennsylvania 15282

No part of this book may be used or reproduced,
in any manner or form whatsoever,
without written permission from the publisher,
except in the case of short quotations
in critical articles or reviews.

"Beech," "Sycamore," "The Subverted Flower," "The Most of It," and "Never Again Would Birds' Song Be the Same" are from the book *The Poetry of Robert Frost*, edited by Edward Connery Lathem. Copyright © 1969 by Henry Holt and Company, copyright © 1942 by Robert Frost, copyright © 1970 by Lesley Frost Ballantine. Reprinted with permission.

ISSN 0076-8820
ISBN 978-0-8207-0464-7

∞ Printed on acid-free paper

Contents

Preface   vii

Language, Style, and Form

Universis Christi Ecclesiis: Milton's Epistle for
   De doctrina Christiana   3
     JOHN K. HALE AND J. DONALD CULLINGTON

The Experimental Form of *Lycidas*   17
     JAMES RUTHERFORD

Gender, Law, and Liberty in the Garden

Domestic Adam   41
     ELISABETH LIEBERT

Milton's Natural Law: Divorce and Individual Property   69
     MICHAEL KOMOROWSKI

Miltonic Proportions: Divine Distribution and the
   Nature of the Lot in *Paradise Lost*   101
     JOSEPH WALLACE

Hermeneutics and Interpretation

Pilgrimage in *Paradise Lost*   127
     BEATRICE GROVES

Fighting for Saint Michael: The Typology of Defeat in
   Milton's Celestial and Sublunary Civil Wars   147
     PATRICIA CROUCH

From Judgment to Interpretation: Eighteenth Century
    Critics of Milton's *Paradise Lost* 181
        ESTHER YU

Legacy, Choice, and the Human Condition

Milton as Muse for Keats, Shelley, and Frost 205
    CARTER REVARD

Is There Freedom Afterwards? A Dialogue between
    Paradise Lost and DeLillo's *Falling Man* 235
        RACHEL FALCONER

Notes 257

Index 313

Preface

Responding to the outcry produced by his divorce tracts, Milton deployed the age-old technique of denigrating his critics: "Licence they mean when they cry libertie."[1] Milton's satiric Sonnet 12 recounts how he had "but prompt[ed] the age to quit their cloggs / By the known rules of antient libertie" (1–2), only to find himself misunderstood and maligned, environed by "a barbarous noise.../ Of Owles and Cuckoes, Asses, Apes and Doggs" (3–4). In Sonnet 11, Milton similarly imagined the passersby gawking at the Greek title of *Tetrachordon* in the bookseller's stall ("bless us! what a word on / A title page is this!" [5–6]), while others "in file / Stand spelling fals" [6–7]. With regard to his cherished topic of liberty (domestic, religious, civil), Milton kept a close eye on his readers: sometimes praising, sometimes disparaging, and sometimes despairing over their real or imagined responses.

A number of essays in this volume of *Milton Studies* reconsider questions of reading and interpretation, especially in regard to liberty in Milton's time and its resonance for our own day. Breaking new ground and challenging previous assumptions, the contributors to this volume look at readers of Milton from the seventeenth to the twenty-first century, at Milton himself interpreting and reworking tradition, and at Miltonic characters such as Adam and

Eve as they strive to interpret the nature and limits of their freedom in relationship to one another and to God. In the first section, "Language, Style, and Form," John K. Hale and J. Donald Cullington remind us of the importance of attending to the form, address, style, and etymology of Milton's Latin, with particular attention to the epistle to *De doctrina Christiana*, as it negotiates authority, community, and heterodoxy. Reexamining the form of *Lycidas*, James Rutherford finds not a tripartite structure but a gradual process of resolution, moving from irregular to regular rhythms, rhyme patterns, and paragraph forms, and he argues that this process has both ontological and political meaning, adumbrating Milton's revolutionary prose and the monism of *Paradise Lost*.

Beginning part 2, "Gender, Law, and Liberty in the Garden," Elisabeth Liebert brings domestic conduct books to bear on the much-debated separation scene of book 9 of *Paradise Lost*. For Liebert, conduct book advice on modes of marital address and management of disputes serves as a lens for evaluating Adam and Eve's domestic exchange. Michael Komoroski examines how, as a part of natural law, divorce for Milton takes precedence over marriage as a positive law, contributing to Adam and Eve's fatal confusion over the limits of natural law and helping to bring about the Fall in *Paradise Lost*. Joseph Wallace shows how the delicate balance of hierarchical relationships and human freedom in the seventeenth century discourse of lots shapes Milton's representation of gender, proportionality, and freedom in Eden and makes particularly effective Satan's deployment of chance and the lot in tempting Eve.

Part 3, "Hermeneutics and Interpretation," includes both Milton's revisions of earlier traditions and practices and the uses of biblical hermeneutics to interpret Milton's own texts. Opening this part, Beatrice Groves situates Adam's misunderstanding of place in his lament for the garden in book 11 of *Paradise Lost* as part of Milton's larger critique and transformation of place-pilgrimage into spiritual growth and discipleship. Patricia Crouch examines the role of the Archangel Michael in Milton's war in heaven alongside a visual and interpretive tradition of Michael as rival to the Son of God, demonstrating how Milton's reworking has political significance in the context of the English revolution. Esther Yu shows a shift in critical analysis from eighteenth century readers (including the notorious Richard Bentley) who construed Milton's text using the aesthetic precepts of Aristotelian principles to other readers who turned to biblical hermeneutics and scriptural exegesis to develop close readings of the Miltonic text, strikingly aligned with mid-twentieth-century New Criticism.

In part 4, "Legacy, Choice, and the Human Condition," Carter Revard explores how later poets, including Keats, Shelley, and Frost, use the "classic" work of Milton to amplify their own voices, appropriating Miltonic keywords, characters, and situations to construct their own poetic identity and to delineate shared struggles. Finally, Rachel Falconer examines Milton's *Paradise Lost* and DeLillo's *Falling Man*, a novel on 9/11, as meditating on human freedom in the face of tragedy, constituting a choice to embrace one's fall, whether from a burning tower or on the brink of heaven, pursued by a wrathful deity.

Essays in this volume, by both newer and more established scholars in the Milton community, thus meditate on hermeneutics and freedom, on Adam and Eve themselves engaged in hermeneutical endeavor (not least to understand and implement their own free choices), on Milton negotiating with earlier practices and traditions, and on Milton's own voice appropriated and revised. If a far cry from the ruminations of the gawking customers in the seventeenth century London bookseller's stall, our debate on Miltonic texts and ideas continues. Indeed, Milton's views can speak to modern views of liberty and to modern pressures and realities that could not have been imagined in his own day.

Laura L. Knoppers

Language, Style, and Form

Universsis Christi Ecclesiis: Milton's Epistle for *De doctrina Christiana*

John K. Hale and J. Donald Cullington

Our edition of John Milton's unorthodox, still controversial systematic theology appears as volume 8 of the new Oxford University Press *Complete Works of John Milton*.[1] It seeks a greater fidelity to Milton's manuscript, by dint of a complete new transcription, fuller edition and notes that keep close to the dictated words, and a translation more literal (and again fuller) than preceding ones. Not that these are the only useful ways to present the work, but they do give new information and emphases, building on the strengths of predecessors, or assuming them in order to offer readers a new scope and methods.

Those predecessors have been three. After the manuscript had lurked unpublished in a cupboard in Whitehall for 140 years, the *editio princeps* was brought out in 1825, with translation and notes, by Charles R. Sumner.[2] The next edition was that of the Columbia *Works* of the 1930s, heavily dependent on Sumner's work.[3] Although no further edition of *De doctrina* has followed until now, the Yale prose works volume took huge strides forward, in the translation of John Carey and the annotations of Maurice

Kelley.⁴ It is not a full edition, however, since it has no Latin text. It lacks Milton's own words. Consequently, our work seeks to take readers back to the original, to the manuscript, back past even Sumner's modernizing and harmonizing of the Latin.⁵

We do this, not on a principle, as the only right way to edit, but as what this text needs now. Four emphases in particular inform our approach to Milton's text. They are needed at once, for its opening epistle, and are illustrated in the following discussion: *linguistic*, with particular attention to his Latin idiolect; *epistolary*, since his choice and stance of address are unique; *allusive*, chiefly scriptural; and *etymological*, since as elsewhere Milton himself wielded etymology to prove his point.⁶

Linguistic or Philological

Here are the opening words, as transcribed from the manuscript (fig. 1) and translated:

> [IO]ANNES MILTONUS Anglus
> Universis Christi Ecclesiis, nec non omnibus
> Fidem Christianam ubicunque Gentium profiten=
> tibus pacem & Veritatis agnitionem, salutemque in
> Deo Patre, ac Domino nostro Iesu Christo
> sempiternam.

> [John Milton Englishman *To all the churches of Christ*, and also to all who profess the Christian faith anywhere among the peoples, [declares] peace, and recognition of the Truth, and everlasting salvation in God our Father and our Lord Jesus Christ.]

The address is to two groups of readers, who are joined by *nec non*. Translators render *nec non* by the English "and." They do the same for the three further connectives in the address, *et*, *-que*, and *ac*. A fourfold "And" homogenizes the four links, though Milton had differentiated them, and makes the syntax tamely additive. But the double negative of *nec non* ("and-not-not") becomes a strong positive in Latin. It means "and indeed," or "and furthermore," to go by the *Oxford Latin Dictionary*, s.v. *neque*. *Nec non* does not meekly add, or set things in simple parallel: it extends, corroborates, or pushes the speaker's emphasis forward from the first onto

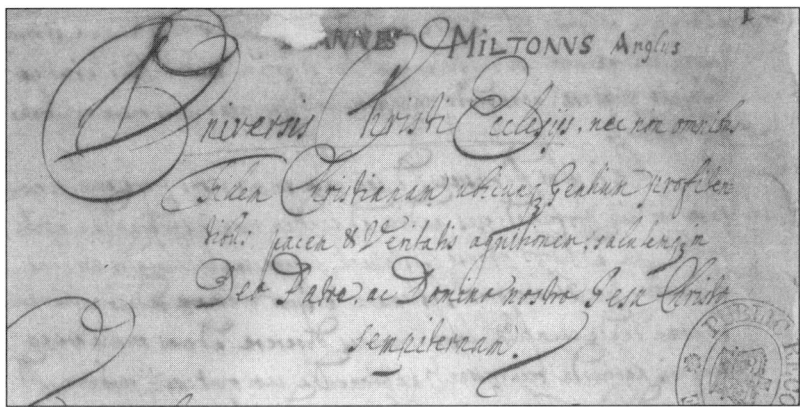

Fig. 1. Opening (superscription), p. 1 (detail), *De doctrina Christiana*. State Papers 9/61. By permission of the National Archives, London.

the second part of the connection. In the present case, therefore, Milton is not merely addressing *Universis Christi Ecclesiis* (as if that were not bold enough). More than that, he is addressing believing individuals, wherever they may be among the *Gentes,* nations. A Latinist should insist that the second group outweigh the first in the speaker's intention; and might infer that such believers, to be found anywhere, might not be found inside the churches; or that readers of a book are individuals, placed willy-nilly in a Protestant or solo reader posture, where Milton as he writes is greeting them but has already begun working on them, to engineer a devout and open-minded suspension of set belief. The inferences are speculative, but based on a firm and new observation.

In that case, what about the next three connectives, all rendered by a further colorless "and" in translations? Do the three different connectives repeat one another, though *Nec non* had a different and greater force? Why do these three come in this sequence, *et* (written &), suffix *-que,* then *ac*?

The general explanation is that stylish Latin, such as this clarion call to believers, observes the general principle of *variatio*. Rhetorically speaking, the humanist Latinist either builds a series of equal *ets*, for a cumulative effect like that of Blake in "A Poison Tree"; or resorts to synonyms to avoid inert repetition.

But a particularizing explanation is more convincing, that Milton's speaking voice and innate sense of verbal rhythm may lie behind (or at least partly account for) the use of varying copulas and the insertion of commas. The comma before *salutemque* both separates *salutem* from *agnitionem* and makes it almost equal in weight to that word. The *-que* rolls on beautifully to *in Deo*; the comma after *Patre* separates the first member of the Trinity from the second, while the use of *ac*, on the other hand, ensures that the two are less separated than if *et* had been used.

Should we furthermore draw in wider contexts, like Milton's theological axioms, to infer that the presence of the first two persons of the Trinity alerts us to the absence of the third, in whom he is always less interested? This seems like illegitimate inference from extraneous knowledge, or from the hindsight of reading book 1, chapters 5–7. There must be good reason for any argument from silence. One such good reason might be the habits of New Testament writers when opening or closing some address to churches and believers. But their habit is to speak of God and Christ, and leave it at that, although the close of 2 Corinthians is an exception. Accordingly, we must answer no to our question. The reasoning from silence is to be resisted. We raise the issue, nevertheless, to call attention to lines of argument that are regularly opened up by a close, linguistic reading of the original Latin words.

Overinterpretation of another sort is a risk. Literary appreciation that feeds off linguistic observation can glorify the words of the text and assume they are the best possible—as in a Whiggish interpretation of history, where only the actual winners could ever have won, and oh what a good, good thing. In reply, one could reason, meekly, that after so many years of underinterpretation, Milton's Latin style as prominently displayed in the superscription might benefit from a little excess of zeal. A stronger reply is that to an informed, close reader the signs of authorial polish and flair are plain enough. Can it be an accident that the whole superscription is a virtual tricolon, or that successive limbs expand, with any apparent retreat followed by further advance, like the waves of an incoming tide? Or that the final limb is poised between the balancing of *salutemque* with *sempiternam*—alliteration, consonance, rhythm, and grammatical agreement, all cooperating sonorously? These should be *heard*, and relished. Milton is in top form, to please and so persuade.

Epistolary

Maurice Kelley observes, "Renaissance theologians tended to address their works to noblemen, patrons, friends, or to the reader; and I have not noted another Renaissance systematic theology directed, like Milton's, to the combined churches of Christ and all Christians" (YP 6:117n2). Working in Princeton, Kelley had access to many more such theologies than the present writers do, but it is naturally very hard to prove uniqueness.

Certainly, if one looks at the prefatorial matter of Milton's known structural models, those of William Ames and of Johann Wollebius,[7] he is manifestly as unlike them in this regard as he is in his way with biblical citations (see next section). The other English theologies examined do as these two, addressing patrons humbly, and readers "praemonitorially." They do not come near to Milton's epistolary trumpet blast. We do not exaggerate: its envoi is no less confident, righteous, or uncompromising. This accords with Milton's stance and voice within controversy, not to mention his combative personality: the message, *Candido lectori* or not, is that here comes the whole man.

Kelley continues, "Both this universality and his form Milton derives from Paul. Romans, Milton suggests [MS 386], was addressed not merely to that church but to believers in general; and Milton's awareness of Paul's epistolary openings is indicated by his comment [MS 7], '*Paul, a servant of Jesus Christ*—in this way he begins nearly all the rest of his epistles.' And also below [MS 63]."[8]

Kelley's first comment ("not merely...believers in general") resembles what was said in our first section about *nec non*. But it is not the identical point. Milton at MS 386, in his chapter on Scripture, says that Peter says Paul wrote not only to the church at

Rome but also to all believers ("scripsisse tamen non illis solùm, sed omnibus fidelibus hîc ait Petrus"). But Milton cites passages from 2 Peter which do not actually show this. It seems that Milton is making an inference that is not made explicit in Scripture itself, but that nonetheless tallies with his superscription.

Kelley's astute but elliptical comment is matched by his second, Milton's "awareness of Paul's epistolary openings," at MS 7 and 63 (YP 6:117n2). What exactly is he aware of, in his own opening? It is not only Paul, and not only openings, that shape Milton's epistle.[9] For example, the "recognition of the Truth," *Veritatis agnitionem*, echoes John more than Paul, truth being a continuing keyword of 2 John, while *agnitionem* for *epignōsin*, "recognition" not general or straightforward "cognition," is a general New Testament subsong. Milton's awareness and applications extend beyond Paul, as one would expect.

Similarly at the ending, or envoi (fig. 2), Milton combines good wishes or even benediction for his "brothers" (*fratres*) with admonition:

> De caetero, fratres, veritatem colite cum charitate; de his, prout Dei spiritus vobis praeiverit, ita iudicate: his mecum utimini, vel ne utimini quidem, nisi fide non dubia scripturarumque claritate persuasi; in Christo denique Servatore ac Domino nostro vivite ac valete.
>
> [For the rest, my brothers, cultivate the truth with charity; judge of this writing according to the spirit of God guiding you; use it with me, or indeed do not use it, unless I have persuaded you with full conviction by the clarity of the Bible; last of all, live and thrive in Christ our Saviour and Lord.] (MS 5, OM 8:10, YP 6:124, CM 14.14)

Peter's letters close with benediction, as does Jude doxologically (the "*general* epistle of Jude," says this copy of the KJV). "Cultivate the truth with love" echoes John again, both the Gospel and Epistles that bear his name. Interspersed with benediction and admonition we read an admonition that is all Milton's own, both in style and substance. The double litotes has both: "his mecum

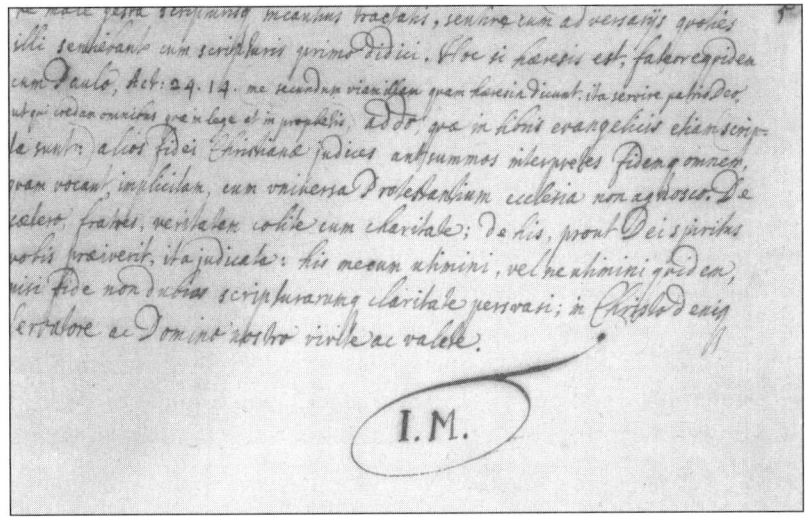

Fig. 2. Envoi, p. 5 (detail), *De doctrina Christiana*. State Papers 9/61. By permission of the National Archives, London.

utimini, vel ne utimini quidem, nisi fide non dubia scripturarumque claritate persuasi" ("use it [this writing of mine] with me, or indeed do not use it, unless I have persuaded you with indubitable conviction by the clarity of the Bible"). "Join me, but only if you agree with me" is said in Milton's habitual voice of candor. Then he signs off with a flourish: "in Christo...vivite ac valete" pairs the alliterative imperatives to make a godly hendiadys.[10]

Do these various other voices diminish the centrality of Paul as exemplar in Milton's epistle? Quite the contrary, as will emerge in the third and fourth sections. But we do find other New Testament letter writers contributing to the epistolary character of the superscription, and to the ending. They do it less when the epistle itself begins. The lengthy hypotactic contextualizing and apologia are Ciceronian after the manner of humanist theological writing. The chief exception to this statement is where the text becomes allusive.

Allusion to Scripture

Allusion is a complex and disputatious concept, in Milton as elsewhere. For example, his majestic epic simile, comparing the fallen angels to the leaves of Vallombrosa, then to the drowned soldiers of Pharaoh, is allusion as much as it is simile; it is the length that makes it "epic" simile. But because it has such power, so many points of contact, actual and imaginable, between the leaves or soldiery and the angels, readers will disagree forever about how many of the lesser details Milton intended us to notice. The position resembles allegory in Spenser or prophecy in Revelation (or Nostradamus). For our present purposes, which concern Milton alluding to Scripture, only three of the safer possibilities are being examined.

All three exhibit the character summed up by George Caird, who discusses allusion among "cohesive" uses of language. Even phatic communion is not necessarily trivial, for it "may tap deep springs of conduct, reminding us of early influences and lost loves." Caird goes on, "Consider the allusive use of the word 'cross' in the letters of Paul." We have not, yet, noticed it as part of Milton's Pauline mindset. But these further words do apply: "Much of the use of the Old Testament in the New is of this allusive kind, establishing rapport between author and reader and giving confidence in a background of shared assumptions. A quotation may be the basis of an appeal to authority, but an allusion is always a reminder of what is held in common."[11] Milton certainly exploits this use of allusion. He knows that he needs this rapport, confidence, and sharing, even while he assumes that his knowledge of Scripture will bring a derivative or delegated authority.

First, there are the undeclared but striking allusions just assembled from the pastoral epistles. These are localized, not ubiquitous, and belong with the chosen genre, the letter—Milton's "epistle general." Second are the less striking and short words or phrases which arise within the flow of Milton's narrative, first contextual, then personal. Some may not be felt as allusion, being in the first instance ordinary Latin or unemphatic metaphors. Since these may go unrecognized or unconsidered, we offer them as possibilities, ones that accord with Milton's mind and imagination in other places, hoping, too, that other readers will propose further specimens. The mental habit suits that Bible-steeped age. Third, we consider the few explicit citations of Scripture within the epistle. All are of Paul. They exemplify Milton's proclaimed method, and foreshadow the teeming proof-texts of the treatise proper.

Since in general the epistle is reliant on New Testament letters, it deserves comment that the second sort of allusions comes from the Gospels. At MS 3 (OM 8:6, YP 6:121, CM 14.8), Milton speaks of his labors to compile a theology thus: "I had by God's good help gained a great strengthening for my faith, or rather, I had stored a treasure." His words are *subsidium* and *thesaurum*. We have translated the former as "a strengthening," but the word might mean a "help" or "support" for his faith. The uncertainty in translating prevents us from connecting it to scriptural images found in the Psalms and widely: "a very present help in trouble," or the parable of the houses with secure and insecure "foundations." Similarly, images of "standing" firm or of the "light of truth" come readily to the devout, but are too common and brief to be reckoned as full allusion. They are better read as Caird's reassuring shared diction. But the treasure-house image more directly alludes to Gospel teaching, wherever Jesus speaks of householders who store up treasure, build treasure houses, or store up treasure in heaven. *Reposuisse* with *thesaurum* makes this plainer, corresponding to Beza's *recondere* at Matthew 6:19. And the following allusion to spiritual wealth corroborates, "haec, quibus melius aut pretiosius nihil habeo" ("this my best and most precious possession"). Ensuing mentions of "truth" and "the light of truth" confirm a felt presence of John's formulations.

Citations, fortunately, are unmistakable. All three of them come in the later, more argumentative portion of the epistle, and all derive from Paul. One comes from 1 Thessalonians 5:21 at MS 3; one from Romans 16:17–18 at MS 4; and one from Acts 24:14 at MS 5. The first quotes Paul without giving the reference, the second quotes with the reference, and the third is Luke reporting

Paul's words. As allusions, the three seem to come in ascending order of fullness and importance. Whether that is intentional we cannot know, though the rhetorical surroundings make it likely, and something may emerge from inspecting each allusion. At the least, we should note a gravitational pull back to Paul as the epistle enters on more energetic apologia.

First, "explorare omnia iubeamur" (we are enjoined to "investigate all things"). The pronoun "we" is working cohesively, in obedience to Paul's words. Whether Paul meant the same things by "all things" as Milton does is less likely, given the indefiniteness of "all." It may not mean absolutely all, only all of what the speaker is thinking about. Nor does Milton explore all, in practice drawing some axiomatic boundaries. But in context, he uses Paul's phrasing to win readers over to his side, against people who claim that controversy sets the church in undesirable uproar.

The Romans passage has to pull more weight, because Milton has begun an urgent, climactic defense against charges of heresy. It reads in full:

> Quibus Ego, id solum fuisse haeresin, quoties hoc nomen in vitio ponitur, aetate Apostolorum, quicquid eorum doctrinae, viva voce traditae, cum libri Evangelici nondum extarent, repugnabat; eosque solos fuisse haereticos, qui, iuxta illud Rom: 16. 17. 18. *dissidia et scandala praeter doctrinam Apostolicam faciebant; non Domino nostro Iesu Christo servientes, sed suo ventri:* conscriptis demum libris evangelicis, pari ratione nihil nisi quod iis repugnat, posse iure nominari haeresin respondeo. (MS 4)

> [To such people I answer, that in the time of the Apostles, when the Evangelical books did not yet exist, whenever the word heresy was used as an accusation, the only heresy was what contradicted the Apostles' teaching as orally transmitted; and the only heretics were those who, according to Rom. 16: 17–18, *were causing disagreements and offences contrary to the Apostolical teaching; not serving our Lord Jesus Christ, but their own belly.* By the same reasoning, then, I answer that after the Evangelical books had finally been put together in writing, nothing can rightly be termed heresy except what conflicts with *them.*]

Neatly, Milton aligns himself with "the Apostolical teaching." He sees it as a teaching older and (by implication) more authentic than the Gospels. He lines up with Paul in a stern and dismissive mood. And if we press the fact that he continues his citation into Paul's final condemnation of those undoubted heretical troublemakers ("undoubted" because we cannot doubt Paul), we may feel an incipient allusion of our previous type, aligning the belly-servers with anyone now who doubts Milton's orthodoxy; for he has Paul and the "Apostolical" teaching on his side, doesn't he? Milton does not make this final step, let alone voice it explicitly; but if you read slowly and responsively, it does hang in the air.

The epistle is coming up the home stretch, into head-on rebuttal of any accusations of heresy (which it is clear he is anticipating, and which are made likely by some of the ideas that will appear in the treatise). He launches, finally, into a definition or redefinition of the Greek word for heresy, *hairesis*. The argument is by etymology, but also by adducing Paul yet again, this time the Paul of Acts. So once again, our four methods are not working in isolation, but in forceful conjunction.

Etymological Proof

Now Milton nails his colors to the mast, his theses to the church door: the passage is given in its entirety:

> De me, libris tantummodo sacris adhaeresco; haeresin aliam, sectam aliam sequor nullam; haereticorum, quos vocant, libros perlegeram nullos, cum ex eorum numero, qui orthodoxi audiunt, [MS 5] re male gesta scripturisque incautius tractatis, sentire cum adversariis quoties illi sentiebant cum scripturis primo didici. Hoc si haeresis est, fateor equidem cum Paulo, Act: 24.14. *me secundum viam illam quam haeresin dicunt, ita servire patrio Deo, ut qui credam omnibus quae in lege et in prophetis*, addo, quae in libris evangelicis etiam scripta sunt: alios fidei Christianae iudices aut summos interpretes fidemque omnem, quam vocant, implicitam, cum universa Protestantium ecclesia non agnosco.

> [As for me, I cleave to the holy writings alone; I follow no other heresy, no other party line; I had read no books by the heretics, so-called, when I first learnt from the blunders and incautious scriptural interpretations of those who are known as the orthodox, [MS 5] to agree with their opponents whenever those opponents agreed with scripture. If this is heresy, I for my part confess, with Paul, Acts 24:14, that *following the path which they call a heresy, thus I serve the God of my fathers, since I believe all the things which are written in the law and in the prophets;* to which I add, the things too which are written in the evangelical books: along with the whole church of Protestants, I refuse to recognize any other judges of Christian faith or paramount interpreters, and all implicit faith, as people call it.]

This argument has several steps, but its climax comes where Milton quotes Paul,[12] to equate "following the way of our fathers" with true and right *haeresis*, choice. How etymological is Paul (or Luke) being, and how decisive does Milton make etymology? We take these points in order.

Milton says, "I follow no other heresy, or party, than the holy writings alone." So he cannot be a heretic. "Nor have I been influenced by the writings of the so-called heretics, for I had not read them when I learnt the true principle, of sifting misinterpretations by the so-called orthodox so as to find myself agreeing with their opponents when the latter had got scripture right." The explanatory force comes from two linguistic points, that the *orthodox*, whose self-assigned name in Greek means *right-thinking*, can be wrong, so implying that their name for opponents is pejorative and self-serving. So are their opponents heretics, and what *is* heresy? Call his belief heresy, but it is that of Paul answering Tertullus before Felix; it is the way of our fathers, which he follows: the law and the prophets, to which add the "things written in the evangelical books"—presumably not only the four Gospels, but the rest of the New Testament, hence of necessity Acts 24:14 itself.

These steps include one about the true—etymological, from *etymos logos*, "true account" or "truth of words"—versus partisan use of names, the struggle for ownership. What is less evident is that Milton is exploiting the Latin translation of the Greek by Beza (which, by the way, differs from that of the Syriac by Tremellius). For the words "haeresin aliam, sectam aliam sequor nullam" ("I follow no other heresy, no other party line"), Milton found no word in the Greek which means "follow"; only Beza's preposition *secundum* for Luke's *kata*. But *secundum* derives from the same root (*sec-*) as appears in Milton's *secta* ("path" or "way") and in the verb *sequor* itself. What in Greek you "choose" is your *hairesis*, from the verb *haireō*: in Latin what you "follow" is the same thing, in a distinct, buried metaphor and actually closer to Paul's *hodon*, corresponding to Hebrew *derek*. The "way" matters more than the choosing or choice. This is clearer in Paul than in Milton, perhaps because charges of heresy were not quite such a bugbear as they since became.[13]

In any event, what Milton does, multilingually, is to harness both metaphors at the outset, before finding them in the Latin of Beza's Paul: "secundum viam illam quam haeresin dicunt." The argument pivots on etymology, but not on pedantry. So annotators, for their sins, must supply the pedantry. Otherwise, the echoes and puns of Milton's key paragraph would be missed, as they certainly are in English translation. For the passage had begun "De me, libris tantummodo sacris adhaeresco; haeresin aliam": the words *adhaeresco* and *haeresin* stand cheek by jowl, and bilingually signal that "I stick to my heresy; stand by my choice." The glancing pun is part of the turbulent arguing, but lost in translation.

So etymology is not decisive but pervasive. It contributes among Milton's many verbal arts. They are wielded and welded together in this example. The same things are happening throughout his eloquent, passionate epistolary apologia. Laboriously and belatedly, the new edition of *De doctrina Christiana* charts some of them, and supplies material and method for readers to "wade further" for themselves.

University of Otago

The Experimental Form of *Lycidas*

James Rutherford

As Thomas H. Luxon observes in his widely read online edition of the poem, "the structure of *Lycidas* remains somewhat mysterious" despite an enormous body of critical literature purporting to explain it.[1] In this essay I plan to untangle some of that mystery. Certain facets of the poem seem designed to provoke uncertainty about its structure, and Milton deliberately undermines the reader's expectations about the metrical and formal structures of *Lycidas* in order to generate complex meanings and reactions. Such a claim entails reconsideration of some perennial questions about verse form, including the possibility or desirability of expressive acoustics, the tension between narrative movement and stanzaic organization, and the political and philosophical implications of metrical and formal choices. *Lycidas* is *about* such questions, and particularly their difficulty, if not in some cases their ultimate insolubility.

Most discussions of *Lycidas*, beginning with Samuel Johnson's notorious attack, have focused on the poem's style and structure. Indeed, determining the formal principles underlying the poem's construction has been one of the great collaborative projects of contemporary criticism. Edward Weismiller's masterful and comprehensive reviews of the scholarship on the verse form of Milton's poems for the variorum are like good mysteries, or detectives' reports on elaborate crimes that have just been solved. There is drama in the recounting of early stumbles with foot prosody and quantitative metrics before the gradual revelation of what metrists commonly refer to as the "two-line approach" to versification.[2] In his review of scholarship about *Lycidas*, Weismiller seems excited when he discusses Thomas Keightley's discovery of the ottava rima stanza at the end of the poem, and Keightley's own doubts that it is intentional after having learned that there is a second ottava rima section within a longer verse paragraph earlier in the poem.[3] When subsequent critics see in this repetition not accident but a transition from "drift to discipline," or even "the inevitability and logic of a mathematical progression," one feels that, despite all the remaining critical disagreements about the poem's structure, new problems have been identified, and progress has been made.[4] By the middle of the century, the editors of the Milton variorum could feel satisfied that the gradual improvement in the collective understanding of Milton's metrical and formal techniques mimicked a pattern of prosodic improvement within the poem itself: in reading *Lycidas*, ontogeny recapitulates phylogeny.

The complex pattern of prosodic development that Milton invents for *Lycidas* reflects a deep change in his conception of the political and philosophical implications of verse form. While most studies of the prosody of *Lycidas* examine the poem in relation to antecedent literary contexts, including the seventeenth century reemergence of the Pindaric ode, the Italian canzone and madrigal tradition, and the neo-Spenserian movement of the 1620s and 1630s, I suggest that the most crucial facets of Milton's compositional strategy anticipate theoretical reflections on creativity in his polemical prose tracts and *Paradise Lost*.[5] In particular, Milton's idiosyncratic approach to prosodic composition in *Lycidas* is in keeping with his representations of the construction of a Christian temple in *The Reason of Church-Government* and *Areopagitica*, and God's creation of the universe in *Paradise Lost*. Through a comparative analysis of these images of various kinds of building manufacture, I will suggest that the verse form of *Lycidas* provides the earliest intimation of Milton's mature thoughts about human and divine creativity, and of the nature and human consequences of his much-discussed metaphysical monism. With respect to its form, *Lycidas* looks forward as much as it looks backward.

The Metrical Line

The meter of Milton's poem is more of a problem than it should be, if one compares it to most of the other poetic compositions of its moment. By the 1630s, when the controversies over the accentual or quantitative bases of English meter had died down, there were few outstanding conceptual problems pertaining to metrical form. It should be emphasized that seventeenth century readers tended to learn about meter through practice rather than theory. There is negative corroboration for this proposition in the relative lack of theoretical statements about English prosody after the 1590s. In addition, there is ample evidence that educators often sent their students to read poetry rather than handbooks. Simon Daines, for example, begins his conventional grammatical treatise, *Orthoepia Anglicana*, with some commonplaces about the typical four-part division of grammar into orthography, etymology, syntax, and prosody. In order to understand the last two subjects, he leaves the student to "practice in reading such oratours and poets as our tongue affords, wherewith every stationers shop is amply repleat."[6] In his own Latin grammar book, Milton briefly observes that "Prosodic, after this Grammar [is] well learnt, will not need to be Englisht for him who hath a mind to read it."[7] Milton seems to have practiced what he preached, observing in *Apology against a Pamphlet* that he mastered the rhythms of the elegiac poets through imitation (YP 1:889). Milton's grammar-school teacher, Alexander Gill, similarly emphasizes practice over precept when it comes to understanding the prosody of words and verse scansion. Although he supplies some rules concerning poetic meter and rhyme, he makes numerous allowances for deliberate transgressions (to achieve *cacemphaton*, or expressive "ill-sounding," for example), and endorses what he calls the "mixed form" in English poetry.[8] Major critics, such as Julius Caesar Scaliger, tended to demystify perennially problematic concepts like rhythm and meter: a poem's meter is simply its "measure," a standard of mere length, and the writing of rhythms is a kind of practical, even physical, affair.[9] Torquato Tasso, an important influence on Milton, influentially compared composing a poem to building a ship.[10] In general, early modern writers employed rhythm and meter like tools, and readers appreciated their effects through habitual experience of them and through comparison, just as they do with any other piece of craftsmanship.

There is evidence that many early readers did keep track of a poem's rhythms as they read along, though they often did not pay the kind of attention a poet like Milton would have desired them to. In her recent contribution to the Oxford edition of the complete works of John Milton, Laura Lunger Knoppers describes the kinds of handwritten marginalia that can be found in extant early copies of *Paradise Regained* and *Samson Agonistes*. She shows that early readers of these poems sometimes *did* notice Milton's unorthodox metrical techniques, but that their only concern seemed to have been to *correct* them.[11] There is, however, evidence that more sensitive readers were prepared to notice when a poet included eight strong beats in a single pentameter line, and to think about how such an unusual metrical structure might reinforce or extend the semantic content of the poetry. Thomas Fuller, Milton's contemporary, gives some indication of the kind of complex response that one poet might have had toward the metrical choices made by another. At the beginning of the third chapter of his *Church-History of Britain*, Fuller quotes a "monkish" epitaph for the ancient king Lucius—in Latin, because it has "nothing worthy of translating": "*Lucius* tenebris priûs Idola qui coluisti, / Es merito celebris ex quo Baptisma subisti" (You, Lucius, who formerly in the darkness worshipped idols, are justly famous from the day you underwent baptism). While it is not strictly necessary to his historical narration, Fuller engages in some brief stylistic analysis: "It seems the *puddle-Poet* did hope, that the jingling of his *Rhyme* would drown the sound of his *false Quantity*. Except any will say, that he affected to make the middle Syllable in *Idola* short, because in the days of King *Lucius* Idolatry was curb'd and contracted, whilest Christianity did dilate and extend it self."[12] This is the first instance I know of in which an early modern reader clearly admits that there may be deliberation and meaning behind a metrical irregularity. Nevertheless, we can probably assume that this type of metrical allegorizing is not unique to Fuller since he himself implies that it is not.[13]

The opening of *Lycidas* would have challenged any reader, however. Outside of some previous poems by Milton himself—including "On Time," "Upon the Circumcision," and "At a Solemn Music"—and selected poems by Edmund Spenser and John Donne, it is difficult to find accentual-syllabic lines exemplifying a degree of prosodic freedom comparable with these:

> Yet once more, O ye laurels and once more
> Ye myrtles brown, with ivy never sere,
> I come to pluck your berries harsh and crude,
> And with forced fingers rude,
> Shatter your leaves before the mellowing year.
> Bitter constraint, and sad occasion dear,
> Compels me to disturb your season due:
> For Lycidas is dead, dead ere his prime,
> Young Lycidas, and hath not left his peer:
> Who would not sing for Lycidas? he knew
> Himself to sing, and build the lofty rhyme.
> He must not float upon his watery bier
> Unwept, and welter to the parching wind,
> Without the meed of some melodious tear.   (1–14)

The very first line of *Lycidas* presents conceptual problems for a method of scansion. Historically, many critics have been concerned that it does not comport with foot prosody; as Henry Cotterill puts it, one cannot find five iambic rhythms without "so altering the natural length of a word that one shudders as at a note in music."[14] Even though the line is susceptible to a flat metrical pronunciation, its apostrophic character, the presence of heavy assonance, and the two strong caesuras probably make a more unorthodox rendering preferable (such as "Yét ónce móre, Ó ye laúrels, ánd ónce móre"). Such distortions were permissible, though hardly common, in the early modern period.[15] In any case, it is easy to imagine an early reader, conditioned by the previous poems in the collection in which *Lycidas* originally appeared, which are almost unrelentingly iambic, stumbling right at the outset as a result of a powerful expectation for a sequence of regular rhythms. The line also presents difficulties because the terminal word "more" lacks a rhyme in the paragraph. On his or her first encounter with the poem, a reader might even have been confused about whether or not it is supposed to be treated as a partial rhyme for "sere," since the next four lines comprise rhymed couplets. This response would be particularly appropriate given that all the other English obsequies for Edward King are in rhymed couplets.[16] The first line of *Lycidas* thus thwarts any reasonable presuppositions about its rhythmic structure and its place within a rhyme scheme.

The fourth line is even more obviously problematic than the first, both as a result of its shorter length and the presence of only one pair of syllables that is clearly iambic. The trimeter structure of the line and alliteration serve to intensify the jarring quality of the first four syllables, despite the ubiquity of what Derek Attridge calls the "rising inversion" in English poetry; indeed, in this case, we might prefer George T. Wright's more contemptuous terminology for the same metrical phenomenon: "lurching rhythm."[17] There are other rhythmic reversals, including initial trochees and the deadening *epizeuxis* in the eighth line, and the presence of dramatic enjambments and a second end-word lacking a rhyme further obscures the integrity of the decasyllabic line, especially in a vocal performance. Only gradually over the course of the paragraph does the rhythmic structure repair itself, culminating in an unenjambed, and perhaps "melodious," line.

It is, of course, easy to find semantic justification for the rhythmic dissonances present in the first verse paragraph of *Lycidas*, and indeed in many places in which they appear throughout the remainder of the poem. In *Lycidas*, as in the monodic musical compositions of sixteenth and seventeenth century Italy, there are clear indications of word painting and of the adjustment of metrical technique to the mood or psychological state of the poem's speaker.[18] The poem weaves in and out of coherent rhythmical and rhyme patterns so that at any moment smooth versification may suffer a "heavy change" (37). The "dread voice" (132) of Peter, in particular, is grating, and Neil Forsyth observes that "it is central to the pastoral convention of the poem that bad preaching should be equated with bad singing and that the lines stand out vividly in the midst of this mostly mellifluous verse."[19] Nevertheless, underlying this occasional alternation between iambic regularity and expressive deviation from the iambic norm there is a clear progression from disorder to order, represented by the initial chaos of *Lycidas*'s opening, and the security of iambic pentameter and ottava rima at its close.

The reader, even an ideal reader, ought to be confused by Milton's prosody at the beginning of *Lycidas*. It is one thing for a poet to deviate from a firmly established rhythm for expressive effect, but it is quite another to transgress a pattern the existence of which the reader might not yet have apprehended. The metrical line and the various deviations from it that one encounters in the first paragraph are easier to understand in retrospect, after having proceeded further through the poem. This is because, after shifting in and out of a relatively regular rhythmic pattern over the course of the entire poem, Milton only demonstrates conventionally defined mastery at the very end. In the final paragraph, there is for the first time an unbroken succession of regular iambic pentameters, without conspicuous rhythmic substitutions, and without enjambment. Milton *withholds* a close approximation of the abstract metrical structure of his verse until the very end of his poem; rather than providing a theme and variations, he provides variations followed by a theme.[20]

The Verse Paragraph

Milton's approach to form in *Lycidas* is comprehensive, affecting every element of his prosody. There is a sense in which the metrical line puts itself together over the course of the poem, achieving full clarity only at the end. Meter is intimated before it is embodied.

The developmental character of the metrical line is replicated on a larger scale in the gradual improvement of selected paragraph forms and rhyme schemes. Such a complex, all-embracing pattern of prosodic development is potentially captured by Milton himself in the phrase "build the lofty rhyme," since the word "rhyme" could signify both rhyme and rhythm in the early modern period, and was frequently a synecdoche for a whole poem.[21] On the level of the verse paragraph, as in the line, it is useful to retain a concept of building that is akin to kinds of material craftsmanship like carpentry or architecture. Milton begins with rough material, works and fashions it, only gradually producing an object that possesses symmetry and proportion.

The use of semantically and structurally parallel verse passages is the key to the design of *Lycidas*. In making this claim, this essay differs from previous detailed accounts of the prosody and structure of the poem in marked ways. Most obviously, it offers an alternative to A. E. Barker's extremely influential—indeed, almost unchallenged—discussion of the tripartite form of *Lycidas*. In his classic essay, Barker argues—on the basis of patterns of imagery and early thematic anticipations of the Christian climax prior to paragraph 10—that the poem possesses three distinct "movements" that are "practically equal in length and precisely parallel in pattern."[22] In contrast, I am describing a twofold pattern, in which there are two five-paragraph sections followed by a coda. The presence of paragraphs of the same length at the beginning and conclusion of each of the main sections establishes this symmetrical pattern. The first section begins and ends with sonnets, the second of which corrects formal deficiencies in the first; the second section possesses 21-line paragraphs, and replicates the pattern of formal improvement discernible in the first half of the poem.

In examining Milton's handling of the verse paragraph in *Lycidas*, it is useful to consider the theory and practice of Torquato Tasso, whose writings—cited positively in *The Reason of Church-Government* and *Of Education*—may indeed have been a direct influence on Milton's thinking about prosody in the 1630s. Tasso, like many other early modern theorists, emphasizes how the poet must select his subject, which he calls the "rough material" (*materia nuda*), and gradually bring it to perfection of form. Throughout his *Discourses on the Art of Poetry* and the later *Discourses on the Heroic Poem*, Tasso places a great deal of emphasis on the word "size" (*la quantita*). Near the end of the first discourse in his *Art of Poetry*, for example, Tasso summarizes his analogy between "what we have come to call the raw material with what philosophers call primary matter": "Just as these philosophers, in considering primary matter (entirely without form though it is), nonetheless take account of its size, which is its constant and eternal attribute, evident before the birth of form and remaining after form decays, so the poet, likewise, should attend to the size of his subject; for when choosing any subject for treatment, he must choose it together with a certain size, this consideration being inseparably part of it."[23] This is, in the first instance, a caution against choosing a subject too large for the chosen poetic medium, lest the poet lapse into excessive digression or confusion in the plot. Nevertheless, it is likely that, in addition to this comparatively unusual usage, Tasso also has the poem's prosody in mind, especially given his own habits of composition. In *Il mondo creato*, for example, Tasso describes the subject of his hexameral narrative in an introductory paragraph of 77 lines, and concludes his poem with a 77-line passage in praise of the finished creation.[24] The two comprehensive statements of the poem's contents occur in paragraphs of the same size. It would be interesting to know if Milton, when he read his predecessors, was attentive to such formal patterns; and whether or not, for example, Tasso's beginning and concluding his cosmological poem with paragraphs of the same length prompted him to do the same in *Paradise Lost*.[25] At the least, it is a suggestive structural correspondence, indicative of the kind of influence that metaphysical ideas had on practical considerations of prosody and verse construction.

In *Lycidas*, Milton introduces new kinds of complexity to Tasso's method of ring composition. It is a peculiar consequence of the design of the poem that one may be haunted by a pattern in a paragraph that one is only able to comprehend at a later stage of one's reading. Despite the prosodic difficulties that critics have found in the first verse paragraph of *Lycidas*, for example, many have been able to perceive in it a "broken sonnet."[26] It is true that the paragraph is 14 lines long, but it fails even to approximate the division into an octave and sestet that is characteristic of all of the independent sonnets Milton published over the course of his life. It is therefore surprising that critics do not discuss the sonnet form of the fifth verse paragraph:

> Where were ye nymphs when the remorseless deep
> Closed o'er the head of your loved Lycidas?
> For neither were ye playing on the steep,
> Where your old bards, the famous Druids, lie,
> Nor on the shaggy top of Mona high,
> Nor yet where Deva spreads her wizard stream:
> Ay me, I fondly dream!
> Had ye been there... for what could that have done?
>
> What could the muse herself that Orpheus bore,
> The muse herself for her enchanting son
> Whom universal nature did lament,
> When by the rout that made the hideous roar,
> His gory visage down the stream was sent,
> Down the swift Hebrus to the Lesbian shore. (50–63)

There are some technicalities about the versification in this passage that may be troubling, including the anacoluthic syntactical structure of line 57, the lack of a rhyme for the word "Lycidas," and the presence of a trimeter line prior to the main semantic division of the paragraph—and yet it more perfectly approximates the sonnet form than the first paragraph does. The fifth paragraph contains 14 lines, and could be divided into two segments that are eight and six lines long.[27] There is a conventional distribution of thematic content in the octave and the sestet: the first eight lines concern the nymphs and their failure to rescue Lycidas while he is stranded at sea, and the following six concern the similar failure of Calliope to aid Orpheus. There is, thus, a typically Miltonic transition from terrestrial to divine concerns at the main division of the paragraph.

There is another way in which the fifth paragraph may improve upon the first: in the presence of three rhyme-words—"bore," "roar," and "shore"—for the word "more," which is unrhymed in the first paragraph. The earliest surviving work on *Lycidas* in the Trinity manuscript draws attention to this detail.[28] The verso side of the last page of *Comus* contains work on three paragraphs. The first is complete, and the phrase "build the lofty rhyme" is underlined. After some draft work on what would become the ninth paragraph, there are the six concluding lines of the fifth, which may be taken as further evidence that these should be treated as a unit. The close juxtaposition in the Trinity manuscript of the first verse paragraph and the final six lines of what would become the fifth is tantalizing evidence of their early connection in the poet's mind.

The rough isomorphism of the first and fifth paragraphs indicates, I believe, that they are closer in meaning than is customarily understood. The fifth paragraph in a sense completes the thoughts in the first, just as it more fully realizes the form and thematic function of the sonnet. These formally and thematically related paragraphs serve to demarcate all the paragraphs in the first half of *Lycidas* as a group. In the first five paragraphs of the poem, the muse is the main subject: the speaker affirms that he will sing for Lycidas even though he is not ready, hopes that some "gentle muse" will do the same for him, and considers in retrospect how Lycidas exemplified the ideal poet—only to conclude these meditations with a despairing sense that no human muse, nor even "the muse herself," can forestall death.

The second half of *Lycidas*, in which there is a transition from human to heavenly perspectives, possesses an analogous but more complex formal organization than the first. It is bracketed by paragraphs that are similar in form and content. The paragraphs are 21 lines in length, and both subdivide into sections of approximately 13 and 8 lines in length. As is the case with the two sonnets, the second of these paragraphs more closely approximates an ideal form only imperfectly manifested in the first.[29]

Jon S. Lawry observes that, in the sixth verse paragraph, "for the first time in the poem, synthesis—in the partly disclosed theme of resurrection and right judgment—tentatively reveals itself."[30] The tentativeness of Apollo's argument is consistent with the imperfection of the formal organization of the paragraph as a whole:

> Alas! What boots it with uncessant care
> To tend the homely slighted shepherd's trade,
> And strictly meditate the thankless muse,
> Were it not better done as others use,
> To sport with Amaryllis in the shade,
> Or with the tangles of Neaera's hair?
> Fame is the spur that the clear spirit doth raise
> (That last infirmity of noble mind)
> To scorn delights, and live laborious days;
> But the fair guerdon when we hope to find,
> And think to burst out into sudden blaze,
> Comes the blind Fury with th' abhorred shears,
> And slits the thin-spun life.
>
> But not the praise,
> Phoebus replied, and touched my trembling ears;
> Fame is no plant that grows on mortal soil,
> Nor in the glistering foil
> Set off to the world, nor in broad rumour lies,
> But lives and spreads aloft by those pure eyes,
> And perfect witness of all-judging Jove;
> As he pronounces lastly on each deed,
> Of so much fame in heaven expect thy meed.   (64–84)

I have introduced a boundary at the middle of line 76, where there is a grammatical stop, and a transition in subject akin to the one I described in the fifth verse paragraph. The larger first section concerns the unceasing efforts of the true artist, his need to abstain from worldly delights, and the compensatory attractions and dangerous elusiveness of fame on earth. The shift to a divine perspective could not be more clean-cut: at the very end of the first sentence the blind fury "slits the thin-spun life," and at the start of the next we are immediately confronted with the voice of Apollo. Despite the clarity of this paragraph's organization, the form may be seen to be slightly imperfect, because the main division comes partway through a line, and there is a word, "Jove," that is lacking a rhyme.

The tenth paragraph of *Lycidas* corrects formal deficiencies of the sixth, in ways that should by now be predictable:

> Weep no more, woeful shepherds weep no more,
> For Lycidas your sorrow is not dead,
> Sunk though he be beneath the watery floor,
> So sinks the day-star in the ocean bed,
> And yet anon repairs his drooping head,
> And tricks his beams, and with new spangled ore,
> Flames in the forehead of the morning sky:
> So Lycidas sunk low, but mounted high,
> Through the dear might of him that walked the waves;
> Where other groves, and other streams along,
> With nectar pure his oozy locks he laves,
> And hears the unexpressive nuptial song,
> In the blest kingdoms meek of joy and love.
>
> There entertain him all the saints above,
> In solemn troops, and sweet societies
> That sing, and singing in their glory move,
> And wipe the tears for ever from his eyes.
> Now Lycidas the shepherds weep no more;
> Henceforth thou art the genius of the shore,
> In thy large recompense, and shalt be good
> To all that wander in that perilous flood.   (165–85)

Whereas in the earlier paragraph the main division came after the sixth syllable of line 177, this one has major and minor sections that are thirteen and eight lines, respectively. These passages subdivide into halves, as the scene changes from the "watery floor" to heaven, and from heaven back to the "perilous flood." There is also a parallel in what I have described as the corrective use of rhyme. Just as the fifth paragraph contains three rhyme words for one that is unrhymed in the first, this paragraph has three rhymes for the word "Jove": "love," "above," and "move." Moreover, as many critics have noticed, there are five "more-rhymes" at the poem's climax, which is suggestive of the final reparation of discordant elements from the very beginning of the poem.[31]

The parallel use of form in the sixth and tenth paragraphs is concomitant with numerous semantic and verbal echoes. Of course, the entire poem is dense with inner allusions, but there is an impressive—almost line-by-line—series of correspondences between these paragraphs in particular. The despairing question about the utility of meditating the thankless muse with "uncessant care" in the first line of the sixth paragraph is paralleled by the injunction to "weep no more" in the first line of the tenth. The "homely slighted shepherds" have their counterparts in the "woeful shepherds." There are similar oscillations between images of light and darkness: in the sixth paragraph, the speaker juxtaposes the laborious days he actually goes through with the sport he might find in the shade; in the tenth the day-star sinks in the morning bed, only to flame in the forehead of the morning sky. Both paragraphs have capillary images: the negligent poet might play with the "tangles of Neaera's hair" while the ocean laves the "oozy locks" of Lycidas. According to Apollo, "Fame is the spur that the clear spirit doth raise"; in the tenth paragraph, Lycidas is "mounted high, / Through the dear might of him that walked the waves." Jove witnesses and judges with his "pure eyes," but the sweet societies of saints "entertain" Lycidas and "wipe the tears for ever from his eyes." In general, images in the sixth paragraph are repeated with variations in the tenth, usually with more lofty diction, and carrying more serious connotations. In the end, the cumulative weight of these invidious comparisons causes the "meed" described in the sixth paragraph to be overwhelmed by the "large recompense" of the tenth.

The apprehension of invisible forms can aid our interpretation of *Lycidas*. The use of corrective metrical and verse-paragraph structures has implications for understanding the tone of Milton's language. The majority of critics have concurred that Milton represents his psychological recovery, following his recognition of his own mortality and his doubts concerning his vocation, over the course of the poem, finding final consolation through his recognition of the redemptive power of Christ. Nevertheless, there have always been readers who believe that this traditional solution is too pat, and perhaps even ironic. For example, in his challenging essay, Neil Forsyth suggests that paragraph 10 contains "a deliberately false climax."[32] However, if we are willing to say, as a result of the presence of irregular meter and the confused disposition of thoughts in the first paragraph, that both the speaker and the sonnet are "broken," it seems reasonable to correlate improvements in metrical and paragraph forms with the resolution of the speaker's, and perhaps the poet's, emotional equilibrium. The prosodic reparation evident in the tenth verse paragraph of *Lycidas* echoes the optimistic note that many critics hear in its language. In this case, I would suggest that deeper familiarity with Milton's formal artifice only deepens the emotional register of the poetry.

In a famous early article, G. Wilson Knight characterizes *Lycidas* as "an effort to bind and clamp together a universe trying to fly off into separate bits," and Stanley Fish admonishes critics for trying to do the same thing to the poem itself.[33] However, I hope that my focus on reparative patterns in a sampling of lines and structurally significant paragraphs provides further evidence for the discernment by many critics of unity in *Lycidas*. Despite its manifold difficulties in terms of meter, tense, point of view, logic, psychology, and so on, the perception of unity is not merely the result of formalist bias, but rather is reflective of Milton's deliberate prosodic invention. The movement of *Lycidas* is anything but entropic: after a radically defamiliarizing opening, it drives toward increasingly well-ordered formal designs. This has a significant impact on how the reader approaches the poem. Metrical irregularities can encourage readers to participate in the formation of the verse that they are reading: they might desire to correct problematic rhythms in accordance with a preconceived notion of what a metrical line should sound like, or find a semantic justification for them, or deliberately alter the natural emphasis of words to give them greater dramatic force. All of these possibilities are open to the reader at the beginning of *Lycidas*; only gradually is one educated in the proper nature of versification as the poem achieves its

Christian climax. Similarly, the reader is exposed to an imperfect version of a paragraph form before being introduced to an improved version at a subsequent stage of the poem. It is a significant innovation of Milton's method of composition to make meter and paragraph forms follow an analogous pattern of development. Indeed, Milton may be the first poet in the English language (perhaps in any language) to distribute, systematically and deliberately, imperfect and corrected versions of the same prosodic form in the same poem for rhetorical effect.

The Meaning of Miltonic Invention

After having encountered Milton's Trinity manuscript for the first (and presumably only) time, Charles Lamb was appalled: "I wish they had thrown them in the Cam, or sent them after the latter Cantos of Spenser into the Irish Channel. How it staggered me to see the fine things in their ore! interlined, corrected! as if their words were mortal, alterable, displaceable, at pleasure! as if they might have been otherwise and just as good! as if inspiration were made up of parts, and these fluctuating, successive, indifferent!"[34] Lamb's comments reflect disappointment that Milton is like many of us, making mistakes and alterations in the course of composition. Nevertheless, in the previous section of this essay, I indicate that what is more remarkable about the draft work on *Lycidas* is that it gives hints of a rationale for some of the most disruptive prosodic features in the final version of the poem, including, most obviously, the irregular appearance of end-rhymes. It should also be noted that Milton himself evinces some pride rather than embarrassment in a slow process of composition characterized by frequent deletion, revision, and reordering of material.

One of Milton's early biographers, Jonathan Richardson, reports his having been told that Milton "would Dictate many, perhaps 40 Lines as it were in a Breath, and then reduce them to half the Number." Gordon Campbell observes the Virgilian precedent for such behavior, slyly suggesting that "it would seem that the same muse that visited Milton's slumbers when the morn purples the east had many centuries earlier visited Virgil's bedside."[35] Virgil's painstaking methods of composition, and his final dissatisfaction with his *Aeneid*, were immortalized in Donatus's famous biography, though Milton may well have read in his acquaintance Franciscus Junius's *De pictura veterum* (The Painting of the Ancients; Latin 1637, English 1638) about how Virgil "brought forth his verses after the manner of Beares, which bring forth their young ones without shape or beauty, and afterwards by licking, fashion what they have brought forth; that such were the new births of his wit, rude and imperfect to looke on, untill he by handling and polishing gave them perfect lineaments." Junius's book, which is generally concerned with "the beginning, progresse, and consummation" of poetry and painting, contains many examples of this kind, often emphasizing how artists "outwardly fashion" works until they are gradually made to conform to "exemplarie and supernall numbers." This kind of casual artistic Platonism was, of course, pervasive in the early modern period, and examples could be multiplied.[36]

Milton probably had these ancient images of artistic creation in mind when he composed *Lycidas*, but his achievement gives them a new force. The views about artistic creation collected above reflect a similar limitation: writers like Virgil and Cicero, Augustine and Plutarch, explain what goes on in the artist's mind *before* he or she puts pen to paper, brush to canvas, or chisel to rock. Milton's art of perfection, which he inaugurates in *Lycidas*, incorporates this thought process into the fabric of the poem itself. In opposition to Philip Sidney's observation about the creative process, it seems that Milton's technique stands not in the idea or fore-conceit of his work, but in the work itself. Milton, that is, breaks down the barrier between planning his poem and building it.

It has not been remarked how significantly Milton's representations of "spiritual architecture" differ from the normative architectural theory of his contemporaries. Marvin Trachtenberg describes how Leon Battisti Alberti and subsequent early modern architects and theorists originally opened up the "unbridgeable chasm between designing and building" that has been with us ever since.[37] This change is evident in seventeenth century English texts, including the *Elements of Architecture* by Henry Wotton, who Milton met shortly before his journey to the Continent in 1638. In this work Wotton, drawing on the theories of Vitruvius and Alberti, contrasts natural and mathematical reason, giving precedence to the latter. The work of the common laborer is minimized, indeed almost irrelevant in comparison with the intellectual work done by the architect, "whose glory doth more consist, in the designement and idea of the whole worke," and whose "truest ambition should be to make the forme, which is the nobler part (as it were) triumph over the matter."[38] The real work of architecture is in making the design for a project, which is to be imitated carefully as the artisans gradually bring form to matter. The artisans play merely an instrumental role in the architectural project; they do not introduce significant changes to a building's design.

Milton's conception of the building process, particularly in his descriptions of the perfection of the Christian church, is different. Milton, in effect, reintroduces the older notion of the master builder, who revises plans in accordance with the exigencies and pressures of the moment. That is to say, he includes the practical difficulties and accidents of the process of construction in his notion of an architectural plan. The material processes of manufacture and the abstract elements of design become blurred. In the following passage, taken from *The Reason of Church-Government*, there is a much greater role for extemporaneous innovation:

> If sects and schismes be turbulent in the unsetl'd estate of a Church, while it lies under the amending hand, it best beseems our Christian courage to think they are but as the throws and pangs that go before the birth of reformation, and that the work it selfe is now in doing. For if we look but on the nature of elementall and mixt things, we know they cannot suffer any change of one kind, or quality into another without the struggl of contrarieties. And in things artificiall, seldome any elegance is wrought without a superfluous wast and refuse in the transaction. No Marble statue can be politely carv'd, no fair edifice built without almost as much rubbish and sweeping. Insomuch that even in the spirituall conflict of S. *Pauls* conversion there fell scales from his eyes that were not perceav'd before. (YP 1:795–96)

The work is in "doing," not designing, and so it is unsurprising that the perfected church will possess features that "were not perceav'd before." Milton basically repeats the metaphor in *Areopagitica*, when he likens men "cried out against for schismatics and sectaries" to artisans building the "Temple of the Lord." Milton states in this work, as he did in *The Reason of Church-Government*, that it is both inevitable and desirable that a series of schisms and dissections will occur before the whole structure can be completed. Even in the end there is no simple uniformity: "And when every stone is laid artfully together, it cannot be united into a continuity, it can but be contiguous in this world; neither can every peece of the building be of one form; nay rather the perfection consists in this, that out of many moderat varieties and brotherly dissimilitudes that are not vastly disproportionall arises the goodly and the gracefull symmetry that commends the whole pile and structure" (YP 2:555). It is easy to pass over such passages as these, which can seem to be casual repetitions of contemporary theoretical preferences for complex kinds of harmony. It is mistaken, however, to see them as conventional endorsements of *concordia discors*. Milton, in contrast with many contemporaries, identifies with the worker, rather than the architect, when he describes how Christians should build the lofty temple.[39]

Many scholars have been sensitive to the relationship Milton's prosody has to his temperament, his ideas about liberty, and his mistrust of domestic political authority. In making a comparison with Milton's earliest radical exhortations to a "perfect" reformation, it is my intention to change our conception of the political—and, perhaps, ontological—implications of Milton's prosody. Milton does not just endorse deviations from a conventional form, but asserts that imperfect, and even anarchic, actions may be required before political progress is possible. It is important to recognize the implications of Milton's belief that, in poetic and church matters, imperfections may speed up reformation. As he says in *The Reason of Church-Government*, "those many Sects and Schismes by some suppos'd to be among us, and that rebellion in *Ireland*, ought not to be a hindrance, but a hastning of reformation" (YP 1:794).[40]

Such statements as these, which basically encourage violent protests against the state, are related to the invention of a prosodic art that is predicated on the deliberate incorporation of imperfect versions of metrical and paragraph forms. Milton's practical innovations in poetics precede, and in some sense underlie, his revolutionary politics.

It is no accident that some of the most radical elements of Milton's mature theology are communicated in scenes involving architectural design and building in *Paradise Lost*. John Rumrich's influential ideas about Milton's monism suggest that "for Milton the created order of material being in time cannot advance without disorder."[41] Rumrich is especially useful in drawing attention to the monistic implications of the architectural images in *Paradise Lost*. He defends the creative potential of chaotic primordial matter by pointing out that it is not God, but Satan, Sin, and Death who impose order on Chaos, in the form of a bridge extending from earth to hell. Rumrich counterintuitively observes that "the Fall has imposed a created order on his [Chaos'] realm: the tyrannically oppressive, ontologically shriveled structure of evil."[42] It is worth dwelling on the complex imagery of this moment, which derives some of its force from Milton's rethinking of the role of the architect in the 1630s and 1640s. Milton not only depicts different consequences of building in Chaos, but different antecedents for it; heavenly and satanic *processes* of building manufacture are radically opposed. When the Son set out on his "great expedition" to build the universe, "all his Father in him shone" (7.196). Indeed, at no point is God altogether apart from the Son during the Creation: it is the Father who speaks at the beginning of every day of the Creation, and on the seventh day we learn that the Father "also went / Invisible, yet staid" (7.588–89). Satan, by contrast, is an utterly detached—indeed, unconscious—architect, taking no part in Creation though he reaps all the credit. Following the construction of the bridge, Sin tells Satan of "[his] magnific deeds, / [His] trophies, which [he views] as not [his] own" (10.354–55), and of how his "virtue hath won / What [his] hands builded not" (10.372–73). Despite Satan's ignorance of the plan or building of the bridge, Sin assures him that he is "their author and prime architect" (10.356).

There is a deep conceptual cohesion in Milton's depictions of architectural fashioning over the course of his career, from the early 1640s to the completion of *Paradise Lost* more than two decades later. In each of these depictions, there is disproportionate emphasis on the process of manufacture rather than its planning or even completion, especially in the images of temple construction from *The Reason of Church-Government* and *Areopagitica*. For Milton, it is the gradual process of repair, without necessarily having a definite conception of what one is working toward, that makes all the difference. When Samuel Butler mockingly writes of the Puritan belief that "religion [was] intended / For nothing else but to be mended," he may well have had Milton in mind.[43]

Simon Jarvis asserts the centrality of a detailed analysis of meter and verse form to poetics, even when it does not bear a clear mimetic relation to linguistic content, and despite the generally acknowledged fact that, "far from having been solved, most of the main descriptive questions concerning what rhythm and meter actually are and how they work remain controverted."[44] In this essay, I have tried to go beyond traditional techniques of mimetic prosody in order to provide evidence for Jarvis's suggestion that prosodic analysis can help us to appreciate more than occasional instances of onomatopoeia. A growing body of criticism shows that Milton's metaphysical monism affects modes of representation and verse form in *Paradise Lost*; my work extends such research by showing that the prosody of *Lycidas* prefigures, and in some sense instantiates, monistic principles that Milton, as far as we know, only consciously affirmed many years later.[45] Milton's compositional methods both reflect and influence his philosophical principles, thereby demonstrating his frequently stated idea that poems can teach us as well or better than metaphysicians can.

Princeton University

Gender, Law, and Liberty in the Garden

Domestic Adam

Elisabeth Liebert

In the bitter aftermath of the Fall, accused by her husband of indulging an inexplicable wanderlust that precipitated their mutual misery, Eve attempts to defend herself by blaming him. The Fall, she suggests, resulted from her husband's lapse in domestic responsibility, from his permissive weakness. As her head and knowing her nature, he should have forbidden her "absolutely" to leave his side.[1] Eve's accusation is significantly unsupported by other textual voices within the epic: rather than criticizing Adam, the narrator, so quick to trace discrepancies between Satan's rhetoric and inward truth, instead confirms Adam's "care / And matrimonial love" (9.318–19), while in book 10 the Son condemns Adam's choice to sin with Eve but not his earlier decision to allow her to work alone. Even Eve implicitly retracts her charge when, repentant, she promises Adam "I never from thy side henceforth [will] stray, / Where'er our day's work lies" (11.176–77). Invoking her freedom to choose a place beside her husband, Eve's words invest her former as well as her future actions with the weight of individual responsibility.

In his 1712 series of essays on *Paradise Lost,* Addison had no trouble recognizing the essential innocence of the debate in book 9, claiming, "It proceeds from a difference of judgment, not of passion, and is managed with reason, not with heat. It is such a dispute as we may suppose might have happened in Paradise, had man continued happy and innocent."[2] Modern readers, however, have often been less charitable, especially to Adam. While scholars such as Diane McColley have sensitively reappraised Eve's role in Eden, supporting her decision to work alone, Adam's behavior at this crucial juncture has been the target of frequent criticism.[3] His failure absolutely to command his wife's obedience and his apparently unmotivated capitulation in the face of her persistence have been seen as the results of "his passion for Eve"[4] or his "narcissistic dependency,"[5] foreshadowing the fatal uxoriousness that would, short hours later, determine his fall. Having argued against the wisdom of separating, having urged the delight and edification he enjoys in his wife's company, Adam commits a "fatal blunder."[6] Instead of "demand[ing] that Eve's love produce her obedience," in a sudden about-face he not only gives his permission but "virtually challenges her to leave," effectively "abrogat[ing] his husbandly authority by refusing to act as Eve's 'Guide and Head.'"[7] While most readers who find fault with Adam side with Eve, a few condemn him for the opposite fault, suggesting that his attitude toward her reasonable suggestion that they work alone is cavalier. Thus, addressing her near the end of their discussion as "O woman," he "assumes the authoritative tone of superior, condescending patriarchy, exhorting Eve to obedience with a principle of wifely conduct of conspicuously unidentified authority."[8]

Is Adam too firm and fixed in his dissent, or is he not firm and fixed enough? And why, where Addison found only innocence, are modern readers inclined to apportion blame? Had Milton produced a series of treatises on marriage rather than on divorce in the early 1640s, the answers to such questions might be straightforward. Nevertheless, textual clues within the epic and their striking congruency with an ideal of marital behavior promoted in contemporary treatises direct the reader to a context that sheds light on Adam's behavior. I suggest that Milton's initial description of Adam and Eve in book 4 engages a paradox that troubled many seventeenth century discussions of marriage and establishes a relational paradigm that succinctly recapitulates the ideal toward which readers of such discussions were urged to aspire. Despite the wide divergence of modern responses to the first couple's first debate, a reappraisal of Adam's behavior in this context absolves him of the charges of both weakness and patriarchal bluster, representing the titles he fashions for his wife and the advice he gives her as consonant with an ideal of rational, humane governance.

The paradox that *Paradise Lost* explores is the infinitesimal degree of hierarchical difference between husband and wife, the paradigm a balance of authority and submission that honors and maintains that difference. To Puritan writers on marriage, gender hierarchy was an inescapable reality endorsed by Scripture: Eve's secondary creation, her prior transgression, the terms of her punishment, and Saint Paul's advice to women were all adduced as evidence that female subordination and male superiority were divinely sanctioned. However, the exact degree of difference resisted definition, and although the marital relationship was frequently compared to the union of Christ with the church, the common humanity of husband and wife complicated that ubiquitous analogy. In the words of William Gouge, whose treatise *Of Domesticall Duties* (1622) devotes 426 pages to the deportment of man and woman in matrimony, "of all degrees wherein there is any difference betwixt person and person, there is the least disparitie betwixt man and wife."[9] Puritan doctrine further complicated the matter by insisting that, despite their hierarchical difference, man and woman were equal in the sight of God. As William and Malleville Haller remark in their classic review of Puritan treatises on marriage, "Woman was inferior to man in nature but equal...in grace. Her soul was as worth saving as his, and its experiences had equal significance."[10] Moreover, the Genesis account itself encouraged egalitarianism: treatises repeatedly drew attention to the fact that Eve was not created from Adam's head, signifying superiority, nor yet from his foot, signifying inferiority, but from his side. She was, therefore, "of middle condition, his fellow and companion, not his servant or slave...of bone neare to his heart, to put him in minde of dilection and love, from under his arme of protection and defense."[11]

The near equality of man and woman implied by the materials of Eve's creation was elaborated through various suggestive metaphors. Alexander Niccholes, who, like Milton, believed that Eve was created to alleviate "the solitude and silence which [Adam's] lonlinesse would else have been subject unto," offers a range of images to explain marital interdependence: "he that hath no wife is said to be a man unbuilt that wanteth one of his ribbes, asleepe as Adam was till his wife was made, for marriage awaketh the understanding as out of a dreame, and he that hath no wife is said to be a man in the midst of the sea, perishing for want of this ship to waft him to shore: Is saith to be parched in the heate of the Sunne, that hath not this Vine to rest him under her shadow."[12] Although conceding the hierarchical superiority of the husband, Niccholes's descriptive prose stresses the man's need of a partner for completion, succor, and success. Similarly, the Elizabethan divine Henrie Smith describes man and wife as "partners, like two oares in a boat" in his immensely popular *A Preparative to Mariage* (1591). In another passage he explains that husband and wife "must be fit, like two Oxen which draw the yoke together, or else all the burthen will ly upon one."[13] Marriage, as these attempts to define it suggest, was an endeavor that required a close degree of similarity, albeit a similarity that was best appreciated imaginatively.

Maintaining the diminishing disparity between two individuals called to serve as oxen under one yoke or oars in one boat required that authority and subjection coexist in delicate balance. For this reason, perhaps, domestic conduct literature, unlike conduct manuals designed for children, is seldom a simple series of rules.[14] Rather, it attempts to resolve the paradox of hierarchy and close similarity by urging both partners to participate in the production of a workable compromise. Judging from the number of pages devoted to its analysis, wifely submission was easier to define but more difficult to elicit than husbandly authority. The wife was to be content with her husband's status, live where he chose, undertake whatever business he required, and avoid spending more on clothing than his income might support.[15] Prescribing the inward attitude from which such outward duties proceed was more problematic, for, as Gouge explains, subjection cannot be forced. A king captured in battle might be "compelled to yeeld homage to the conqueror" but, not thinking himself inferior, will not yield "a subjects dutie to him," rather spending his time planning escape and revenge; a wife might similarly be forced to outward compliance but remain inwardly antagonistic (270). True subjection, however, is as natural and voluntary as the hyacinth's following the sun.[16] It is produced by the Christian wife as a devout response to her husband's divinely sanctioned superiority, so that "though there were no other motive in the world to move her to subjection, yet for conscience sake to Christ she should yeeld it" (Gouge, 333).[17] It is active, evidenced in her swift and cheerful acquiescence to her husband's desires, her obedient performance of his commands, and her willingness to accept rebuke and "endevour to redresse what is justly reproved" (Gouge, 315, 319–20).

Although eliciting wifely subjection is perhaps more challenging, husbands are also rigorously schooled in the exercise of authority. Again, there is no simple list of rules. Rather, love is the husband's first duty, and love should determine his behavior in all facets of his relationship with his wife. Thomas Carter reminds his readers that "a man may draw more from a woman by loving and kind using of her, then any way by force,"[18] while Henrie Smith once again uses imagery to urge husbands toward gentleness and patience: "As we do not handle glasses like pots, because they are weaker vesselles, but touch them nicelie, and softlie for feare of crackes, so a man must intreate his wife with gentlenesse and softnesse; not expecting that wisedom, nor that faith, nor that patience, nor that strength in the weaker vessell, which should be in the stronger."[19] The recurring message is that for a marriage to succeed, wifely submission must be voluntarily produced and husbandly authority must, in Milton's words, be exercised through "gentle sway."

In his works on divorce, Milton claims familiarity with the contemporary canon of Puritan writings on marriage. Although he mentions by name only William Perkins, his education at Cambridge must have fostered an interest in emerging Puritan ideologies that survived his being "Church-outed by the Prelats."[20] In *Tetrachordon*, for example, he explains that his own seemingly radical view on divorce is no more than the logical conclusion of Puritan "Expositers," who, like ostriches, have left "their own mature positions like...eggs...in the dust" (YP 2:598). The philosophical egg Milton refers to here is the Puritan identification of "fitness" within marriage as a spiritual and personal quality, a belief that is central to his suggestion that marriage is dissolved not for adultery or desertion but when partners are no longer inwardly compatible. This is clearly not a reference to Perkins, whose *Christian Oeconomie* (tr. 1609) addresses the question of how to find a person "fit for marriage" by devoting 30 pages to prohibitive degrees of consanguinity and only four to spiritual parity. Rather, it is illustrated by writers like Gouge, who passes quickly over consanguinity to observe that "Mutuall love and good liking of each other is as glue" (197). It is exemplified by Smith, who explains that a spouse must not only be godly but individually "sutable; for divers women have many vertues, & yet do not fit with some men; & divers men have many vertues, & yet do not fit to some women."[21] And it is shared by Niccholes, who emphasizes the "mutuall society and comfort of life, without which [marriage] could neither subsist nor continue" and for whom "fitness" meant not the avoidance of consanguinity but "a fitnesse in affection" without which "there is either a falling off from the bond of duty, or a shrinking up of the joy and felicity therein."[22]

If Milton responds to such contemporary ideologies in *Tetrachordon*, the description of Adam and Eve in book 4 of *Paradise Lost* participates with equal transparency in the ideal of marital behavior disseminated through Puritan sermons and treatises on marriage:

> Two of far nobler shape erect and tall,
> Godlike erect, with native honour clad
> In naked majesty seemed lords of all,
> And worthy seemed, for in their looks divine
> The image of their glorious maker shone,
> Truth, wisdom, sanctitude severe and pure,

> Severe, but in true filial freedom placed;
> Whence true authority in men; though both
> Not equal, as their sex not equal seemed;
> For contemplation he and valour formed,
> For softness she and sweet attractive grace,
> He for God only, she for God in him:
> . . . .
> She as a veil down to the slender waist
> Her unadornèd golden tresses wore
> Dishevelled, but in wanton ringlets waved
> As the vine curls her tendrils, which implied
> Subjection, but required with gentle sway,
> And by her yielded, by him best received. (4.288–309)

In these lyrical lines, Milton reprises pages upon pages of prose in which conduct writers defined the nature, source, and consequences for both husband and wife of marital hierarchy.[23] The reader's initial glance is led to the "neere conjunction which is betwixt man and wife," rather than their disparity (Gouge, 372). Milton's description of Adam and Eve as both stamped by the divine image echoes the sense of spiritual equality that complicated gendered hierarchy for his contemporaries, while Adam's own description of Eve's origin, "out of my side...nearest my heart" (4.484), resonates with the commonplace observation that Eve was formed from Adam's side rather than his head or foot. As William and Malleville Haller suggest, "To the contemporary pious reader nothing in all this, except the beauty of language and verse, would have seemed unfamiliar.... Up to a point Milton was merely presenting in the poetic idiom of *Paradise Lost* what most men and women in his day, certainly most Puritans, thought about marriage, had often heard from the pulpit, and could have read in a large number of edifying books."[24] Audiences familiar with such books would have been attuned to the delicate negotiation of near equality in book 4 of *Paradise Lost*. They would surely have appreciated the paradigm epitomized in this prelapsarian relationship with its complementary "gentle sway" and willingly yielded submission. And, reading further, they would have discovered that the paradigm established in this initial description was not static but permeated the ongoing interaction of unfallen Adam and Eve, informing their physical, sexual, and verbal interactions.

"Dutiful Titles"

Adam's first address to Eve in the moments after her creation includes her name, a simple, unelaborated vocative that calls her into relationship and social identity much as his naming of the animals must have given them identity within the garden. However, any reader of *Paradise Lost* will have remarked upon the relative infrequency of the simple vocative as Adam and Eve converse. Before the Fall, they address each other with florid apostrophe, often omitting the other's proper name in preference for elaborate terms of address that identify the spouse in relation to the speaker. A critical tendency following Lacan to focus upon dialogue as an index of ego development in the speaker has led to what Addison once praised as "the gallantries of Paradise" being viewed with scholarly suspicion.[25] Adam's lyrical nomination of Eve as "Sole partner and sole part of all these joys / Dearer thyself than all" (4.411–12), for instance, has been criticized for betraying a "suspicious, Imaginary over-evaluation of Eve" or a "subtle hint of his weakness for his wife" that Satan does not fail to notice,[26] while Eve's address to Adam as "my guide / And head" (4.442–43) ominously suggests "an absence of autonomy and separate selfhood for Eve, and for Adam as well."[27] Furthermore, those scholars who call attention to reciprocity in Eden note that the first couple's "reciprocal courtesies" promote mutual love and respect but offer no rigorous analysis of how specific "courtesies" achieve this effect.[28] But as readers of seventeenth century conduct literature were aware, the specifics of address, rather than its generalities, are of utmost importance: when numerous variants are available (and in Eden they unarguably are) the speaker's choice of salutation carries significant messages, actively projecting identity for the addressee and insisting that identity is a social rather than an individual creation.[29] Thus, while it could be argued that the elaborate vocatives of Edenic speech simply follow the epic practice that resulted in such name clusters as "Agamemnon leader of men" or "Menelaus of the loud war cry," the seventeenth century reader would also have heard in these vocatives a verbal behavior that parallelled the prescriptions for couples in Puritan sermons and treatises on marriage.

This brief but pertinent advice falls into two categories: that given generally to the couple and that given more specifically to each partner. The main thrust is the same, however: terms of address must preserve the precarious equilibrium between authority and submission and confirm the identity of each partner not autonomously but within relationship, as each exists in relation to the other. Thus, explaining the importance of the first year of marriage in their *Houshold Government,* John Dod and Robert Cleaver specifically recommend the use of names that acknowledge marital function: "But if they shall use taunts or words of reproach and despite one against another, much hurt then may ensue thereof: *For a little leaven sowreth the whole lumpe.* And therefore let them use to give one to the other, their dutifull names and titles, and to eschue and shunne the contrary."[30] A century earlier, Erasmus had urged the reader of *De civilitate morum puerilium* to use such nonspecific titles as "worshypfull maysters" and "reverende fathers" *only* "if that privat names come nat to mynde."[31] By the seventeenth century, however, and within marriage, titles deriving from duty were actually preferred above the use of private names, for such titles recognize and reaffirm social roles. The identity of each partner within the marriage is determined by their relationship, and the reiteration of that social contract in verbal address exerts a powerfully formative influence upon them both, reminding them of their relative, not autonomous, identity. As Dod and Cleaver assert, "many times the very name of husband, or wife, father, or sonne, master, or servant, &c. doth greatly helpe to perswade the minde, and to winne the affection; yea, the very mentioning of these names, doth oftentimes leave a print of dutie behind in the conscience."[32]

Beyond the general exhortation to both partners to use titles that derive from and acknowledge marital duty, husband and wife are to observe specific verbal behaviors toward each other. The virtuous seventeenth century wife is to use forms of address that indicate subjection and reverence, and the verbal habits of godly women from the Old Testament, particularly those of Abraham's wife Sarah, are repeatedly adduced as models. Maintaining that the wife's speeches to and about her husband must be "dutifull and respective," William Whately plays Sarah as his trump card in *A Bride-Bush:* "Shee must not call him by light names, nor talke of him with any kinde of carelesnesse and slightness of speech, much lesse with despitefull and reproachfull termes. Heerein the godly fact of *Sarah,* commended to our imitation, must be followed in practice. When shee thought of her husband in the absence of all company, shee intituled him by the name of *my Lord.* If in her private conceit shee gaue him so good and honourable titles, what would she have done in company? what in his owne presence? what unto himself?"[33] Whately leaves these questions unanswered, and the reader is left to imagine for herself what Sarah might have called Abraham to his face. Perhaps the vocatives fashioned by Milton's unfallen Eve fill that imaginative vacuum.

In *Of Domesticall Duties,* Gouge explores a more eclectic sweep of possibilities. Aiming to be respectful "in their thoughts, words, deeds, and whole conversation towards their husbands," wives should avoid all "tokens of familiaritie as are not withal tokens of subjection and reverence" (284). The vocatives they particularly ought to avoid include: "those compellations which argue [the husband's] equalitie or inferioritie rather then superioritie, as *Brother, Cosen, Friend, Man,* &c.... Not unlike to those are such as these, *Sweet, Sweeting, Heart, Sweet-heart, Love, Joy, Deare,* &c. and such as these, *Ducke, Chicke, Pigsnie,* &c. and husbands Christian names, as *John, Thomas, William, Henry,* &c. which if they be contracted (as many use to contract them thus, *Jack, Tom, Will, Hall*) they are much more unseemly: servants are usually so called" (283). The use of such names fails to demonstrate subjection and reverence, while the names themselves are "tokens of familiaritie...unbeseeming a wife" (284). Gouge's disapproval seems to be firmly based on the power of speech to reveal attitudes in the speaker, for his main objection against such endearments is that their use indicates an undesirable insubordination in the woman.[34] However, the potential of apostrophe to shape the recipient by suggesting what he or she *should* be may well underlie Gouge's injunctions. His earlier assertion that a wife's proper exercise of reverence "cannot but much worke on the heart of a good and kinde husband, and make him the more to respect [her]" (279) leaves open the possibility that "unseemly" forms of address might also work dangerously in the husband's heart, eliciting from him equally unseemly responses to his wife. Lurking beneath Gouge's disapproval, then, is the semiarticulated fear of the performative force of words. If expressions of reverence "cannot but much worke on the heart of a good and kinde husband," what might such disrespectful names as Jack and Tom do? Might they not, by verbally enacting a marriage devoid of hierarchical respect, effect in him an attitude of inferiority and reduce him to the level of a servant?[35]

Gouge prefers wives to use those titles that come with the legitimizing stamp of scriptural precedent, including those terms of address that some readers are concerned to find on the lips of Milton's Eve: "*Head, Guide, Master, Man,* and the like." But, like Dod and Cleaver, he wholeheartedly approves of "husband" as the "fittest and meetest title" (284) "Husband" certainly seems to be the title of choice. Not only prescribed in treatises and sermons on marital conduct, it is also ascribed to those who, like Katherine Stubbs, were celebrated in eulogizing literature as paragons of domestic virtue. Speaking with her husband Philip Stubbs on her deathbed, Mistress Stubbs addresses him not by his Christian name but as "Beloved husband" and "sweet husband."[36]

Although wives are the primary recipients of advice on how to address their spouses, Gouge also has specific advice for husbands:

> Among other *titles* the most ordinary and usuall title *(wife)* is a milde and kinde title, and least offensive of all other: if an husband give any other *title* to his wife, it must be such an one as manifesteth kindnesse, familiaritie, love, and delight. Such are all the titles which Christ giveth to the Church, as *Spouse, Love, Dove,* with the like. I doe not deny but that in the Song of

> *Salomon*, and in other places of Scripture many titles are given and speeches used by Christ to the Church which are not meet to be used by husbands to their wives, because they are metaphoricall, and hyperbolicall: but yet in them all we may observe tokens of amiablenesse, kindnesse, and mildnesse, which is the end for which I have alledged his example.
>
> But contrary are such titles as on the one side set the wife in too high a place over her husband, as *Lady, Mistresse, Dame, Mother*, &c. And on the other side set her in too meane a rancke, as woman, wench, &c. And their Christian names contracted, as *Sal, Mal, Besse, Nan*, &c. and names of kindred, as *Sister*, and *Cosen:* and, opprobrious names, as *slut, drab, queane;* and names more befitting beasts then wives, as *Cole, Browne, Muggle*, &c. (371–72)

Again, Gouge's warning is informed by an understanding of the power of words to enact rather than simply refer. It is not the referential inaccuracy of addressing one's wife as one's mother that concerns him but rather the power of names to effect hierarchical, intersubjective identity. Ill-chosen names set the wife in an undesirable relation to her husband, creating for her a distorted persona that threatens the desired social identity of them both by eroding the delicate balance of authority and subordination required in marriage.

Gouge allows a wider range of titles to the husband than to the wife, stipulating only that they convey proper affection and in their "amiablenesse, kindnesse, and mildnesse" reflect the mysterious marriage of Christ to the church, projecting for the wife an ideal and nonthreatening identity. That Milton's Adam uses vocatives from the Song of Solomon as he whispers Eve awake at the opening of book 5 has not gone unremarked by critics.[37] Interestingly, however, and seldom noted, in echoing the divine Lover of the Song, Adam also parallels the ideal of matrimonial behavior advocated by conduct literature, for the interaction of the divine Lover with his Beloved is frequently cited as exemplary for the married man.[38]

Throughout the unfallen books of *Paradise Lost*, the first couple's salutations exemplify the ideals set out above. Although neither deploys the preferred "ordinary and usuall title" of "husband" or "wife" (and perhaps such titles do not sit easily with the sublimity demanded of epic diction), Adam makes full use of his "prompt eloquence" (5.149), rivaling the creative latitude granted husbands to express "kindnesse, familiaritie, love, and delight," while Eve fashions apostrophes that are preeminently, invariably "dutifull and respective." Their "dutifull titles" acknowledge their respective roles as husband and wife, reflecting on the way their human society determines who they are and are becoming, while acknowledging their precedent and enabling relationship with the Creator. Further, they choose terms of address that are appropriate to the matter and purpose of their conversation, actually using epithets to introduce topics for discussion. And, as their prelapsarian conversation develops, epithets are answered by epithets in a chain of echo and reiteration.

Adam's opening apostrophe in book 4, "Sole partner and sole part of all these joys, / Dearer thyself than all" (4.411–12), dignifies Eve with an essential role in his own being and happiness. It acknowledges their close equality without setting Eve too high or too low: she is his sole partner and, of all the joys of Eden, she alone is part of him, as well as summing up in herself "what seem[s] fair in all the world" (8.472).[39] Moreover, containing as it does a pun on "sole" and "soul," the apostrophe recalls to mind the reflections of domestic conduct literature upon the materials and manner of Eve's creation, that "she which should lye in his bosome, was made in his bosome," not of his head or foot.[40] Made in his image, Eve partners Adam's soul and fills his self-confessed need for fellowship.

Adam's apostrophe projects for Eve an identity in which she is defined primarily in relation to him. In her responsive address Eve accepts the defining pressure of that relationship and in turn names him in relation to herself, willingly producing her own subordination:

> O thou for whom
> And from whom I was formed flesh of thy flesh,
> And without whom am to no end, my guide
> And head, what thou hast said is just and right.

> For we to him indeed all praises owe,
> And daily thanks, I chiefly who enjoy
> So far the happier lot, enjoying thee
> Pre-eminent by so much odds, while thou
> Like consort to thyself canst nowhere find. (4.440–48)

Eve's choice of vocatives responds to the implicit need of Adam's address, affirming her love and emphasizing her reciprocal dependence upon him by identifying him as the source and purpose of her being. It also answers the suggestion of close equality by which Adam honored her with an assertion of hierarchical difference, not as a repressive burden but as a reality that permeates and enables their relationship: Adam is her "guide" and "head," two titles that Gouge approved on the grounds of scriptural precedent. Echoing Adam's description of her as dearer than all the joys of Eden, Eve describes him as the summation of *her* enjoyment and, asserting her greater gratitude for a greater happiness, honors him by freely acknowledging his superiority in the hierarchy of Eden. As Adam set her apart and above the rest of the created world, so she sets him apart and above herself.

As Adam and Eve converse in Eden, they recall and repeat each other's words, engaging in responsive iteration that confirms relationships and ratifies character traits by reflecting them in speech.[41] Eve concludes the story of her nativity by affirming that she now sees "How beauty is excelled by manly grace / And wisdom, which alone is truly *fair*" (4.490–91; emphasis mine). Adam recalls this assertion and Eve's deferential suggestion that he cannot find "like *consort*" to himself and shapes these two utterances into a courteous affirmation of her value: she is, he tells her, his "Fair consort" (4.610). The vocative gently undermines any self-deprecation in Eve's previous speech, reestablishing the egalitarianism that characterized Adam's opening words and reassuring Eve that her choice to yield accrues only to her honor. His sharply drawn differentiation between the activities of man and animal underlines his characterization of Eve as his consort by acknowledging her joint responsibility to reform and govern the garden.

Again, Eve's response answers Adam's generous egalitarianism with titles that are "tokens of subjection and reverence" and verbally perform her willing subordination. Her vocatives recall her own earlier narration of Adam's material and verbal authoring of her, reassuring him of her willed obedience by repeating the choice she made on meeting him after her nativity: "My author and disposer, what thou bidst / Unargued I obey; so God ordains, / God is thy law, thou mine" (4.635–37). Further, her address places in Adam's hands the disposition of human knowledge and so prepares the way for the question that concludes her speech by representing him as capable within the terms of their relationship to remedy the limits of her own knowledge.[42] It serves, in other words, as *laudando praecipere,* that subtle anticipatory praise "when by telling men what they are, they represent to them what they should be."[43] Eve not only describes Adam as he is (her physical author and her guide) but also as she desires him to be (the author and disposer of wisdom who will answer her question about the universe). Moreover, the theme and variation interplay that emerges as a characteristic of prelapsarian conversation is again present: Eve's aubade takes as its point of departure Adam's earlier claim that their relationship is a source of sweetness that surpasses all else in Eden (4.439), reversing the compliment he paid her. Adam's absence has the power to annul any actual pleasure: none of the beauties in Eden would be sweet without him.[44]

Criticism of Adam's discursive style as authoritarian and purged of feeling must surely have overlooked the whispered endearments with which he wakes Eve at the beginning of book 5, which are among the most eloquent and tender in the epic: "Awake / My fairest, my espoused, my latest found, / Heaven's last best gift, my ever new delight" (5.17–19).[45] As was noted above, the names Adam fashions for his sleeping wife echo those in two passages from the Song of Solomon (2:10–13, 7:11–12). And aptly so, for Eve's dream participates in a drama of waking and search that parallels that of the Song of Solomon. On waking finally to daylight, Eve welcomes with embraces and loving names the beloved whose presence she had sought in vain in sleep, naming Adam in relation to herself as she rejects the dreamed experience of separation and temptation: "O sole in whom my thoughts find all repose, / My glory, my perfection" (5.28–29).[46] Removed from Adam in her dream and urged to perfect herself alone by sinning, she reiterates her preference for perfection *in* rather than *without* her "other self." Moreover, she names him once again in that particular relation to herself and characterized by those precise attributes that she urgently requires him to exercise: physical repose has yielded only spiritual unease, but with Adam's sole (and soul) interpretive assistance, her thoughts might find the rest they seek.

Adam's explanation of faculty psychology has most frequently been cited as the method by which he comforts Eve.[47] But faculty psychology is not all that allays Eve's anxiety, for the apostrophe that introduces it also offers reassurance. The names by which Adam addresses Eve after hearing her story assure her of his continued affection and the validity of their relationship to confer and protect identity. The voice of the dream had addressed her as "happy creature, fair angelic Eve" (5.74), suggesting an autonomous and isolated identity. Adam renames her "Best image of myself and dearer half" (5.95), answering rather than avoiding the subversive tenor of the dream with its call to individualism and self-glorification. The dream angel promised Eve happiness as a goddess among gods. Eating and then obliging her to eat, the angel forced her unwilling mimicry of itself and snatched her from the garden to flight above the earth. Adam's words draw Eve back to Eden, reasserting her reflection of and participation in his own being and reassuring her that the dream has tainted neither her nor their relationship.

"O Woman"

As an examination of Adam and Eve's prelapsarian epithets illustrates, their discursive behavior reveals the willingness with which they negotiate the subtle challenges of marital hierarchy. Unlike Satan, who argues for self-determinacy, Adam and Eve understand themselves as they participate in and are determined by relationship. They select terms of address to reflect and encourage each other's burgeoning identity, to respond to the theme of a partner's speech, to preface a variation on that theme, or to encourage the exercise of particular, timely traits. Verbally they enact the compromise advocated by domestic conduct literature, Adam choosing titles that mitigate his superiority, Eve those that demonstrate her voluntary submission. This pattern changes, however, at the beginning of book 9 and again, irreversibly, after the Fall.

The book 9 exchange begins with a simple vocative from Eve: "Adam" (9.205). Gouge, it will be remembered, advised against the wife's use of proper names, for they erode the subtle hierarchy of marriage and have the potential to effect subordination in the husband. Although Eve has previously addressed her husband as "Adam," that usage differs significantly from her first address in book 9. In book 5, about to correct his mistaken views on household economy, Eve begins with the apostrophe, "Adam, earth's hallowed mould, / Of God inspired" (5.321–22). Interestingly, at that moment and for the first time in the epic Adam's relationship to herself is not the focus of her apostrophe. Rather, she seeks to improve his understanding of God's bounty, fulfilling "that maine end for which a wife was given a man, namely, *to be a helpe*" (Gouge, 368–69). From the wealth of epithets available to her, she selects those that best introduce the substance of her speech and soften her correction of his mistake, for just as she understands and wisely manages earth's fruits in general, so she understands and manages this divinely inspired product of earth's mold. Now, however, in book 9, her use of the proper name "Adam" (9.289) serves not to instruct him gently in household management. Rather, her opening words initiate a startling deviation from the patterns of verbal behavior established through books 4 and 5: of her four speeches in the book 9 discussion, two (those beginning lines 322 and 378) lack any vocative forms at all, while her second speech, which begins with an echo of her former elaborate apostrophe, concludes with a repetition of the proper name to attach rebuke more pointedly to her addressee: "Thoughts, which how found they harbor in thy breast, / Adam, misthought of her to thee so dear?" (9.288–89). Closest her husband's heart, where she should be cherished, lurks suspicion.

Moreover, the one instance of elaborate address that Eve now deploys compares uneasily with her earlier vocatives that set

Adam in intimate relation to herself and their Creator. "Offspring of heaven and earth, and all earth's lord" (9.273) seems to acknowledge Adam's hierarchical superiority but actually isolates him from intimate relationship, for his position as *her* lord, the theme of her vocatives throughout book 4, remains unarticulated or is at best assumed in his general lordship of the earth. At this moment of crisis, Eve selects titles for her husband that, while accurate and ostensibly respectful, are also peculiarly exalted and remote. Furthermore, the specificity and intimacy of the origins invoked by the apostrophe in book 5 ("earth's hallowed mould / Of God inspired") are here replaced by a general and impersonal derivation. The process of Adam's generation is left undefined, no longer the result of divine inspiration of sacred matter. Notable, too, is Eve's subsequent description of God not as "*our* maker" but, impersonally, as "*the* maker" (9.338; emphasis mine).

This sudden depersonalization in Eve's choice of vocatives, reflecting, perhaps, her new desire to explore the possibilities of autonomy, is highlighted by the consistency with which Adam affords her "dutifull and respective" titles. Responding to her suggestion that they work alone, he addresses her in familiar terms: "Sole Eve, associate sole, to me beyond / Compare above all living creatures dear" (9.228–29). The apostrophe reprises his first address in book 4 and, as it did there, the suggested pun on sole/ soul reminds Eve of her unique importance. Now, more explicitly than in book 4, it also serves as *laudando praecipere*, urging the continued solace and association he will request in his ensuing speech. His next apostrophe reestablishes the repetition that played an important part in their earlier vocatives. Responding to Eve's "Offspring of heaven and earth, and all earth's lord," Adam echoes her syntax but uses the echo to reassert the intimacy and specificity of identity within relationship, naming her "Daughter of God and man, immortal Eve" (9.291). The impersonal "offspring" of Eve's address becomes the personal "daughter," while God, not heaven, is reestablished as the author of being. The narrator informs us that Adam addresses Eve with "healing words." That healing begins in his choice of vocatives and his gentle substitution of the personal and social for the impersonal and autonomous in determining identity.

But Adam's style of address, too, alters in his final response to Eve: "O woman, best are all things as the will / Of God ordained them" (9.342–43).[48] His persistent use of elaborate epithets through the debate until this moment makes this last apostrophe the more striking. "Woman" is one of the titles that Gouge advised the husband to avoid because it "set [the wife] in too meane a rancke" (372). But does this shift necessarily reveal "superior, condescending patriarchy"? Until this point, Adam's terms of address have been generously egalitarian; now instead of emphasizing close similarity, he selects a form of apostrophe that exaggerates hierarchical difference and by doing so conveys rebuke. However, that rebuke need not be read as originating in personal affront nor as insisting on Eve's hierarchical inferiority to himself. Adam has been happy until this point to repair Eve's neglect of domestic etiquette with loving epithets; his vehemence is aroused not by her responses to him but by her remark that "Eden were no Eden thus exposed," with its implication that the very design of creation may be flawed. His "O woman" echoes—or more properly anticipates—Saint Paul's response to the straw man of Romans 9:20 who questions God's justice: "Nay but, O man, who art thou that repliest against God? Shall the thing formed say to him that formed *it*, Why hast thou made me thus?" Adam's "O woman" conveys a similar rebuke, reminding Eve not so much of the respective status of man and woman but, more importantly, of the vast hierarchical difference between creature and creator.

"The Principles of Humanity"

If this single aberration in Adam's mode of addressing his wife during the debate arises, as I suggest it does, from his jealousy of God's honor, not his own, what of his final, dismissive speech? Moments after his vehement defense of the Creator's wisdom and creation's perfect order, having suggested that Eve might be safer by his side, Adam apparently changes tack. Having urged his wife to remain with him, now he yields to her desire to separate: "But if thou think, trial unsought may find / Us both securer then thus warned thou seemst, / Go; for thy stay, not free, absents thee more" (9.370–72). These, of course, are the words Eve will later recall as she accuses him of failing in his domestic responsibilities. These are the words that for some critics witness his abrogation of "husbandly authority" and constitute his "fatal blunder."[49] I would not for a moment deny that Adam's passion for Eve determines his fall. But to blame him at this point is to overlook the fact that once again his verbal behavior delicately negotiates the paradox of near equality, echoing protocols established in early modern conduct literature for handling domestic disputes.

Beyond the names he might give his wife, the husband's behavior toward her, especially in the duties of instruction and rebuke, receives extended attention in conduct literature. The first point conduct writers are concerned to establish is that his execution of these duties is to be verbal, not physical. "Her cheekes," writes Henrie Smith, "are made for thy lippes, and not for thy fistes. The verie name of a wife, is like the Angell which stayed *Abrahams* hand when the stroke was comming."[50] While all conduct writers eschew violence, they also closely prescribe the husband's verbal behavior: Whately devotes 18 pages to instructing husbands how to instruct and rebuke their wives, while Gouge's advice on these topics stretches to 24 pages.

Again, because Milton turned his attention in the 1640s to the problems of divorce rather than a description of marriage, it can be difficult to determine to what extent his views on marital disputes coincide with those of his Puritan contemporaries. His response to Mary Powell's long absence in Oxford indicates a degree of personal tolerance, and his attitudes toward women in the divorce tracts are also suggestive. Although he insisted that Moses granted divorce for the benefit of the husband, the marital ideal that emerges through the divorce tracts strongly promotes mutual compatibility and happiness and necessarily entails considerable respect for women. This respect emerges all the more decisively when one compares the limits Milton sets to female subordination to the limits set by his contemporaries in two frequently debated scenarios: the godly wife married to an unbeliever and the wise woman married to an inept husband.

Milton's contemporaries, wary of the ramifications of their belief that marriage was most importantly an internal, spiritual union, not only denied the dissolution of marriage for spiritual incompatibility but also insisted that marital hierarchy remained in force in such cases. When Gouge, for example, asks whether a "wise, sober, religious Matron" must consider a husband "of lewd and beastly conditions, as a drunkard, a glutton, a profane swaggerer, an impious swearer, and blasphemer...her superiour, and worthy of an husbands honour," his answer is brief and unambiguous: "Surely she must" (273). Milton's response is notably more compassionate: "the wife also, as her subjection is terminated in the Lord, being her self the redeem'd of Christ, is not still bound to be the vassall of him, who is the bondslave of Satan: she being now neither the image nor the glory of such a person, nor made for him, nor left in bondage to him; but hath recours to the wing of charity, and protection of the Church; unless there be a hope on either side; yet such a hope must be meant, as may be a rationall hope, and not an endles servitude" (YP 2:591). Unlike Gouge, who condemns a Christian woman to a life of unrelieved misery, Milton insists that spiritual disparity does terminate the marriage and makes a particular point of liberating the woman, as well as the man, from a relationship that would reduce close equality to intolerable vassalage.

The second scenario sheds further light on the essential humanity of Milton's marital ideal. Although the state of female education meant that women's intellectual inferiority was often a sad reality, writers of domestic conduct literature did contemplate the possibility of "a wise, vertuous, and gratious woman...maried to an husband destitute of understanding, to a very naturall...or a frenzy man, or to one made very blockish, and stupid, unfit to manage his affaires through some distemper, wound, or sicknesse" (Gouge, 287–88). Henrie Smith has no hesitation in advocating a course of behavior for the wife of such a man: "she must not examine whether he be wise or simple, but that she is his wife, and therefore they which are bound must obey."[51] Gouge, perhaps more practically, suggests that in cases of "impotencie" or "impossibilitie," or when a husband fails to make appropriate arrangements for the management of his household prior to an extended absence, the wife might govern. Significantly, though, she does so without her husband's prior knowledge or approval; his condition means that his "consent is not to be expected," and he remains oblivious of her inversion of marital hierarchy (288).

Milton's response, in contrast, emphasizes mutual understanding, openness, and humanity. Although he acknowledges that scriptural authority places the wife beneath her husband, he suggests that "particular exceptions may have place, if she exceed her husband in prudence and dexterity, and he contentedly yeeld, for then a superior and more naturall law comes in, that the wiser should govern the lesse wise, whether male or female" (YP 2:589). Instead of forbidding the wife to question her husband's authority or endorsing a covert usurpation under the conditions of husbandly impotence, Milton suggests a solution that is both rational and radical: an amicable agreement between individuals that prioritizes natural capacity above scripturally endorsed gender hierarchy. For Milton, "the principles of humanity" determine what behavior is appropriate within marriage and require that neither husband nor wife be "enthrall[ed]...to duties or to sufferings" (YP 2:592). While Milton's works on divorce remain silent on the issues of marital disputes, then, their deep humanity suggests that the advice given by his Puritan contemporaries might serve as an imperfect prototype for Milton's own.

Two key elements in the husband's verbal behavior, both elaborated at length by conduct writers, have particular bearing on Adam's words to Eve in book 9. In the first place, conduct writers agree that in all instances the wife's essential humanity and particular disposition must be respected. Instructions must be moderated by "the understanding and capacity of thy wife" and intermingled with "sweet and pithy perswasions, which are testimonies of great love" (Gouge, 373). (The reader might recall that Milton's Eve prefers her husband's tutelage to that of Raphael because of his intermingling of such "perswasions.") Similarly, rebukes must be reserved until the wife is in an appropriate frame of mind to receive them. Until she is, the husband is to refrain from exercising this duty, even if that means that in the interim he remains silent while she scolds: better, Whately suggests, "that she have the last word, then both multiply worse words."[52]

Secondly, although husbands have been given authority by God, they must temper that authority with meekness, reserving direct commands for situations of gravity and not desiring to "bee Lord in every thing."[53] Gouge describes husbands who demand that their wives obey their every whim as wielding their authority "like a swaggerers sword, which cannot long rest in the sheath, but upon every small occasion is drawne forth" (378). The picture is of a husband addicted to control and verging on violence. Such husbands, when their wives fail in instant obedience or understanding, "will be angry with them, and in anger give them evill language," behavior that is not only nonproductive but also damaging. "This harshnesse," Gouge writes, "is ordinarily so fruitlesse, and withall so exasperateth a womans spirit, as I thinke he were better clene omit the duty then doe it after such a manner" (373). Similar advice is found in Whately's *Bride-Bush,* which exhorts its reader "so carry thy selfe to thy wife, that she may perceive herselfe to have entred, not into servile thraldome, but loving subjection."[54] Both writers agree that it is better that the husband defer his duty to instruct or rebuke his wife than that he do so in a manner that causes her distress.[55]

Underpinning these injunctions to temper authority with mildness and consider at all points the impact of instruction or rebuke on its recipient is, once again, the commonplace that "the man is to his wife, in the place of Christ to his Church."[56] As Whately explains, "Christ beseecheth his Church most an end, which hee might with most right command. Let the husband imitate that best husband, and beware of, *Doe it, or you had best;* and, *You shall whether you will or no: I will have it so to crosse you.*" Rather, like Christ, the husband should so "governe his wife, & provoke her to accomplish his will with quiet, pleasing and insinuating termes, rather than open and expresse, much lesse violent commandings."[57] Similarly, Gouge states that a wife's submission should be requested rather than openly commanded: "As the use of an husbands authoritie in commanding must be so rare, so when there is occasion to use it, it must be with such mildnesse and moderation tempered, so as (according to Saint *Pauls* example) though he have power to command that which is convenient, yet *for loves sake he rather intreat it*" (378). If conduct literature, urging the example of the divine bridegroom's interactions with his spouse, advises the early modern husband to entreat where he might command and to desist if he sees his wife unresponsive, would a contemporary reader have condemned Adam's decision to allow Eve to leave? Might not such a reader have rather applauded his exemplary forbearance? Adam's words are designed to preserve the balance of authority and submission that Eve's momentary resistance seems to imperil: soliciting rather than demanding compliance, he uses "quiet" and "pleasing" terms, entreating Eve to stay "for love's sake" rather than resorting to "open and express" commands.

What, then, is the husband to do when the wife refuses his instruction or ignores his rebuke, as Eve seems to do the morning of the Fall? Should he persist, as Joan Bennett suggests Adam should have done, until his superior reasoning allows her to correct her own faulty logic?[58] According to conduct literature, there are some "extraordinary" circumstances that require more than mild entreaty from a husband, such as the wife's fall into "an heinous notorious sinne." In such instances, Gouge allows that "some sharpnesse may be used" (384). Similarly, Whately sets limits to the husband's Christ-like willingness to overlook faults, but only if and when the wife "comes to some wilfulnes in sinning" or proves herself to "be more than ordinarily unruly."[59] But even when in debates over spiritual issues the wife rejects her husband's instruction and acts with apparent wilfulness, her husband must still consider the impact of restraint upon her conscience. According to Gouge, "Though the husbands command be sufficient warrant to the wife, and if he peremptorily presse her to this or that, she ought to yeeld, yet the love and mildnesse required of an husband should make him so to tender her as to remit something of his power, and when he seeth her conscience troubled about his command, to releeve her conscience by forbearing to presse that which seemeth so burthensome to her" (375). The wise husband, realizing in such instances that his instructions directly impinge upon his wife's ability to follow the promptings of her conscience, will desist from exerting authority and allow her to make her own decision.

Liberty of conscience was, of course, one of the great ideals in whose service Milton expended both energy and ink. The final question to be asked in exoneration of Milton's Adam, then, is whether Eve's conscience, rather than simply her powers of reasoning, is troubled by the advice he gives her during the debate. The narrator tells us that she "thought / Less attributed to her faith sincere" (9.319–20) and, disturbed by what she perceived as insult to her integrity, claimed that to suppose her insufficient alone to overcome temptation would make a mockery of their "happy state" in Eden. What is at stake is Eve's belief in the divine gift of human sufficiency, the subject of the Father's opening disquisition in the divine colloquy of book 3. Eden as an exterior, physical reality is indeed "frail," its best defenses easily breached by the enemy, its angelic guard at least temporarily baffled. But, as Lewalski notes, this "perilous exposure of Eden" is central to the vision of "moral reality" outlined in *Areopagitica* and enacted in *Paradise Lost:* "physical or external protections cannot really safeguard man from the attractions of evil, so that his only true security is in watchfulness and constant growth in virtue and wisdom." Eden, for man or woman, is, in the final analysis, an inward state.[60]

As we have seen, Adam corrects Eve using "some sharpnesse":

> O Woman, best are all things as the will
> Of God ordained them, his creating hand
> Nothing imperfect or deficient left
> Of all that he created, much less man,
> Or aught that might his happy state secure,
> Secure from outward force; within himself
> The danger lies, yet lies within his power:
> Against his will he can receive no harm. (9.343–50)

But a simple assertion of the divinely created sufficiency of the will would be an inadequate response to Eve's concern if Adam, having explained that man is indeed capable of repulsing evil without outward aid, should then insist that Eve remain with him. Such imposed restraint would only enforce her suspicion that her own sufficiency is still in doubt. Instead, Adam judges it better "to remit something of his power" and to "releeve her conscience by forbearing to presse that which seemeth so burthensome to her." Having urged her to stay for love's sake, he allows her to leave for her own, affording her the autonomy her terms of address and her argument for separation seek. Had Eve returned unfallen to receive Adam's garland of roses, she might, as conduct manuals suggest a wife might under such mild and loving governance, have freely admitted her error and the wisdom of his advice. She might have expressed regret for words "so erroneous" without that sad addition obliged by the Fall: "thence by just event / Found so unfortunate" (10.969–70).

In the brief narrative interlude after Adam's penultimate speech and before Eve's response, the narrator describes Adam's attitude and motivation with the simple, yet eloquent summation: "So spake domestic *Adam* in his care / And matrimonial love" (9.318–19). Perhaps our belief that modernity is characterized by a superior egalitarianism persuades us to overlook the narrator's guiding voice and to read Adam's words that fateful morning as evidence of uxoriousness or patriarchal superiority. The context of conduct literature obliges us to reappraise such readings. Although Milton's familiarity with any specific treatise on marriage must remain a matter of speculation, his creation of Adam and Eve clearly engages with the paradox of near equality that perplexes the writings of his Puritan contemporaries and offers as a paradigm a marriage of rational humanity in which authority is gently urged and submission willingly produced. Here, as in so many other passages of his great epic, resonates Milton's claim in *The Reason of Church-Government* that poetic ability is "of power beside the office of a pulpit, to imbreed and cherish in a great people the seeds of vertu, and publick civility" (YP 1:816). An early reader familiar with Puritan ideologies would have found in the loving and respectful names that "domestic *Adam*" fashions for his spouse, in his gentle entreaties and his respect for her struggling conscience, a literary exemplar of the ideal early modern husband.

Louisiana State University, Shreveport

Milton's Natural Law: Divorce and Individual Property

Michael Komorowski

In imagining Adam and Eve's marriage in *Paradise Lost*, Milton, as has long been realized, drew heavily on the ideal of companionate marriage that he had developed in his divorce tracts. With a disastrous marriage of his own and a political and religious atmosphere charged by contentious calls for resistance to authority, Milton sent his divorce tracts of 1643–45 into an ideological fray much larger than their immediate subject would suggest. Eventually, Milton found his way to a justification for divorce in the natural law by promoting a natural freedom of individual conscience that would become the trademark of his polemics. In *Tetrachordon* (1645), he argued that marriage joined two parties so that each would be a "help meet" to the other. Marriage was best understood as an "outward good," a means to companionship and communal holiness, that should be entered into and disengaged from according to the dictates of conscience (YP 2:665).[1] Milton accordingly formulated marriage in *Tetrachordon* as a contractual bond, much like ownership of property. In *Paradise Lost*, marriage is the only such contract that Adam and Eve can freely enter and freely leave, and the narrator fittingly describes it as "sole propriety /

...of all things common else" (4.751–52).[2] Marriage removes both spouses "from the community of nature" so that each becomes the exclusive possession of the other (YP 2:665). Only the creation of a better society composed of two "meet helps" could justify this radical appropriation of communal property (YP 2:621). Any marriage that fell short of that high standard ought to be dissolved, Milton claimed. With characteristic boldness, this argument effectively implied that the burden of proof rested with those who defended marriage as indissoluble rather than with those like himself who pointed to the natural logic of divorce.

Milton constructed a theoretical edifice in *Tetrachordon* to support these brave assertions, which depended heavily on an account of the origins of divorce in natural law. Although an appeal to the natural law in the 1640s offered a common strategy for political and religious controversialists to bolster their positions, Milton's version takes an unusual form when pressed into the service of his argument. In defending the right to divorce, Milton read in the law of nature a strong protection of individual agency that allowed for—and even demanded—the constant evaluation of social relationships. Because marriage instituted a form of property ownership, and not an unbreakable bond, it could be dissolved. This idiosyncratic turn allowed Milton to make an impassioned appeal that located divorce in natural law while marriage, by contrast, pertained to the positive law, or those statutes created secondarily to the natural law. While reason revealed the contents of the natural law, only divine or human fiat could promulgate the positive law. Only the acquisition of a "help meet" could be natural, Milton stressed. The marriage contract had allowed spouses to "appropriate" each other, but that form of ownership only held as long as their exclusive proprietary claim to each other facilitated their mutual help and sociability. Once a spouse no longer fulfilled that godly role, the only natural—and therefore just—action was divorce.

When Milton turned to the subject of his epic some years later, his representation of marriage and of the corresponding necessity for divorce under certain conditions offered him a powerful means to explain the fall of Adam and Eve. The natural law and the first couple's misunderstanding of the limits of that law lie at the heart of their separate decisions to fall. *Paradise Lost* imagines marriage as an outward good, or a form of exclusive property by which one spouse owns the other, and it is because of this capacity for ownership that Adam and Eve are individuals. But while in Eden, they have extreme difficulty viewing themselves and their marriage in these terms. Milton represents Adam and Eve's choice to sin as one arising from the competing claims of the law of nature and what appears to be an arbitrary positive law. This distinction, though, is one that only becomes readily apparent to the unhappy couple after—and as a result of—their fall. Although they seem to distinguish the natural law from God's positive law, they do not understand that the arbitrariness of the positive law prevents them from comprehending it rationally. Both are tempted to assimilate that law within the natural logic of creation with which they are intimately familiar. Their interactions with each other and with the garden around them convince them to transgress the command: Eve reasons that all things are permitted to her in nature while Adam decides to fall because his love for Eve encourages him to believe that their marriage is naturally unbreakable. Both only vaguely understand their actions as decisions that they undertake as individuals.

After discussing Milton's increasing reliance on natural law arguments during the 1640s culminating in *Tetrachordon*, my argument will visit the separation colloquy at the beginning of book 9 of *Paradise Lost* as Adam and Eve attempt to resolve their distinct views of marriage. It is at this point that the competing desires of collective action in marriage and individual choice begin to be felt most strongly. Their decision to work separately for a few hours leads narratologically to the Fall, but does not cause it. Adam and Eve each decide to disobey God's command for different reasons and, I argue, it is their misunderstanding of their individual agency that causes them to sin. One of the consequences of this misunderstanding of themselves is a misunderstanding of marriage. It is because marriage appears to them to be part of the natural law that they are led into sin. But their marriage represents a unique species of love in Eden that cannot be reduced to natural or rational attraction or to reflexive self-love. Rather, Edenic marriage constitutes a personal possession, a special kind of property, the legitimacy of which is only guaranteed by the possibility of divorce.

Propriety in Marriage: The Divorce Tracts and Natural Law

Although Milton's career-long intellectual commitments to individual liberty, civic virtue, and biblical hermeneutics all suggest that his interest in the question of the civil and religious permissibility of divorce was more than personal, it has been equally clear to several generations of Milton scholars that this topic was one that "the spurre of self-concernment" drove him to address, as Stephen Fallon aptly notes.[3] At least since the discovery that Milton was married in 1642 and not 1643 and the recovery of the suggestive and sordid details of the royalist Powell family's financial debts to the elder John Milton, there can be little doubt that Milton wrote in favor of divorce with the farsighted hope that he himself would be first in line to secure one.[4] These two inspirations for Milton's clamorous publications on divorce are not at such cross-purposes as it may seem. By the time he completed his fourth divorce tract in early 1645, Milton's personal wish to obtain a divorce harmonized with his ostensibly more altruistic commitment to liberate his compatriots from the bondage of maddeningly interminable marriages. This union was greatly aided by Milton's discovery and heavy use of arguments that located an individual's free agency and consequent right to terminate a marriage in the natural law.

Both parliamentarian and royalist arguments for political legitimacy in the mid-1640s increasingly found recourse to the law of nature to buttress their positions. Appeals to a natural, and therefore divine, order of the universe as a justification for either royal or parliamentary supremacy leveled a powerful critique at opposing arguments.[5] But with just about everyone making appeals to the law of nature, the concept had fast become slippery. Although it appeared to many that the natural law comprised more or less the secular commandments that God had given Moses (that is, the second table), a new minimalist conception of this law as simply the right to self-preservation was gaining traction. By the time Milton wrote his impassioned antimonarchical treatises at the end of the decade, he had thoroughly imbibed these appeals to the natural law, but it is his divorce tracts of several years earlier that first present sustained natural law arguments. *Tetrachordon* argues that the natural law guarantees everyone the right to determine how best to live according to God's commands. Divorce must therefore occupy a privileged place within the natural law lest an evil spouse lead the otherwise blameless party only farther from God. An indissoluble marriage, no matter how burdensome or sinful, could never have been in the divine plan for aiding humans to live godly lives. Marriage, therefore, must be "not a naturall, but a civill and ordain'd relation," that is, a positive law (YP 2:601). But Milton was initially slow to appeal to these concepts, and his first publications on divorce take a decidedly different tack.[6]

These first attempts at arguing for divorce depended to a large degree on sustained close readings of a very select number of scriptural passages. Milton argued that Jesus' apparent disapproval of divorce could best be understood as a rebuke of the Pharisees (Matt. 19:3–9). To their selective obedience of the law, Jesus responded, "Moses because of the hardness of your hearts suffered you to put away your wives: but from the beginning it was not so." He concludes by appearing to prohibit divorce in all cases "except it be for fornication."[7] Dismissing these words as a very specific response to the Pharisees, Milton then proceeds to emphasize the Mosaic law governing divorce, Deuteronomy 24:1–2, which allowed the dissolution of marriage for reasons Milton argued had to do with the incompatibility of the spouses.[8] The extreme precision with which Milton had construed the Gospel passage suggested, however, a glaring logical weakness. If Jesus' words were uttered merely "either to convince the extravagance of the Pharises on that point, or to give a sharp and vehement answer to a tempting question," it becomes difficult to understand the context of Matthew 5:31–32, which repeats the prohibition and the single exception of fornication to a much broader audience during the Sermon on the Mount (YP 2:282). Milton had been attacked on precisely this point in the anonymous reply to his tract published in November 1644.[9]

Milton, though, appears already to have been refining the evidence for his thesis. The process of near constant revision of his case for divorce in 1644 forced Milton not only to sharpen his arguments but more importantly to reappraise the relationship between the old and new laws, Edenic and contemporary marriage, and the scope of natural law. Much later, Milton would articulate in *De doctrina Christiana* the more radical position, "that the whole Mosaic law is abolished by the gospel" (YP 6:531). In *Tetrachordon*, as he had to a lesser degree in *The Doctrine and Discipline of Divorce*, Milton takes pains to demonstrate that natural law validates the Mosaic law on divorce. "The Statutes of the Lord are all pure and just," Milton writes, "and if all, then this of Divorce" (YP 2:620).[10] With this assertion in mind, he embarks on a 12-point defense of the Deuteronomic divorce law that begins by distinguishing natural from positive (here "ordain'd" and "civill") law:

> if Mariage be but an ordain'd relation, as it seems not more, it cannot take place above the prime dictats of nature; and if it bee of natural right, yet it must yeeld to that which is more natural, and before it by eldership and precedence in nature. Now it is not natural that *Hugh* marries *Beatrice*, or *Thomas Rebecca*, beeing only a civill contract, and full of many chances, but that these men seek them meet helps, that only is natural; and that they espouse them such, that only is mariage. But if they find them neither fit helps, nor tolerable society, what thing more natural, more original and first in nature then to depart from that which is irksom, greevous, actively hateful, and injurious eevn to hostility. (YP 2:621–22)

Since marriage is authorized by a positive law, it is impossible that it should infringe upon natural right. Those rights have been guaranteed by the Gospel, allowing Milton to read much of the Mosaic law as a confirmation of natural law. Christ has released believers from slavish adherence to the arbitrary parts of the law, "having cancell'd the hand writing of ordinances which was against us," distilling its essence to "the fulfilling of all through charity" (YP 2:587) or, as Milton was to express later, "love of God and of our neighbor" (YP 6:531).[11] The homespun names of Milton's hypothetical couples reinforce his central point that true marriage must promote loving companionship and piety, the ends for which it was intended.

In light of this fuller explanation of the natural law, the new trajectory for Milton's argument for divorce becomes clear. *Tetrachordon* deemphasizes the reading that since Christ addresses only the Pharisees in the Gospel prohibition on divorce, the statute in Deuteronomy therefore remains intact. He contextualizes this narrow argument as merely one part of a larger biblical justification for divorce that finds its rationale in the law of nature, given by God in the Mosaic law and then delivered in a distilled form in the Gospel. Clearly, Milton gauged the logical weakness of a position that so narrowly restricted the addressees of Christ's words and perceived that his argument would demand a fuller and more analytical treatment of the relationship between Old and New Testaments.[12]

Tetrachordon is both more wide ranging in its use of sources and broader in the implications of its argument. The four-stringed lyre named in the Greek title joins the four places in Scripture that address divorce to create what Milton supposes will be the harmonious sound of the natural law. But not all of the notes are played equally in his exegesis. James Turner summarizes, "Deuteronomy may be an important support of the edifice of divorce law, but Genesis is its main pillar," although this contrast is far truer of *Tetrachordon* than it is of any previous iteration of Milton's argument.[13] *Doctrine and Discipline*, especially in its second incarnation of February 1644, had pushed heavily on the more expansive Deuteronomic prescription, even at times appearing to denigrate the relationship between Genesis and the Gospel. Milton, for instance, dismisses Christ's apparent proscription by assaulting the ambiguity of his scriptural citation: "*What God hath joyn'd let no man put asunder*, is as obscure as any clause fetcht out of *Genesis*" (YP 2:301). In this formulation, the precision of Deuteronomy supplements the vagueness of Genesis, but in *Tetrachordon*, Genesis provides a key justification for the conditional legitimacy of marriage: "*therefore* shall a man leav father and mother...and they shall bee one flesh" (YP 2:613; my emphasis). Milton read this crucial verse as evidence that marriage formed a new social relationship between two persons, bound by "love fitly dispos'd to mutual help and comfort of life" (YP 2:613). Genesis describes the consequences of a true marriage, which "cannot either in Religion, Law, or Reason bee bound, and posted upon mankind to his sorrow and misery, but receiv what force they have from the meetnes of help and solace" (YP 2:613). The ideal of "one flesh" cannot be invoked to prevent the dissolution of a failing marriage. Milton insists that "Mariage is not true mariage by beeing individual, but therfore individual, if it be true Mariage" (YP 2:610). Indissolubility is a consequence of true marriage, but not certain evidence of true marriage since it may be imposed artificially. Those who cite Genesis in support of the absolute integrity of marriage have confused cause and effect. It is only natural, then, that distancing oneself from an obstacle to closer union with God must assume priority over any outward attainment of good, even the good provided by a marriage.

The logic of *Tetrachordon* rests on the theological point that God's covenants last forever and that the secondary law of nature that governed human behavior from the moment of the Fall is unchanging. Despite base desires to sin, human reason can apprehend this secondary law and, by following it, live harmoniously and righteously in civil society. Since marriage exists so that a man's wife may be "his image and helpe in religious society," the natural law must allow divorce to redress those situations in which this spousal aid is not forthcoming (YP 2:592). It is because the marriage makes two into one and unites both parties with the entire body of believers that divorce ought to be permitted, for if it were not, those who remain in unfulfilling marriages would sin against the ideal oneness at which the marriage had aimed. In *Doctrine and Discipline*, Milton found a ghoulish image to convey the point as he urged his readers to consider the miserable spouses "instead of beeing one flesh, they will be rather two carkasses chain'd unnaturally together" (YP 2:326). In *Tetrachordon,* he resurrects the spouses, but reduces them to mere animals who "live as they were deadly enemies in a cage together" (YP 2:599).

Establishing this point, Milton reads Christ's words in the Gospel of Matthew as a justification for divorce. Christ elucidates the Mosaic law in the Gospel so that what appears to be an abrogation of that law is in fact only a refinement. "Moses because of the hardness of your hearts suffered you to put away your wives," he tells the Pharisees, "but from the beginning it was not so" (Matt. 19:8). Arguing that hardness of heart merely refers to the weaknesses inherent in all humans after the Fall rather than to any particular sin, Milton can then contextualize divorce as one law among "the *secondary law of nature and of nations*" (YP 2:661). Because humans had fallen, God permitted this secondary natural law, or law of nations, that allowed warfare, social hierarchies, government, and "propriety to divide all things by severall possession, trade and commerce, not without usury" (661). Had they persevered in their perfect state, this secondary law would have been "most unjust" (661). Since that law included permission for divorce for incompatibility, Milton argued, "we may as well abolish the whole law of nations" were civil authorities to forbid divorce (662).[14] This argumentative thrust required Milton to take a renewed look at the relationship of paradisal and postlapsarian marital relations and, somewhat surprisingly, to fashion an innovative conception of marriage as a special kind of property.

The nature of that property only becomes clear for Milton as he articulates the character of marriage after the fall of Adam and Eve. A less stringent law governs fallen humans in accordance with their sinful nature: "In the beginning, had men continu'd perfet, it had bin just that all things should have remain'd, as they began to *Adam* & *Eve*. But after that the sons of men grew violent & injurious, it alter'd the lore of justice, and put the government of things into a new frame" (YP 2:665). The postlapsarian world demanded new relationships between individuals in marriage and, indeed, among all in a community. Milton was able to clarify the means by which marriage created a form of private property only by considering the legal guarantee for its dissolution. The secondary law of nature "for mans good and quiet, reduc't things to propriety, which were at first in common," thereby underwriting the Deuteronomic divorce law (YP 2:625). Milton explains the logical ramifications for marriage when spouses regard each other as property:

> While man and woman were both perfet each to other, there needed no divorce; but when they both degenerated to imperfection, & oft times grew to be an intolerable evil each to other, then law more justly did permitt the alienating of that evil which mistake made proper, then it did the appropriating of that good which Nature at first made common. For if the absence of outward good be not so bad as the presence of a close evil, & that propriety, whether by cov'nant or possession, be but the attainment of some outward good, it is more natural & righteous that the law should sever us from an intimat evil, then appropriate any outward good to us from the community of nature. The Gospel indeed tending ever to that which is perfetest, aim'd at the restorement of all things, as they were in the beginning. And therefore all things were in common to those primitive Christians in the Acts, which *Ananias & Sapphira* dearly felt. (YP 2:665)

A spouse, as an "outward good," is property that has been appropriated by another from the communal property of all. The Gospel calls for a new Eden, "the restorement of all things, as they were in the beginning," that is, the restoration of the community of nature. But marriage is special since it necessarily requires the appropriation of another; the "outward good" it creates is not one that can be held in common. (What is more, Milton acknowledges frankly, Christians no longer hold much property in common as in the early days, and it makes little sense to apply the letter of the Gospel to a changed world [YP 2:666].) Christians, living after the promulgation of the Gospel, must make certain that any appropriation of another person from the communal property of all is justified by the acquisition of a help meet. Hence, Milton's focus in this passage on divesting oneself of evil, lest one suffer the fate of Ananias and Sapphira, who retained part of the money they had received for their land and immediately collapsed dead when Peter confronted them (Acts 5:1–10). Those who remain in a loveless marriage commit the same crime, Milton implies. Marriage is no more than property, "but...some outward good." When spouses are unfit companions for each other, they unjustly withhold their property from the community. As a result, the Deuteronomic law on divorce guarantees the high standard of the Gospel. It ensures that righteous spouses can end their marriages and thereby free themselves of evil as they return the companionship of their partners to the community of all believers.

Marriage is "propriety," something one owns "by cov'nant or possession," and it is therefore always incumbent upon both spouses to ensure that this private, exclusive relationship brings real, tangible benefits that could not be otherwise obtained. Milton's argument implies that marriage, by the very nature of its exclusivity, robs a larger community of companionship; it resembles an appropriation of formerly public lands by enclosure. Nature makes all goods common at first—both property and immaterial benefits such as companionship—and if a compelling reason is required to appropriate any person or thing from nature for exclusive use, so much more obvious would it appear that any private appropriation ought to be relinquished the moment it no longer fulfills its original purpose.[15] Marriage, then, must necessarily pertain to the positive law since it is merely an option for living a holy life, while the natural law guarantees a right to divorce since a loveless marriage always imperils individual piety and communal harmony.[16]

The Positive Law of Eden

Tetrachordon leaves no doubt that Milton found the distinction between natural and positive laws his most potent intellectual weapon in asserting his case for divorce. This distinction also proved crucial for his justification of the divine interdiction on the tree of knowledge in both *De doctrina* and *Paradise Lost*. In *De doctrina*, Milton's yoking together "Of the Special Government of Man before the Fall: Dealing also with the Sabbath and Marriage" in a single chapter may at first seem odd, but the interdiction, Sabbath worship, and marriage all count as arbitrary, positive laws for Milton.[17] The interdiction and marriage are, additionally, linked by their concern with respect for property (and discussion of these two laws takes up the vast majority of the chapter in question in *De doctrina*). The original sin was, among much else, a sin of theft according to biblical commentaries, and marriage, as we have seen, institutes a form of property ownership. Disobedience to God in the form of eating the fruit violates God's property just as remaining in a loveless marriage misuses a special form of property that allows for companionship and domestic harmony. In *Paradise Lost*, Milton brings this analogy into sharp focus, especially after the Fall, as Adam and Eve suffer the consequences of sin against God and against each other.

In the epic, the first sin contains all sins, not simply or primarily theft; hence, Adam and Eve are "manifold in sin" after their fall (*PL* 10.16).[18] Nevertheless, Milton's explanation in *De doctrina* of God's punishment for the transgression of the divine command figures the Fall as a sin against property. Justifying humanity's inheritance of the original sin, Milton likens Adam and Eve to "a man convicted of high treason, which is only an offence against another man, [who] forfeits not only his estate and citizenship (*fundum aut civitatem*) but also those of all his family."[19] The legacy of their punishment through all generations can be understood by likening the banishment from Eden to the forfeiture of real property. For Milton, the forfeiture of something concrete, the *fundus*, explains the concomitant loss of the abstraction *civitas*.

Milton's thinking in this regard was no doubt indebted to the major republican theorists of the previous century from Machiavelli forward who had held that a republic granted citizenship on the basis of land tenure.[20] But he also would have found it necessary to engage with a tradition of scholarship on the natural law both when writing political tracts in the aftermath of the regicide and when composing his epic some years later. In both of these undertakings, Milton strove, like his contemporaries Samuel Rutherford, Anthony Ascham, and most other polemicists, to describe the original state of human society and its government as reason dictated it must at some very early time have existed. Milton used this strategy to brilliant effect in *Tetrachordon* and *The Tenure of Kings and Magistrates* to argue for the rights of spouses and citizens that had been theirs since time immemorial. In *Paradise Lost,* Milton reflects not only on the legacy of these original rights but also on the first humans' understanding of the freedom that these rights grant to them. Milton takes great care that his Eden should accurately embody a natural law in which respect for property, including the special case of marriage, is at the center of Adam and Eve's relationship with each other and with God.

The preeminent European theorist of natural law of the previous generation was Hugo Grotius, the Dutch humanist who in 1625 published *De jure belli ac pacis* on the rights of nations in an international arena.[21] Milton had made a point of visiting Grotius in Paris in 1638 during his continental sojourn and quoted his works approvingly at several points in his divorce tracts. Milton would have known (and presumably admired) him as an Arminian and an advocate of religious toleration. For Grotius, the natural law governed human behavior as a necessary consequence of the Creation and not because God explicitly elucidated its precepts. Humans were naturally sociable, and in order to live in society certain indisputable rules of conduct were necessary even if (*etiamsi daremus*), Grotius boldly proclaimed, God did not exist.[22] Behind this startling, though conditional, assertion lay his avowed aim to discredit the position that law was nothing more than institutionalized protection of self-interest (*iura sibi homines utilitate sanxisse*) and that therefore no basis existed for universally binding codes of behavior.[23] Where the skeptical tradition had claimed self-interest as the basis of law, Grotius proposed respect for the property of others, and it was from this principle that he could elucidate universal tenets of conduct for individuals and states alike.

Grotius began with the proposition that the innate sociability of humans necessarily required the mutual respect of everyone living in a society. Although property did not exist at the Creation when humans had little need for the exclusive use of very much of anything, shortly thereafter they began to apply themselves to the artificial improvement of their environment. It was these "various Arts, whereof the Symbol was *the Tree of Knowledge of Good and Evil*, that is, of the Knowledge of Things which one may use either well or ill" that led to the specialization of labor, or "Diversity of Inclination," as Grotius calls it, and that bred covetousness, avarice, and violence. It was only when nature was improved through human labor that there arose any desire or need to restrict its use. And it was at this point, entirely without intervention by any human or divine legislator, that Grotius located the "Original of Property," and with it, the law of nature.[24] By utter necessity, the natural law instituted a respect for differences among individuals and among states that became more marked with the passage of time as the original primitive equality of all faded into myth. These differences included hierarchical social relations as between master and slave, husband and wife, or parents and children, and Grotius suggested that liberty was best considered as a kind of property since the liberty of an inferior was governed by his or her superior.[25] The natural law established a rational guide for social living that, by respecting private property, in turn preserved the liberty of individuals and nations alike.

Grotius's conception of the natural law was minimalist to the extreme. His works demonstrated a pronounced skepticism about the existence of universal moral truths and instead substituted for these a right of self-preservation that was grounded in self-ownership. It was on this basis that Grotius argued for a limited right to resist temporal magistrates. But Grotius's links between property ownership—particularly the ownership of liberty—and self-preservation remained hazy for many thinkers during the decade of the English civil wars.[26] Anthony Ascham, who may have fought for the parliamentary army during the wars and who afterward was sent abroad by the new government as a diplomat, sought to clarify the issue by recasting the question of legitimate resistance to authority as a simple matter of respecting the natural rights of possession. Ascham warned the Levellers and other assorted radicals that, although revolutions might "take down the greatest Colossuse's, and whatever else might be ombragious in the excrescencies of Civill Pomp," to abolish or even tamper with the right of private property would violate the natural law.[27]

Ascham proposes to the Levellers as well as to moderate Independents and formerly sympathetic Presbyterians the organizing and civilizing virtues of property ownership. He sets out to prove two points: first, that only property ownership can guarantee a right of self-preservation, and second, that property ownership has been a crucial part of human existence from the very beginning. On the first point, he posits a state of nature in which the most powerful arrogate property to themselves since no one can impose obligations on others without physical force or the threat of it. The most powerful individuals, from Nimrod to William the Conqueror, owned the most property and prospered accordingly, he notes dryly.[28] Secondly, in order to substantiate his account of the beginnings of property, Ascham invents a clever, and as far as I know, original exegesis of the positive law of Eden:

> When *Adam* was alone in the Garden of *Eden,* he was in a state of property, for of one tree thereof he might not eat: so that his first sin was a sin against property, and therefore theft, or at least a sin of Ambition by theft; as Ambition ever since is maintein'd by usurping some other thing also which belongs to another. For that reason he hid himself as fearing to be punish't for that theft; as if Gods command Thou shalt not eat, had been Thou shalt not steale. If *Adam* had not had enough without the allowance of that tree, he might have pleaded as *David* did, when he eate of the sacrifice or shew-bread.[29]

For Ascham, God's installation of Adam as a *dominus* of the entire earth—but for a unique, crucial exception—was to be taken quite literally. God had instituted property rights from the very beginning. If living in Eden necessitated communal ownership of property, as Levellers and assorted radicals had claimed, there could be no dominion and therefore no sovereignty. Adam's recognition of God's sovereignty and of the limits of his own depends on the existence of property. Dominion and sovereignty are distinct but interdependent concepts. God will not allow his property to be violated, because to do so would be to abdicate his kingship, in effect to admit that something other than a natural right of self-preservation would justify Adam's resistance to his authority. This is absurd, and consequently Adam loses possession of his own land when he steals. By arguing that property was part of the divine intention from the beginning, Ascham demonstrates that the right to rule derived from the possession of land. Since the Parliamentarians now possessed the nation, they possessed a lawful right to rule as well.

Although Ascham's resourceful use of Genesis lends a measure of godly authority to his argument that critics had charged was lacking, his reading of the key event is a hasty one. His myopic focus on Adam misrepresents the element of temptation so crucial to the Fall as it suggests that Adam's ownership of Eden extends to Eve as well since she fails to merit even a casual reference in Ascham's exegesis. According to Ascham, Adam sins while "alone in the Garden of *Eden*," a baffling factual inaccuracy that suggests Ascham was eager to cast more responsibility for the Fall on Adam than most scriptural commentators would allow. Without Eve or the serpent, Adam's self-possession is never in doubt. He is the archetypal contracting subject who freely enters a contract with God and then equally freely breaks it.

In *Paradise Lost*, Adam and Eve's forfeiture of their dominion follows as a necessary consequence of both their failure to respect the divinely ordained limits on their behavior and their misunderstanding of marriage as instituting mutual ownership of each other. As Eve will say, she has sinned against both God and Adam in disobeying the prohibition, but Adam, too, fails to hold Eve and himself to the high Miltonic standards of marriage (10.930–31). Milton, though, differs sharply from the contentions of Ascham and Grotius on the origins of property. If the tree of knowledge can represent God's private property in *Paradise Lost*, it is only because God has explicitly ordained it as something that the law of nature does not govern. For Milton, the tree functions less as a marker of the importance of property itself than it signals God's sovereignty and his power to differentiate himself from the laws of the natural world that he has created. Milton is adamant, both in *De doctrina* and in *Paradise Lost*, that the command not to eat the fruit can have no basis in natural law. Neither is this command a symbol or a sacrament of God's law as, notably, William Ames and his followers claimed.[30] Milton exposes the logical inconsistency of this line of reasoning by pointing out that since Adam and Eve were naturally good it would have been meaningless for God to have evaluated their loyalty to the natural law. God could only have required their adherence to one or more positive laws that imposed an entirely arbitrary restriction in order to test their obedience. Milton, therefore, insists that the fruit is a thing indifferent and God's command not to eat it must be explicit and arbitrary, in other words, a positive law.[31] Abdiel will tell Satan just before he delivers the first ceremonial blow in battle that "God and nature bid the same," but the relationship between natural law and the prohibition in Eden is clearly more complex (*PL* 6.176).

Milton followed the famed Hebraist and legal scholar John Selden in his argument that the fruit was a thing indifferent, and his understanding of the relationship of reason to the natural law owes much to Selden as well. Selden's extensive work on the rabbinic understanding of natural law asserts that this law is apparent to humans not only by means of their rational faculties, but also via the direct command of God. Selden argues that God must have uttered the commands of the natural law first to Adam and then again to Noah. Subsequent generations could understand this law by means of the *intellectus agens*, or active intellect, by which Selden means the capacity of human reason when aided by divine inspiration to apprehend truth.[32] Selden's formulation of natural law contrasts with the Grotian and Hobbesian models, which posit natural law as simply those constraints on behavior that necessarily arise from the desire for self-preservation and, for Grotius, the concomitant need for society. Their reconceptualization of natural law as reason derived from self-interest diverges sharply from older classical and Thomist formulations of the natural law as a series of objective rational principles that could be drawn up as a list, the most famous of which was, of course, the second table of the law that Moses received on Sinai.[33]

Paradise Lost harmonizes these differing approaches to the natural law. God never outlines the precise tenets of the natural law for Adam and Eve since to do so would be redundant according to Milton's theology, but he does explicitly warn them about the fruit. It is this positive law that guarantees that Adam and Eve are free to obey or disobey God. The prohibition governing the fruit, then, can be read as a kind of seed of the Mosaic law: it is an explicit intervention by God that supplements the natural law and, by supplementing it, renders it distinct. While the second table clarified the natural law for the Israelites, the prohibition likewise renders the natural law meaningful in Eden. The tree of knowledge must have been chosen arbitrarily since, had it possessed innate qualities harmful to Adam and Eve, their obedience would simply have resulted from following the natural law. As Genesis makes abundantly clear, God made his creatures naturally good, and mere obedience to the natural law would require no active choice to accept God's sovereignty. Only an object indifferent, which is "something which was in itself neither good nor evil," and which "had nothing to do with the law of nature," could truly test their obedience. Commands governing things indifferent are contained in the positive law (*ius...positivum*), as Milton notes (YP 6:353; CM 15:116).

When Adam recalls for Raphael his first memories, he relates God's solemn interdiction as one piece of knowledge about paradise among many. "I come thy Guide / To the Garden of bliss, thy seat prepar'd," Adam remembers God telling him, and that divine guidance includes both the prohibition as well as an assurance that Adam remains master over the animals and plants (8.298–99). Accordingly, Adam named the animals "and understood / Thir Nature, with such knowledge God endu'd" (8.352–53). The promulgation of the natural law occurs simultaneously with the positive law, as it must if Adam is to have a real choice to sin. Milton hints, then, that the prohibition signals the Seldenic original moment at which the deity transmits the natural law to humans. Milton's unique perspective on that moment, though, has God utter a secondary, positive law in order for human reason to orient itself properly vis-à-vis the natural law. But Milton's fierce defenses of personal liberty led him toward the Grotian and Hobbesian camp as well, as he represents Adam's conflict before eating the fruit as one between his self-preservation and his natural sociability with Eve.[34]

The human understanding of the distinction between natural and positive law, though, is not ordinarily of much consequence to Adam and Eve's daily routine while in Eden. In *Paradise Lost*, the first couple takes their cues from the natural world, understanding that God's law is the ultimate origin of all of their actions. At the end of their first day in paradise, Adam tells Eve,

> th' hour
> Of night, and all things now retir'd to rest
> Mind us of like repose, since God hath set
> Labor and rest, as day and night to men
> Successive.   (4.610–14)

He concludes that the prodigious growth of the garden will beckon them to work in the morning but, for the moment, "as Nature wills, Night bids us rest" (4.633). Eve's response here is notorious as a site of Milton's misogyny in the poem, but she simply ratifies Adam's wholesale representation of their daily routine as a logical effect of the dictates of nature, and through nature, God: "what thou bidd'st / Unargu'd I obey; so God ordains, / God is thy Law, thou mine" (4.635–37). Adam expresses the natural law, which is itself a reflection of God's volition. Eve understands that Adam's words, and presumably the natural world that she observes around her, can have no meaning other than what "God ordains," even if her grammar leaves it unclear whether God has ordained that she obey Adam or merely that she has no objection to Adam's logic on this particular point. By conflating God's words with Adam's, Eve leaves little room for distinguishing the signs of nature (and therefore of God) from their own (or God's) arbitrary will.

When we meet the happy couple about to begin their daily labors in book 9, Eve has found a voice with which to assert her own desires even though she never manages to differentiate fully the natural law from the arbitrary promptings of her will. Eve's argument for the division of their labor appeals to the apparent backlog of gardening that awaits them everywhere they turn. She suggests that she understands obedience to nature as entailing more, and harder, work than they might undertake ordinarily:

> the work under our labor grows,
> Luxurious by restraint; what we by day
> Lop overgrown, or prune, or prop, or bind,
> One night or two with wanton growth derides
> Tending to wild.
> . . . .
> Let us divide our labors. (9.208–12, 14)

Obedience for Eve consists in following the dictates of the natural world around them even though it would be strange for God to have mandated so much work. Adam's rejoinder gently chides Eve for taking their work too seriously and points out that amorous looks are just as natural and reasonable as the labor that they need to perform in the garden:

> Yet not so strictly hath our Lord impos'd
> Labor, as to debar us when we need
> Refreshment, whether food, or talk between,
> Food of the mind, or this sweet intercourse
> Of looks and smiles, for smiles from Reason flow,
> To brute deni'd, and are of Love the food,
> Love not the lowest end of human life. (9.235–41)

Although Adam thinks it absurd that they might literally be choked by the garden's growth however torrid—"These paths and Bowers doubt not but our joint hands / Will keep from Wilderness with ease," he argues (9.244–45)—brief separation might actually help to enliven their relationship. This relationship, too, demands a kind of work that Adam reminds Eve is at least as important as their gardening. He suggests that perhaps Eve tires of always hearing his apparently more sage advice and therefore that "solitude sometimes is best society, / And short retirement urges sweet return" (9.249–50). Adam may find Eve's compulsion to keep busy unsettling and discovers at this point his own introversion as a validation of Eve's argument if not of her reasoning. Perhaps as a result of these mild neuroses, perhaps because the concept of willful, arbitrary action is itself difficult to fathom in Eden, all action appears to Adam and Eve as if governed by the natural law. Eve sees that law at work in the garden's apparent inducement to separate labor, while Adam finds it expressed in the necessary periodic renewal of their marriage. Overgrown pathways offer the natural evidence for Eve, as conversation and smiles furnish the same for Adam. Both suggest, in their own ways, that they understand their work and their separation not as things indifferent but as reactions to the intimate promptings of nature.

Just as the separation scene shows Adam and Eve's difficulty in putting literal distance between them, so too does it represent their difficulty at conceiving of the choice as entirely the result of individual action, free though it may be. Adam seems to win the first part of the argument easily enough as he dismisses Eve's notion of uncontrollable and dangerous growth, but her counterresponse, which asserts convincingly that true freedom requires the possibility of temptation, proves less easily refuted (9.322–41). Reasoning from mutual benefit, Adam argues that Eve ought to leave if she believes that remaining together would merely insulate her from an impending threat: "if thou think trial unsought may find / Us both securer [i.e., more careless] than thus warn'd thou seem'st / Go" (9.370–72). Although Eve's argument that "Faith, Love, Virtue unassay'd" is of little meaning neatly echoes the most resounding passages encouraging individual trial in *Areopagitica*, her separation is hardly one of principled individualism (9.335).[35] At the end of their conversation Eve remains "yet submiss" and still seeks Adam's "permission" to leave his side (9.377, 78). For Adam, the issue that seems to trouble him most is the possibility that they might not be in harmony, and he takes pains to ensure their final agreement, however strained that accord may be. Adam and Eve both seem to grasp imperfectly their own autonomy at this point. For both, free will remains a theoretical abstraction that the concrete benefits of more productive work or of closer companionship in marriage overshadow.

Eve's declaration that she must test herself in order to remain virtuous signals the impending threat. When Satan finds Eve shortly afterward, her incomplete sense of herself as an autonomous entity separate from Adam and her uncertainty about the limits of natural and personal volition become the entry points for his temptation. She does not fully understand that the natural law governs nature while both natural and positive laws govern human behavior. Her initial response to the tempting serpent is one of shock that the linguistic boundary between human and beast should have been broken: "Language of Man pronounc't / By Tongue of Brute, and human sense exprest?" she wonders (9.553–54). Eve's passive grammatical construction in describing the serpent "with human voice endu'd" suggests both her confusion about the ontological similarities between herself and the serpent and uncertainty over the agency behind this change (9.561). Since almost everything in Eden has been governed by natural law in accordance with the creative power of God, and since the only two positive laws of Eden also originate with God, it is reasonable for her to assume that the serpent's speech ultimately derives from God as well.

Nevertheless, Eve does differentiate God's interdiction from her reason as guides for conduct. Telling Satan that she can neither "taste nor touch" the tree since "God so commanded, and left that Command / Sole Daughter of his voice," she adds that "the rest, we live / Law to ourselves, our Reason is our Law" (9.651–54). Similarly, Adam implies that he understands the special nature of the command when he recounts for Raphael the moment that he heard God pronounce it. Telling the archangel that "the rigid interdiction [still] resounds / Yet dreadful in [his] ear," he contrasts that admonition with the placid natural world around him and with the "clear aspect" of the divine countenance that soon reappears (8.334–36). Eve, however, hears this interdiction secondarily via Adam and in a more measured tone (4.419–35). She has already acknowledged that Adam acts as a conduit of God's law for her: "what thou bidd'st / Unargu'd I obey; so God ordains, / God is thy Law, thou mine" (4.635–37). In the crucial separation scene, though, Eve does argue with Adam about the nature of their work, and her rational arguments, in part, gain for her a victory. It is not so clear that what Eve understands as law and what she understands as opinion or suggestion remain entirely distinct. If Adam's word is her law and she has just negotiated that law with him, it becomes plausible for her to imagine that a divine command might be similarly negotiable under the right circumstances.

It is precisely this opportunity for debate that Satan exploits by framing his temptation as an appeal to reason when Eve's understanding of the difference between divine ordinance and human choice informed by reason is cursory at best. When Eve reminds Satan of God's prohibition, he asks her, "hath God then said that of the Fruit / Of all these Garden Trees ye shall not eat, / Yet Lords declar'd of all in Earth or Air?" (9.656–58). Eve did not say that *all* of the trees were forbidden, but Satan implies that perhaps he might understand a divine natural logic if God had extended a blanket prohibition. Masking his insinuation as a question asking for clarification, Satan attempts to muddle Eve's distinction between God's positive and natural law. Since positive law governs nothing in Eden except the tree of knowledge and their marriage, and since Adam and Eve, by definition, act in accordance with natural law, there is no possible way in which she can rationally evaluate the justness of the positive law. Satan had grasped this point instantly upon learning that the fruit of the tree had been proscribed: "Knowledge forbidd'n? / Suspicious, reasonless" (4.515–16).[36] Accordingly, he tempts Eve with ringing oratory "impregn'd / With Reason" (9.737–38). Reason, though, is a tool insufficient for this particular test of obedience, as Milton shows plangently in Eve's final speech before she tastes the fruit as she argues that God could never have intended to debar her from knowledge; "such prohibitions bind not," she concludes (9.760).

This is the crux of the poem's theodicy: how can Adam and Eve understand the basis of God's completely arbitrary prohibition when neither their reason nor their complete sense of union with the natural world provides them with tools adequate for that task? Adam and Eve must intuit the basis for this positive law, but unlike the angels, as Raphael explains, they are not yet accustomed to this mode of apprehending knowledge. Reason is mostly intuitive for angels, but mostly discursive for humans (5.486–90). Since Adam and Eve have not encountered any other explicit positive law with which to compare God's prohibition, the discursive use of reason to evaluate that law's intent and scope is inadequate. Positive law operates paradoxically in the poem: it validates the natural law that provides freedom for human action by guaranteeing that Adam and Eve have a real chance of failure. The Blakean and, later, Empsonian traditions of reading the poem, though, would argue that God has weighted the die for failure, and the assertion is difficult to deny given Milton's polemics that defend resistance to positive laws that contravened the natural law. Satan's temptation of Eve follows the same logic: he argues that Eve ought to eat the apple because the prohibition is an arbitrary statute with no basis in nature and that eating the apple is an act that would accord better with God's gift to her of dominion over nature.

Eve's fall occurs when she reasons that natural law supersedes the law governing the tree of knowledge, thereby absolving her of obedience to it, and in a similar way Adam explicitly locates in nature his justification for joining Eve in sin. When she returns bearing a branch with the fruit, Adam cries out, "I feel / The Link of Nature draw me" (9.913–14); "I feel / The Bond of Nature draw me to my own" (9.955–56). Although in pointing to the natural bond between them he merely points back to himself and to his own free will, Adam finds it difficult to distinguish between a choice that he makes entirely of his own accord and one that Eve has already made for him. The "Link" or the "Bond" of nature that Adam feels implies that only some heroic force could liberate him from this captivity, just as Paul will emphasize that only Christ could liberate the Jews from the bondage of the law (Gal. 4:1–31). The terms also recall the legal formula for a divorce *a vinculo matrimonii;* marriage is a durable bond but not an unbreakable one under the right conditions, although Adam does not seem to admit any circumstances that could possibly end his marriage.[37] Indeed, Adam implies that he understands his sin as having already occurred as he wonders skeptically about the possibility that he might "another Rib afford" should he decide to abandon Eve (9.912).

This odd anxiety about a future operation reveals a deeper uncertainty about Adam's own medial position as created being and creator. At first, he appears for a moment to cut God out of the creative act and to take responsibility for Eve's creation himself, but then attempts to quiet his nerves by suggesting that "God, Creator wise / ...[would never] so destroy / Us his prime Creatures" (9.938–40).[38] In the end, Adam casts his lot with Eve by finding more similarities with her as created being than with God as Creator. But this interpretation demands that he believe himself already to have sinned and that he mistake the symbolic "one flesh" for literal truth. Adam gravely compromises his sense of himself the moment that he decides that his self resides within Eve and not within his own autonomous being. His hyperbolic rhetoric in which all creation is "dependent made" on Eve and him and, therefore, that "God shall uncreate, / Be frustrate, do, undo, and labor lose" were they to fall completes the process (9.943–44). Adam's hermeneutical approach is backwards: he reasons that the symbol of marriage has caused him to sin when, in fact, his misrepresentation of that symbol as natural fact actually leads him into sin.

Jason P. Rosenblatt shows that Adam's understanding of his marriage is backward in another sense as well. Telling Eve that "to lose thee were to lose myself" (9.959), Adam echoes Milton's conclusion in *Tetrachordon* that the desire to remain in an uncompanionate marriage is the "servil temptation of loosing our selves" (YP 2:681).[39] Adam's words immediately before this moment, though, suggest his extreme uneasiness with the concept of the self: "My own in thee, for what thou art is mine; / Our State cannot be sever'd, we are one, / One Flesh; to lose thee were to lose myself" (9.957–59).[40] Milton takes extreme care with Adam's language here: he will fall with Eve because she is, he says, "my own in thee," that is, something of him possessed in her substance.

And, likewise, something of her that he possesses: "for what thou art is mine." He does not say, "for what thou art I am"; they are not a single essence. Milton is careful to grant Adam the autonomous choice to fall (and implies that had he thought it through a bit more, he might not have), but Adam's words have the effect of obscuring the nature of his connection with Eve rather than clarifying it. Indeed, had he followed the logic of "what thou art is mine," he would have been led back to marriage as property and to the possibility of alienating that property, even if he might still have found it extraordinarily difficult to cast off the one he loves. Milton's poetic solution to Adam's dilemma requires a much more complex process of reasoning than the theological solution to an uncompanionate marriage that he had outlined in the divorce tracts. Eve is not an abstraction like the unnamed sinful marriage partner in *Tetrachordon*, but a living spouse bound to Adam not simply by marriage, but by love.

When Adam does decide to fall, the narrator excises the ties of love from the account, supplying a stark description of the act:

> She gave him of that fair enticing Fruit
> With liberal hand: he scrupl'd not to eat
> Against his better knowledge, not deceiv'd,
> But fondly overcome with Female charm.   (9.996–99)

Adam fully retains his capacity to reason, but it is by an abstract "Female charm" that he is finally subdued. How does the poem suggest that we reconcile the narrator's adamant assertion here that Adam was "not deceiv'd" with the Father's equally resolute declaration, "Man falls deceiv'd" (3.130)? A literalist reading would point out that Eve falls for corporate man and is deceived by Satan, while Adam, individually, is undeceived in his resolution to fall with Eve. But the account here is so much colder than Adam's anxious deliberations immediately before he eats the fruit. In echoing Paul's words that "Adam was not deceived," Milton shifts the register of the poem back to one of justification for God's punishment of sin (1 Tim. 2:14).[41] Both Adam and Eve must fall for humanity to fall, and the narrator's pronouncement of a clear-sighted Adam suggests that he does not see himself as fully autonomous from Eve: her deception is his deception, he tells himself, though he understands this line of reasoning to be fallacious. In choosing her, he literally chooses death, enacting Milton's lurid image of the marriage partners not as godly spouses but as two carcasses.

Adam enthralled by "Female charm" recalls the uxoriousness, as Milton often puts it, of many of the heroes whom he had once considered as subjects for his biblical epic, notably Samson and Solomon.[42] The crucial difference between Adam at the moment of his fall and these later figures lies in his conflicted sense of his physical and spiritual unity with Eve. Adam feels at once extreme self-love and self-loathing—and surely this intensity of emotion must have been one of the reasons why Milton recognized the superiority of Adam and Eve to any other biblical subject—which spurs his decision to confirm the oneness he feels he ought to share with Eve. Adam seems to understand that he has not yet participated in Eve's sin, but "against his better knowledge" and driven by his own form of *philautia*, he can find no means of alienating a part of himself.[43] By construing the idea of "one flesh" too narrowly, Adam relinquishes his own individuality for a deluded sense of what constitutes himself.

Adam's extremely literal interpretation of "one flesh" is understandable, especially given Milton's investment in presenting Eden in proleptic terms. Though the morally correct decision for Adam must be the assertion of his own individuality, his relationship with Eve and with the garden around him implores our sympathy for the extraordinary difficulty of this choice.[44] Adam and Eve's colloquy immediately before the Fall reiterates the durability of representing marriage as indissoluble because of the acute distress Adam feels at the prospect of losing Eve. And yet, Adam enacts what his narrow-minded descendants will do when interpreting Christ's words on divorce in a similarly restrictive fashion. The colloquy provides an explanation for Milton's need to reformulate his argument for divorce between the publication of the second edition of *Doctrine and Discipline* and *Tetrachordon*. In the earlier tract he dismisses the scriptural evidence that "what God has joined, let no man put asunder" as too obscure. But the enduring legacy of that apparent command, emblematized for Adam in the creation of Eve, suggests the potency of that line of reasoning. Clearly, Eve cannot serve as a help meet when she offers the branch of forbidden fruit to Adam, but she may still be one flesh with his. It is not hard to see how Adam's intense emotions cause him to override God's prohibition against the fruit by appealing to a prohibition against divorce that seems to be present in nature.

The more theologically mature and more difficult decision available to Adam is the one at which Milton arrives in *Tetrachordon*, though Adam has not the luxury of having bushwhacked through three divorce tracts first in order to set his argument straight. Marriage is a kind of property, an "outward good," as *Tetrachordon* insists, that can draw Adam closer to God and to nature, although the benefits of this "outward good" never outweigh the potential of marriage to cause imminent harm. By figuring marriage as "propriety," both what is fitting and what one owns, Milton crystallizes the importance of each marriage partner's individual nature before and during a marriage. In order to understand the paradisal meaning of marriage as "sole propriety / ... of all things common else," Adam must recognize that his marriage is fundamentally different from every other attraction that he feels in Eden (4.751–52). The narrator's gloss on marriage as "sole propriety" refers not to their monogamy (Adam is, after all, a patriarch), but to the special addition of law outside the natural law that applies only to them (it is *proprius*).[45] Although Adam is drawn to every other living thing by the natural law, Raphael cautions him explicitly to regard Eve as a separate, individual being and to make his own decisions based on "self-esteem, grounded on just and right / Well manag'd" (8.572–73). Adam's natural reason may not have been entirely sufficient to distinguish himself from Eve, but with an explicit, divine intervention Adam becomes fully capable of understanding his proper place in marriage. Eve's fall sets God's arbitrary demarcation of the limits of lawful action alongside the marriage bond, and when these two positive laws conflict, Adam is understandably distressed. He chooses to take solace not by trusting the word of God, inscrutable as it seems, but in the familiar comfort of imagining himself as permanently connected to everything in nature.

It is fitting that when the Son arrives in the garden to confront Adam and Eve and to discharge the Father's (or nature's) will in disciplining them, he does so individually. There is scriptural authorization for this, but Milton surely means to emphasize that specific punishments for Eve and for Adam indicate that their marriage no longer remains the "one flesh" that had pertained as a consequence of their companionship in paradise. As their sin alienates them from God, so too does it alienate them from each other. Their mutual recriminations at the end of book 9 lead nowhere, and the Son must explicitly specify their labor and their generative functions. They must rely on each other, and their marriage will require that each act as a help meet to the other. The choice to reconcile will remain with them as they descend from the mountain of paradise to make their way in history.[46]

There remains the further, strange punishment of the serpent in whose "offense" the Son seems peculiarly interested only after the fact (10.171). The curse bestowed on the serpent is, of course, biblical in origin and Milton was bound to include it in his epic, though he appears uneasy as his narrator clarifies that the animal was "unable to transfer / The Guilt on him who made him instrument" (10.165–66). The narrator explains the curse in a very brief line and a half: "justly then accurst, / As vitiated in Nature" (10.168–69), a curious phrase that seems to occlude more than it explains. There is something profoundly unnatural about its physical shape, the Son implies, and it is therefore fitting that it be permanently vitiated or arbitrarily disadvantaged.[47] The words of the curse, sentencing as they do the serpent to eating dust and to a pathetic means of movement, set it apart from nature for eternity. The serpent remains as a sign of a perpetual positive law in contrast to the world around it governed by the natural law. The lines that immediately follow, "more to know / Concern'd not Man (since he no further knew) / Nor alter'd his offense" (10.169–71), may seem like an ungraceful exit from the explanation on the narrator's part but remind the reader that the serpent's relevance is as a sign of God's positive law. Adam and Eve need only remember that God can intervene arbitrarily in nature as he wishes. This deliberate intervention will then serve as a sign of their eventual salvation.

Like the prohibition governing the tree of knowledge, the vitiation of the serpent can be understood as a classic instance of what Milton elsewhere calls with reference to the tree "a declaration of power" (YP 6:352). The punishment of the serpent teaches Adam and Eve that God can do it. It creates an indelible differentiation between natural and positive laws and finally makes obvious to Adam and Eve a distinction that would have been helpful to them before the Fall. The knowledge they gain by eating the fruit includes this crucial distinction, and the vitiated serpent becomes living evidence of the freedom they have lost. The serpent represents the necessity of a positive law to guarantee human freedom and a way for Michael to teach the meaning of the protevangelium. As a metaphor of the arbitrary and constraining positive law of the Old Testament, the serpent reminds the faithful of a future intervention in human history when Christ will abolish the old law by writing a new one in the human heart (Ezek. 11:19, 36:26; Rom. 2:14–15; 2 Cor. 3:3; and *PL* 12.485–90). The woman's descendants will bruise the head of the serpent, while it shall strike at their heels. The serpent becomes at once a sign of the promise of a new law and a punishment for disobedience to the old law while it is in force.[48]

Paradoxically, Adam's decision to fall with Eve evacuates the warmth from the poem's representation of marriage, and it becomes necessary to understand that bond in the harsher terms of an abstract positive law. Adam is overcome not so much by Eve, the narrator intones, but by a faceless "Female charm" (9.999). His incomplete understanding of marriage prevents him from articulating the meaning of individuality. Had he fully appreciated marriage as a positive law he would have understood its divine purpose as the joining of two helpmates who draw each other closer to God. Raphael had offered hope that paradisal marriage could one day exhibit the same signs of the angelic commingling of bodily substance even if, for the moment, Adam cannot truly understand what angelic intimacy really looks and feels like. Since human reason is by nature discursive and may become in time, according to Raphael, more intuitive, only with a partner can this change be effected. Marriage is the only other positive law in Eden to which the positive law governing the tree of knowledge could have been compared. Although not an explicit positive law, Adam and Eve could have used their discursive reasoning and Raphael's words to probe the meaning of their love for each other. It is not the same as love of nature, as Eve seems to think, nor is it the same as self-love, as Adam convinces himself. Marital love is the free and arbitrary love of another, of a person beyond the self, and Milton's theodicy accordingly requires that Adam and Eve's marriage bond be the primary bulwark against their fall. Far from causing the Fall, their love for each other could have led them to greater love of God.

As it is, that path toward God becomes much more circuitous as a result of the Fall. The reality of the vast and newly dangerous world indeed deepens the mutual love of Adam and Eve, but it does so out of necessity. Adam and Eve need each other as the at once terrifying and quiet final lines of the epic insist. Their marriage not only ought to bring them closer to a godly life but, crucially, aid in their survival. The positive law of marriage after the Fall suggests a new and equally valid basis for the law of nature. In accordance with Selden's account of its origins, Milton has Michael narrate the strange ways of a fallen world to equip Adam with revealed knowledge about the law and his descendants' transgressions of it. But as it is for Grotius and Hobbes, Milton's fallen world is one in which the first law is that of self-preservation. Adam speaks more than he realizes at the time when he declares to Eve, "to lose thee were to lose myself" (9.959). By disobeying the positive law of God in eating the fruit, Adam rationalizes obedience to what he supposes is the natural law. But in misunderstanding the natural law of Eden, he utters the words of the stern new law that will govern the fallen world.

Yale University

Miltonic Proportions: Divine Distribution and the Nature of the Lot in *Paradise Lost*

Joseph Wallace

In book 9 of *Paradise Lost*, Satan tells Eve that he has attained a "life more perfect...than fate / Meant me, by venturing higher than my lot."[1] Eve, having tasted the fruit of the forbidden tree, then urges Adam:

> Thou therefore also taste, that equal lot
> May join us, equal joy, as equal love;
> Lest thou not tasting, different degree
> Disjoin us. (9.881–84)

Adam's reasoning fluctuates thereafter, but eventually he is resolved:

> However I with thee have fixed my lot,
> Certain to undergo like doom, if death
> Consort with thee, death is to me as life;
> So forcible within my heart I feel
> The bond of nature draw me to my own,
> My own in thee, for what thou art is mine. (9.952–57)

The repetition of the word "lot" in these passages indicates its particular importance for the logic of Satan's temptation and its palpable effect on both Eve and Adam. It is significant that Eve's deployment of Satan's term accompanies her anxious repetition of the word "equal" in her plea to Adam. Satan has persuaded her to look for inequality in God's dispensation. Both Adam and Eve eventually misconceive the structuring function of inequality within God's creation; the Fall partly results from their own attempts to bridge the gaps of an uneven cosmos.

By characterizing his inheritance from God as his "lot," Satan raises an issue that preoccupied seventeenth century religious and political thinkers alike, namely, the rationale behind God's unequal distribution of his essence in the created world and the impact that inequality had on human political and social relationships. Lots have a long history of commentary as occasional instruments of God's will but also as mechanisms of political representation; in both cases they function as tools of division and selection, whether of God's division of tribes and selection of elders, or of the division of goods and selection of officers.[2] Milton was certainly aware of the vibrant seventeenth century discourse on lots, and in *Paradise Lost* he engages it to describe the relationship between God's will and the inequality that God institutes among his creatures.

The nature of this inequality matters in the poem; its presence both in the natural order and in arbitrary divine decree causes no end of confusion for the first humans. Lots represent one way to ameliorate the perception of inequality; a lottery preserves inequality but also relies on a contingent, egalitarian principle to function. Characterizing the divine will as a distributor of lots goes some way toward introducing contingency, and mobility, into the cosmos. The discourse surrounding the lot in the seventeenth century informs arguments about the interaction between the inequality of divine distribution and proportional human responsibility in *Paradise Lost*. In the poem, the idea that God gives each person a "lot" leads naturally to the imperative for humans to interpret their relationship to God proportionally, literally, "according to one's share" (Lat., *pro portione*). Milton coordinates theological and mathematical models of proportional thinking about divine and human relationships in the garden, and uses them to define Adam and Eve's experience therein. Reading the discourse of lots in the poem reveals some of Milton's most complex thinking about the imperfect alignment between divine dispensation and the human ability to interpret and structure that dispensation. The "lot" becomes a site where religious belief in a just and all-powerful God intersects with the political and social necessity of understanding and enacting the inequalities inherent in a hierarchical universe.

As Eve indicates with her association of lot with equality, casting lots was often intended as an impartial way to create inequality among things that were previously equal. Just as God could assign different portions to different tribes in the Old Testament by lot,[3] so too human legal and political systems could utilize lots to create a fair method of division among those of equal standing.[4] The question of God's unequal dispensation has become central to scholarly discussions of the relationship between religious duty and political identity in *Paradise Lost*. The idea that Milton might set liberty in opposition to equality has proved to be enduring. According to some scholars, Milton's monism, along with his Arianism, tended to produce a view of the cosmos in which hierarchical differentiation is always somewhat at odds with material unity.[5] Just as Milton in his other works advocates social equity even as he dismisses political equality, Milton the author of *Paradise Lost* was more interested in examining equality in terms of proportional relationships than in terms of political subjectivity.[6]

In Milton's system of hierarchies, morality can only be relational and proportional, not constructed radically, in the sense of attempting to arrive at a fundamental egalitarian position. In the poem, human beings come into being, according to Victoria Kahn, "if not fully formed, at least already created," a view she opposes to the Hobbesian one that we "construct ourselves and our obligations ex nihilo."[7] Obligation, therefore, does not inhere merely in the interaction between autonomous rights and natural or divine laws, but rather in the duties enjoined by the proportional relationship between human inheritance and divine will.[8] In the world of *Paradise Lost*, respect for hierarchical inequality must also acknowledge the original source of embodied equality represented by a God who creates *ex deo*.[9] But this acknowledgment has a destabilizing influence on relationships conceived within one rung of the celestial hierarchy, which is why Satan can confuse Eve with the illusion of movement and the potential for equality represented by knowledge.

In terms of gender, the critical discussion has turned on the relative amount of inequality that exists between Adam and Eve and the effect that this has on the Fall. The tension between the two accounts of Creation in Genesis inaugurates a similar tension in the poem: in the priestly account of Genesis 1 Adam and Eve are created simultaneously, while in the Yahwist account of Genesis 2 Eve is created from Adam's rib.[10] This tension has generated a range of critical opinion on the question of whether Milton intends the original state of inequality to be a constant or something to be ameliorated within human relationships.[11] The degree to which Milton integrates gender equality or inequality within the theology of the poem has proved to be a focal point for scholars debating Milton's views of equality.[12] The couple's differences clearly lead them to different conceptions about their relationship to God and to each other, and yet the question remains whether their differences are qualitative or quantitative. In other words, do they possess the same abilities but in different degrees, or are they imbued by God with different abilities? Even the Son, as is made clear in book 3, relates to God more properly by "merit" and duty rather than solely by "birthright" (3.309). Adam and Eve struggle to understand the nature of their duty to God in terms of their own inequality and proportional relationship to him and each other. The fall of the first couple comes about partly because of their perception that inequalities among beings are more rigid than they are, which is why Satan's use of the term "lot" works so well. It crystalizes Eve's, and the reader's, worry that the signs of God's will might be revealed only in discrete instances, rather than at every moment within the human will and consciousness. Satan portrays God's will as static and confined, which actually helps Eve to conceive of her own subjectivity as mobile, though Satan encourages her to misunderstand the inequality within the poem's monist cosmos.[13]

This long-standing critical discussion about God's methods of differentiation and distribution might profitably be channeled through seventeenth century debates about lots. Lots often were the focal point of a complex discourse in the seventeenth century about the relationship between God's will and the religious and political structures of the created world. One of the most important connotations of the "lot" was that of the special privilege that God bestowed on some of his subjects but not others. Furthermore, many in the seventeenth century would have been aware that "lot" was a shibboleth specifically for clerical privilege. The Greek word for "lot" is κλῆρος, which was transliterated into Latin as *clerus*, the word for a clergyman or a clerical order. The origin of this usage lies in the appointment of Matthias as an apostle in the first chapter of Acts. There were two candidates, but only one could be chosen, and so the other apostles cast lots: "And they gave forth their lots; and the lot fell upon Matthias; and he was numbered with the eleven apostles" (Acts 1:26). Since they called upon the Lord before they cast their lots, the implication was that God himself had selected the clergy for a special place in his church. Thus, the term "lot" came to stand in for God's method of showing his will to his creatures. This derivation was also enshrined in canon law in chapter 21 of Gratian's *Decretum:* "Cleros, & clericos hinc appellatos credimus, quia Matthias sorte electus est, quem primum per Apostolos legimus ordinatum. Κλῆρος enim graece, sors latine, vel hereditas dicitur. Propterea ergo dicti sunt clerici; quia de sorte Domini sunt; vel quia Domini partem habent" (We believe that clergymen are called that because Matthias was chosen by lot, as we read that he was the first to be ordained by the apostles. For *klēros* in Greek and *sors* in Latin mean inheritance. On account of this therefore they are called clerics; because they come from the lot of the Lord; or because they have a portion from the Lord).[14] Thus, one of the prime defenses of prelacy was that God gave clerics a special inheritance or portion in his church.

Understandably, Presbyterians reacted against this logic in the 1640s. The Scottish Presbyterian George Gillespie argued in 1641, "For there is none of the faithful, who may not say with *David, Psal.* 16.5. *The Lord is the portion of my inheritance;* and of whom also it may not bee said, that they are the Lords inheritance, or lot: for *Peter* giveth this name to the whole Church, 1 Pet. 5.3." Gillespie contests the appropriation of the lot by those defending episcopacy: "But *Matthias* the Apostle was chosen by lot. What then? By what reason doth the Canon law draw from hence a name common to all the Ministers of the Gospell?"[15] Milton, too, joined this attack on the priestly lot. In *Of Reformation*, Milton argues that in the time of Elizabeth, the bishops convinced the queen that their existence as intermediaries functioned as a safeguard for her prerogative. And because of their success, "They had found a good Tabernacle, they sate under a spreading Vine, their Lot was fallen in a faire Inheritance."[16] In his *Reason of Church-Government*, Milton portrays both Lucifer and Adam as priests, because both overstepped their lot: "For Lucifer before Adam was the first prelat Angel, and both he, as is commonly thought, and our forefather Adam, as we all know, for aspiring above their orders, were miserably degraded" (YP 1:762). Of course, these very orders were justified, in the later church at least, by means of the priestly lot.

That Milton's Satan possesses the characteristics of an ambitious cleric is not surprising.[17] In book 4 of *Paradise Lost,* he is compared to a hireling priest infiltrating the church: "So clomb this first grand thief into God's fold: / So since into his church lewd hirelings climb" (4.192–93). But Satan's recourse to the language of lots in book 9 signifies more than his priestly ambition. It is also part of a long-standing argument about how God distributes justice to his creations and how he reveals his will to them. For exhaustive information on lots, seventeenth century readers would have turned to the scholar and clergyman Thomas Gataker, who composed a treatise on lots in 1619 and revised it in 1627. Gataker argues that there are some lots, such as those cast by God, that are not technically up to chance at all. These are divinatory, or "extraordinary" lots. However, divisory, "ordinary" lots are used in mundane situations to choose between two fundamentally similar options. With a divinatory lot, one expects "to have the division by Lot made exactly and precisely according to the right of the thing divided in regard of those among whom it is divided, or according to the truth of some thing that is thereby enquired into."[18] When God casts a lot, for example, it is extraordinary in that it shows his will directing chance. Gataker explains that when God casts a lot the result will be the same every time: "Herein is the difference betweene the one and the other, betweene the extraordinary Lot, wherein there is an immediate hand of God for speciall purpose, and the ordinary Lot, wherein there is not; that the one could not but fall certainely, were it never so oft cast, as in the Lots used for the discovery of *Achan* and *Jonas,* and in the election of *Saul* and *Matthias,* and the like." Gataker argues throughout his treatise that the one type of lot has no relevance to the other; that is, ordinary lots do not reveal God's will, just his "ordinary providence."[19] They simply provide an equitable standard of choice when faced with two indifferent options.

The theological implications of this position were apparent to those interested in the legitimacy of the clerical inheritance. Gataker's delineation of the two types of lots left room both for a privileged clergy instituted by an "extraordinary" lot and for a civic realm in which magistrates often relied on lots to maintain social equity. Gataker eventually advocated a mixture of Episcopal and Presbyterian systems of church governance when he served in the Westminster Assembly. Others, especially those inclining more toward Presbyterianism and Independency, tried to reposition the role of lots in ecclesiastical conflict. For many, the division between "ordinary" and "extraordinary" lots was an artificial one; any cast of a lot was an appeal to chance and, indirectly, to God the director of chance. Milton enters the debate about lots, albeit briefly, in *De doctrina Christiana*. There he argues, "The casting of lots is in effect an appeal to the divine power for explanation or arbitration in uncertain or controversial matters" (YP 6:690). But he also defends the indeterminacy of lots with recourse to God's unpredictable will: "The casting of lots is sometimes attacked on the grounds that, when it is tried more than once the result is found to vary, and so must be mere chance. But this is a poor argument, because when God himself has been tried more than once by some insistent questioner, he has sometimes given conflicting replies, (as he did to Balaam, for instance, Num. xii. 12, 20: *do not go with them...Get up, go with them*)" (YP 6:690). Milton contends that relying on chance is implicitly an appeal to God, but that God only reveals himself in a way that would allow us partial, not systematic, knowledge of him and his will.[20]

Milton's strategy was one way to argue against the special privilege of the priestly class: the lot mimics the indeterminacy of God's responses to the same question, and thus lots cannot be used to determine God's absolute will. Rather, the lot is a tool that mitigates the human tendency toward willfulness. In 1678 Vincent Alsop, a Presbyterian, could write of "a great, and solemn Ordinance of God, viz. *The Lot,* wherein the Alseeing and Alruling God Controuls the Contingency of the voluble Creature."[21] For Alsop, the lot is a mechanism of control over chance because it is an equitable standard of arbitration that eliminates the perception of inequality in decisions of "voluble," or willful, creatures. But Alsop, like Milton, is blurring the distinction between ordinary and extraordinary lots. The danger for Presbyterians was that the separation of ordinary and extraordinary lots could make room for the special privileges of a clerical order. In other words, if contingency is made into a legitimate ethical and theological force, then it would have to be admitted that there is one realm in which God exercises absolute discretion and one in which, as Gataker argued, the discretion of contingency is left to human authorities interpreting God's will. Better, thought some, simply to ascribe all contingency to God's will.[22]

The origins of this debate about contingency lie in the early seventeenth century and the rise of anti-Calvinist sentiment among the clergy.[23] As early as 1613 Thomas Jackson could argue that uncertainty about God's providence was the chief impediment to "professing true religion." Therefore, "Unto this purpose much would it avail, to be resolved whether all things fall out by fatal necessity, or some contingently; how fate and contingency (if compatible each with the other) stand mutually affected, how both subordinate to the absolute immutability of that one everlasting decree."[24] Robert Shelford stated plainly in 1635, "[God] hath given to man free-will; and to maintain this, he hath ordained contingencie."[25] The increasing trend in Arminian theology of positioning contingency as an analogue of free will prompted the Independent minister John Owen to respond in 1643 with *A Display of Arminianisme: Being a Discovery of the Old Pelagian Idol Free-Will, with the New Goddesse Contingency*. For the Calvinist Owen, "the ancient casting of lots" represents the supreme example of God's control of contingency, because lots are "a thing as casuall and accidentall as can be imagined... yet God overruleth them to the declaring of his purpose." However, Owen does acknowledge that God makes a place for things properly contingent: "And yet this overruling act of Gods providence, (as no other decree or act of his) doth not rob things contingent of their proper nature: for cannot he who effectually causeth that they shall come to passe, cause also that they shall come to passe contingently."[26] The debate thus turned on the extent to which God institutes contingency and permits it within his cosmos; the extent to which, in other words, contingent events were signs of his will. And again, Owen wants to blur the distinction between ordinary and extraordinary lots. Partly, this is so that he can argue against clerical privilege: if God controls all contingent events, it does not make sense to speak of different kinds of lots, since all contingent events are signs of his will. Indeed, if every cast of a lot is actually an appeal to God, as Milton thought, then this further argues against dividing chance occurrences into signs of God's will on the one hand and indifferent ethical indicators on the other.

Milton plays on the difference between the two types of lots in book 4 of *Paradise Lost*. When Uriel comes down to Eden to warn that some evil spirit has escaped, it turns out that in heaven, as in the Hebrew temple, ministerial duties are assigned by lotteries: "Gabriel, to thee thy course by lot hath given / Charge and strict watch that to this happy place / No evil thing approach or enter in" (4.561–63). This lot functions as a divisory lot; among the angels of heaven the lot allows choice without the accompanying pride of election. For the heavenly hierarchies, chance functions as an indicator of God's will that duties be done, but also that those duties do not limit the freedom of the angels. Satan, of course, disjoined freedom and duty to God. Thus, we are meant to contrast the selection of Gabriel by lot with the devils' system of voting in book 2.[27] "With full assent / They vote" (2.388–89) on whether or not to seduce man. They then start to vote on the agent they will send to earth. As Beelzebub describes the ideal candidate, "Here he had need / All circumspection, and we now no less / Choice in our suffrage" (2.413–15). It is a neat reversal that Satan, who has remarked on his distaste for service, volunteers for this duty. However, for him elections are not about service but about pride, while for Gabriel, selection by lot underscores the union of duty and equality in heavenly government.

At the end of book 4, Milton introduces a divinatory lot during the confrontation between Gabriel and Satan. The confrontation is all the more meaningful because it consists of the angel chosen by lot and the angel who elected himself. And indeed, the contest is decided by lot once again, albeit a different kind of lot. Gabriel explains:

> Satan, I know thy strength, and thou knowst mine,
> Neither our own but given; what folly then
> To boast what arms can do, since thine no more
> Than heaven permits, nor mine, though doubled now
> To trample thee as mire: for proof look up,
> And read thy lot in yon celestial sign
> Where thou art weighed, and shown how light, how weak,
> If thou resist. The fiend looked up and knew
> His mounted scale aloft.   (4.1006–14)

His "lot" is the sign of Libra, the scales. God himself weighs the two consequences of Satan's leaving or staying; Satan's "lot" is thus a sign of God's will rather than an indication of his own strength. God's scale is simply a representation of his will that Satan not fight Gabriel but rather leave to tempt Adam and Eve. However, it becomes evident to the reader, and perhaps to Satan as well, that the battle between Gabriel and Satan would not have been decided based on their immutable "lot" of strength, which heaven had ordained; rather, God changed Gabriel's portion of strength, and the resulting situation became Satan's lot. Gabriel rightly argues that his agency is paradoxically both his own and dependent on divine allotment, which God can change based on the freely made decisions of his creatures. God permits a certain degree of contingency in the "lot" that ends book 4.

Here, as elsewhere, Milton's God is self-limiting, allowing for the potentiality and contingency with which his creatures exercise their own, self-limiting freedoms.[28] Thus, to speak of a fixed "lot" in a monist universe is somewhat nonsensical and at least rests on a misunderstanding of the way that God's distribution partakes of contingency. But it is also a mistake to align one's "lot" completely with contingency. In book 2, the fallen angels misunderstand God's distribution by invoking a Stoic ethic of resignation to fate even as they replace God's will with pure chance. Belial argues that changing their "lot" depends on the interaction between chance and their own mental resolve:

> Besides what hope the never-ending flight
> Of future days may bring, what chance, what change
> Worth waiting, since our present lot appears
> For happy though but ill, for ill not worst,
> If we procure not to ourselves more woe.   (2.221–25)

For Belial, it makes sense to speak of a "present lot" because chance may offer him and the others an opportunity to change it. Mammon, too, constructs a false binary of fate and chance:

> him to unthrone we then
> May hope, when everlasting fate shall yield
> To fickle chance, and Chaos judge the strife:
> The former vain to hope argues as vain
> The latter: for what place can be for us
> Within heaven's bound, unless heaven's lord supreme
> We overpower?   (2.231–37)

Mammon does not sufficiently integrate chance into the complete scheme of God's creation. The devils paradoxically see their position as at once strictly fixed and contingently mutable. They have not encountered the abyss of Chaos, as Satan will later on, and thus assume that chance is a force existing outside of divine dispensation.[29]

Because God's universe is monistic, there is a sense in which it is correct to speak of contingency holding sway over some parts of it. For, as Satan sets out on his voyage, he meets Chance and Chaos.[30] Over the "eternal anarchy" (2.896),

> Chaos umpire sits,
> And by decision more embroils the fray
> By which he reigns: next him high arbiter
> Chance governs all.   (2.907–10)

Satan is fascinated by this "wild abyss" (2.917) with its "embryon atoms" (2.900). It may be at this very moment that Satan decides to tempt humanity with chance; the lack of limits in the abyss seems to destabilize the legitimacy of hierarchical station. What happens next only strengthens Satan's notion that chance might form a way to combat God's will. Satan falls into the abyss,

> and to this hour
> Down had been falling, had not by ill chance
> The strong rebuff of some tumultuous cloud
> Instinct with fire and nitre hurried him
> As many miles aloft: (2.934–38)

Satan, armed with the knowledge that God does permit chance within his orderly universe, proceeds to tempt Eve with the same possibility that intrigued the rebel angels: that chance might also permit fundamental, radical equality.

Yet, the idea that God allows things to occur contingently also grants Eve the license to eliminate such contingency by making herself "more equal" (9.823) to Adam. In book 9, Satan portrays his own inheritance from God as mutable, granting him license to venture beyond the fixed lot he has received. And yet, he also implies that by doing so he has found a way to stabilize and even eliminate contingencies by changing his lot. Knowledge of causes is, for Satan, a kind of technology that would correct the uncertainty that accompanies the perception of inequality, which itself stems from being a creature inhabiting a certain place within the cosmic whole. Satan's "science" is the power "not only to discern / Things in their causes, but to trace the ways / Of highest agents, deemed however wise" (9.681–83). This knowledge of causes would apparently grant one a vantage point from which to observe the entire chain of cause and effect in the cosmos. From this vantage, inequalities would come to seem contingent in themselves, merely the result of the inexorable series of proximate causes, which only increase in complexity and effect as the distance from God increases. Satan perceived that inequality is easily characterized as contingent; and so his venture beyond his contingent position supposedly makes him equal to those above him. Similarly, after Eve tastes the fruit she begins to think that if Adam also eats then they will have an "equal lot," along with "equal joy" and "equal love" (9.881–82). Satan persuades Eve to see inequality as a kind of absence of awareness that has come about by chance, but that can be stabilized by means of some sort of knowledge or art that can eliminate the power of chance.[31]

That Satan's temptation plays on the idea of inequality is especially appropriate, because one of the central ideas of the middle books of *Paradise Lost* is that God orders his creation proportionally and therefore institutes proportional inequality. But this proportionality is not immediately apparent to the first couple. When Eve is gathering food for Raphael, she says that she intends to bring back such a variety "as he / Beholding shall confess that here on earth / God hath dispensed his bounties as in heaven" (5.328–30). Eve intuitively understands God's monistic universe better than Adam, who later wonders if angels enjoy food as humans do. And yet Raphael answers them both by explaining the concept of a hierarchical yet monist cosmos in terms of proportion:

> All things proceed, and up to him return,
> . . . .
> As nearer to him placed or nearer tending

> Each in their several active spheres assigned,
> Till body up to spirit work, in bounds
> Proportioned to each kind. (5.470, 476–79)

Raphael tells Adam that even though all things are linked to God materially, God nevertheless has proportioned that material so that each species has a unique relationship to it. His explanation also obliquely addresses Eve's notion that God "dispenses" things on earth as in heaven. Indeed, God does dispense all things in the same way, though only materially and not formally; for, as Raphael explains later on, the material "kind" of God's dispensation is the same for humans and angels, while the "degree," or form, of access may be different (5.490).

However, the underlying confusion about the limits of God's proportional creation remains in both Eve and Adam. In book 8, Adam asks Raphael about the heavenly bodies:

> reasoning I oft admire,
> How nature wise and frugal could commit
> Such disproportions, with superfluous hand
> So many nobler bodies to create. (8.25–28)

Raphael's response mystifies rather than clarifies the issue of proportion: "Dream not of other worlds, what creatures there / Live, in what state, condition or degree" (8.175–76). He further muddies the notion of proportionality between humans and God later, when he says to Adam, "For God we see hath honoured thee, and set / On man his equal love" (8.227–28). God sets his love equally on angels and on man, but equality in God's eyes is still, strangely, proportional. As a further illustration of the paradoxes of a proportional cosmos, Adam recounts to Raphael his request to God for a mate:

> Among unequals what society
> Can sort, what harmony or true delight?
> Which must be mutual, in proportion due
> Given and received; but in disparity
> The one intense, the other still remiss
> Cannot well suit with either, but soon prove
> Tedious alike. (8.383–89)

The tension in this passage is between Adam's desire for an equal and his recognition that "harmony and true delight" proceed "in proportion due." Through his language of musical harmony, Adam implies that whenever there is musical unison there must also be a proportional difference: two voices joining together depend on this proportion to make harmony.[32] Adam further recognizes that two beings of absolute "disparity" cannot relate to each other; rather, the difference that Adam accepts is a "mutual," proportional difference that nevertheless works together to create harmony. God's response asks Adam to differentiate himself from God, which Adam does by further delving into the paradox of equality springing from inequality:

> No need that thou
> Shouldst propagate, already infinite;
> And through all numbers absolute, though one;
> But man by number is to manifest
> His single imperfection, and beget
> Like of his like, his image multiplied,
> In unity defective, which requires
> Collateral love, and dearest amity.   (8.419–26)

Man's "single imperfection" comes from "number"; in other words, man cannot reproduce himself as God can but must join in "collateral love" with another being. And yet, this coupling somehow produces "like of his like." This tradition of associating perfection with singularity stretches back to antiquity. As one of Virgil's shepherds says, "numero deus impare gaudet" (God delights in an uneven number). Servius provides the rationale: "et impar numerus inmortalis, quia dividi integer non potest; par numerus mortalis, quia dividi potest" (an uneven number is immortal, because it is a whole and cannot be divided; an even number is mortal, because it can be divided).[33] Human reproduction, similarly, is "in unity defective" because it proceeds from a union. Thus, Adam says he needs an equal and yet acknowledges that fundamental equality is impossible in a proportional universe.

And while Adam tends to define equality too narrowly through the horizontal relationships within each rung of this proportional universe, Eve tends to look for equality vertically in the integrated dispensation God has given to heaven and earth.[34] Both of their perspectives turn out to be flawed. Satan's temptation sets both of these perspectives on equality within the ameliorative function of later, postlapsarian human legal and political systems. These systems, too, often set up standards of "equality" that must be enforced by laws and political mechanisms. When Raphael begins to recount the war in heaven, we hear Satan spouting this very language of proportional equality, which becomes a justification of representative equality. He asks his fellow angels,

> Will ye submit your necks, and choose to bend
> The supple knee? Ye will not, if I trust
> To know ye right, or if ye know yourselves
> Natives and sons of heaven possessed before
> By none, and if not equal all, yet free,
> Equally free; for orders and degrees
> Jar not with liberty, but well consist.
> Who can in reason then or right assume
> Monarchy over such as live by right
> His equals, if in power and splendour less,
> In freedom equal? (5.787–97)

Satan confuses liberty and equality in a persuasive though superficial way. His circular logic associates freedom with proportional equality to God, and that proportional equality then turns into a "right" to be his equals. Indeed, this logic turns God's differentiation of "orders and degrees" into an act of distribution of individual rights that, all of a sudden, are divorced entirely from the duties entailed by those very orders and degrees. That God's differentiated cosmos implies duty is confirmed by Raphael in book 7, when he recounts God's response to Satan's rebellion:

> I can repair
> That detriment, if such it be to lose
> Self-lost, and in a moment will create
> Another world, out of one man a race
> Of men innumerable, there to dwell,
> Not here, *till by degrees of merit raised*

> They open to themselves at length the way
> Up hither. (7.152–59; italics added)

In the postlapsarian world, God will similarly exercise a proportional method of salvation, like the proportional duties he enjoins on his prelapsarian creatures.

But the relationship between two types of dispensation—pre- and postlapsarian—is nevertheless marked by different types of equality. The famous lines on the ant society in book 7 present a picture of what postlapsarian equality might look like:

> The parsimonious emmet, provident
> Of future, in small room large heart enclosed,
> Pattern of just equality perhaps
> Hereafter; joined in her popular tribes
> Of commonalty. (7.485–89)

The word "tribes" is especially significant here; and there is reason to believe that Milton intended a reference to the Israelite tribes of the Old Testament, whose government in the wilderness Michael describes to Adam in book 12: "In the wide wilderness, there they shall found / Their government, and their great senate choose / Through the twelve tribes, to rule by laws ordained" (12.224–26). The ant's "just equality" points to an ideal synthesis of individual justice and egalitarian social structure. Yet, the qualifying "perhaps / Hereafter" points out that in a postlapsarian world the process of "equality" becoming "just" is a troubled one, requiring complex social and political structures, tribes and senates, to enact the laws that God ordains.[35]

The Jewish Sanhedrin set about approaching this "just equality" by employing mediators who could interpret God's will and apply it in human laws. Moses himself is represented as a necessary mediatory presence in book 12:

> But the voice of God
> To mortal ear is dreadful; they beseech
> That Moses might report to them his will,
> And terror cease; he grants them their desire,
> Instructed that to God is no accéss
> Without mediator. (12.235–40)

Often, Moses' mediation of God's will took the form of lots, as was well known in the seventeenth century. In his work on the Jewish Sanhedrin, John Selden quotes a talmudic commentary on Numbers 11:16, when Moses used lots to enforce equality:

> Tempore quo dixit Deus O. M. Mosi, congrega mihi septuaginta viros e presbyteris, seu senioribus, Israel, dixit sibi Moses, seu secum cogitavit, Quomodo hoc faciam? Si ex qualibet tribus selegero sex, numerum imperatum superabit is numerus binis. Erunt enim 72. At si selegero ex qualibet tribu quinque, deerunt numero imperato decem. Ita enim fient 60. Et demum, si ex tribu altera quinos, atque ex altera senos selegero, inter tribus conflabo invidiam.
>
> [When God said to that most excellent and great Moses, bring to me seventy men out of the elders of Israel, Moses said to himself, How will I do this? If I select six out of every tribe, the number will exceed the requested number by two and there will be seventy-two. But if I select five out of every tribe, ten will be missing from the requested number and there will be sixty. And finally, if I select five from every other tribe and six from the remaining tribes, I will stir up jealousy among the tribes.][36]

Moses then selected 6 from each of the 12 tribes and wrote "Presbyter" on 70 lots, leaving 2 lots blank. He put them into an urn and each potential presbyter drew lots. As Selden remarks, "Sortes ejusmodi non raro apud eos adhibitae" (they often employed lots of this kind) (1:1259). Selden is interested, along with his talmudic sources, in the conjunction of human ingenuity and divine decree. Maintaining a "just equality" among the tribes is Moses' imperative, a duty entrusted to him as mediator of God's will.

Thomas Hobbes was also interested in this passage from Numbers, commenting on it in his *Leviathan* in order to show that God's will was channeled through Moses as human administrator. When God told Moses to select the 70, God intended them to be "such as Moses himself should appoint for Elders and Officers of the People." That Moses selected them through a lottery was especially appropriate, because as Hobbes notes immediately thereafter, "God spake also many times by the event of

Lots; which were ordered by such as he had put in Authority over his people."[37] Hobbes's purpose is to demystify God's working, but even for Hobbes "lots" were a site where the divine and human came together to decide the best order for human society. This is especially important for Hobbes, for whom the equal use of indivisible things through lot was a law of nature: "in things, therefore, indivisible and incommunicable, it is the law of nature, *That the use be alternate, or the advantage given away by lot;* because there is no other way of equality; and equality is the law of nature."[38] Lots would thus seem to respect the potential equality of persons while also providing an impartial standard of division and distribution. Jean Bodin implies as much when he cites the same source that Hobbes likely had in mind, Euripides' *Phoenissae,* in which Jocasta thinks "a lawfull equalitie to be most agreeable unto mans nature."[39] And yet, as Bodin also notes, this "lawfull equalitie" creates more problems than it solves because it does not respect the natural divisions among people, divisions that must show up in social and political arrangements.

In these texts, Selden and Hobbes were both more concerned with the complex relationship between human politics and divine, with positive law rather than with prelapsarian understandings of inequality.[40] But in Milton's garden the problem of inequality adumbrates these larger and later debates about political representation and social justice. The recognition that proportional inequality must exist within social relationships informs one of Eve's earliest speeches, after Adam has explained the divine prohibition and the duty to praise God:

> For we to him indeed all praises owe,
> And daily thanks, I chiefly who enjoy
> So far the happier lot, enjoying thee
> Pre-eminent by so much odds, while thou
> Like consort to thyself canst nowhere find.   (4.444–48)

This represents a significant challenge to Adam's plea for an equal in book 8. Eve's recognition of her own individuality, her own differentiated "lot," accompanies her recognition of the proportional relationship between her and Adam. But her choice of the word "odds" is especially important because it emphasizes the degree of difference between Eve and Adam in terms of their radical, indivisible subjectivity. An odd number cannot evenly be divided. But she also implicitly argues that proportional advantage is very real indeed; Adam is "pre-eminent" by odds, which precludes Eve from being his "like consort."

Indeed, Eve's speech reminds us that there is more than one way to understand proportional relationships. Eve introduces what many in the seventeenth century would call a principle of "arithmetical" proportion. This kind of proportion partakes of an absolute view of inequality: if two things are different numerically, they are unequal. For Eve to be Adam's equal, she implies, there would have to exist no "odds" between them. Geometrical proportion, on the other hand, sees equality as the relative difference in magnitude between two numbers. So, 3:6::6:12—this is a geometrical equality because the difference in relational magnitude is the same; each set is twice the other. For Eve, proportional inequality is absolute and numerical; for Adam, however, equality depends on the degree of difference.

The political implications of these two types of proportion were evident in the seventeenth century. As Francis Theobald argues, geometrical proportion privileged monarchical hierarchy while the arithmetic was more conducive to a popular government: "Divine *Plato* saith, God doth καλῶς γεομετρείν [*sic*]: Which he meant in this sense; because, The Geometrical proportion was more agreeable & suitable to Regal Power, because this makes no Confusion of all-together, but giveth unto every one according to his desert and worthiness; whereas the other, *viz.* Arithmetical proportion, giveth equally unto all, according to number: and therefore it was, that *Lycurgus* chased out of *Lacedemon* Arithmetical proportion, as a popular thing, turbulent and apt to make Commotions."[41] Within the arithmetical dispensation, the only way to effect equality is by redistribution among different parts of the social hierarchy; hence the dangerousness of this system of apportionment. Lots were not inherently aligned with one or the other type of proportion, though some worried that they tended toward the arithmetical because of their indifference to social position.[42] Plato, the great opponent of popular government, wrote that lots should only be used "on account of the discontent of the masses"; their use represents "an infringement of the perfect and exact, as being contrary to strict justice."[43] However, even though the difference between arithmetical and geometrical proportion was clear in postlapsarian politics, Milton was not content to import the distinction wholly into the prelapsarian world of *Paradise Lost*. There, the two types of proportion function as two ways of understanding the human duty to fulfill God's commands.

In 1689 the theologian John Alexander provided an explanation of prelapsarian duties that could function as a gloss on Milton's poem. Alexander makes much of the fact that he is a "converted Jew," and thus attentive to the way that God's covenant with the Jews proceeded from the Fall. However, as Alexander notes, there was no covenant before the Fall: "The transaction, that passed between GOD and Adam in Eden, Gen. 2, was a meer Sanction on God's side."[44] Alexander links prelapsarian obligation to the two types of proportion. "Commutative Justice is when an equal proportion is observed between giving and receiving, between the merit and the reward, between the injunction and the performance." This kind of divine justice existed only before the Fall, because afterward humankind had need of a "*Covenant*, which, as to us, hath always a proportion *Geometrical*, as being grounded upon distributive Justice, 2 *Tim*. 4. 8. By *Grace purchased* for us, through the satisfaction of an equal in Nature, even by Christ Covenanting for us with the Father."[45] Humanity's relationship to proportion is different from God's, who contains all proportions within. As Thomas Jackson defined the divine essence in 1628, "In that he is indivisibly *one*, and yet eminently *all*, he is immutable, contrariety itself unto contrarieties; arithmetical equality itself to things equal; geometrically equal to things unequal according to every degree of their unequal capacities in what sort soever."[46] And yet, as becomes clear in the middle books of *Paradise Lost*, both Adam and Eve have trouble understanding the proportional relationship between themselves and God, and even between each other. Adam desires an equal—for "Among unequals what society / Can sort"? (8.383–84)—but an equal that is different enough from him to give him delight "in proportion due" (8.385). Ultimately, he underestimates the difficulty of creating harmonious communication out of proportional differences. By contrast, although Eve sees the equalizing effects of duty to God and Adam, she acknowledges the insurmountable "odds" (4.447) between herself and Adam.

Returning to Satan's temptation of Eve and the Fall in book 9, these concepts of proportional relationships coalesce around the correct interpretation of the "lots" distributed by God. Satan's primary goal is to associate God's proportional dispensation with ameliorative representative mechanisms in the postlapsarian world. Milton gives us a hint of Satan's strategy before Satan's final speech to Eve, comparing him to "some orator renowned / in Athens or free Rome" (9.670–71). Milton's narrator links Satan to the political systems of those great empires, and most importantly to "free Rome"; Satan's method of temptation will be to imply that sophisticated political knowledge can lead to a free society of equals. But Satan separates political representation from divine distribution; in his schema, one's "lot" (9.690) is the element of natural chance that "knowledge" extirpates (9.687). He had overheard Eve's remark in book 4 that she enjoyed the "happier lot" (4.446) and that she considered her lot to preclude her from being Adam's "like consort" (4.448). He uses this confusion of proportion to imply that movement between levels of cosmic hierarchy is not only possible, but that it also remains proportional; thus, the change from serpent to man and from man to angel is "but proportion meet" (9.711).

For Eve, this notion of radical change that remains proportional would solve the problem of equality between her and Adam. The knowledge of good and evil becomes a leveling force for her, which would provide them both with "equal lot" and "equal joy, as equal love" (9.882–83). The basic misunderstanding afflicting both Eve and Adam, after Satan's temptation, is that they assume that God's proportional universe is geometrically ordered when really, for them, it is arithmetically ordered. Obedience to God and the reward of eternal life exist as a 1:1 ratio. Adam and Eve, encouraged by Satan, confuse arithmetical duty with a geometrical political relationship in which equality is artificially derived from covenant and contract. However, for the first couple the element of chance in their assigned position in the universe is not mutable but rather constitutive of proportional freedom and equality within an unequal cosmos.

As Satan realizes, however, chance as manifested in the concept of "lot" formed a potentially destabilizing force because it blurred the lines of communication between God's will and his creatures. This was the case in seventeenth century discussions of the power of lots as well. With the repetition of "lot" in book 9 and throughout *Paradise Lost,* Milton recognizes the complex interplay between postlapsarian methods of political, representative equality and a theological position that must explain inequality within a materially unified cosmos. This tension allows for two interrelated conclusions applicable to the poem and to the fallen world it imagines. First, it is clear that the political manipulation of equal representation is insufficient without a recognition of the proportional inequality that God institutes. But, more importantly, the contingent expression of God's will never completely aligns with the human ability to comprehend and incorporate proportional thinking into political and social relationships. Thus, after the Fall the inequality that existed in the garden becomes hardened into institutional inequalities, such as clerical privilege. And while lots can function to maintain equity within divine commands, postlapsarian human institutions will forever imperfectly mediate God's will and human knowledge.

University of North Carolina, Chapel Hill

HERMENEUTICS AND INTERPRETATION

Pilgrimage in *Paradise Lost*

Beatrice Groves

Blake's *Milton: A Poem* is prefaced by a lyric (popularly known as "Jerusalem") that appears to invoke the myth that Joseph of Arimathea brought Jesus to Albion: "And did those feet in ancient time, / Walk upon England's mountains green."[1] Blake's emphasis on Christ's feet here is entirely in accord with the medieval pilgrimage narratives evoked by these lines—texts that likewise imagine a landscape transformed by the presence of the godhead and display an initially surprising obsession with feet and footprints.[2] However, precisely because feet are dusty and ordinary, they revive the wonder at God's condescension in becoming flesh, and footprints become memorials of the Incarnation, recording the spot where the divine and earthly once met.[3] Pilgrimage literature, like Blake's *Milton*, focuses "sharply on the feet that repeatedly indicate encounters of one realm of existence with another."[4] The opening sentence of *The Book of Sir John Mandeville* (ca. 1356)—the most popular of all pilgrim narratives—avows that the Holy Land is holy because God had chosen "to envyroun that lond with his blesside feet."[5] One late-fifteenth-century pilgrim narrative anticipates Blake's Glastonbury myth by claiming that one of the imprints left by Jesus' feet at the Ascension "is taken awaie from thence and brought to Westmynstre in Englond."[6] Both narratives are strikingly literal attempts to relocate the sanctity of the Holy Land (incandescent with Christ's footprints) to England. Blake's *Milton*, however, although attracted by the myth, states that the transformative power of the Incarnation is not restricted by place: whether or not Christ trod on English soil, the speaker can follow in his spiritual footsteps and forge a new Jerusalem—a renewed society—in his homeland.

In Milton's *Paradise Lost*, likewise, Adam's attachment to his homeland is expressed in the traditional terminology of geographical pilgrimage that he must learn to translate into an active spirituality. Adam articulates the desire to remain in a place where God has walked, where he can "trace" God's "footstep."[7] Milton is deeply antagonistic to the practice of pilgrimage and this passage is one of Adam's "many errors in the course of his instruction" by Michael.[8] But Adam's imagined pilgrimage around Eden's sacred sites brings forward a concept fundamental to the final books of the poem. The ubiquitous metaphor of the Christian life as a pilgrimage (the epistle to the Hebrews states that faithful are as "strangers and pilgrims on the earth," Augustine that "the City of God...is on pilgrimage in this world")[9] underlies the final action of *Paradise Lost:* from the allusions that connect Adam with the archetypal holy wanderer, Abraham, to the famous closing lines.[10]

Out of Eden

Adam's imagined pilgrimage in book 11 of *Paradise Lost* embodies humankind's "overfond" (*PL* 11.289) attachment to place and calls forward one of Milton's most radical additions to the Genesis story: the destruction of paradise. When Adam appears unresponsive to Michael's arguments against idolatrous attachment to his home, he is informed, "this mount / Of Paradise" will be destroyed "to teach thee that God attributes to place / No sanctity" (11.829–30, 836–37). Milton connects Adam's love of Eden with that of pilgrims for the Holy Land, so that when paradise is destroyed Adam becomes a pilgrim without a physical goal, a pilgrim ready—like

Abraham—to leave the land he knows and trust that God will lead him to a heavenly home. Milton's striking decision to destroy the garden highlights (and enables) Adam's growth from his initial desire for place pilgrimage to an understanding of the spiritual pilgrimage he will undergo. Under Michael's tutelage, Adam learns that he must transmute his overliteral desire to remain where he can "trace" God's "footstep" into spiritual understanding of what it is to follow in the "track divine" (11.329, 354).

Despite the important, if implicit, pilgrim theme in the final books of *Paradise Lost,* there has been some critical resistance to the idea of Milton's use of such imagery. The editors of the Yale edition of Milton's prose argue that the original language of "the true wayfaring Christian" in the printed text of *Areopagitica* (1644) (which has been changed by a contemporary hand to "the true warfaring Christian") cannot be the correct reading because "the image of the Christian pilgrimage, frequently found elsewhere, never occurs in Milton."[11] In fact, there is another (albeit fleeting) example of such imagery in *Areopagitica* itself when Milton calls living an honest and faithful life "Christian walking" (YP 2:537).[12] But the significance for *Paradise Lost* of the biblically based trope of the Christian life as a journey (in which physical movement stands for the striving of the soul) has perhaps been obscured for modern critics by the poem's explicit denigration of geographical pilgrimage. Satan's wandering takes him through the barren limbo of "The Paradise of Fools" (*PL* 3.496) where "pilgrims roam, that strayed so far to seek / In Golgotha him dead, who lives in heaven," whirled thither with all their "relics, beads, / Indulgences, dispenses, pardons, bulls" (3.476–77, 491–92). The asyndeton expresses a curt contempt for the practice of pilgrimage and, at first sight, such a passage seems to support the view that there is something inherently unlikely in Milton's use of "wayfaring" as a metaphor for the spiritual life.

The literary history of the trope of pilgrimage, however, suggests the opposite. In the medieval church there had been a "precarious harmony between moral, interior and place pilgrimage" and widespread disagreement over the efficacy of geographical pilgrimage in the wider scheme of the spiritual pilgrimage of a Christian's life.[13] The Protestant suppression of the practice of pilgrimage, however, freed the metaphor from these tensions and in doing so made it into an even more vibrant devotional and poetic image. Bunyan's *Pilgrim's Progress* (1678) is only the most famous example of an outpouring of early modern divinity which—following in the footsteps of Arthur Dent's best-selling *Plaine Mans Path-Way to Heaven* (1601)—figured the Protestant Christian life as a "godly and ghostly pilgrimage."[14] Antagonism to the practice of pilgrimage promoted the use of pilgrimage as a spiritual trope because it imbued it with a new clarity.[15] For Protestants there was only one kind of pilgrimage, only one route to Jerusalem.

Place Pilgrimage in *Paradise Lost*

For Milton, as for many Protestants, there was something inherently suspect about place pilgrimage, and Adam's imagined peregrination around the mount of paradise is rendered spiritually dubious through its connection with the practice and lore of geographical pilgrimage. As Adam describes what he desires, he is unknowingly tracing the stations, stones, and altars of what will become the pilgrim route around Jerusalem:

> here I could frequent,
> With worship, place by place where he vouchsafed
> Presence divine, and to my sons relate;
> On this mount he appeared; under this tree
> Stood visible, among these pines his voice
> I heard, here with him at this fountain talked:
> So many grateful altars I would rear
> Of grassy turf, and pile up every stone
> Of lustre from the brook, in memory,
> Or monument to ages.   (11.317–26)

Adam longs to remain in the place that communion with God has rendered sacred, and he imagines setting apart the mountains, trees, and fountains where God had "vouchsafed / Presence divine" by building "grateful altars" or piles of stones over them. Like the

Franciscan friars who conducted pilgrims around the sites of the Holy Land, Adam imagines leading others around these holy sites and relating to them God's actions in these places.

The marking of holy sites with altars and piles of stones was ubiquitous on the pilgrim route around Judea, and one early-sixteenth-century English pilgrim (the chaplain to Sir Richard Guylforde who visited the Holy Land in 1506) notes that stones are used to memorialize the locations of scriptural events: "therby is the place shewed, by token of a stone, where Judas betrayed our Savyoure to the Jewes with a kyssse."[16] These stones are placed, like Adam's, "in memory, / Or monument to ages" and sometimes, like his, they form altars. Egeria (ca. 381–84), the first pilgrim to leave a full narrative of her journey, notes of one holy site: "there is no building there, but it is an enormous round rock with a flat place on top where the holy men are said to have stood, and a kind of altar in the middle made of stones."[17] Indeed, the stone that covered Christianity's holiest place—the site of the Resurrection—is likewise an altar.[18]

In the Church of the Nativity at Bethlehem altars mark every place of importance. Adam's imagined procession "place by place" between the altars he has raised to mark the sites where God "vouchsafed / Presence divine" is reminiscent of that described by Guylforde's chaplain between the altars of this church:

> And firste the sayd processyon broughte us to a place at an aulter in the southe yle, where our Savyour Criste was circumsised, &c.
>
> And from thens we come to an other aulter on the northe syde, where the thre kynges made redy their offerynges to present unto our Savyour Criste.
>
> And from this place descendyng by certyne stone grees we come into a wonder fayre lytell Chapell, at the hyghe aulter wherof is the very place of the byrthe of our Lord.[19]

Adam's route, like that of those pilgrims who "with a fulle reverent procession...circuett abowt the same glorius cherch visiteng and declaryng alle the forewriten hooli places,"[20] has an "incipient liturgical pattern."[21] Egeria, for example, always read the Bible passage "proper" to the place when visiting sites as well as reciting appropriate psalms and prayers.[22] In the Holy Land, as in Adam's paradise, place is understood as sacred because of the history that has been enacted on that spot: a history that is memorialized through reciting it on the very spot where it occurred in a ritual that confirms the reciprocal holiness of place and story.

Adam's holy places—like those in Jerusalem—are natural phenomena that act as contact relics, marking sites of theological memory rather than owning any inherent sanctity. The mountain, fountain, and trees of Adam's imagined route around paradise are strikingly close to the most important pilgrimage sites in the Holy Land. Mountains—such as the Mount of Olives and Mount Tabor—were major sites for pilgrims because of their importance in scriptural narratives.[23] Fountains are less biblically prominent, but those struck from the rock by Moses and sweetened by Elijah were augmented with apocryphal examples, such as the "very clere fountayne somwhat under therthe, where our blessyd Lady was wonte many tymes to wasshe ye clothes of our blessyd Savyour in his childehode."[24] Despite the more problematic nature of trees (Protestant travelers often ridiculed the idea that these could have survived since biblical times), they mark the pilgrimage route in profusion. In 333 the Bordeaux pilgrim (the first to leave an account of his journey) saw "the palm-tree from which the children took branches and strewed them in Christ's path," the sycamore that Zacchaeus climbed, and the plane trees "planted by Jacob."[25] Later pilgrims were likewise shown the tree under which Jesus and Mary rested, balm trees that Jesus watered at Mary's request, the terebinth at Mamre, and the burning bush out of which God spoke to Moses, "which is still alive and sprouting."[26]

Adam's reification of trees, mountains, and running water is in part a primitive response, linked to the sanctity of place and the natural world in paganism, and rejected by Milton as such.[27] It has been argued that with the conversion of Constantine in the fourth century "came a reaffirmation of the spiritual significance of 'place,' a development which probably owed something to the pagan background of the emperor."[28] Once it had a Christian emperor, the church was able to openly designate its holy sites, and Milton's distaste for the establishment of the church under Constantine was allied to his rejection of this emphasis on the sanctity of place (YP 1:944). It may indeed be a sign of a residual pagan sensibility that led Constantine to build four temples in the Holy Land at the site of a tree (the terebinth of Mamre), a mountain (the Mount of Olives), and two caves (Bethlehem and Christ's tomb).[29]

Milton's critique of Adam's desired proto-pilgrimage route around Eden appears likewise to imply that Christianity has been tainted by a pagan sense of the holiness of place. Adam is rebuked by Michael: "Adam, thou knowst heaven his, and all the earth. / Not this rock only; his omnipresence fills / Land, sea, and air" (11.335–37). Adam's localized devotion is corrected with words that recall Jesus' warning to the woman of Samaria: "the houre commeth, when yee shall neither in this mountaine, nor yet at Hierusalem, worship the Father" (John 4:21). Geographical pilgrimage is one of the strongest indicators of a belief in sacred places and hence the allusion to it in Adam's words (*PL* 11.317–26) is an implicit criticism of what Milton considered the overly physical worship of the Roman Catholic and, presumably, the Restoration Church.

The undercutting of papal authority is manifest in Milton's substitution of "rock" for "mountain," a substitution that "hits at the successors of St. Peter (the *rock*) for their attempt to confine God's presence with the *narrow bounds* of local pieties and institutionalized forms."[30] It is striking, however, that Michael's use of John 4:21 to rebut a neophyte's enthusiasm for worshipping God in holy places should have a direct analogue in a letter of Saint Jerome. Jerome is writing to Paulinus of Nola, attempting to cool the latter's ardent desire to visit the Holy Land: "I do not presume to limit God's omnipotence or to restrict to a narrow strip of earth Him whom the heaven cannot contain.... The true worshippers worship the Father neither at Jerusalem nor on mount Gerizim."[31] It is a parallel that alerts us to a surprising aspect of this exchange between man and angel in book 11 of *Paradise Lost*. Adam's desires show Milton unexpectedly deploying his knowledge of the stones, altars, mountains, trees, and protoliturgical character of the pilgrimage route, but they also have a poignant beauty entirely lacking from the satirical description of pilgrims in the Paradise of Fools.[32] The elegiac cast of Adam's lament recalls the lyricism with which other seventeenth century poets (of rather different theological persuasions) had mourned the falling away of the Old Testament's easy converse with God. Henry Vaughan's "Religion," modeled on George Herbert's "Decay," is a threnody for divine intimacy, suffused—like Adam's speech—with longing for a time when the Lord spoke to humankind beside fountains, under trees, and shared meals in shady groves.

The numinous landscape of the Old Testament, mirrored in Adam's description of Eden, is one in which there is a conversational intimacy between humankind and God. It is a relationship that would have held particular appeal for Milton for it required no mediating authority; and indeed, half of *Paradise Lost* is taken up with converse between humankind and God's angelic messengers. When the conversation with the affable archangel is over, the subsequent book opens with a lament over the divorce the Fall will create:

> No more of talk where God or angel guest
> With man, as with his friend, familiar used
> To sit indulgent, and with him partake
> Rural repast, permitting him the while
> Venial discourse unblamed.   (9.1–5)

Fowler finds a problem here—"God talked with Adam (viii 316–51), but no common meal is mentioned"—but the passage is clearly referring to Adam's intercourse with Raphael, which, as it is modeled on the visit of the three angels to Abraham (Gen. 18:1–15), explains the phrase "God or angel guest." Abraham's encounter was understood as both an angelic and a divine visitation: "And the LORD appeared unto him, in the plaines of Mamre: and he sate in the tent doore in the heate of the day. And hee lift[ed] up his eyes and looked, and loe, three men stood by him" (Gen. 18:1–2).[33] Abraham's angelic visitors were universally understood in Christian exegesis as a "mystical sign of the Trinity": pilgrims visiting the oak that marked the site at Mamre claimed to have seen the place where "the Holy Trinity appeared to the Patriarch Abraham, and did eat with him."[34] (It is attractive to speculate that Milton's reduction in the number of angels from three to one is indicative not merely of the drive toward narrative simplicity, but also of unorthodox Trinitarian theology.)

The most significant evidence of heavenly condescension in the biblical account is that the angels share a meal with Abraham, but in Vaughan's version (like Milton's), verbal exchange becomes equally important:

> In *Abr'hams* Tent the winged guests
> (O how familiar then was heaven!)
> Eate, drinke, discourse, sit downe, and rest
> Untill the Coole and shady *Even*.[35]

"Familiar" and "discourse" are likewise Milton's words (*PL* 9.2, 5): the conviviality of conversation expresses for these seventeenth century poets what sharing a meal symbolized in biblical culture. Adam believes that the loss of Eden comprehends the frustration of his desire for direct conversation with God: "among these pines his voice / I heard, here with him at this fountain talked" (*PL* 11.321–22). The closeness—in tone and choice of biblical allusion—of Vaughan's poem to Adam's words and the opening of book 9 suggests that Milton's epic is sensitive to the loss inherent in its iconoclastic destruction of paradise.[36]

Divining the Track: The Vision of God

The ultimate desire of Adam's imagined pilgrim route is identical with that of pilgrims to the Holy Land: to "trace" God's "footstep" (*PL* 11.329). On viewing the imprint of Christ's feet on the Mount of Olives, a mid-fourteenth-century English pilgrim wrote, "we might say with David: '*We will go into his tabernacle: we will adore in the place where his feet stood.*'"[37] "Where his feet stood" is a somewhat free translation of Psalm 131's *hadom raglayw* ("footstoole," 1:7), and it was understood as giving biblical sanction for the practice of pilgrimage, as well as intensifying interest in sites where Jesus' footprints were believed to be still visible. Although these places were esteemed some of the most holy (they became, for example, the places most likely to be plundered by pilgrims seeking relics of earth to carry back home), "the land of Jerusalem is throughout holy and sanctified, seeing that the prophets, the Apostles, and the Lord Himself walked therein."[38] The whole of Jerusalem was one vast contact relic, sanctified by the touch of Christ's feet. Pilgrims such as Felix Fabri (ca. 1480) believed that to venerate the earth anywhere in Jerusalem was to kiss Christ's "footsteps."[39] Paulinus of Nola (ca. 354–431) wrote, "no other sentiment draws men to Jerusalem, but the desire to see and touch the places where Christ was physically present, and to be able to say from their very own experience: *We have gone into His tabernacle, and have adored in the places where His feet stood*. Though a deeper meaning may be read into this passage, we must not ignore the simple and literal sense when apposite.... the desire is a truly religious one to see the places in which Christ walked, suffered, rose again."[40]

The spiritual benefit of walking where Christ had walked would have been impressed upon pilgrims by their Franciscan guides who, through their official role as the conductors of pilgrims around the Holy Land, literally embodied their rule's command to follow in Christ's footsteps.[41] As late as 1601, the Protestant traveler Henry Timberlake recorded in his immensely popular *True and Strange Discourse of the Travailes of Two English Pilgrimes* (1603) the Franciscan sermon to which he had listened on arrival in Jerusalem, "tending to this effect: how meritorious it was for us to visit the Holy Land, & see those sanctified places where our Saviours feete had trode."[42] The explosion of pilgrimages to Jerusalem between 1300 and the mid-sixteenth century suggests that pilgrims, like their guides, believed that tracing Christ's footprints in the soil of Judea would aid them in their search to become his spiritual disciples.[43]

It was intended that pilgrims would be inspired by viewing the literal footsteps of Christ to walk his spiritual path, but for Milton such physical traces were a distraction from the business of discipleship. Adam desires to continue to reside in the place where God has walked, rather than to forge a new communion with him in a land without the comfort of his physical presence:

> In yonder nether world where shall I seek
> His bright appearances, or footstep trace?
> For though I fled him angry, yet recalled
> To life prolonged and promised race, I now
> Gladly behold though but his utmost skirts
> Of glory, and far off his steps adore. (*PL* 11.328–33)

The primary meaning of "promised race" is Adam's posterity, but the accompanying "footstep" and "steps" make explicit the punning relation of the phrase to the life Adam is to lead: "let us run with patience the race that is set before us" (Heb. 12:1). The Pauline epistles regularly use metaphors of journeys and contests for the spiritual striving of a Christian life—"Know ye not that they which runne in a race, runne all, but one receiveth the price [prize]?" (1 Cor. 9:24)—and the double meaning of Adam's "promised race" comes to fruition when Adam is promised that some of his posterity will die their "race well run" (*PL* 12.505), recalling Paul's affirmation "Ye did runne well" (Gal. 5:7).[44] These layers of meaning in "promised race" are rendered profound rather than simply playful by the evocation in Adam's complaint of Moses' vision of God.

Toward the end of Exodus Moses asks God to "shew me thy glory," and God accedes with the proviso that he will not be permitted to see his face: "it shall come to pass, while my glory passeth by, that I will put thee in a clift of the rock, and will cover thee with my hand, while I pass by: And I will take away mine hand, and thou shalt see my back parts: but my face shall not be seen" (Exod. 33:18, 23). At first Adam's (pre-) echo of this passage appears simply to be a sign of the separation that the Fall has brought between God and humankind: Moses is shown God's "back parts" because he could not sustain viewing his full "glory," and the postlapsarian Adam, who had once been capable of God's "bright appearances," must likewise learn now to view only his "utmost skirts." But the allusion also suggests that Adam has intuited the deeper meaning of Moses' vision. As Gregory of Nyssa explains, at the heart of this story is a narrative not of separation but of discipleship: "he who follows sees the back."[45] Moses sees God's "backe parts"—or "utmost skirts"—because he has become God's disciple: "all trace of an external and static relationship between God and believer is expunged.... The vision of God *is* discipleship."[46] (While the literal-minded pilgrims of the Paradise of Fools "fly o'er the backside of the world" [*PL* 3.494], the true pilgrim will be granted a view of the "back parts" of God because he has become his follower.)

Both Adam's words and Gregory of Nyssa's exegesis of Exodus describe the desire for a vision of God through the Pauline language of discipleship in which the Christian life involves athletic striving for salvation. For Gregory of Nyssa, Moses standing in the cleft of the rock is actually competing in the race of discipleship: "when he promised that he would stand him on the rock, he showed him the nature of that divine race.... For truly he who has *run the race*, as the Apostle says, in that wide and roomy stadium, which the divine voice calls 'place,' and has *kept the faith* and, as the figurative expression says, has planted his feet on the rock; such a person will be adorned with the *crown of righteousness* from the hand of the contest's judge."[47] Gregory of Nyssa sees in this moment an intimation of a Pauline understanding of discipleship, as shown by his quotations from the Second Epistle to Timothy: "I have finished my course, I have kept the faith. Henceefoorth there is layde up for me a crown of righteousnesse" (2 Tim. 4:7–8). Adam's "footstep," "steps," and "promised race" bring forward the answer to his thwarted desire to remain immured, like Moses, on a "rock" (*PL* 11.336), and his echo of Exodus 33 holds the solution to his quandary; he will "trace" (the word means both "find" and "follow")[48] God's "footstep" not by remaining in paradise but by living the life of a true disciple, running his "promised race" and placing his own feet in the "track divine" (11.354).

Wandering Steps and Slow

Adam and Eve walk with "wandering steps and slow" (12.648) as they set out in the final lines of *Paradise Lost*, but—despite their apparent waywardness—in their forward motion they anticipate the biblical tropes of discipleship. Walking suggests growth in the spirit, for the correct moral stance begins merely with standing.

The underlying metaphor in *Paradise Lost* of sin as "Fall" puts ethical pressure on the fact that humankind, alone among the creatures, stands upright. Man is "Godlike erect" (4.289): his distinctive posture implying moral rectitude and a divine capacity for reason and rule. In man God creates

> a creature who not prone
> And brute as other creatures, but endued
> With sanctity of reason, might erect
> His stature, and upright with front serene
> Govern the rest, self-knowing.   (7.506–10)

Milton knits together the classical idea that man's heaven-facing stance reflects a truth about his moral nature and the Christian metaphor of "the Fall" (which the bible literalizes in the punishment inflicted on the belly-creeping serpent).[49] Man is made "sufficient to have stood, though free to fall" (3.99), and at his creation Adam instinctively leaps up:

>   raised
> By quick instinctive motion up I sprung,
> As thitherward endeavouring, and upright
> Stood on my feet.   (8.258–61)

(The poet treads carefully here: the enjambment of "upright / Stood on my feet" enacts the slight unsteadiness of Adam's first upstanding, while the strong initial "Stood" expresses the confidence with which Adam remembers the moment). The Holy Spirit desires "the upright heart" (1.18), and while the forces of Satan will end the poem "prone" just as they began it (1.195, 10.542), Adam and Eve, after their Fall, learn to stand again through penitence: "Thus they in lowliest plight repentant stood" (11.1). The inevitable Fall of *Paradise Lost* is balanced by endless upward striving: the 105 occurrences of "up" are extended by 60 compound uses ("upbore," "upheave," "upraised," "upreared," "uprooted," "uptore," etc.), including two Miltonic coinages ("upsent" and "upwhirled"). "Lapsèd" humankind is "upheld" by God (3.176, 178), and redemption will return humankind to the "upright" (8.260) state in which it was created. Once humankind is upstanding once more at the end of the poem, "wandering steps" can follow the "track divine." As Fowler notes, "wandering" "implies 'erring' as *slow* implies 'reluctant'"; however, the submerged pilgrim motif, which casts Adam and Eve's departure from paradise in the Pauline mold of a spiritual journey, keeps the less obvious, optimistic senses of the word in play.[50]

Initially, "wandering" was a morally neutral word in English, meaning merely "to move hither and thither without fixed course or certain aim." Over time this ungoverned physical movement began to accrue dubious associations both literal—"to deviate from a given path, or determined course; to turn aside from a mark"—and figurative: "to turn aside from a purpose, from a determined course of conduct, or train of thought; to digress; to pass out of the control of reason or conscience; to fall into error (moral or intellectual)."[51] There are 35 occurrences of "wander" and its cognates in *Paradise Lost*, and the word is frequently connected with the Fall, which is the result of Satan's "wandering quest" (2.830) and Eve's "desire of wandering" (9.1136). However (unlike, for example, Spenser's quest-epic in which to wander is to stray from the true path), in *Paradise Lost* "wander" remains a richly textured word that holds potential despite its fallen nature.[52] Notwithstanding his fear of being left "erroneous, there to wander" (7.20) on the Aleian field, the narrator of *Paradise Lost* glories in the mental freedom that allows him "to wander where the Muses haunt" (3.27) (a freedom perhaps particularly grateful to a blind man who would not have been able to wander unaided without danger of pain or indignity in the material world). In *Areopagitica*, Milton likewise exalts in this freedom, stating that it is God (not the devil) who "gives us minds that can wander beyond all limit and satiety" (YP 2:528).[53]

Milton also returns the word to its neutral signification in order to describe God's creation. The innocence of Eden's "wandering" rivers (7.302) is echoed in the "mystic dance" of the planets' punningly "wandring fires" (5.177–78; *planeo*, "I wander"), creating a landscape in which gods might "wander with delight" (7.330). When Raphael describes the waters of Eden as in "serpent error wandering" (7.302), the reader's foreknowledge of the Fall contaminates the ingenuousness of the rivers' undulations. But this audacious piling of words allows the reader to glimpse—as out of the corner of his or her eye—a pristine, prelapsarian world in which even such words as "serpent," "error," and "wandering" convey only the innocence of their literal meaning. As Ricks argues, Milton's Latinisms reach "back to an earlier purity"—to a time when *error* could mean simply "wandering (not to err)," and *lapse* "falling (not the Fall)."[54] This poetic tool creates a vivid word picture of a prelapsarian world by simultaneously evoking and excluding the reader's knowledge of the transgression now seemingly inherent to serpents, error, and wandering. There is an obvious dramatic irony in this intimation of the Fall, but Milton is also imitating the pedagogical method he finds in Eden itself: "it was from out the rinde of one apple tasted, that the knowledge of good and evill as twins cleaving together leapt forth into the World. And perhaps this is that doom which *Adam* fell into of knowing good and evill, that is to say of knowing good by evill" (YP 2:514). Milton gives his reader a glimpse of the prelapsarian purity of unfallen language, not simply (*pace* Fish) to awaken in them a consciousness of their own sin, but also to inspire in them a "conative" virtue: a virtue that finds itself through striving against sin.[55] The pure words of Eden confront readers with their own sin not simply to shame them but to remind them of the inherent purity of creation, to encourage them to use the knowledge of evil in pursuit of "knowing good": to strive, as the poet has done, imaginatively to recover innocence in the fallen world.

The striving of Milton's Latinisms for an earlier purity is a theological, as well as a poetic, stance. Protestants insisted that their faith was, as John Foxe puts it (in the preface to his edition of the Anglo-Saxon Gospels), "no new reformation of things lately begonne, which were not before, but rather the reduction of the Church to the Pristine state of olde conformitie."[56] Protestantism sought to lead the church back to its "ancient puritie,"[57] and in doing so it looked back not only to the apostolic church but also, ultimately, to the origins of the church in God's founding covenants with Abraham and Adam. According to some seventeenth century Protestants, the "first Church was the Garden of Eden," for "the Church had a beeing in all ages, ever since the Promise was given to our first Parents in Paradise."[58] Milton's attempt to reinvigorate prelapsarian meanings connects with Protestantism's theological desire to return to the earliest, purest forms of worship. Adam and Eve's daily morning orison (5.153–208) enacts worship in which the spontaneous outpouring of the heart is uttered in the formal eloquence of the church's liturgy: "for neither various style / Nor holy rapture wanted they to praise / Their maker" (5.146–48). In Eden there is no disjunction between emotional truth and rhetorical skill.[59] Despite the accretions of sin that have infected humankind's relationship with the divine—a lapse rendered audible in the debasement of words such as "wander"—Milton's revival of etymological innocence strives after an original purity in the hope that, through grace, humankind can return to the true worship of God.

In attempting to reclaim "wander" from its negative semantic change, Milton is following in the first footsteps of the English Reformation. Wycliffe likewise tried to purify "wandering" by using it to render the morally neutral *ambulare* of the Vulgate. When preaching on Galatians Wycliffe described how, "In this epistle techith Poul how wey-ferynge men that lyyven here shulden go the streight wey that ledith men to the blisse of hevene.... Poul biddith men, *Waundre in spirit, and so not fulle desires of the fleishe*. That man wandrith in spirit, whose spirit is led bi the Holi Goost."[60] Wycliffe's striking version of the famous injunction to "Walke in the Spirit" (Gal. 5:16) alerts his auditors to the way in which "wey-ferynge men," lacking the fleshy temptations of hearth and home, are more likely to be receptive to the promptings of the Holy Spirit: "that man wandrith in spirit, whose spirit is led bi the Holi Goost."[61] In *Paradise Regained* the Son follows the promptings of this Spirit—"Thou spirit who led'st this glorious eremite / Into the desert"[62]—and in *Paradise Lost* the "true wayfaring Christian" is given other exalted archetypes for God's guidance through the desert places. In Milton's epic both Noah's ark and the Ark of the Covenant travel under Providence's guiding hand in their "wandering" (11.779, 12.334).

In their chastened, repentant state, eschewing their "overfond" (11.289) attachment to place and knowing they will die before redemption comes but knowing too that it will come, Adam and Eve are the image of the patriarchs they will beget: "These al died in faith, not having received the promises, but having seene them a farre off, and were perswaded of them, and embraced them, and confessed that they were strangers and pilgrims on the earth" (Heb. 11:13). The author of the epistle to the Hebrews, as Philip Edwards argues, "was transposing the sense of exile which suffuses the Old Testament—the Jews seeing themselves as a displaced people, enforced wanderers in search of the Promised Land, longing for return to Zion, or Jerusalem—and allying it with the spirit of alienation from the life around them which inspired the early Christians."[63] This biblical metaphor of journeying for the faithful life is likewise embraced by *Paradise Lost*. When Adam is told that Jesus will "bring back / Through the world's wilderness long wandered man" (12.312–13), Israel's exile is, as in Hebrews, understood as metonymic for the wandering of humankind. Just as Abraham, the father of Israel, had been told by God to "walke before mee" (Gen. 17:1), so Adam, humankind's progenitor, learns "to walk / As in his presence" (12.562–63).

Abraham and Adam have been connected throughout *Paradise Lost*, most significantly in the modeling of Raphael's visit to Adam in book 5 on the visit of the three angels to Abraham (Gen. 18: 1–15).[64] Abraham was noted in Hebrews as one who was not a citizen, but rather "By faith he sojourned in the land of promise, as in a strange countrey, dwelling in tabernacles" (Heb. 11:9). In *Paradise Lost*, Abraham's abandonment of his lands in Canaan and "wandering" (12.133) in the desert becomes an image for humankind, lost until Jesus comes to "bring back / Through the world's wilderness long wandered man / Safe to eternal paradise of rest" (12.312–14). Abraham's faithfulness is expressed by his leaving his home and setting out into the unknown, and the connection between Adam's exile and Abraham's "wandering" (12.133) gives an optimistic coloring to the final, famous, occurrence of the word "wander" in the poem:

> The world was all before them, where to choose
> Their place of rest, and providence their guide:
> They hand in hand with wandering steps and slow,
> Through Eden took their solitary way. (12.646–49)

Eve's "wandering" has been underscored by the poem—she whose "will / Of wandering" (9.1145–46) has led to the Fall (see also 9.1136, 10.875). But just as her earlier dangerous desire for independence—"from her husband's hand her hand / Soft she withdrew" (9.385–86)—is recalled and redeemed here (the awkward repetition of "hand her hand" becomes the warm familiarity of "hand in hand"), so likewise her earlier "wandering" has the potential to be transformed. As Fish argues, "in Book XII, 'wand'ring' undergoes a final transformation and is absorbed into the Christian vision.... Wandering is now the movement of faith, the sign of one's willingness to go out at the command of God."[65]

It is Eve, the first to wander, who is the first to repent, and her final words show that she has fully internalized Michael's injunction against attachment to external place, telling her spouse, "thou to me / Art all things under heaven, all places thou" (12.617–18).[66] Eve's loving paradox—"with thee to go, / Is to stay here" (12.615–16)—is an implicit correction of Adam's fallacious reasoning at his fall ("if death / Consort with thee, death is to me as life" [9.953–54]). Through her love for Adam, Eve has found that a truly loving relationship (with Adam, as with God) is independent of place. Eve's final words echo, as Barbara Lewalski notes, Ruth's declaration to Naomi: "whither thou goest, I will goe; and where thou lodgest I will lodge: thy people shall be my people, and thy God my God."[67] Ruth's journey with Naomi leads her to the true God and the "erring" implied by the final occurrence of "wandering" in *Paradise Lost* is tempered by the biblical resonances of those who wandered in the desert and found their way home. The echo of Ruth's and Abraham's "wandering" (12.133) in book 12 keeps in play the spiritual possibilities of unfettered movement and retains the exquisite balance of the poem's final lines, which enact God's command to Michael, "send them forth, though sorrowing, yet in peace" (11.117).

As N. H. Keeble persuasively argues, in the Old Testament Israel's history is told through narratives in which "religious dedication and desert journeys are so interconnected that the landscapes of nomadic wanderings become emblems of moral conditions and the journey the means by which spiritual destinies are fulfilled. In the two traditions of Israel's origins, in the Abraham legends and the Exodus saga, is repeated the same pattern of decision to leave, journey under divine guidance, testing in the wilderness and covenant. This pattern came to control the narrative shape of the Protestant—still more, Puritan—imagination, for here was a Biblically authorised model for the representation of experience."[68] In the histories of patriarchs such as Abraham, Moses, and Noah, migrancy becomes the natural state of the faithful. Adam and Eve have erred in their previous "wandering," but there is another path for the word, and one that with "providence their guide" they may follow. Humankind, like the exilic Israel, may "gain by their delay / In the wide wilderness" (12.223–24).[69] Despite the pejoration of "wandering" there remains latent in the postlapsarian world the innocence it owned in Eden. To wander can be, like the patriarchs, to be detached from the pleasures of the flesh, to acknowledge oneself a stranger and pilgrim upon earth, searching for the New Jerusalem under the guidance of the spirit: "Adam fallinge out of that earthly Paradise, that was a figure of the heavenly, fownd a way into the true one by faith in Christ."[70]

Many seventeenth century Protestants found spiritual succor in the Pauline combination of spiritual pilgrimage and the vigorous race for the heavenly crown. Bunyan, ever the strenuous spiritual athlete, wrote in his *Heavenly Foot-Man* (1698), that "they that will go to Heaven, they must run for it.... I say, there are many steps to be taken by those that intend to be Saved, by running or walking in the steps of that Faith of our Father *Abraham*. Out of *Egypt*, thou must go thorow the *Red Sea*; thou must run a long and tedious Journey, thorow the wast howling Wilderness, before thou come to the Land of Promise."[71] There is something of *Areopagitica*'s hot and dusty race here ("the race, where that immortall garland is to be run for, not without dust and heat"), but the poetics of *Paradise*

Lost seem more trusting that God will eventually gather in "long wandered man" and that "the destiny to which the Christian hero accedes is not burdensome but fulfilling."[72]

It has been convincingly argued that in Christian epic, "movement away from God may in the long run be movement toward him. With this principle Augustine gives new meaning to the circuitry that characterizes the movement of the epic hero: 'circumflectere cursus,' the injunction under which the epic hero moves, translates into the Christian precept that to be saved one must first be lost."[73] In his commentary on the Psalms, Augustine writes that we are all "wandering" to that heavenly Jerusalem where "the angels await us wanderers" (civitate Jerusalem caelesti, unde nos modo peregrinamur, adtendunt nos peregrinos).[74] Augustine's "unde" (both "from which" and "to which") creates a circular narrative that makes homecoming inevitable for the errant citizens of God's city. Adam and Eve leave Eden but through their wandering Providence will lead them back to their heavenly home for, as Fowler notes, the "wandering steps" and "solitary way" of Milton's final lines recall a hopeful biblical analogue: "They wandred in the wildernesse, in a solitarie way: they found no city to dwell in.... Then they cried unto the Lord in their trouble: and he delivered them out of their distresses. And he led them foorth by the right way: that they might goe to a citie of habitation."[75] For Milton, as for Augustine, the motif of spiritual pilgrimage sets the reader on the right track.

Trinity College, Oxford

Fighting for Saint Michael: The Typology of Defeat in Milton's Celestial and Sublunary Civil Wars

Patricia Crouch

Milton's God moves in mysterious ways. In book 6 of *Paradise Lost*, Raphael quotes him as follows:

> Go Michael of celestial armies prince,
> And thou in military prowess next
> Gabriel, lead forth to battle these my sons
> Invincible, lead forth my armèd saints
> By thousands and by millions ranged for fight;
> Equal in number to that godless crew
> Rebellious, them with fire and hostile arms
> Fearless assault, and to the brow of heaven
> Pursuing drive them out from God and bliss,
> Into their place of punishment, the gulf
> Of Tartarus, which ready opens wide
> His fiery chaos to receive their fall.   (6.44–55)[1]

God's imperatives here are two: the loyal angels are to "assault" the rebels and then "drive them out" of heaven. Only a breath's pause separates the two commands. There is nothing to indicate that another entity will intervene in the battle, nothing to suggest that Michael and his angels will not be victorious. And yet, as Raphael proceeds to narrate the details of the assault and expulsion, it becomes clear that no direct relation obtains between the two acts. The opposing sides, as God subsequently explains it, are "Equal in their creation...formed" (6.690–91). The warring angels are doomed to an implacable stalemate, a "perpetual fight" that "needs must last / Endless, and no solution...found" (6.693–94). God has misdirected Michael and Gabriel with his rousing speech, if only by omission. And Michael, at least, is led astray. He misreads God's Word as presaging the loyal angels' total victory over the rebels. During the first day of the conflict, Satan approaches this "prince of angels" (6.281) in order to challenge him to single combat. Michael is "glad," for he "hop[es] here to end / Intestine war in heaven, the arch-foe subdued / Or captive dragged in chains" (6.258–60). Armed with his adamantine shield and his infallible sword "from the armoury of God," Michael has every reason to be confident that he will prevail (6.321). What he does not and cannot know, for he has been given no hint of it, is that God has stage-managed the war in heaven for the greater glory of his Son. Michael and his angels can and do win a battle, but they cannot and do not win the war. Only the appearance of the Son in his chariot, a Christian deus ex machina, can end the conflict once begun.

Virtually all Christian readers, artists, and hagiographers before Milton imagined the war in heaven quite differently. Whether their hermeneutic was literalizing or allegorizing, Catholic or Protestant, their understanding of its dynamic as an uninterrupted sequence of assault-and-expulsion anticipated Michael's in *Paradise Lost*. Where Milton's fictionalized archangel bases his interpretation upon the Word of God spoken directly to him, theirs was rooted in the Word transmitted to them in the Bible, especially in the book of Revelation:

> And there was warre in heaven, Michael and his Angels fought against the dragon, & the dragon fought and his angels,
> And prevailed not, neither was their place found any more in heaven.

> And the great dragon was cast out, that old serpent, called the devill and Satan, which deceiveth the whole world: hee was cast out into the earth, and his angels were cast out with him. (Rev. 12:7–9)²

Although theologians for centuries had been divided sharply over what they took to be the passage's seeming signification of Michael as the passive agent responsible for "cast[ing] out" the "great dragon" in verse 9, the grammatical crux that enables Milton's own heterodox solution to this problem does not seem ever to have been disputed. Underlying the poet's idiosyncratic exegesis is the implied pronoun reference at the start of verse 8, which all major early modern English translations preserve from the Greek. From a purely grammatical standpoint, the "they" in "And [they] prevailed not," because of its failure to differentiate, might be interpreted either as referring to the fallen angels alone (because of syntactical proximity) or to the fallen and unfallen angels alike. Because verse 9 unequivocally establishes that the rebel angels alone are cast from heaven, the implied pronoun in the previous verse would seem to indicate the same group. Yet Milton, without apparent precedent, takes it to refer not merely to Satan and his minions but to the whole of the warring angels. He affirms this interpretation in *De doctrina Christiana* when he writes, "Michael is introduced as leader of the angels and ἀντίπαλος (antagonist) of the prince of the devils: their respective forces were drawn up in battle array and separated after a fairly even fight, Rev. xii. 7, 8."³ What *De doctrina Christiana* does not do is explain the theological grounds of this unconventional exegesis, which surely must involve more than an arbitrary grammatical choice or unspoken semantic quarrel with the Greek word, ἀντίπαλος. Nor does it explain why in his epic poem Milton should have Michael commit precisely the same interpretive error that the author believed his contemporaries did, only to correct that reading within the space of the same book.

Despite the great care that Milton takes in book 6 to foreground the archangel's role as an interpreter of the divine Word, few critics have sought to locate Michael's failures as a warrior and exegete within a cohesive hermeneutic schema. Although critical discussions of books 5 and 6 abound, most engage the poet's unusual treatment of the celestial war in terms of aesthetics, topicality, or religious allegory. The war has been interpreted variously as driven by artistic rather than theological concerns, as a reflection of the "secondary attack" battle tactics employed during the English civil war, as a parody of earthly warfare, as an allegory of the militant church's unrelenting war against the forces of evil, and as a "somber" Restoration expression of the poet's political or millenarian disillusionment.[4] Those scholars who do attempt to situate the war within Milton's broader hermeneutic make no mention of Michael's function as a reader in book 6. This oversight is puzzling given the vast amount of scholarship devoted to the archangel's exegetical, and explicitly prophetical, role in books 11 and 12. Because the poem's closure is dependent entirely upon Michael successfully discharging his role as scriptural exegete, no critical account of the war in heaven can be fully satisfactory unless it explains both why and how Milton in book 6 reads Revelation as he does and why he makes the figure of Michael bear such crucial interpretive weight.

Taking its cue from *Paradise Lost*, this essay offers a new way of looking at the celestial war, one that positions Michael, rather than Christ or Satan, at the interpretive center of book 6. Obliquely following Stanley Fish, I will argue that the poet "ostentatiously calls...up" two interpretations of the war in heaven in order to provide both the archangel and the epic's readers "with the shock of their disappointment" at discovering their own hermeneutic failure.[5] By invoking these competing versions of the celestial war, Milton dramatizes and seeks to bridge the gulf, as wide as Tartarus itself, stretching between the Word and its significations. His representations of the war remain true to the Bible, on the one hand, and elaborate the difficulties presented by any attempt to read it transparently, on the other. Read as a cautionary tale about reading, God's education of the archangel in book 6 should be seen as preparing Michael to lead Adam through his own scriptural exegesis lesson in books 11 and 12, a lesson that extends equally to Milton's fallen readers.

As I will demonstrate, Michael's inadequacies as champion and reader, while rooted in abstract theological matters, speak directly to the religio-political events of the English civil wars and their aftermath. The archangel's misreading of God's speech regarding the war in heaven replicates the eschatological misreading made by millenarian English dissenters who believed that they were ushering in the thousand-year reign of Christ on earth under a succession of earthly Michaels, including Essex, Manchester, and Cromwell. By having Michael misread, and then having Raphael reread, Revelation 12, the poet offers an illuminating, retrospective adjustment to the millenarian expectations of the English revolutionaries. Yet he does so not to repudiate but to recuperate them. Although the degeneration and eventual collapse of the revolutionary project during the 1650s and 1660s may have led Milton to relinquish his belief in the imminence of the millennium and his radical contemporaries' role in portending it, his doctrinal certitude in the eschaton's eventuality remained unshaken. "War wearied" may have "performed what war can do" (6.695) on English soil, but the military failures of the revolution, read correctly, had not been for nought, any more than Michael's failures had been for nothing in the celestial war.

Milton's characterization of Michael in *Paradise Lost* emerges at the convergence of preterist and historicist applications of theology. The first restricts itself to the archangel's identity as it is inscribed in the pages of the Bible and other religious writings. It recognizes Michael as an independent actor in his own right as well as a type of Christ, but it grants him no agency in the temporal world outside the bounds of biblical history.[6] The second reaches beyond Scripture; it searches human history, past and present, for one or more earthly manifestations, or quasi-typological incarnations, of the archangel. Central to both approaches is the theory of typological resemblances, which propounds that the images of the Old Testament are "shadow[s] of things to come" in the New Testament[7] or, in the historicist mode, potentially in the future course of history. Early modern millenarians often combined the two approaches to recognize Michael as an actor participating in heavenly and sublunary events alike. The multivalent typological hermeneutic enabled English radicals to identify the historical actors and events of their own time as repetitions, or even fulfillments, of types delineated in the Bible. Yet those repetitions were always marked by difference. Typology asserts an identity between remote things; it does not imply an identicalness. The space of uncertainty generated by the tension between like and unlike, between same and different, always leaves open the possibility of conflation (mistaking type for antitype) or error (misidentification).

When Milton stages Michael's misreading of God's Word in book 6, he metatheatrically negotiates this space of theological uncertainty. Anxiously underwriting every debate concerning Michael's agency were worries about the potential for mistaken identity. Although apparently unremarked by Milton scholars, since the time of the primitive church, the confluence of Judaic and early Christian beliefs had engendered a wholly inappropriate rivalry between the Son and Michael that was nearly as pronounced as the adversarial relationship between the Son and Satan. Michael, whose name translates as the interrogative "who is as God, or who is lyke unto God?,"[8] emerges in the writings of Jewish angelologists and the Old Testament bearing striking functional, titular, and visible likenesses to Christ. In Hebrew texts, Michael is portrayed as "a mediator between God and men for the peace of Israel,"[9] a role that the New Testament explicitly ascribes to Christ alone.[10] Both Michael, in the Judaic tradition, and Christ, in the Christian one, share claim to the titles of protector of the church, commander of the heavenly host, and prince of the angels.[11] The imagery surrounding the archangel and the Son also exhibits remarkable similarities.[12] These resemblances were troublesome for several reasons. For one thing, Michael's central role in the eviction of Satan from heaven was seen as an infringement upon the Son's divine prerogative.[13] At the same time, by drawing attention to the Son's absence from the expulsion, the archangel's exemplary heroism opens the possibility that Christ may have had no existence prior to his incarnation and hence that he, like the angels, is a created rather than eternal being.¹⁴ Michael thus threatens the Son in the very same ways that Satan does,¹⁵ even as his heroic and cultic stature makes him potentially more dangerous to the Son than even the demonic adversary is.

In a 1640 critique of the Michaelmas Day collect and epistle prescribed by the *Book of Common Prayer* (outlawed by Parliament in 1645), the Church of England clergyman Lewes Hughes makes explicit the blasphemous potential of a literal interpretation of Michael's agency in Revelation 12:7–9. The Church of England's prescription that these verses be read to honor "*S. Michael and all the Angels*" as ones who "succour and defend us in [sic] earth" distracts churchgoers' attention from their true champion and defender, the Son, dimming his just glory.¹⁶ The verses, Hughes argues, are "appointed to be read...of purpose to pervert the meaning of our Saviour Christ, by misse-applying to Michael and all Angels in the highest Heaven, the victory that Christ hath...fighting the battell against Antichrist."¹⁷ It is precisely this misreading that Milton stages for us in book 6 when he has Michael infer a guarantee of his success, rather than the Son's, from God's command to "assault" the rebels and "drive them.../ Into their place of punishment" (6.51–53). We are not passive as this erroneous exegesis unfolds and then later unravels. The poet and the archangel himself invite us to misread Revelation. The fact that Milton allows us to harbor our hermeneutic delusions for much of the book before finally exposing them as fallacious suggests that there is a method, and a lesson, in what he does.

In *Paradise Lost*, Michael neither flouts nor questions Christ's authority over him, as Satan does, yet there is a momentary suggestion of hubris in Milton's archangel, as though he has temporarily forgotten his place. Even though God addresses both Michael and Gabriel in his speech, and then only in their roles as captain and lieutenant, respectively, of the angelic host, Michael concludes that he will single-handedly overcome Satan and, with him, the rebel forces as a whole. For most of the first day of the war, the loyal and rebel forces remain at a stalemate. As the narrator Raphael tells us, the "battle hung" (6.246) until Satan approached the heroic Michael, who with "two-handed sway" of his sword was busily inflicting "Wide wasting...destruction" upon the rebel squadrons (6.251, 253). Once brought face-to-face with Satan, Michael hastily comes to surmise that he personally will turn the battle and thereby "end / Intestine war in heaven" once and for all (6.258–59). While clearly Michael recognizes intellectually that his power derives solely from God, in practice he metonymically relocates that power, investing it in the sword of justice that he carries. The symbolic weight of the weapon is so great that Michael demands of Satan, "Hence then, and evil go with thee along / Thy offspring, to the place of evil, hell,.../ Ere this avenging sword begin thy doom" (6.275–76, 278). Yet the "Author of evil" (6.262) is far from cowed by the archangel's bold words, which he perceives, rightly as it will turn out, to be mere "airy threats" (6.283). Satan not only dismisses Michael's warning out of hand but also challenges the archangel's entire interpretation of the celestial war when he remarks, "The strife which thou callst evil,...we style / The strife of glory" (6.289–90). From the rebel forces' point of view, their struggle is noble and just; it seeks to restore them to the place of glory that they believe the Son has usurped from them. While the reader presumably knows better than to sympathize with the rebels, Satan, in turning Michael's characterizations of the sword and the war against him, nevertheless gestures toward the flexibility and potential for error inherent in every act of interpretation.

Although Michael never openly quests for the kind of "glory" that Satan does, his desire is implied, not only by his forwardness in assuming his own exemplary role in the battle, but also by his belief that his single-handed defeat of Satan will cause the mass of the rebel forces to turn tail and flee the battlefield. Given Michael's overconfidence in the singularity of his agency, however fleeting it may be, Satan's rendering of the war as fame-driven ultimately implicates the archangel as well as the fiends whom he battles. If we compare Michael's behavior with that of Abdiel at the opening of the celestial war, the aptness of Satan's characterization of the conflict becomes clear. Readers certainly would recall that fewer than 100 lines before he approaches Michael, Satan is facing Abdiel in single combat. Then, Satan accuses his opponent of being "ambitious to win / From me some plume, that thy success may show / Destruction to the rest" of the fallen forces (6.160–62). Abdiel's duly humble response to Satan's allegation acts as a foil to the presumptuousness of Michael. Although Abdiel smites Satan, as the prince of the angels will later do, he recognizes that the value of the stroke is wholly emblematic, just as his reasoned defiance of Satan's seduction of the angels to sin had been. Abdiel never loses sight, as Michael does, of whose hand will finally bring down the archfiend and his cohort. As he explains to Satan, God easily could "Have raised incessant armies to defeat" the rebels "or with solitary hand" finished them off (6.138, 139). Instead, he chose to stage the war in heaven as a lesson for all of his angels, fallen and unfallen alike. God decreed that the opposing forces should be equal in strength and number (6.227–29) precisely because this created a state of equilibrium within which he could unfold his didactic mystery play at his leisure. When, as a consequence of Abdiel's "noble stroke" (6.189), Satan "back recoil[s]" until he comes to rest "on bended knee" (6.194), the loyal angels are right to see this symbolic enactment of the fiend's subjugation to God and the Son as a "Presage of victory" (6.201). Where they go wrong is in interpreting it as a sign of their own victory in battle. For Satan to bow to the Son would be entirely appropriate; for him to bow to Michael or the other angels would be completely inappropriate, given that the angels are his equals, "save what sin hath impaired" (6.691). As Michael will do in his parley with Satan, the angels put too much confidence in their own, inimitable battle power, and too little in the "solitary hand" of God that supplies them with that power.

Michael is distracted by the materialism of his own physical battle, so much so that he loses sight of the godhead's behind-the-scenes exercise of his invisible, spiritual agency. A painting by Peter Paul Rubens (1577–1640) entitled *The Fall of the Rebel Angels* (fig. 1) offers a useful visual representation of Michael's perspectival position. Though the colorful figure of the heroic dragon-trampler looms large in the painting's foreground, an ethereal God directly above him peers down from a mass of unformed clouds

Fig. 1. Peter Paul Rubens, *The Fall of the Rebel Angels* (1621/22). Alte Pinakothek, Bayerische Staatsgemaeldesammlungen, Munich, Germany. Reproduced with permission of bpk, Berlin / Alte Pinakothek Bayerische Staatsgemmaeldeslungen, Munich, Germany / Art Resource, NY.

into which he almost dissolves. With his eyes turned downward as they are, Michael seems caught up in the moment, as indeed he is in *Paradise Lost*. The visual arrangement of the painting, in a way analogous to the Michaelmas Day collect about which Lewes Hughes complained, threatens to distract the viewer's attention sufficiently that he may "misse-appl[y] to Michael and all Angels in the highest Heaven, the victory that Christ hath...fighting the battell against Antichrist."[18] And, in fact, many artists, including virtually all sculptors and the painter Raphael (fig. 2), fail to include even a hint of heavenly involvement in Michael's battle against Satan.

If we, as readers, miss the point of Milton's juxtaposition of Abdiel's and Michael's respective fights with Satan, and hence the implicit gesture toward a higher power, we too may be led to believe that the battle involving Michael will end the war, and that the archfiend and his minions will be expelled as a consequence. The narrator Raphael, however, intervenes at this point, as he often does, to destabilize our certainty in our reading. Reiterating his earlier anxiety (5.564–76) about the impossibility of accommodating celestial events to the language and concepts of the sublunary world, Raphael informs us that he must now "with the tongue / Of angels" speak the "Unspeakable" (6.297–98). As his account of the physical fight between the leaders of the warring forces unfolds, Raphael's paradoxical vocal voicelessness speaks directly to Michael's and our temptation to mistake the sign for the real thing. If we see Michael not as a *figura* of Christ, as we see Abdiel, but as one who fulfills Christ's dragon-trampling role, then we are perceiving too close a resemblance between things that are at least as dissimilar as they are alike. To put it another way, we are assuming an equivalence between what is voiced (the material) and what cannot be voiced (the spiritual) that can never exist. We are mistaking Michael for the godhead. Raphael's caution in describing Michael and Satan as merely "likest gods" who only "seemed" "Fit to decide the empire of great heaven" (6.301, 303) reminds us that the two captains are most emphatically not gods. Because each possesses a merely "next to almighty arm" (6.316), neither is

Fig. 2. Raphael, *St. Michael Confounding the Devil* (1518). Louvre, Paris. Reproduced with permission of Scala / Art Resource, NY.

capable of implementing heaven's fate. Only the "Almighty arm" itself can deliver heaven from the scourge of the rebels.

Raphael's warning to us introduces a potentially powerful dramatic irony, assuming, of course, that we have heeded his message. When he remarks that "Michaël and his angels," after driving Satan from the field, "prevalent / Encamp[ed]" (6.411–12), Raphael opens to interrogation the textual crux embodied in Revelation's "And [they] prevailed not" (12:8). Eliding the gap between what God says and what he means, the loyal angels mistakenly assume that they indeed have prevailed, and that the rebel angels in all likelihood already will have "fled" heaven (6.531). Sage readers, having been educated by Raphael not to make this mistake, will not be surprised when the fruitless war resumes, reasserting the stalemate. At this stage, though, the readers' knowledge remains limited, for it is impossible to predict how the standoff will be broken, and hence how the war finally will end. All that we do know is that it will not be effectuated by Michael and that Revelation 12:7–9 therefore must be read in some other way.

Protestant theologians would have agreed. Most often, they recuperated the Bible's threatening allusions to Michael by appropriating them in some fashion to Christ. But they did not do so in the same way that Milton does. Following the precedent established by the early church fathers, the majority of commentators of the sixteenth and seventeenth centuries responded to the challenge posed by the archangel by "transform[ing] Michael traditions" in such a way that writings from the Bible or other religious texts "which originally referred to Michael could be understood messianically."[19] Most commonly, they did so by stripping the archangel of his individual agency by treating his appellation, "Michael," as a mere signifier of Christ. Because Michael's name means one "who is as God, or who is lyke unto God?" and because it was believed that only Christ could be said to share God's nature, the designation "Michael" was interpreted as a title for the Messiah rather than as the proper name of some discrete entity.[20] To avoid any appearance of too close a resemblance between Michael and Christ, commentators who adopt this approach collapse the two figures in such a way that the first is erased altogether. Repudiating the literal sense of the Revelation passage, those who effect such a reassignment invariably read the battle between "Michael" and the "dragon" allegorically. The notion of a literal war in heaven is deemed oxymoronic. After all, "heaven...is no place of dragons or quarrels" but a place of peace.[21] Such theologians deny that the Revelation verses depict the fall of the rebel angels at all.[22] Instead, they interpret the prophet John's vision as a sign either of Christ's Crucifixion and Resurrection or, more generally, of his metaphorical ousting of Satan from the true church.[23]

By contrast, while Milton acknowledges in *De doctrina* that a "lot of people are of the opinion that Michael is Christ," he rejects this reading as nonsensical (YP 6:347). In his view, "it would be very strange for an apostle of the Gospel to talk in such an obscure way, and to call Christ by another name, when reporting these odd and unheard-of-things about him" (YP 6:347).[24] From the poet's perspective, when Protestants erased Michael in this way, they merely reversed the problem of misinterpretation. In order to prevent the pious from naïvely misrecognizing Michael as Christ, they foolishly misrecognized Christ as Michael. What Milton seeks to do in *Paradise Lost* is to preserve both figures while making their similarities and differences explicit. Considered from a dispassionate hermeneutic standpoint, Michael could be allowed to retain his angelic identity if he was understood correctly as a type, or partial prefiguration, of Christ, rather than as a usurper of the Son's divine powers and prerogatives. In the terms that Milton sets forth in *Paradise Lost*, Michael needs to be seen to look a bit more like Abdiel and a bit less like the Son.

The problem with the typological approach to Michael was that it was rarely viewed in this dispassionate way by Protestants, whether radical or conservative. To most, it seemed to bear the indelible taint of popery. There was good reason for this, since this strategy was precisely the one favored by Catholics. The seventeenth century Jesuit theologian Robert Bellarmine makes Michael's and Christ's typological power relations explicit when he explains, "in the universal Catholic Church there are two supreme pontiffs established under Christ the Lord, one a man and visible [the Pope], and one an angel and invisible, who we believe is the Archangel Michael. As once the synagogue of the Jews revered him as a patron, so now does the Church of Christians."[25] Putting aside for the moment Protestants' obvious objections to Bellarmine's view of the pope, we may observe that the theologian preserves Michael's traditional role as set forth in the Old Testament and other Judaic writings. At the same time, he insists upon the archangel's subjection and inferiority to the Son, whom Bellarmine believes has installed him in the office of the church's protector. Michael's actions, whether on earth or in the celestial battle, parallel and indeed presage Christ's victories, but those actions are never successful in the way that Christ's are in the New Testament and finally will be at the eschaton. Bellarmine's assertion of Michael's subordinate role would seem to solve the problem posed by the archangel's potential for conflation with Christ. But Bellarmine also introduces new problems. His positioning of the pope as Michael's earthly counterpart, and his linking of Michael to the institution of the Catholic Church—which here becomes indistinguishable from the "Church of Christians"—would have appeared to Protestants as a coopting of the archangel for sinister ends. Even as Bellarmine's formulation forestalls the inordinate exaltation of Michael by refusing to treat him as equivalent to Christ, it proposes a quasi-typological resemblance between the pope and Michael, and therefore between the pope and Christ.[26]

From a Protestant perspective, there were other problems as well. The Catholic insistence upon Michael's inferior status is belied by the prayers and reverence offered to the archangel within the institution of the church. The Michaelmas Day collect and epistle prescribed by the *Book of Common Prayer*, discussed above, was perceived as inherently idolatrous, one of the remnants of Catholicism that remained to be stripped from the Church of England. Until 1644, parishioners in some English churches still knelt before images or statues of the archangel Michael in what appeared to be a form of worship.[27] The fact that Michael was most often visually represented in the guise of the heroic dragon-trampler of Revelation, in a pose very nearly identical to one occasionally used to depict Christ (fig. 3),[28] further blurred the distinction between the two figures, paradoxically reaffirming the troublesome conflation that Bellarmine and other Catholics purportedly had sought to undo through the application of typology. Although Catholics insisted, rationally enough, that the veneration paid to saints and angels (*dulia*, a form of respect) was of a different character from that paid to the godhead (*latria*, a form of reverence), for the most part "such niceties...were lost on puritans."[29] As the English dissenters saw it, the papists, despite their protestations to the contrary, treated "the Angells...as halfe goddes"[30] even as they sought to cover over their idolatry with typological sophistry.

Because of Milton's antipathy toward Catholicism and his deep-seated iconoclasm, it would be preposterous to conclude that his depiction of Michael as an active agent in *Paradise Lost* reveals Catholic sympathies on his part.[31] What Milton does in book 6 is retain the literalizing and typological aspects of the Catholic reading while preventing his reader from making the elisions that the Catholics were believed to make in practice. In short, he treats the war in heaven as a teachable moment. As we have seen, he initially invites his readers, along with Michael himself, to make this slippage by misreading the scriptural account of the celestial war as it is voiced by God in the poem (6.45–55). In doing so, he implicitly tempts us to commit precisely the same error that Catholics did when they glorified Michael too much.

In the final act of his military drama, however, Milton proceeds to scrutinize this interpretation. Once Raphael has hinted to the reader that the loyal angels' perception of their victory may not be as it seems, and once the bootless battle resumes, proving him right, the scene changes. God, who at the opening of the war had ordered Michael and Gabriel to "Pursuing drive them [the rebels] out from God and bliss, / Into their place of punishment, the gulf / Of Tartarus" (6.52–54), now repeats these instructions to the Son, whom he commands to "Pursue these sons of darkness, drive them out / From all heaven's bounds into the utter deep" (6.715–16). Like the typologically congruent figures of Michael and Christ, the

Fig. 3. *Christ Militant* (sixth century). Museo Arcivescovile, Ravenna, Italy. Reproduced with permission of Erich Lessing / Art Resource, NY.

two speeches on the surface appear virtually the same, but they are not identical. God's words on both occasions mean precisely what they say, but only in Christ's case do his words mean *only* what they say. In God's speech to Michael and Gabriel, there is a lacuna stretching between his commands to "assault" the rebels and then "drive them out" of heaven (6.51–52). This lacuna can be filled only by the Son, since only the Son can instantiate God's Word, and since only Christ can defeat the dragon. Whereas Michael possesses only a "next to Almighty arm" (6.316), God himself tells the Son, "my almighty arms / Gird on" (6.713–14).

When God addresses the Son in the final scene of book 6, he iterates rather transparently the didactic purpose implicit in his tempting of Michael to hermeneutic error. It becomes clear for the first time that God has not engineered the angelic impasse between the warring forces merely to admonish Satan and the rebels. When God tells the Son that he has "ordained" his victory so "that all may know / In heaven and hell thy power above compare" (6.700, 704–05), the deity's dual motives become clear. God has tested Michael and found him wanting; the archangel, like Satan, needs to remember that he is subordinate to the Son, and that he is no more a god than is the posturing archfiend, though both on the surface "likest gods...seemed" (6.301). Strictly speaking, the archangel has not misread God's words to him; rather, he has failed to supply what is absent. This is true in terms of both Scripture and script. What is missing is not only the textually incarnate form of Christ potentially implied by the scriptural "And [they] prevailed not" (Rev. 12:8) but also the embodied form of Christ as the agent to whom Satan will bow. Michael has been called upon to perform a literalizing reading, but he has also been expected to supplement that reading with his larger knowledge of the Word. He has been asked, so to speak, to turn and face the aeriform figure hovering above him in the clouds in Rubens's pictorial depiction of him (see fig. 1).

In *Paradise Lost* the intertextual key to filling the lacuna in God's initial command to Michael and Gabriel to "assault" the rebels and "drive them out" (6.51–52) of heaven is the scene of the

Son's exaltation in book 5. Through the careful application of geometric imagery, Raphael's narrative at the close of book 6 restores the Son to his rightful places, both literal and symbolic, at the center and at the apex of the spiritual order. As we witness Christ's appearance on the battlefield, we are meant to recall that when God summoned the angels to hear his declaration of Christ's elevation, the angels gathered around him and the Son in "circuit inexpressible.../ Orb within orb" (5.595–96). Viewed from above, God and the Son are at the midpoint of a celestial circle. Viewed from the side, they are at the vertex of a heavenly triangle. In their singular "brightness," it is as if the Father and Son are at the "top" of a "flaming mount" that manifests, below, the lesser brightness of the angels who form the triangle's base (5.599, 598). This imagery of verticality is reinforced, but also complicated, by the fact that the angels carry "ten thousand thousand ensigns high advanced" (5.588) which

> for distinction serve
> Of hierarchies, of orders, and degrees;
> Or in their glittering tissues bear imblazed
> Holy memorials, acts of zeal and love
> Recorded eminent.   (5.590–94)

The Miltonic "or" in these lines is critical. It points up the fact that these banners would seem to offer two possible models of angelic identity—one determined by the angels' hierarchical relationship to the godhead and their peers, the other determined by the honorable actions they have performed. But these two classes of identity markers are not meant to be mutually exclusive. The angels' heroic deeds should arise solely from their desire to serve and glorify the godhead. As such, they also signal, though in a more oblique way than the explicitly hierarchical ensigns, the angels' acquiescence and subjugation to the proper order of things.

Raphael's reintroduction of the imagery of encirclement and verticality in book 6 allows us to recognize that Michael in the heat of battle has mistakenly interpreted all of the signs—God's Word to him, the emblems of angelic virtue, and Satan's prophetic kneeling before Abdiel—as signifiers of his own potency, rather than the Son's. He has lost the ability to distinguish between the *dulia*, or respect, to which he is entitled, and the *latria*, or reverence, due to the godhead alone. Recalling the imagery of book 5, Raphael describes the Son as seated atop a chariot-throne "flashing thick flames" and shining so brightly that the loyal angels can see him from "far off" (6.751, 768). He is again "attended with [the] ten thousand thousand saints" who before had surrounded him and the Father (6.767). No longer, though, do the angels carry flags advertising their own virtues and hierarchical standing. Now, only "the great ensign of Messiah blazed / Aloft by angels borne, his sign in heaven" (6.775–76).

Despite the prophecy implicitly contained in God's speech to the whole of the heavenly host that the Son will be the one before whom Satan bows (5.607–08), Michael is "surprised" when the Messiah appears on the battlefield, as are the other loyal angels (6.774). Importantly, though, it is a surprise marked by "unexpected joy," for the angels instantly realize that Christ has come to deliver them from the futility of the celestial war (6.774). As soon as he realizes that his interpretation of his own dragon-trampling role has been mistaken, Michael acts quickly, and properly. He "soon reduced / His army" under the Son, so that they were "circumfused on either wing, / Under their head embodied all in one" (6.777–79). Once again, the angels find themselves encircling Christ, even as they stand beneath him, rehearsing once more the visual hierarchies that they performed in book 5. By contrast, whereas Michael rejoices in discovering and remedying his error once it is revealed to him, the fallen angels merely "envy" the Son more (6.793). The reprobates cling to their hermeneutic failure, fueled by their unrelenting desire for the glory that belongs to the Son alone. Hence, the only possible outcome for them is to be cast out of heaven and sent to "their doom" (6.817). The restoration of the Son's, Michael's, and Satan's proper places is symbolically enacted in the pathetic fallacy of a self-reordering nature. The destruction that accrued from the angels' warfare is undone with a Word from the Son. Just as the angels had returned to their rightful positions of their own volition, "at his command the uprooted hills retired / Each to his place" (6.781–82). God's will that all things should bow before the Son is reiterated when the hills defer, "obsequious" (6.783). Sharing the loyal angels' joy at the coming of the Messiah, every "hill and valley smiled" with a profusion of "fresh flowerets" (6.784). When the Son drives Satan and the rebels out of heaven, all is again right with the heavenly world.

Like his mainstream Protestant contemporaries, Milton ultimately rereads, and rectifies, Michael's agency in the celestial war by appropriating his role to the Messiah.[32] The end result, at least, is the same: Michael is stripped of his efficacy, and his potency as described in Revelation is transferred to Christ. Yet Milton's hermeneutic is quite different from that of his more conservative contemporaries. He neither elides Michael nor reduces the celestial war to mere allegory. The poet's belief in the efficacious intervention of angels on earth, combined with his millenarianism, situates him not with his conservative Anglican contemporaries but in the camp of radical Protestant figures like Joseph Mede and Thomas Brightman, whose works were translated and published in England at the direction of Parliament during the early 1640s.[33] Throughout the English civil war and Protectorate, radical religious dissenters identified themselves with the army of "saints" described in Revelation 13:7, whom they believed would usher in Christ's visible reign on earth.[34] Typologically speaking, they believed that they were the chosen people of "Israel," God's "firstborn, whom he will not have any longer kept in bondage" and on whose behalf he "rebuketh kings and Parliaments, armies and Councils."[35] Michael, as the "great prince" of the Israelites (Dan. 12:1), was their "chiefe patron" and "Defender."[36] The conservative Protestant elision of Michael had the advantage of containing and depoliticizing a figure who occupied a prominent place in the millenarian narratives of English revolutionaries. By disavowing Michael's role in the celestial war that demarcated the beginning of human history (the Creation), mainstream Protestant commentators also disclaimed his apparent usurpation of Christ's precedence in the eschaton signaling the end of the temporal world.[37] Milton's treatment of the archangel, which is far more nuanced than his contemporaries', enables the poet to preserve Michael as a discrete figure even as he reassesses Michael's typological roles in the celestial and sublunary civil wars that provide the text and subtext of books 5 and 6.

Although their responses to the figure of "Michael" in Revelation 12:7–9 are not uniform, all early modern millenarians share a belief in the celestial battle as a "double warre," one signifying on both earthly and spiritual levels.[38] The English clergyman Thomas Brightman (1562–1607) argues with most of his Protestant contemporaries that the reference to "Michael" in Revelation is to be interpreted as a title for Christ, while the celestial war itself is to be interpreted as an allegory of the "battell in the Church upon the earth." At the same time, however, he urges that "*Michaell* by communication of name is [the fourth-century Roman emperor] *Constantine*, the faithfull souldier of Christ" who defended the primitive church against the advances of the pagan emperors Maxentius, Maximinus, and Lucinius, collectively representing the "*Dragon*...by whose tyranny the Devill powred forth his hatred against the Church." Writing in 1611, and historicist in his outlook, Brightman believes that a renewed battle against the dragon by Michael's/Constantine's successors, including Thomas Cromwell, Thomas Cranmer, and Elizabeth I, has already begun and will continue to rage until 1650. At that time, the reformation of the church will be complete: the papacy will be overthrown, the Jews will be converted, and a New Jerusalem will be established on earth. Brightman invites his contemporaries as well as the later English civil war revolutionaries to imagine themselves, like Constantine, as "faithfull souldier[s] of Christ...warring under the banner" of their captain "Michael" in a protoapocalyptic battle on earth.[39] The closest early modern analogue to Milton's reading of Revelation, though, is to be found in Joseph Mede's *The Key of the Revelation* (1650). Between 1610 and 1638, Mede served as a fellow of Christ's College, Cambridge, where Milton may have studied under him.[40] As Brightman does, Mede interprets Michael as historically signifying the Emperor Constantine and his early modern English heirs. Unlike Brightman, but like Milton, Mede also preserves Michael's distinct identity as the leader of the angels who engages Satan in a literal, celestial battle.[41]

Milton's *De doctrina Christiana* is entirely consistent with Mede's theology and the apocalyptic narratives of the poet's civil war and Protectorate contemporaries. The author argues in his sixth book that certain "signs" common to "the destruction of Jerusalem, the type of Christ's second coming, and his second coming itself" will herald the millennium. He notes immediately after that "some authorities" believe the millennium will be announced by "the calling of the entire nation not only of the Jews but also of the Israelites" (YP 6:617), the latter term encompassing the international community of saints that Milton envisioned in *The Second Defence* (YP 4:554–55). In *Areopagitica* (1644), Milton describes the English people as the vanguard of this holy host. A "concurrence of signs," he argues, has made it apparent that the nation has been "chos'n before any other, that out of her as out of *Sion* should be proclam'd and sounded forth the first tidings and trumpet of Reformation to all *Europ*" (YP 2:552). The English saints, like Constantine before them, have been called to war against the dragon, and they will usher in "some new and great period in [God's]...Church, ev'n to the reforming of Reformation it self" (YP 2:553). While it is true that in *Areopagitica* Milton's focus is upon truth and spiritual warfare, his language has strong militaristic overtones. Though the England of *Areopagitica* is indeed "a City of refuge, the mansion house of liberty, encompast and surrounded with [God's]...protection," "the shop of warre" that supports it also is kept busy with "anvils and hammers waking, to fashion out the plates and instruments of armed Justice in defence of beleaguer'd Truth" (YP 2:553–54). As *The Second Defence* (1654) demonstrates even more clearly,[42] the English army in Milton's view fights a "double warre," one both literal and spiritual. Neither can be separated from the other. When he stages in *Paradise Lost* Michael's misreading of God's directive to him, Milton therefore should be seen as attending as much to his politico-religious convictions as to his theological ones.

Given the indebtedness of the revolutionaries' prophetic schema to the book of Revelation,[43] it is perhaps inevitable that the figure of Michael should occupy a central place in their millenarian readings of the English civil war. From the onset of hostilities through the Protectorate, the mantle of Michael was passed to a succession of parliamentary champions.[44] A military banner carried by the parliamentary forces beginning in 1642 (fig. 4), for example, depicts an armed man trampling a bishop's mitre beneath his feet, a sword upraised in his hand, with the motto "Pro deo et patria," or "For God and country."[45] Eventually, the archangel's dragon-trampling role came to be associated with Oliver Cromwell, a fact that I will argue is central to Milton's depiction of the war in heaven. During the early years of the conflict, though, the most prominent military figure on the parliamentary side was Robert Devereux, the third Earl of Essex. John Taylor unequivocally alludes to Essex's assumption of Michael's office in a 1643 satirical tract. In this text, Taylor describes his purportedly autobiographical "conversion, confession, [and] contrition" from his former state as "a misled, ill-bred, rebellious round-head." Before he regained his senses, casting off puritanism and returning to the bosom of the Church of England, Taylor writes, "I was at *Boston, in Lincolnshire,* where I heard M*ʳ Anderson* the diligent Preacher say, that the Earle of *Essex* was *Michaell* the Archangell, and that the King was the Dragon, which he must Tread under his feet. verily [sic] it was strange doctrine to me, and I (like an asse) beleeved him."[46] A year later, the royalist John Cleveland complained that the dissenters thought Edward Montague, second Earl of Manchester, "so sanctified a Thunderbolt, that Burroughs, in a... blasphemy to his Lord of hosts,... stile[d] him the Archangel, giving Battel to the Devil."[47]

Ultimately, however, the Michael-like military leader who most captured and sustained the imaginations of the English dissenters in general and Milton in particular was Oliver Cromwell, who had served under both Manchester and Fairfax. As Laura Lunger Knoppers demonstrates, the English during the war became accustomed to seeing Cromwell depicted as a glorious, conquering military hero. Such portraiture quickly became conventionalized, persisting even after the Protector's death in 1658.[48] Some republican depictions of Cromwell associate the parliamentary

Fig. 4. *Banners of the Parliamentary Army, in the time of Charles I, with the Arms of the Captains.* © British Library Board, MS. Sloane 5247, fol. 71v.

forces' leader with Michael overtly. In a 1655 pamphlet, for example, the Quaker leader George Fox addresses Cromwell as the one "into whose hands God hath committed the Sword of Justice, that under thee all may be Godly and quietly governed. A terror to the evil doers, and for the encouragement of them that do well; and to the rest of the Army, whom the Lord hath set above all your enemies."[49]

While Milton never directly equates Cromwell with Michael, as Fox does, his praise of the renowned general is uncustomarily effusive. In "Cromwell, Our Cheif [sic] of Men" (1652), the poet commends Cromwell for having "reard Gods Trophies" and for having "his [God's] work pursu'd."[50] In the *Second Defence* (1654), Milton declares Cromwell England's "defender," a "strong and faithful...pillar" to its glory, and a "support of English interests." The author gushes, "For while you, O Cromwell, are safe, he does not have sufficient faith even in God himself who would fear for the safety of England, when he sees God everywhere so favorable to you, so unmistakably at your side" (YP 4:670). Milton endows Cromwell with virtually all of the archangel's most revered qualities. Cromwell is the "defender of liberty" and "father" of his country (YP 4:670). Milton elaborates at length upon Cromwell's role as the "general of England's armies," declaring, "he traversed the entire realm of Britain with uninterrupted victory" and exhibited a "rare and all-but-divine excellence." Indeed, "there flourished in him so great a power, whether of intellect and genius or of discipline (established not merely according to military standards, but rather according to the code of Christian virtue) that to his camp...he attracted from every side all men who were already good and brave, or else he made them such, chiefly by his own example" (YP 4:668).[51] As the favored object of the divine regard and a man of "all-but-divine excellence," Cromwell sounds a great deal like the angelic "halfe goddes" once honored in the *Book of Common Prayer*.

As the Interregnum during which Christ's return was anticipated got underway, though, many of the English revolutionaries began to suspect Cromwell's unworthiness as the saints' champion. The regicide, for one thing, led many to abandon or lose faith in the cause, including Essex. The king's execution generated an outpouring of rhetoric and images that depicted Cromwell as a perverter of justice and a greedy and duplicitous usurper of Charles I. Royalists, of course, were responsible for most of this vitriol.

Yet even to those who supported the regicide, the pure figure of a Cromwellian Michael appeared to degenerate over time as the Protector increasingly adopted the very temporal dignities that had been seen as emblematic of the corruption of the Stuart king and the Church of England. More and more, he seemed to live up to the archangel Michael's name, meaning one "who is as God," but only in the sense that he looked surprisingly, if only outwardly, like the English monarchs who had associated their office strongly with presumptions of divine right. The ceremonial rites of Cromwell's 1657 investiture ceremony especially jarred many iconoclasts, including the Puritans. The visual spectacle of the Protector's installation seemed to bear out the postregicide wave of anti-Cromwellian propaganda.[52] An illustration contained in *A Further narrative of the passages of these times in the Common-wealth of England* (1658) reveals that the Protector received at his investiture an impressive array of monarchical accoutrements. According to the caption, "Mr. Speaker. in ye name of ye Par^{mt}. presented Seuerall things to his Highne^{s}s Viz: a Robe of Purple Velvet Lined wth Ermine: a Large Bible Richly Guilt & Bossed: Next a Sword & Lastly a Septer of Massie Gold."[53] From the viewpoint of many, Cromwell's mock-coronation mirrored his spiritual degeneration. In the Puritan Lucy Hutchinson's view, Cromwell had once been "so uncorruptibly faithful both to his trust and the people's interest that he could not be drawn" in by King Charles's "trinkling" during the latter's captivity at Hampton Court.[54] By the time of his accession to Lord Protector, though, Cromwell had all but abandoned the Good Old Cause and become little better than a usurper of the crown. As Hutchinson describes it,

> Cromwell and his army grew wanton with their power, and invented a thousand tricks of government.... He weeded, in a few months' time, above a 150 godly officers out of the army, with

whom many of the religious soldiers went off, and in their room abundance of the King's dissolute soldiers were entertained; and the army was almost changed from that godly religious army, whose valour God had crowned with triumph, into the dissolute army they had beaten, bearing yet a better name. His wife and children were setting up for principality, which suited no better with any of them than scarlet on the ape; only, to speak truth of himself, he had much natural greatness in him, and well became the place he had usurped.[55]

Though Milton in 1654 praised Cromwell for having "spurned" the "name of king...from your far greater eminence," by 1657 it was in name only that the Protector was perceived by many to differ from his royal predecessor (YP 4:672). Parliament's restoration of Charles II to the Stuart kingship in 1660 was almost anticlimactic, for Cromwell's perceived pride and power-grabbing already had shaken radically many dissenters' hopes that England, under Michael's leadership, was destined soon to fulfill its role as the harbinger of the Second Coming.

Although English millenarians found it increasingly difficult after 1649 to reconcile the historical Cromwell with his biblical persona, they clung to the larger typological schema in which the figure of the English Michael was embedded because it underwrote in significant ways their revolutionary narrative. Michael's interpretive failure in *Paradise Lost,* and Milton's subsequent exposure of that failure, rehearse, but also recuperate, the dissenters' millenarian misreading of Cromwell's agency. A 1658 engraving by William Faithorne (fig. 5) positions Cromwell unambiguously as a quasi-typological incarnation of Michael. *The Embleme of Englands Distractions*[56] depicts the Protector standing astride both a serpent ("Error") and the body of a prone woman (recalling Psalm 91:13) with a crown and rosary cast to the ground beside her head (the whore of "Babilon" of Revelation 17). The upraised sword in Cromwell's right hand and the unclasped book in his left suggestively evoke the apocalyptic war described in the "seal[ed]...books" of prophecy, which according to Daniel 12:4 would be opened with the arrival of the end of days. Surrounding Cromwell are several typologically significant Old Testament scenes. Above the Protector

Fig. 5. William Faithorne, *The Embleme of Englands distractions* (1658). Reg. No. 1848,0911.242. © The Trustees of the British Museum.

and to his left, Noah's ark is pictured, while the dove of the same story, an olive leaf in its beak, hovers directly overhead. The inclusion of this imagery of the Flood evokes, in Milton's words, the moment when "God vouchsafe[d] to raise another world /...and all his anger to forget" (PL 11.877–78). As such, it prefigures the new world that would begin at the time of the Second Advent, when Christ would commence his reign on earth.

A raised hill to Cromwell's left makes explicit the millenarian foreshadowing implicit in the imagery of the flood. The hill is identified as Mount Sion, normally taken as a synecdoche for Jerusalem, where in the last days God will gather together the remnant of his faithful and establish "the house of the Lord" (Mic. 4:1). Pictured below are various scenes, glossed by Micah 4:3, depicting both the Judgment and the eventual peace that will ensue from Christ's Second Coming when "he shall judge among many people...and they shall beate their swords into plowshares." At that time, no longer will any "nation...lift up a sword against nation, neither shall they learne warre any more." The implications of the engraving are clear: Cromwell, by making war against the serpent and the Roman Catholic Church with the sword and Bible that he carries, has ushered in the culmination of the Old Testament narrative of the chosen people and an end of war forever.

The iconography of Faithorne's engraving threatens to transfer Christ's glory and agency to the twinned figures of Michael and Cromwell. Streaming from the triple crowns of England, Scotland, and Ireland upheld on the martial hero's sword are the words, "I will never faile thee, nor forsake thee" (Josh. 1:5) on one side and "Bee still, and know that I am GOD" (Ps. 46:10) on the other. Although the streamers extend from the sword into heaven, and thereby assert that the sword and the power of Cromwell and Michael derive from the "almighty arm" of the godhead rather than from the martial hero's merely "next to almighty arm" (PL 6.316), the iconography's assertion of a heavenly hierarchy is so subtle as to be easily missed, even taking into account the overwhelming vertical visual orientation of the drawing, which parallels the emphatically hierarchical imagery that Raphael deploys in books 5 and 6 of *Paradise Lost*. Like Milton's fictionalized Michael, the illustration's interpreters are hermeneutically positioned between two competing representations of authority, the one embodied in the Word, the other in the sword: in the first, agency is vested solely in the godhead, while in the second it is *in*vested in a material weapon. If readers fail to recognize that the latter is a mere *figura* for the former, they may inadvertently mistake the type for the antitype, as Milton's Michael does.

The three figures occupying the right-side column in the illustration reiterate the ambiguity inherent in the millenarians' bivalent hermeneutic. Although their eyes are turned upward, presumably toward heaven, they also are turned toward—and perspectivally positioned beneath—the figure of Cromwell/Michael, so that the figures appear to be bowing reverentially before him. Their apparent worship of Cromwell/Michael presumably should be interpreted as merely emblematic, that is, as directed not to the type but above him to the antitype, just as Satan's bow before Abdiel in the epic prefigures the fiend's submission to Christ alone. Nevertheless, because the figure of Cromwell so dominates the scene, the engraving tempts its beholders to see Cromwell not as one "who is as God, or who is lyke unto God,"[57] but as the very referent of the "I am GOD" that appears on his sword's banner. As such, it stages, but fails to contain, the very challenge that Michael in the sacred texts was seen to pose to Christ's prerogatives and uniquely exalted status.

In his depiction of Michael in *Paradise Lost*, Milton acknowledges and responds to the interpretive difficulties engendered by the millenarian reliance upon typological resemblances or correspondences. Arguably, had the poet followed the lead of his orthodox Protestant contemporaries and elided Michael's role in the celestial war altogether, he could have erased the troublesome failures of Cromwell by redirecting the reader's attention solely to a heavenly world where wars are fought only allegorically by the perfect figure of Christ. But to do so would be to deny the very millenarian narrative that undergirded the dissenters' earthly revolution. However disillusioned Milton may have been with Cromwell's failures, he never wrote against the Protector in the ways he had written against Charles I. As David Loewenstein notes, "Milton himself never represented the ambiguities of Cromwell's character and religious politics in satanic and opportunistic terms: despite his godly republican ideals and his likely disappointment with the Protectorate, there is not a shred of evidence that Milton came to envision Cromwell himself as a 'false dissembler,'" a term applied to Satan in *Paradise Lost*.[58] Since Cromwell, in the eyes of the poet and his revolutionary contemporaries, stood as the champion of truth and liberty, he could not be renounced without admitting that the claims supporting the millenarians' violent crusade all had been lies. Milton would permit no such apostasy.

Instead, he reread his source text, Revelation 12:7–9. He determined that the failures of the revolution demonstrated that the English radicals had mistakenly presumed too close an identity between type and antitype, between the archangel's war against Satan and the Son's. During the millenarian fever of the 1640s and 1650s, the dissenters' military leaders had looked like the angel who defeats Satan in Revelation 12, who in turn looks like the Christ of Revelation 20. But these seventeenth century military leaders were not Michael any more than Michael is Christ. The English champions, and especially Cromwell, needed to be recognized as imperfect. Rather than denying Michael's agency as so many of his more traditional contemporaries did, the poet in *Paradise Lost* and *De doctrina Christiana* clarifies the nature of the archangel's role as a type of Christ and establishes the limits of his efficacy. Against an artistic and hagiographic tradition that exalts Michael's exemplary heroism, Milton draws a clear boundary between him and Christ. Rather than focusing on the apparent similarities between the two figures, he emphasizes their differences. As he does so, Milton illuminates the standing of Oliver Cromwell as a historical, seventeenth century manifestation of Michael.

The political and religious failures of the English revolution, along with the moral failures of Cromwell, offered a humbling lesson to the dissenters. Milton reminds his disillusioned readers, to borrow from *The Souldiers Pocket Bible*, that "all of us upon such occasions" of defeat in battle must "search whether we have not put two [sic] little confidence in the Arme of the Lord, and too much in the arme of flesh."[59] To commit this error is to confuse, and indeed conflate, one reality with another. This does not mean that Michael's battle, or the parliamentarian rebels', signified nothing or served no purpose beyond humiliating the war's otherwise righteous participants. As the Son explains to his angelic "saints" in *Paradise Lost,* their offerings of "faithful...warfare" and "fearless[ness] in his righteous cause" are "accepted" by God as signs of their loyalty and fidelity to truth (6.803–04). The workings of the "arme of the flesh," in both Milton's celestial and sublunary civil wars, remain "type[s] of Christ's second coming," announcing "the calling of the entire nation not only of the Jews but also of the Israelites" (YP 6:616–17). But the "doom" of Satan's forces rightly belongs to Christ alone (6.817). Christ and only Christ will exact due "vengeance" (6.808) when he fulfills the typological promise in the celestial angels' and earthly saints' struggles. Like Michael, Cromwell and his followers are revealed to be imperfect, as all angels and humans are. But these imperfections do not negate the symbolic value of the respective champions' victories. They merely need to be interpreted properly. Time, rather than the trappings of visible success, Milton urges, ultimately will prove the justness of their cause.

Framingham State University

From Judgment to Interpretation: Eighteenth Century Critics of Milton's *Paradise Lost*

Esther Yu

In the fateful separation scene of book 9 of *Paradise Lost*, Eve surveys the abundant growth in the garden before her and suggests to Adam that a more effective way of tending to the garden might be devised:

> Let us divide our labors, thou where choice
> Leads thee, or where most needs, whether to wind
> The Woodbine round this Arbour, or direct
> The clasping Ivie where to climb, while I
> In yonder Spring of Roses intermixt
> With Myrtle, find what to redress till Noon:
> For while so near each other thus all day
> Our taske we choose, what wonder if so near
> Looks intervene and smiles, or object new
> Casual discourse draw on, which intermits
> Our dayes work brought to little, though begun
> Early, and th' hour of Supper comes unearn'd.[1]

In his examination of this passage, Christopher Ricks demonstrates the technique of close reading to brilliant effect. He turns a critical eye upon individual words, searching for secondary and tertiary definitions that enrich the sense of the entire passage. He seizes, for example, upon Eve's desire to "redress" nature. The most obvious definition of "redress" in a botanical context relates to setting or raising a plant to an upright position. "But it seems improbable," Ricks writes, "that Milton is unaware of the moral resonance of the word—its moral meaning is also ancient, and found in Chaucer. Eve may believe that she is going to set the plants upright and erect. In fact, she 'herself, though fairest unsupported flower,' will be 'drooping unsustained'" (9.432, 430). Eve's reference to the "casual discourse" that would prevent the pair from working similarly invites Ricks's scrutiny. For "casual" may signify not only that "which befalls" but also that "which falls"—a denotation only too appropriate for reminding us that the discourse that ultimately distracts Eve not only brings the "day's work ... to little," but precipitates the fall of humankind.[2] By exploring the different registers of key words, Ricks goes well beyond a literal understanding of what Eve communicates to detect the undercurrents of language that seem to reveal the irresistible force of some greater design, be it God's or the poet's. Readers armed with Ricks's insights are better prepared to grasp the poignancy of a scene in which Eve remains tragically unaware of the dangers attendant upon her suggestion.

Ricks's use of new critical methods in his reading of *Paradise Lost* serves, of course, as a pointed vindication of Milton's style against well-known New Critics like T. S. Eliot and F. R. Leavis, who had accused Milton of neglecting sense for sound. The early-twentieth-century movement of New Criticism in which these critics played a part, as we recall, elevated the text into a self-sufficient unit for critical analysis and emphasized the value of textual analysis over belletristic, historical, or biographical approaches to literary studies.[3] The main work of literary analysis, the New Critics insisted, should consist of careful, sustained attention to selected portions of a text in order to achieve a deeper understanding of the work as a unified whole. By the time the methodology was codified in William Wimsatt and Monroe Beardsley's 1954 essay, "The Intentional Fallacy," the central stance of New Criticism could be formulated in this way: "poetic analysis and exegesis" was to be considered no less than the "true and objective way of criticism." The textual meaning so highly prized by New Critics was to be uncovered through examining a poem's internal features; in Wimsatt and Beardsley's words, such meaning could be accessed "through the semantics and syntax of a poem, through our habitual knowledge of the language, through grammars, dictionaries, and all the literature which is the source of dictionaries, in general through all that makes a language and culture."[4] Ricks's analysis, as we have seen, explores meaning in just this manner, as the poet's language becomes the principal point of departure for acquiring interpretative insight.

If New Criticism today tends to be dismissed as a state of innocence—or willful ignorance—before the sophistication of theory and New Historicism, the techniques associated with the movement are still readily employed in professional journals and deeply entrenched in American educational institutions. The legacy of New Criticism has been largely pedagogical and powerfully so; as John Guillory and others argue, the New Critics shaped literary criticism into the form that made it acceptable to twentieth century universities as an academic discipline.[5] A genealogical exploration of New Criticism's pedagogical dimensions takes us to Cambridge University in 1929, when I. A. Richards called attention to the shortcomings of literary education with the protocols of *Practical Criticism*; it would, however, fall to his pupil William Empson to further develop the interpretive procedures of close reading in such works as *Seven Types of Ambiguity*.[6] Across the Atlantic, a group of American Southerners took up the formulation of close reading and gave the practice institutional weight, first in southern universities, then elsewhere.[7] The transatlantic origins of close reading are worth considering, if only to complicate the usual alignment of the practice with a particular conservative ideology.[8] The Southern Agrarians who endorsed and eventually codified close reading, after all, found it congenial to a conservative agenda that had little to do with the ideological preferences of the English progenitors of the method. The adaptability of close reading to such distinctly motivated critical enterprises has seldom been acknowledged.

I wish to suggest, however, that the versatility of close reading has allowed it to span historical divides as well as ideological ones. Empson's writing provides compelling evidence that his advocacy of close reading and taste for ambiguity were heavily informed by a much earlier set of practices. In *Some Versions of Pastoral*, he devotes a great deal of attention to the responses of two eighteenth century critics of Milton, Richard Bentley and Zachary Pearce, and virtually builds his argument upon observations they make. Though Empson's conclusions are, as readers have come to expect of him, idiosyncratically original, his engagement with the earlier critics suggests a common approach underlying more apparent differences.[9] Empson mimics the eighteenth century critics' method of subjecting verbal minutiae to scrutiny, and draws his final argument out of the same evidentiary pool of individual word choices and grammatical constructions. Furthermore, he reserves his highest praise for these early critics in the instances in which they advance interpretations of Milton's language—precisely the work that he, and other New Critics after him, would come to see as the main burden of literary criticism.[10]

In his close readings of Milton, Empson drew inspiration from an earlier historical period that was itself a significant turning point in the development of literary criticism. As the focal point of over three centuries' worth of literary criticism, *Paradise Lost* provides an ideal locus from which to examine such historical shifts in reading. My own survey of early-eighteenth-century critics of *Paradise Lost* confirms what a thoughtful reading of Empson's work already suggests: the key principles behind the mid-twentieth-century practice of close reading are far from new. Furthermore, a study of the eighteenth century critics of *Paradise Lost* reveals a perceptible shift in the approach to reading—one that exhibits the same inward turn to the text that New Criticism later recapitulates. On the earlier end of the eighteenth century transition, critics like

Joseph Addison and Richard Bentley produce evaluative readings by relying on principles of classical criticism to assess the poem's aesthetic value; later commentators including Zachary Pearce and the two Jonathan Richardsons, however, explore textual meaning with interpretative practices prefiguring modern techniques of close reading. As the commentators of *Paradise Lost* led the move away from neoclassical modes of criticism, they, in turn drew from another well-established mode of reading—biblical hermeneutics. Our fascination with textual meaning and our sense of the enormous potential of literary works to yield multiple readings cannot be understood apart from recognizing the powerful influence of biblical hermeneutics. Ultimately, my reading provides yet one more way to register the magnitude of Milton's achievement: *Paradise Lost,* for eighteenth century readers, becomes the text that lays bare the insufficiency of existing critical tools and calls forth new approaches to reading.

Judgment

The explosive growth of the literary marketplace in the early eighteenth century produced a newly diversified range of reading materials for a growing community of readers. For Joseph Addison and other prominent men of letters, however, this expansion signaled a crisis of taste. The cultural elite found themselves contending with the increasingly forceful tides of public opinion in deciding questions of literary value. "The existence of a public itself," as David Marshall observes, seemed "to undermine the universal judgment and agreement upon which the standard of taste [was seen to be] founded."[11] Leading literary men like Addison attempted to maintain order in the Republic of Letters by insisting upon guidelines that would allow readers to recognize literary works of distinction. The ancients, by Addison's time, had come to be regarded among the English literati as undisputed authorities on poetry and literary criticism. The French neoclassical critic René Le Bossu, whose work had circulated in translation since 1695, articulates the prevailing view: "Aristotle and Horace left behind them such rules, as make them by all men of learning, to be look'd upon as perfect masters of the art of poetry: and the poems of *Homer* and *Virgil* are, by the grant of all ages, the most perfect models of this way of writing, the world ever saw."[12] Addison's evaluation of *Paradise Lost* thus draws on the principles of classical criticism set forth by Aristotle, Horace, and to a lesser extent, Longinus—the three figures who had most influenced the development of European criticism.[13]

When the classical critics approached works of literature, the plot of any given piece was considered on the basis of its composition and emotional effectiveness. The French neoclassical critics, for example, insisted that each work fulfill two criteria: the plot "must be *admirable,* and it must be *probable.*"[14] It was not enough to fashion a delightful plot; as the French critic René Rapin argues in the spirit of Aristotle, readers are more powerfully affected if the events presented are also believable.[15] Thus, Addison, in keeping with neoclassical principles, praises Milton's work for the most part, and reserves his strongest objections for Milton's depiction of Sin and Death and the Limbo of Vanity. Sin is famously depicted as a woman "to the waste, and fair / But ended foul in many a scaly fould /...About her middle round / A cry of Hell Hounds never ceasing bark'd" (2.650–54). Passages such as these, Addison writes, "are astonishing, but not credible; the reader cannot so far impose upon himself to see a possibility in them; they are the descriptions of dreams and shadows, not of things or persons."[16] Addison rejects these representations as inappropriate to the classical epic; in his own words, these fantastical images "favor of the spirit of *Spenser* and *Ariosto* [rather] than of *Homer* and *Virgil.*"[17] His aversion to these more fanciful depictions accords with the taste of neoclassical critics like Rapin, who dismissed the "visions, enchantments, and prodigious adventures [of poets like Ariosto as] the vain *imaginations of a sick brain* [to be] pitied by all men of *sense*, because they have no color of likelihood. The same judgment must be pronounc'd of the other *Italian* and *Spanish* poets, who suffer their wits to ramble in the romantic way: 'tis too great an honor to call them poets, for they are for the most part but rimesters."[18]

Addison's criticism of Milton reflects a broader concern among neoclassical critics with generic integrity, and a particularly deep investment in defending the dignified form of the classical epic from the corruptions of the epic romance.[19]

For Addison, however, the classical principles decline in power as critical tools over the course of his essays. Aristotle in the *Poetics* enjoins epic poets to avoid lengthy narrative asides and digressive self-references, and commends Homer for being "the only poet who rightly appreciates the part he should take himself." "The poet," he writes, "should speak as little as possible in his own person, for it is not this that makes him an imitator."[20] Addison, in turn, also takes such nonmimetic divagations as evidence of poor poetic judgment, and offers up Lucan's negative example: "*Lucan*," he writes disapprovingly, "was an injudicious poet [who] lets drop his story very frequently for the sake of unnecessary digressions." Milton too, Addison continues, lacks Homeric self-restraint and exposes himself to the same charges: "*Milton's* complaint of his blindness, his panegyrick on marriage, his reflections on *Adam* and *Eve's* going naked, of the angels eating, and several other passages in his poem, are liable to the same exception [of injudiciousness]." Ultimately, however, Addison recognizes that Milton excels despite, and even because of, his transgression of the classical guidelines. "I must confess," he writes, "there is so great a beauty in these digressions, that I would not wish them out of his poem."[21] Addison begins the critical series by drawing upon the classical framework of criticism to prove the merits of *Paradise Lost*, but discards these evaluative standards as they seem increasingly unsuited for arriving at a fair judgment. "Our language," Addison famously wrote, "sunk under [Milton], and was unequal to that greatness of soul, which furnished him with such glorious conceptions." Classical criticism, too, was arguably unequal to the task of measuring his merits.

Addison's efforts are fascinating for the extent to which he relies on classical criticism to prove Milton's genius, while simultaneously demonstrating an awareness that such principles do no justice to what Empson would later identify as the "delicacy and subtlety" of Milton's style.[22] By the close of the series, Addison privileges his own aesthetic sense as a means of specifying the poem's merits. He praises Milton's portrayal of Adam's first waking moments, and explains that these "wonderful incidents...have in them all the beauties of novelty, at the same time that they have all the graces of nature....In a word, though they are natural they are not obvious, which is the true character of all fine writing."[23] Addison never explicitly states that Milton transcends the constraints of classical criticism. As he proceeds, though, he devises a much more loosely formulated concept of the "beauties" of *Paradise Lost*—essentially, his own favorite passages—to extol its virtues. The insights of Irving Howe into twentieth century literary criticism apply equally well to Addison's time in the eighteenth century when the English critical enterprise was beginning: "Criticism became the vehicle through which a cultivated elite...exercised its powers of perception....The critic became the guardian of taste, a priest of values, a protector of the undefiled word. And in some ways he seemed even more accessible to the audience than the poet or novelist, for the critic talked directly about the problems which the poet or novelist presented imaginatively."[24] Addison's critical horizons, of course, lie beyond Milton's poem, for the series of judgments he passes on *Paradise Lost* are also to be read more generally as models for helping readers to develop discriminating literary palates. As Addison directs readers to admire the delicacy and subtlety of the depictions in *Paradise Lost*, however, Homer and Virgil diminish in importance as exemplars, and Milton's poem rises to become a model of tasteful writing on its own merits.

Though Addison's commentary reveals a growing awareness of the limitations of traditional benchmarks, Richard Bentley, in his infamous edition of *Paradise Lost*, takes a rather different view. By the time his emendations were published in 1732, Bentley had secured a reputation as the foremost classicist of his age. A century and a half later his achievements would still inspire the poet A. E. Housman to praise him as "the greatest scholar that England or perhaps that Europe ever bred."[25] "Conjectural criticism," Dr. Johnson once remarked, "demands more than humanity possesses"; Bentley, it seems, possessed more of those requisite abilities than most.²⁶ Bentley's keen intuition and extraordinary knowledge of the classics allowed him to restore long-corrupted passages of classical manuscripts. When he finally turned his critical eye to *Paradise Lost,* he approached it with the same, although in this case somewhat disingenuous, desire to restore authenticity, and proposed more than 800 changes to Milton's text on the basis of a dubious claim that copyists and editors corrupted the text.²⁷ Bentley's edition is now often dismissed as a strange outlier in the history of literary criticism—a monument of intellectual snobbery, yet Bentley employs essentially the same standards of evaluation used by Addison. But where Addison directs our gaze upward to the pillar of classical standards in order to show how *Paradise Lost* rises to a comparable stature, Bentley uses his classical taste as the straightedge against which every metrical foot of Milton's poem is measured for its quality of craftsmanship. Where the text conflicts with Bentley's sense of the classical style, the text is modified.

According to Aristotle in the *Poetics,* critics can justly censure texts on the basis of five criteria, of which one of the most interesting is a concept that has been translated as "artistic correctness."²⁸ Though Aristotle leaves this idea vaguely defined, Bentley asserts a very definite sense of this artistic propriety based on his understanding of the classical tradition. An example from book 4 illustrates the remarkably specific nature of Bentley's aesthetic sense. Milton, in giving us a first glimpse of the lovely pair, pauses to dwell on Adam's majestic features:

> [His] fair large Front and Eye sublime declar'd
> Absolute rule; and Hyacinthin Locks
> Round from his parted forelock manly hung
> Clustring, but not beneath his shoulders broad.   (4.300–03)

Bentley's comments show the extent to which he reads Milton with parallels to the ancient poets in mind. "*Broad shoulders,*" he notes approvingly, "are always assign'd to the antient heroes; in *Homer* they have εὐρέας ὤμους, in Virgil, *latos humeros.*"²⁹ Milton's portrayal of Adam's broad shoulders is appropriate, since the first man in all his perfection should embody ideal conceptions of masculine beauty. Bentley goes on, however, to voice disapproval of what he sees as an oversight: "I wonder," he writes, "that Milton has given no indication that Adam has a beard; nor the least down or blossom on his chin, the first access to manhood; which the *Greek* and *Latin* poets dwell on, as the principal part of manly beauty" (IV.303). The authority Bentley accords to the ancient poets is remarkable. Instead of suggesting that the classical portrayals of beauty are worthy of emulation as Addison might, Bentley makes them the very standard from which the epic poet deviates only in error.

Bentley likewise objects to the description of Eve in book 8 and rewrites it to conform to classical tradition. Adam rapturously reports to Raphael that "to consummate all, / Greatness of mind and nobleness their seat / Build in her *loveliest* and create an awe / About her as a guard angelic placed" (XIII.556–59; Bentley's italics). Bentley finds this description—especially the use of the phrase "her loveliest"—absurd. (*"In her loveliest!"* he bursts out incredulously. "Pray what?") He asserts that Milton actually intended to write, "Greatness of mind and nobleness their seat / Build in her FORHEAD, and create an awe" (VII.557–58). Bentley correctly identifies what the modern reader finds strange about the diction, for it is indeed unclear how exactly this phrase should be interpreted. Is "her loveliest" a noun referring to Eve in a manner comparable to the use of "my dearest" or "her highness?" Is it an adverb? If so, why should it be related to the verb "build"? Bentley perceives this difficulty but fails to examine carefully the context in which the passage appears. Adam, in the course of his discussion with Raphael, is describing an internal conflict: he "understand[s], in the prime end / Of Nature [Eve to be] th'inferior; [both] in the mind / And inward Faculties" (8.540–42). He confesses, though, that her physical beauty so overwhelms him that in her presence, "what she wills to do or say, / Seems wisest, vertuousest, discreetest, best" (8.549–50). The use of "loveliest" in Bentley's contested line clearly echoes these earlier superlatives.

Bentley fails to grasp the subtle way in which Milton's diction participates in the poem's larger reflections upon external beauty and its authority. Eve, upon being created, flees from Adam, who seems "less faire," before God leads her to see "how beauty is excelled by manly grace / And wisdom, which alone is truly fair" (4.478, 490–91). Adam inherently differs from his beautiful wife in that his excellence is primarily manifested through his noble conduct and intellectual strength. That "greatness of mind and nobleness their seat / Build in [Eve] loveliest" is troubling, then: Adam is overcome by a sense that the masculine stronghold of wisdom and magnanimity is best held by Eve instead. The verbal ambiguity that Bentley detects furthermore reflects the suspiciously circular turn of Adam's logic. Wisdom and majesty, he wants to say, are most attractively displayed in Eve's person—perhaps, crucially enough though, as his language betrays, because Eve is loveliest of all to begin with. Raphael must reprimand Adam for such a comparison, urging him to "weigh with her thy self; / Then value" (8.570–71).

Such a reading of the passage is lost on Bentley, however, and he argues instead for a reference to the forehead. As he explains it, "greatness, nobleness, authority, awe, are by all *Greek* and *Latin* poets plac'd in the *forhead*" (VIII.557–58). Bentley, given his immense learning, is probably right with regards to the practice of the ancient poets, but his accuracy in the matter is beside the point. What is important to note here is the way he approaches reading: upon encountering a portion of the text that seems insufficiently lucid, he relies on his classicist knowledge to dictate how it should read instead. This insistence on an Aristotelian "artistic correctness" seems absurd, though again, it is significant to recognize that Addison relies on similar methods when he uses classical principles to evaluate *Paradise Lost*. Both critics, moreover, privilege classical principles over Milton's own style in at least a few instances. Bentley, however, places full confidence in his own interpretation of classical principles, and as a result, presents us with a markedly different text than the one Milton wrote.

Of the five criteria for criticism laid out in the *Poetics*, three are closely tied with the proper use of logic and reason. Passages of the text that are "impossible"—that is, illogical in reality, "irrational," or lacking coherent logical cause, and "contradictory," or logically inconsistent, are all to be condemned according to Aristotle.[30]

Bentley's application of this classical injunction against the illogical in its most harmless form is rather amusing, but in its more subversive form completely undermines the use of poetic language. Bentley attacks the epic simile used in book 1 to describe Satan as he lies partially submerged in the fiery lake. Satan is compared to the Leviathan who,

> Haply slumbring on the *Norway* foam
> The Pilot of some small night-founder'd Skiff,
> Deeming some Island, oft, as Sea-men tell,
> With fixed Anchor in his skaly rind
> Moors by his side.   (1.203–07)

Milton, in the space of five lines, draws for us a vivid picture of the dangers faced by unsuspecting sailors on the open sea, but Bentley focuses in on two problems: "Skaly rind is unlucky here," he writes, "for it falls out contrary, that the whale has no skales, or if he had them; by proportion with other fish, they would be so large, thick, and solid, that no seaman could *fix his anchor* through them." What Milton really intended to say, Bentley tells us, is that the seaman fixed an anchor in the Leviathan's "skinny rind" (I.206). Bentley demands a level of realism from the text that seems wholly unnecessary and idiosyncratic; at its core, though, this objection to the word choice can be understood as a rigid and overly scrupulous application of the Aristotelian demand for logical consistency.

One realizes upon reading Bentley that he is engaging in an entirely different activity altogether. It could be said that Bentley is a close reader of a certain type, but one who probes the text and searches for flaws in its logic and aesthetic representations. It is, of course, quite difficult to define the limits to which an aesthetic standard can be considered valid. Bentley's adherence to classical principles, in a sense, could be seen as a purer, more faithful application of the prevailing aesthetic standard to a work that other English critics defended out of nativist biases. Bentley's work, presumptuous as it is, must yet be recognized as a logical, if extreme, extension of the evaluative critical impulse. If, as classical critics claim, poems aspiring to the status of epic forbears must fulfill certain criteria, then no one would be more qualified to perfect the modern epic than an exacting critic familiar with Aristotelian principles. Bentley called attention to the problem, though he was not the problem itself—instead, as later literary critics recognized, the entire authority of the classical aesthetic either had to be tempered or replaced by a different orientation to reading.

Interpretation

The publication of Bentley's work galvanized the scholars of the literary community, and within two years, valuable commentaries emerged in defense of Milton's text. The writers of these commentaries were less concerned with Bentley's claims of editorial interpolation than with his negative appraisal writ large of *Paradise Lost*. The first of these commentaries, Zachary Pearce's *Review of the Text of the Twelve Books of Milton's "Paradise Lost,"* thus methodically disproves each of Bentley's emendations in turn. Pearce, the vicar of St. Martin-in-the-Fields at the time of writing, assumes an impressively evenhanded tone in giving due consideration to Bentley's proposed changes before drawing upon his classical and biblical knowledge to prove the authenticity and superiority of Milton's text.[31] Two years later, Jonathan Richardson partnered with his namesake son to produce a critical work of *Explanatory Notes and Remarks on "Paradise Lost"* that, notwithstanding the occasional note of exuberant admiration, begins to assume a more familiar scholarly, interpretative approach to the work.[32]

One of the most salient characteristics of Pearce's and the Richardsons' commentaries is the deferential tone of the commentators toward the poet and text. For example, in book 5, Raphael describes to Adam the bliss of heavenly repast, where all partakers are "secure / Of surfet where full measure onely bounds / Excess" (5.638–40). Bentley, in keeping with the classicist emphasis upon clarity and intelligibility, improves Milton's diction. "What the import of *only bounds* excess, is difficult to conceive," he writes disapprovingly, before replacing the offending phrase with "NEVER KNOWS excess" (V.638). Pearce, on the other hand, defends Milton's word choice by exploring the significance of the lines. "The meaning of the expression may be," he suggests, that "full measure has no other effect than to set bounds to excess; and not, as it happens often among men, to tempt to it."[33] "Or rather," he proposes upon further consideration, "the word *only* may belong to full *measure*, and the sense may be this, where excess is not restrain'd and prevented by want, nor by any quantity less than full measure" (5.638). Pearce shows respect for Milton's diction by preserving and justifying his creative use of language; he strives, furthermore, to understand all possible meanings that could be extracted from a potentially ambiguous phrase. His deference to the text is even mirrored in his use of language: "The meaning of the expression *may* be," Pearce ventures to suggest, "or rather, the word...*may* belong to...and the sense *may* be this" (5.639; italics mine). This critical humility—the reluctance not only to intervene in the text but also to legislate a single, definitive interpretation—places Pearce in a strikingly different relationship to the poem.

A backlash against Bentley's heavy-handed approach surely accounts at least in part for the rise of the critical humility that Pearce and the Richardsons exhibit. Even if Bentley's brazen attack on *Paradise Lost* served as an impetus for change, however, it does not explain the choice of this divergent form of criticism with its distinctive conceptual foundations. The key to understanding the central influences here may lie in Pearce's identity: he was a prominent clergyman, and more importantly for our purposes, a biblical commentator.[34] Scriptural exegesis since the Renaissance had served as the mode of scholarship par excellence for theologians as well as other influential thinkers.[35] Leading scholars of seventeenth century Europe, including Hugo Grotius and Daniel Heinsius, weighed in on theological issues from the margins of their own scriptural commentaries, and Milton himself would resort in *Tetrachordon* (March 1645) to arguing in favor of divorce through biblical exposition. Alongside the erudite and polemical works, a tradition of vernacular homiletic commentary existed as well. Such works would have been familiar to a broader base of English Protestant readers since they supplied explicatory and hortative support without the burden of more esoteric debates.³⁶ It was common for the biblical scholars behind these commentaries to express a sense of inadequacy to the task, and to assume a position of humility and deference to the text. In one well-known set of seventeenth century biblical annotations, the author, Henry Ainsworth, expresses a typical attitude toward his work: "But forasmuch as my portion is small, in the knowledge of holy things; let the godly reader try what I set downe, and not accept it, because I say it: and let the learned be provoked unto more large and fruitfull labours in this kinde."³⁷ Ainsworth emphasizes the limitations of his endeavor and urges readers to see his work as only part of a larger effort to advance biblical scholarship and interpretation in general.

More than a century earlier, the Reformation leader Martin Luther had urged readers of Genesis to approach the text from a similarly deferential perspective. In his discussion of the Creation account, he effectively advises readers to refrain from reading as Bentley did: "If we cannot attain unto a comprehension of the reason [for the interval of six days for Creation]...let us remain scholars, and leave all the preceptorship to the Holy Spirit!"³⁸ For Luther, the author of the text implicitly assumes the position of instructor, and readers must strive to learn the text's lessons while recognizing their own inherent limitations as students and scholars. Readers are in no position to insist upon a particular interpretation of the text as final; at best, they can venture provisional readings. When Matthew Poole comes across Genesis 3:1 in his commentary (1683), he attempts to explain what the biblical author means in identifying the serpent as "more subtil than any beast of the field":

> But this text *may* and *seems* to be understood not of the whole kind of serpent; but of this individual, or particular serpent [who] acted...by the Devil....There *seems* indeed to be an allusion here to the natural subtilty of all serpents, and the sense of the sacred Penman *may seem* to be this, as if he said, the serpent, indeed in itself is a subtil creature...but howsoever this be in other serpents, it is certain that this serpent was more subtil than any beast of the field.³⁹

Pearce works within this tradition of qualifying his interpretations as educated conjectures and adopts a similarly tentative tone. The Protestant approach to biblical annotations corresponds with Pearce's preference for providing commentary that aims to be heuristic rather than dogmatic.

In the experience of Milton's Protestant readers, the demand for individual involvement in the act of reading is relatively high. All believers, after all, are expected to take an active role in understanding the Scriptures, though they might contain, as the apostle Peter himself writes, "some things hard to be understood" (2 Pet. 3:16 AV). From such a perspective, readers are expected to persevere despite difficulty in the quest for comprehension.[40] A challenging text is problematic from Bentley's point of view but completely acceptable and even evocative of divine authorship to later commentators viewing Milton's epic through the lens of biblical hermeneutics. Readers are charged with the task of making sense of the author's aesthetic choices—even those more obscurely motivated ones. Thus, the Richardsons, in dealing with the passage that lists inhabitants of the Paradise of Fools, defend Milton's choice to switch abruptly from naming specific classical figures (Empedocles, Cleombrotus) to more general groups, including "Eremits and Friers" (3.474). "'Tis his concise manner," they write in response to Bentley's objections, before offering up a challenge that resonates throughout the expository commentaries: "Let the reader do something for himself."[41] Where Bentley finds fault with the poet, Pearce and the Richardsons put the onus on the reader both to make sense of the text on a literal level and to reflect upon possible motives for distinctive authorial decisions. The New Critics two centuries later promote a view of the active close reader that bears strong resemblances to this eighteenth century concept. When Cleanth Brooks writes in *The Well Wrought Urn* (1947) about the requirements placed upon readers by modern poets, his description serves equally well for elucidating the challenge of *Paradise Lost* to eighteenth century readers: "The modern poet has, for better or worse, thrown the weight of the responsibility upon the reader. The reader must be on the alert for shifts of tone, for ironic statement, for suggestion rather than direct statement.... He is further expected to be reasonably well acquainted with the general tradition—literary, political, philosophical, for he is reading a poet who comes at the end of a long tradition and who can hardly be expected to write honestly and with full integrity and yet ignore this fact."[42] The eighteenth century critics, like the more recent advocates of close reading, are prepared to understand the activity as a potentially challenging one that requires readers to grapple with complex texts.

The conception of an active reader who can both determine the sense of the text and judge between the opinions of commentators is rooted in the Protestant emphasis on the abilities of all readers of Scripture. Milton himself speaks from this position in *Of Reformation* (May 1641), when he insists that all readers can and should attain an understanding of the Bible irrespective of age, class, gender, or level of schooling: "The scriptures protesting their own plainness and perspicuity, [call] to them to be instructed, not only the wise and learned, but the simple, the poor, the babes, foretelling an extraordinary effusion of God's Spirit upon every age and sex, attributing to all men, and requiring from them the ability of searching, trying, examining all things, and by the Spirit discerning that which is good" (YP 1:566). In Luther's writings as well, each and every Protestant believer is accorded a great deal of agency; as he expresses it, "through the Holy Spirit of a special gift from God, anyone who is enlightened concerning himself and his own salvation, judges and discerns with the greatest certainty the dogmas and opinions of all men."[43]

This stress on the capability of the early modern lay reader extends beyond Scripture to secular texts as well, and shapes the role of commentaries for readers of *Paradise Lost*. When the Richardsons in book 5 conclude a lengthy exploration of the representation of celestial bodies, they gesture toward a reader who is conceived of as a fellow scholar and equal: "We have offer'd the several ways which occur to us in which the passage may be understood; the reader is at liberty to make use of any he likes best. Or if he is not yet satisfy'd, he may perhaps find a better; in that case we shall be thankful, if he is so good as to communicate it to us" (5.175). The attitude of critical humility corresponds with a heightened sense of the reader's ability. As seen before, readers are expected to shoulder the largest part of the burden of making sense of the text. Where further assistance is required, readers are to look with a discerning eye upon commentaries to determine whether the suggestions offered therein may be considered valid, and to produce better readings if they exist.[44] Twentieth century New Critics resurrect this relationship between the commentator and the reader in the relationship of critic and close reader. As Wimsatt expresses it, "the critic is...[an] explicator of meanings. His readers, if they are alert, will not be content to take what he says at testimony, but will scrutinize it as teaching."[45] With the proper level of attention, the fit reader in Wimsatt's conception, as well as the one imagined by Pearce and the Richardsons, is capable of correctly evaluating the critical pronouncements of even highly qualified scholars.

For Protestants, the Scriptures are accessible to all, but not without the diligent exercise of individual effort and the aid of the Holy Spirit. As Milton notes, the act of reading Scripture necessarily involves "searching, trying, [and] examining all things" (YP 1:566). This textual probing is a form of close reading that might be stretched to encompass Bentley's detail-oriented criticism, but the crucial difference that distinguishes the latter critics is their reliance upon a scholarly approach. This scholarly focus, which places an emphasis upon determining the meaning of the text, differs from a criticism primarily concerned with aesthetic or experiential issues. The expository critics build instead upon a repository of knowledge to allow readers to rise to Milton's level in terms of literary scholarship, linguistic knowledge, and scientific awareness. Consider, for example, the possible responses to Milton's imaginative description of the Edenic guards closing in around Satan in the garden:

> th' Angelic Squadron bright
> Turnd fierie red, sharpening in mooned hornes
> Thir Phalanx, and began to hemm him round

> With ported Spears, as thick as when a field
> Of *Ceres* ripe for harvest waving bends
> Her bearded Grove of ears, which way the wind
> Swayes them; the careful Plowman doubting stands
> Least on the threshing floore his hopeful sheaves
> Prove chaff.   (4.977–85)

Bentley is incensed by the mixed metaphor. He approves of the first portion in which the phalanx is "compar'd to a crop of ripe wheat, which wav'd with a gentle wind bend all their heads the same way," but protests against the phantom editor who "deserts the notion" and unnecessarily contributes "a tempest, and frightens the husbandman with the loss of all his grain" (IV.983). "What an injury is this to the prior comparison?" Bentley demands, exasperated. "Where's the least similitude?" (IV.983). The Richardsons have none of the same objections. They calmly explain that the angels' spears are "ported" because they are "held sloping toward the enemy, the right hand before, and the other behind [in] a defensive posture, ready also to attack" (IV.980). Ceres, they go on to remind the reader, is the goddess of corn. The Richardsons reroute the discussion of aesthetic propriety by taking it as the very premise for interpretation, and turn to focus instead on advancing the reader's comprehension.

Bentley may disapprove of the use of mixed metaphors, but the expository critics work within a tradition of biblical commentators who have long accepted mixed metaphors in Scripture without questioning their aesthetic merit. Biblical poetry abounds in mixed metaphors; think, for example of the injunction in Psalm 34 to "taste and see that the Lord is good" (Ps. 34:8 AV). Another Davidic psalm uses richly varied imagery to depict the sun: the rising sun "is as a bridegroom coming out of his chamber, and rejoiceth as a strong man to run a race" (Ps. 19:5 AV). In his biblical *Annotations*, Poole offers an interpretation of these lines: the sun is both like the groom in that it is "gloriously adorned with lights as with a beautiful garment, and [smiles] upon the lower world with a pleasant countenance"; it furthermore resembles the athletic champion who has "rested all night, and break[s] forth as it were on a sudden...promising to himself victory...[and setting] upon his work with great pleasure."[46] Had Poole been a literary critic with rigidly classicist tastes, he could have noted that neither metaphor adequately conveys the sun's majesty, and that each metaphor lacks a logical relationship to the other. Instead, aesthetic discussion is entirely subjugated to an exploration of the psalmist's intended meaning. In a similar passage from *Paradise Lost,* Milton borrows from the imagery of the psalm to depict the "glorious Lamp / Regent of Day and all th'Horizon round / Invested with bright Rayes, jocond to run / His Longitude through Heav'n's high rode" (7.370–73). The Richardsons' corresponding note similarly focuses on interpretation of intent: "What Milton means to say here," the Richardsons explain, is "very poetically...[to] tell us that at the sun's first appearance the dawning of that day was in joy, and all the delights of the sweetest season were in their utmost perfection" (8.373). The established framework of biblical hermeneutics thus provides a model for textual criticism that foregrounds the interpretation of poetic language against a tacit respect for its aesthetic achievement.

In another move that foreshadows the close readings of New Critics and Miltonists like Empson and Ricks, early commentators pay a great deal of attention not only to Milton's poetic use of language, but to his diction more generally as they offer probing examinations of etymological significance. In one instance from book 7, the celestial inhabitants hail the return of their king, praising him as "greater now in [His] return / Than from the Giant Angels" (7.604–05). The Richardsons extract a great deal of significance from the single word "giant" by looking beyond the bounds of the English language. "The Hebrew word *Gibbor* rendred giant by the *Septuagint* signifies a proud, fierce, and aspiring temper," they explain, "His readers having it in their thoughts would be assisted by that idea to conceive better of his story" (7.605). Readers familiar with Milton's style could argue that Milton's use of Latinate, Hebraic, and Grecian phrases in his verse naturally gives rise to this etymological commentary.[47] The learned Richardsons possess a wealth of literary and linguistic knowledge that allows them to release what Ricks would call the "enhancing suggestions [of meaning] from the burial-places of memory,"[48] but it does not then follow that such etymological discoveries would be considered legitimate scholarship and literary criticism. Addison in his essays, after all, was not terribly preoccupied with individual words, and Bentley was only so when he detected an instance of improper usage.

Again, biblical commentaries are crucial to understanding the origins and acceptance of this distinctive element of criticism. Although historians often associate the rise of philological scholarship with the restoration of classical texts, biblical scholars initially developed the discipline as a means of working with different scriptural manuscripts.[49] Because these scholars studied a text that had been translated out of Hebrew and Greek and into Latin and English, knowledge of the original languages greatly contributed to a more accurate understanding of the biblical authors' original intent. The literal sense of one Greek word might be successfully translated into English without losing its general meaning, though richer nuances of the phrase could be discerned by returning to the original Greek. Take, for instance, the Authorized Version's translation of the Gospel of Matthew, in which Jesus urges his disciples to "be reconciled to thy brother [before going to] offer thy gift [to God]" (5:24). In his *Annotations on the New Testament* (1659), Henry Hammond provides a fuller understanding of what the reconciliation entails by referring to the active register of the original word: in Greek, the word translated "reconciles" is, "literally, *think thou well*, or *be friends with thine adversary*, [and] clearly signifies *make*, or *get him*, to be *friends* with thee" (Mark 14:54).[50] According to this reading of Scripture, even the most basic units of text—individual words—are replete with meaning. The commentators on *Paradise Lost*, as readers familiar with biblical scholarship, were prepared to encounter words and phrases in English that took on additional meaning when traced back to earlier linguistic roots. Twentieth century critics like Empson have recognized the eighteenth century annotators' contributions in this area as excellent examples of close reading, and have built directly upon their methods. The form of the commentary restricted interpretation to smaller units of analysis, but in doing so, opened up enormous possibilities for understanding texts in their entirety; the methods of verbal analysis used by Empson and Ricks function in much the same way. The eighteenth century commentators grasped the significance of the "potentialities of language" that later New Critics like Brooks so greatly valued.[51]

Conclusion

We in the academy often take it for granted that it would be misguided to impose a uniform set of aesthetic expectations on all literary works, preferring instead to imagine that our aesthetic judgments are the result of objective efforts to describe and interpret the structure and meaning of literary texts on their own terms. Literary studies, however, has not always been thus, and a reflection upon the activities of Bentley and the neoclassical critics reminds us that the history of literary criticism might have developed quite differently if critics like Pearce and the Richardsons had not pioneered a different protocol of reading.

It would scarcely be an overstatement to say that the application of the methods of biblical exegesis to *Paradise Lost* in the early eighteenth century changed the way we read today. It is no accident that *Paradise Lost* played this important role. It took the appearance of a modern, vernacular work whose power seemed to rival that of the classics to encourage readers to conceive of English literature as a body of work that deserved the reverence previously reserved for the ancients. And it took a poem "hid...by its own luster,"[52] as the Richardsons described it, to elicit all the interpretive energies previously reserved for sacred texts.

University of California, Berkeley

LEGACY, CHOICE, AND THE HUMAN CONDITION

Milton as Muse for Keats, Shelley, and Frost

Carter Revard

Canonizing Milton: Dryden Agonistes

In the late seventeenth and early eighteenth century it became possible for English poets to amplify[1] their voices by using Milton's lion-skin as echo chamber. Not until a culture's poets are canonized and classicized can this be done, because it assumes an audience not just familiar with but immediately alive to the actual words of the earlier poets, which is only possible once those poets are recognized laureates, and some of their poems learned by heart—whether in official schooling or by tacit agreement of the literate class as to what poets should be read in the vernacular. In the case of John Milton, the process of canonization can be seen as beginning when would-be rival John Dryden put on the lion's skin and tried to steal Milton's voice for his "opera" *The State of Innocence*—recognizing Milton as king of poets, but marking himself as an ass.[2] It was a typical opportunist and careerist use by Dryden of Milton's *Paradise Lost;* he would later preserve himself in its amber by the laudatory epigram he contributed for its third (1688) edition.[3]

How Milton's literary reputation rose has been exhaustively studied, but here I am concerned only with how his becoming a "classic" made his work usable by other writers to amplify their own.[4] One mark of such classicizing in early eighteenth century England is public discussion of Milton, Shakespeare, and other poets and dramatists in the newly formed media that provided a kind of extension of the educational establishment, guiding manners and tastes and morals after a fashion via *Tatler, Spectator,* pamphlets, books, *Scriblerus Papers,* and the like: a public education alternative to the older forms of courtly, aristocratic, legal/clerical, and university reading and conversation. Another mark is the beginning of "classic" editions of the earlier poets, not just collections of their writings, but annotated editions—Shakespeare was edited by Alexander Pope and Lewis Theobald, Milton was edited by Richard Bentley and Thomas Newton—in classical format, in volumes sold by subscription; not as "hot" contemporary laps for the gossiping groupie-gropers, but as "cool" tomes, upon which one could sit magisterially in coffee-houses. By 1714, when Pope was finishing his *Rape of the Lock,* the mark of classic status had been stamped upon *Paradise Lost:* particular lines were parodied, impressive figures like Satan were mimicked and parodied. Pope's sylph Ariel, though named for a Shakespearean figure, gets from Milton's Satan some of his tempter's genes. Milton, in 1714, was being viewed as the English equivalent of Homer and Virgil, and by the 1730s *Paradise Lost* was being used like the *Iliad* or the *Aeneid*.[5]

And Pope's Satanic Toad(y)

Pope, in the 1730s, expected his readers to have a detailed verbal memory of the fourth book of *Paradise Lost*. In the *Epistle to Dr. Arbuthnot,* Pope stilettos Lord Hervey with an allusion to *Paradise Lost* 4.797–809, then beheads him with a piece of Jewish lore. Here are Pope's lines:

> Whether in florid impotence he speaks,
> And, as the prompter breathes, the puppet squeaks;
> Or at the ear of Eve, familiar toad,

> Half froth, half venom, spits himself abroad,
> In puns, or politics, or tales, or lies,
> Or spite, or smut, or rhymes, or blasphemies.
> . . . .
>
> Eve's tempter thus the Rabbins have expressed,
> A cherub's face, a reptile all the rest.⁶

And here is *Paradise Lost* 4.797–809:

> So saying, on he [Gabriel] led his radiant Files,
> Daz'ling the Moon; these [Ithuriel and Zephon] to the Bower direct
> In search of whom they sought: him [Satan] there they found
> *Squat like a Toad, close at the eare of Eve;*
> Assaying by his Devilish art to reach
> The Organs of her Fancie, and with them forge
> Illusions as he list, Phantasms and Dreams,
> Or if, inspiring venom, he might taint
> Th' animal Spirits that from pure blood arise
> Like gentle breaths from Rivers pure, thence raise
> At least distemperd, discontented thoughts,
> Vaine hopes, vaine aimes, inordinate desires
> Blown up with high conceits ingendring pride.⁷

With a single drop of Miltonic allusion, Pope curdles harmless court gossip into profoundly corrupting behavior. A mere "toady," dressed in Miltonic diction and let into Queen Anne's presence, takes on satanic stature and power. This, Pope wants us to see, is not just the courtly tittle-tattle and rumor-mongering which, in *Rape of the Lock*, he had lightly dismissed ("singing, dancing, ogling, and *all that*"): Lord Hervey, so the Miltonic allusion warns, is corrupting England's queen, the very source of literary patronage and artistic recognition, the true arbiter of national taste. Pope, in this Eden, is like Milton's Ithuriel, guarding Eve: his satiric pen, like Ithuriel's spear, "touches" Satan in his "toady" disguise as Lord Hervey. And that touch exposes, not a magnificent fallen angel, but a low, creeping, poisonous, fawning Lord Hervey—not a daylight Serpent, but a night-time Toad, with whispered rumors and gossip and innuendos "inspiring" (breathing into the queen's ears) his "venom" that would corrupt and pervert her imagination, her judgment, her very reason.

Pope is marvelously deft in nailing down the analogy. Lord Hervey is one of the court's "familiars," just as a toad could be a witch's familiar, sent to spy or to deliver messages. Perhaps the allusive familiar brings in a whiff of Shakespearean supernatural from the "blasted heath" of *Macbeth*, where devil-familiars in the form of cats and toads "call" the Three Weird Sisters, or do their evil bidding—perhaps, indeed, Pope hints that behind the androgynous Lord Hervey are nasty females, court hags who "hold their Sabbaths, less for joy than spite," as he puts it in his *Second Moral Essay, on the Characters of Women*.

Pope certainly implies that such petty court-scene details mask issues comparable to those in the garden of Eden. Since, for Pope, the literary scene was one of very high importance, since the poet was guardian of a nation's intellectual and moral standards, it was more than a trivial matter for the queen of England to be misled by someone like Lord Hervey into the merely personal, the purely gossipy version of issues and events of the time. So the Miltonic allusions let Pope imply a great deal about the beauty, innocence, majesty, and intelligence of the queen, and the evil of Lord Hervey.

Yet what Pope takes as canonized here is still just the poem, not the poet. As a Catholic, Pope would hardly identify himself with Milton the person, and Pope presents himself as Horace rather than Homer (though he did hope to crown his career with an epic, and proposed to write it in blank verse following Milton's example).[8] By Pope's day Milton's poem was classic, but its poet was still a heretic. That would change only when English poets came to think of themselves as *like* Milton—antiestablishment, marginalized, midwives to the future rather than guardians of the past. Not until the Romantic period did poets evoke Milton as patron, friend, and muse to their poetry, and not only did they echo, use, or allude to Milton's poems, but chose those lines in which Milton constructed his own poetic self, and took that self as their model. And a century later, in a United States whose founding fathers took Milton as champion of republican government and model for poetic greatness, so also did the greatest American poet of the twentieth century, Robert Frost.

John Keats, Percy Bysshe Shelley, and Robert Frost made use in different ways of the language and poetic authority of John Milton.[9] The use in each case was friendly, and the relationship of later to earlier classic not one of rivalry, anxiety, or contestation, but friendship and encouragement: the three later poets turned to passages of *Paradise Lost* in which John Milton constructed a heroic model of himself as poet in mortal combat with outward and inward dangers,[10] and by using certain language from these passages the later poets placed themselves alongside Milton in a struggle against common enemies.[11]

Singing in Darkness: Milton and Keats

I will first look at what Keats achieved by using one Miltonic word in "Ode to a Nightingale." To see what Keats saw, we must look first at where he found that word, then at what Milton himself was doing with it.[12] The word is "darkling," used in *Paradise Lost* 3.39, where Milton from his mortal darkness speaks directly to the holy light of heaven. He has just voiced his joy at being done with his account (in books 1 and 2 of the poem) of the realm of Chaos and eternal Night, but now is pierced by the irony of claiming that he, a man gone blind, is safely "revisiting" the deity's holy light:

> thee I revisit safe,
> And feel thy sovran vital Lamp; but thou
> Revisit'st not these eyes, that rowle in vain
> To find thy piercing ray, and find no dawn;
> So thick a drop serene hath quencht thir Orbs,
> Or dim suffusion veild. (*PL* 3.21–26)

In these lines the impersonal epic has been transformed to personal lyric; the all-powerful poet acknowledges himself a blind and helpless man. But Milton refuses to be a victim, will not let his loss of sight deprive him of what is worth seeing—and the first of those sights is where the muses dwell:

> Yet not the more
> Cease I to wander where the Muses haunt,
> Cleer Spring, or shadie Grove, or Sunnie Hill,
> Smit with the love of sacred Song; but chief
> Thee *Sion* and the flowrie Brooks beneath
> That wash thy hallowd feet, and warbling flow,
> Nightly I visit. (3.26–32)

Milton rejoices, having constructed something upon which to rejoice: he turns the dark nothing before his eyes into a sunlit Arcadia, a moonlit Mount Zion. He hears at night the voices of his own daughters, or the daughters of Mnemosyne, giving him the beautiful Greek or Hebrew songs, and he remembers the poets and prophets who made those verses, recalling that some of them were blind like him. Then, as he wishes he might be like them, not only in being blind but also in being a great poet, new poetry moves quietly, like the stream he describes, into him and from him, as he begins to

> feed on thoughts, that voluntarie move
> Harmonious numbers; as the wakeful Bird
> Sings darkling, and in shadiest Covert hid
> Tunes her nocturnal Note. (3.37–40)

Yet this nocturnal note, it turns out, is hardly joyful; Milton drops again into deep sadness at the thought of what blindness has taken from him:

> Thus with the Year
> Seasons return, but not to me returns
> Day, or the sweet approach of Ev'n or Morn,
> Or sight of vernal bloom, or Summers Rose,
> Or flocks, or heards, or human face divine. (3.40–44)

But here, even though these verses do just what the earlier ones had done—that is, while lamenting a loss, they re-create the thing lost—once more the bright imagined scene is snatched away:

> But cloud in stead, and ever-during dark
> Surrounds me, from the chearful wayes of men
> Cut off, and for the Book of knowledg fair
> Presented with a Universal blanc

> Of Natures works to mee expung'd and ras'd,
> And wisdome at one entrance quite shut out. (3.45–50)

The despair Milton has just fought off seems here to have caught and pinned him helpless, with "wisdome...quite shut out"—and Milton well knew that such blindness was read by opponents as God's judgmental withholding of the light of understanding. But Milton will not accept defeat by the monster Despair; he fights him off, reverses his hold, and escapes—or so, as referee, I would judge—with a pin:

> So much the rather thou Celestial light
> Shine inward, and the mind through all her powers
> Irradiate, there plant eyes, all mist from thence
> Purge and disperse, that I may see and tell
> Of things invisible to mortal sight. (3.51–55)

I have gone slowly through this Miltonic passage, because when Keats gets around to using that one word "darkling" in his "Ode to a Nightingale," it holds all the gravitas from Milton's great psalm of lamentation and praise, but collapsed into itself like a neutron star. Keats's poem differs in many dimensions from Milton's, but the crucial likeness is that each poet while trying to sing finds himself in a kind of darkness where singing seems all but impossible. Keats's "Ode to a Nightingale" was written in May 1819, when he had lately abandoned an earlier version of his epic *Hyperion*, which that summer and fall he would try to recast as *The Fall of Hyperion: A Dream*.[13] In May 1819, the reviews of Keats's badly flawed semiepic *Endymion* were flaying him as if he were Marsyas challenging Apollo—and when, one late afternoon, he went out into the garden of Wentworth House, and heard a nightingale begin to sing, it struck him as painfully unlike his poetry, which seemed doomed to perish, whereas the bird's song would go on and be "a joy forever."

Keats begins the ode not in darkness but in late sunlight ("shadows numberless"), and begins by speaking of his own feelings, not his efforts to produce an epic; in fact, he never mentions those efforts. Only the reader of this poem who knows the life it came from would recognize that it is about Keats's efforts to write heroic poetry, to produce a great epic or at least a body of permanently valued poetry. There are parallels with Milton, but also differences. Keats is not blind, and the "embalmed darkness" he moves within seems outward, not inward: he walks in an English garden at nightfall. His first words for his feelings on hearing the nightingale are not words of delight, or happiness, but pain and affliction. Yet he claims this is because the bird's song makes him so happy that he aches; the song, he says, numbs him like an opiate or a drink of hemlock (Socrates dying for teaching too well). Then he denies that envy makes him feel this way—though, of course, we here should begin to realize that a kind of envy is precisely what makes him feel this way: he, an unsuccessful singer, is responding to a mythically successful one. What he hears makes him want to commit suicide—but to join the bird even while doing it, drinking wine whose effect is like the bird's song, so that not only might he "drink, and leave the world unseen," but also might fade *with* the bird "into the forest dim." And when he then says he will join the bird not by actually drinking, but "on the viewless wings of Poesy," we see that he means to get to where the bird is by himself singing, with this poem as his song.

All that is clear enough, and many critical readers have seen it. But I am here looking at how Keats is comparing himself not just to a lyric nightingale but also to a heroic singer. This ode is not a Horatian amble, but a Pindaric flight. He is not putting himself in the company of lesser poets, especially those dithy-Rambos of the later eighteenth century who tried to muscle their way up Helicon with odes to the passions or to the Bard or whatever. As shown by his next moves (in stanza 4), the nightingale he wants to join is John Milton.

His first move is to change the lighting. He had been listening to the bird sing "in some melodious plot / Of beechen green, and shadows numberless," but once he takes wing to join it, night has fallen: "Already with thee! tender is the night, / And haply the Queen-Moon is on her throne, / Clustered around with all her starry fays." And his next move is the Miltonic one: the camera cuts back, from Keats in moonlit heaven with the bird, to himself in darkness on earth: "But here there is no light, / Save what from heaven is with the breezes blown / Through verdurous glooms and winding mossy ways. / I cannot see." Keats has situated and moved himself just as Milton did: first rising into the light of heaven, then falling back into the darkness of human mortality, where all that human eyes can see, or not see, seems cause for despair and proof of defeat. For Milton, it is the physical and spiritual "cloud,...and ever-during dark" that surrounds and cuts him off from "the cheerful ways of men"; for Keats, it is "the weariness, the fever and the fret / Here where men sit and hear each other groan," so that as Keats sits and listens to the nightingale he is tempted to give the whole struggle up.

It is just at this point that Keats uses that Miltonic word: "Darkling I listen, and, for many a time / I have been half in love with easeful Death /... Now more than ever seems it rich to die." If the word, as I believe it does, brings the Miltonic context with it, Keats has set himself alongside Milton, yet carefully differentiates himself: he wears his rue, as Ophelia recommended, with a difference—as a son of Milton, but with a coat of arms that has indeed been differenced. The mark of difference is in the verbs used by Milton and Keats. Milton says, "as the wakeful bird / Sings darkling," whereas Keats says "Darkling I listen." Milton has fully identified himself as a singer in darkness; Keats aspires to join him and even, by poetic imagination, is there for a moment, but falls back. For a moment he is with the bird in the starry heavens, but falls again into a darkness where "there is no light," and recognizes that dying will not bring him closer to its singing.

Yet in his next-to-last stanza Keats speaks without envy, praising the bird for its reaching an audience ranging over the whole social gamut from emperor to clown, for its touching the heart of Ruth, saddest of humans, in her despair, and for opening the narrative vistas of poetry's "magic casements." Then in his final stanza, as he hears the bird's song fading, Keats acknowledges that his own poetic fancy has created much of whatever reality there is in the bird's song and in poetry at large. The whole poem becomes, in the last two lines, part of what may be merely "a vision, or a waking dream." The music has fled, and Keats asks himself, "Do I wake or sleep?"

Keats's ode, then, overtly celebrates the nightingale's powers of song, but covertly evokes the epic poet Milton's achievement. It tells us Keats wants to be such a singer as a nightingale is or as Milton was, but except for a brief moment in the fourth stanza of the poem, Keats carefully assigns himself the role of listener rather than singer. Milton, in his battle with despair, turns to celestial light and asks it to shine inward, but Keats does not have Milton's religious conviction to fall back on, and the art he celebrates as a way out of his own mortality and despair is, he admits, perhaps more fancy than reality. Keats seems really to believe in the muse, but he never quite commits himself. His ode celebrates the range of listeners to great poetry, the healing and cheering powers it has, and the views of enchanted realms it opens, but he gains at best a draw with despair. He calls upon Milton, as heroic poet, to join him in the fight, but does not believe in himself enough, or in the reality of what he was writing, to stay the course as Milton does.

Singing in Sunlight: Shelley and Milton

The story is somewhat different when we look at what Shelley did with Milton's word "unpremeditated" (*PL* 9.24). In 1820, Shelley used it not only in the opening stanza of "To a Skylark," but twice more in his translation of the "Homeric" *Hymn to Hermes*.[14] Milton used "unpremeditated" as he turned from friendly domestic scenes with Raphael, Adam, and Eve, to the tragedy of the Fall itself:

> Sad task, yet argument
> Not less but more Heroic than the wrauth
> Of stern *Achilles* on his Foe pursu'd
> Thrice Fugitive about *Troy* Wall; or rage
> Of *Turnus* for *Lavinia* disespous'd,
> Or *Neptun*'s ire or *Juno*'s, that so long
> Perplex'd the *Greek* and *Cytherea*'s son;
> If answerable style I can obtaine
> Of my Celestial Patroness, who deignes

> Her nightly visitation unimplor'd,
> And dictates to me slumbring, or inspires
> Easie my unpremeditated Verse:
> Since first this Subject for Heroic Song
> Pleas'd me long choosing, and beginning late;
> Not sedulous by Nature to indite
> Warrs, hitherto the onely Argument
> Heroic deem'd, chief maistrie to dissect
> With long and tedious havoc fabl'd Knights
> In Battels feign'd; the better fortitude
> Of Patience and Heroic Martyrdom
> Unsung. (*PL* 9.13–33)

Here as before, the poet, confined in darkness, must fight through doubt and despair to sing "darkling," but this time his self-doubt does not spring from loss of sight, but from the weight of his chosen task—and, also, from fear of being no longer listened to. In the 1660s, many in his (far from fit) audience had apparently turned from Milton's blank verse to Dryden's heroic quatrains and couplets.[15] He needs, therefore, not only inward vision, but also a style that can sustain the great argument he has chosen; and with this he must reach an audience who, though few, will rightly hear his song. These gifts he can only obtain from the Muse: from Urania, the Holy Spirit, his "Celestial Patroness." "Celestial," not "royal": Milton carefully distinguishes his patroness from those of other would-be writers of heroic verse—for instance, the English poet laureate with his merely royal patroness, who might "deign" to allow her adoring poet an evening visit; her laureate might choose to write of earthly wars (*Annus Mirabile* perhaps?). Milton's is no flattering preface to Her Royal Highness, but an austerely casual account of divine inspiration, of being granted an audience with the Holy Spirit.

Milton is fighting royalist/imperialist notions of poetry, particularly epic poetry, which Restoration readers and critics were foisting off on his fellow poets. Milton understood fully that a Cowley or Dryden might take the Bible and—as Marvell feared might happen for Milton himself—"ruin...the sacred Truths to Fable and old Song." Milton must fight in himself the human weakness that might do the same, so at the start of book 9 he asks the Muse to help him avoid this, asks that he might rise to a style high enough to suit his great theme, to write of both the war in heaven and the wars within the human heart, to justify the ways of God to man by matching his epic form to this great theme. This theme, he asserts, is "not less but more heroic" than those of Homer and Virgil,

> If answerable style I can obtain
> Of my Celestial Patroness, who deignes
> Her nightly visitation unimplor'd,
> And dictates to me slumb'ring, or inspires
> Easy my unpremeditated verse. (9.20–24)

With that help, Milton's "higher Argument" will be "sufficient of itself to raise" (9.42–43) the poem and justify its being called "Heroic" (9.29),

> unless an Age too late, or cold
> Climate, or years damp my intended wing
> Deprest—and much they may, if all be mine,
> Not Hers who brings it nightly to my Ear. (9.44–47)

It is worth putting this plainly: a poet now generally considered the greatest writer of his age is here appealing for an audience willing to listen, and for continued support from the Muse, who thus far has inspired his lines, to come into his mind and dictate the "unpremeditated" verses his task demands.

Everything Milton says in these lines fits Shelley's view of himself and his work in July 1820, when he wrote "To a Skylark," echoing in its very first stanza Milton's appeal to the Muse in *Paradise Lost* 9.24:

> Hail to thee, blithe Spirit!
> Bird thou never wert,
> That from Heav'n, or near it,
> Pourest thy full heart
> In profuse strains of unpremeditated art.[16]

"Unpremeditated," for Milton as "Puritan," speaks to the divine source of both poetry and prayer, recalling the inspired song and speech of Adam and Eve as they pray, the morning after Eve's troubling dream:

> Their Orisons, each Morning duly paid
> In various style, for neither various style
> Nor holy rapture wanted they to praise
> Thir Maker, in fit strains pronounc't or sung
> Unmeditated, such prompt eloquence
> Flowd from their lips, in Prose or numerous Verse,
> More tuneable than needed Lute or Harp
> To add more sweetness.   (*PL* 5.145–52)

Once we hear these Miltonic echoes in the first stanza of "To a Skylark," we understand that Shelley is not referring only to "natural" inspiration. True, he hears the bird's song as offering a prelapsarian spontaneity like that of Milton's Adam and Eve. He is indeed a Romantic poet, wishing to break into spontaneous song like the bird—but that is only part of the truth about Shelley, who like Milton was both a classically learned and politically committed poet. The classical dimensions emerge once we realize that in July 1820, when Shelley wrote "To a Skylark," he was also translating the "Homeric" *Hymn to Mercury* ("Hermes" in the Greek original)[17]—and that he used the same Miltonic word "unpremeditated" twice within that translation, each time using it to describe not merely natural but divinely inspired song.

The *Hymn to Mercury* narrates the very origins of lyric song: how Zeus begot Hermes on Maia, and the precocious infant emerges from the cave where he was born, spies a tortoise, kills it, and of its shell makes the very first lyre, stringing it with sheepgut. Immediately the god begins to play this new instrument, and to sing a brilliant and bawdy song:

> When he had wrought the lovely instrument,
>   He tried the chords, and made division meet
> Preluding with the plectrum, and there went
>   Up from beneath his hand a tumult sweet
> Of mighty sounds, and from his lips he sent
>   A strain of unpremeditated wit
> Joyous and wild and wanton—such you may
>   Hear among revellers on a holiday.
>   (*Hymn to Mercury*, stanza 9, lines 63–71)

Hermes, however, is an incorrigible trickster, a "king of robbers" (229), who covets the great wealth that Father Zeus had given to his half-brother Apollo, much of which Hermes argues that he himself should have had.[18] Before long, he lays down the lyre and goes out to steal his brother Apollo's oxen of the sun, two of which he butchers, roasts, and devours. Phoebus Apollo discovers their theft, tracks Hermes back to the cave, and hales him off to Olympus to indict him before the court of Zeus. Protesting his innocence, Hermes nevertheless leads Apollo to where he has hidden the oxen of the sun. Apollo tries to punish him—but Hermes, who is still carrying in his left hand the tortoiseshell lyre, suddenly begins to sing, and by the beauty and power of his song—a Creation song, "illustrating the birth / Of the bright Gods, and the dark desert earth" (571–72)—Apollo is enchanted and overcome, asking in wonder,

> Whether the glorious power you now show forth
>   Was folded up within you at your birth,
> Or whether mortal taught or God inspired
>   The power of unpremeditated song?   (587–90)

Apollo is so ravished by this music that he says not only is it worth the 50 stolen oxen of the sun, but that he will lead Hermes back to Olympus and lavish upon him "many glorious gifts" (619). Whereupon the sly Hermes, with a flattering but quite true praise of Apollo's great powers and wisdom, offers in return to give Apollo the lyre. This Apollo at once accepts:

> And then Apollo with the plectrum strook
>   The chords, and from beneath his hands a crash
> Of mighty sounds rushed up, whose music shook
>   The soul with sweetness; as of an adept
> His sweeter voice a just accordance kept.   (672–76)

Hermes and Apollo, like Shelley's skylark, are divinely inspired singers, and the key word Shelley uses for all their songs, "unpremeditated," he took from *Paradise Lost*.

But what of the political dimensions? These emerge once we recall that earlier in 1820 Shelley had written his "Ode to Liberty," where he speaks of Milton as both inspired poet and champion of freedom. Addressing "Liberty," Shelley says,

> And England's prophets hailed thee as their queen,
> In songs whose music cannot pass away,
> Though it must flow forever: not unseen,
> Before the spirit-sighted countenance
> Of Milton didst thou pass, from the sad scene
> Beyond whose night he saw, with dejected mien.   (145–50)

"Spirit-sighted countenance" echoes Milton's invocation to the Muse in *Paradise Lost*, 9.13–47—precisely where Shelley found "unpremeditated." Shelley, in the "Ode to Liberty," pictures Milton as (during the 1660s) a blind seer, watching Liberty pass from the "sad scene" of England, yet still (though "with dejected mien") seeing beyond that dark night—not only divinely inspired poet, but political prophet, as fearlessly antimonarchist as Shelley himself, and—also like Shelley—someone who for his political views and actions endured obloquy while watching those he considered enemies of a free and just society prevail and flourish. Shelley—like Milton—looked beyond the darkness, asking to sing beyond his despair, so that (as he says in the last line of "To a Skylark") "the world should listen then—as I am listening now."

So, in the summer of 1820, Shelley was keenly focused on poetic inspiration, on finding or creating an audience for his poetry, and on speaking out for political liberty. In his "Ode to Liberty" he references the very lines of *Paradise Lost* that tell of the poet's being visited nightly by a Muse who inspires "easy [his] unpremeditated verse," even as he celebrates the skylark as Nature's own example of inspired singing and asks that it teach him how to sing as perfectly, unselfishly, and usefully—and how to be listened to with like joy and (implied) assent:

> Teach me half the gladness
>   That thy brain must know,
> Such harmonious madness
>   From my lips would flow
> The world should listen then—as I am listening now.   (101–05)

His lyric aspires to the heroic political dimension: he wants, like Milton, to be heard, to win hearts and minds, to change England from a corrupt empire to a clean democracy. He wants to sing like the skylark, like Adam and Eve, like Hermes and Apollo, like Milton—so that his songs might Edenize and deify the world, free it by love from supernatural chains of vengeance.

Milton and Frost: Tree of Knowledge, Witness Tree

The twentieth century American poet Robert Frost, like Keats and Shelley, makes strong use of Milton, but more darkly, as we see in five poems that he put into his 1942 volume *A Witness Tree:* first, "Beech" and "Sycamore," which begin the volume and (in "Beech," line 7) supply the book's title phrase; then, in a later sequence of three poems, "The Most of It," "Never Again Would Birds' Song Be the Same," and "The Subverted Flower."[19]

In "Beech" and "Sycamore," Frost turns to the Bible and Milton to show us the book's central theme: exploring boundaries between a human self and the realms of community, nation, and world of "dark and doubt" that press in upon the self.[20] "Beech" is Frost's statement of where and how he stands, and he makes it by using both biblical and Miltonic language. As it begins, he evokes the Old Testament story (Gen. 31:43–54) of Jacob's setting a boundary between himself and Laban; in its last two lines he echoes Milton's self-presentation in *Paradise Lost* 7.23–31. As for the three later poems, "The Most of It," "Never Again Would Birds' Song Be the Same," and "The Subverted Flower," other scholars suggest that they are thematically related.[21] I propose that in these three poems (as in "Beech" and "Sycamore") Frost draws on the Bible and *Paradise Lost* to adumbrate his own poetic, political, and personal situation in the period 1938–42—and that to see how Frost was using Milton deepens and clarifies our understanding of what Frost was doing not only with the five poems in question but also in the whole of *A Witness Tree*.

Frost took the title of *A Witness Tree* from line 7 of his poem, "Beech":

> Where my imaginary line
> Bends square in woods, an iron spine
> And pile of real rocks have been founded.

> And off this corner of the wild,
> Where these are driven in and piled,
> One tree, by being deeply wounded,
> Has been impressed as Witness Tree
> And made commit to memory
> My proof of being not unbounded.
> Thus truth's established and borne out,
> Though circumstanced with dark and doubt—
> Though by a world of doubt surrounded.

That title, and certain other words and phrases of the poem, point first to the Old Testament, then to the etymological meaning of those words. Genesis 31:43–54 tells how Jacob, after serving his father-in-law Laban for years, departed with his wives, children, servants, and possessions, and when Laban pursued him they made a covenant by which they parted all their possessions and set a stone pillar and heap of stones, which they denominate as "a witness," to mark the boundary between their lands. Laban says (31:44), "let us make a covenant, you and I, and let it be a witness between you and me," so Jacob sets up a stone as pillar (31:45) and tells his kinsfolk to gather stones and make a heap, which he and Laban (31:46–48) call "The Heap of Witness." They share a ceremonial meal beside this "witness heap," after which Laban concludes (31:52), "This heap is a witness, and the pillar is a witness, that I will not pass by this heap to you for harm, and you will not pass by this heap and this pillar to me, for harm."

There was no doubt a New England custom of thus marking boundaries between properties,[22] though perhaps not everyone who set up such a heap of stones, and marked a tree beside it, had the Old Testament story in mind. Still, Frost in "Beech" and "Sycamore" deliberately evokes both Old and New Testament passages. He has moved from the earlier humorous skepticism of "Mending Wall" to a kind of humorous and faintly skeptical fideism. The 1914 *North of Boston* wall between neighbors (one of whom moves in "a darkness" but the other considers himself, humorously, as somewhat more enlightened) has become a 1942 *Witness Tree* boundary marker between individuals that both isolates and protects them from each other, and the boundary is now built with biblical words that separate not only individuals but whole religious bodies (and communities) from each other.

In "Beech" and "Sycamore," every common word rings like a bell with deep overtones and undertones: this wounded witness, in or near a pile of rocks, is a Martyr Tree, for Greek *martyr*, as Frost well knew (he was a prize student of Greek), means "witness." The first Christian martyr, Stephen, was stoned to death. Tree and Cross are twins, and Zacchaeus the publican as witness "Did climb the tree / Our Lord to see": in the King James version of Luke 19:2–10, the tree is a sycamore, and Zacchaeus not only sees Jesus entering Jerusalem, but is called down, asked to be his host, and told that "This day is salvation come to this house, ... for the Son of Man is come to seek and to save that which was lost."

Recall, now, that "beech" and "book" are etymologically the same: in Old English, the singular *boc* took the umlauted plural *bec*, and at an early stage writing was done on wooden tablets—on *beech*. So the "wounded *Witness Tree*" is also *the Book*. As for those rocks, they are not only what martyrs were stoned with, but as Jesus said, "Thou art Peter, and upon this *rock* I will build my church." What Frost says is "established and borne out" is not some personal credo, but "truth," the kind of truth to which martyrdom witnesses: but all is done by hints and voice tones and allusions: like Emily Dickinson, Robert tells it "slant."

Frost thus tells us, in this title poem and teasing little follower, that this book is his wounded witness, has been "impressed" (a word for men forced into military service, but playing on "printed") to establish and bear out the truth of his mortal limits, of his being "bounded" within his "corner of the wild," his "woods."[23] He alludes to the biblical splitting up of Laban and Jacob, developing into two different nations: like them, Frost invokes God as witness to the boundary between human individuals—in spirit, body, property, and all other ways. Frost in his craggy, oblique way is also marking off his self and spirit in particular ways: his book testifies to the suffering of someone who had lately lost a daughter, wife, and son, who as a peculiar conservative is politically alienated from leftist power centers of the 1930s; a teacher who had resigned his position at Amherst College and (like Dante while writing the

Commedia) had not yet found a new patron, nor a new academic or establishment post (like Milton after the Restoration).[24]

Later in *A Witness Tree*, Frost returns to these nested distinctions—skin, house, nation—in the poem "Triple Bronze," remarking, "And that defense makes three / Between too much and me." The "triple bronze," however, with its classical resonances, puts Frost in the company of Achilles and Aeneas, those bearers of shields made by divine powers. The poet is "shielded" by his skin, by his house, by his nation, as those great figures were shielded by the triple bronze of their warrior shields; though playful, Frost's image of his poetic self has epic dimensions, just as does the implied figuring of himself as choosing, like Jacob, to go his "separate" way.

Frost and Milton: In Dark, by Doubt Surrounded

Frost, then, adapted biblical and Miltonic language for the book's first two poems, figuring himself in the early 1940s as an exiled poet and founder of "my own nation." Yet there is more: in the last two lines of "Beech," "Though circumstanced with dark and doubt—/ Though by a world of doubt surrounded," by echoing *Paradise Lost* 7.23-31 Frost evokes Milton's "exile at home" after the Restoration: *A Witness Tree*, published in 1942, sets Frost alongside Milton, who in the 1660s was politically isolated and threatened, poetically at a late and perhaps sterile phase of his career, personally wounded (blind, a beloved wife not long dead, watching other poets gain the laurels and proclaim new canons of verse and morals and power). Here is *Paradise Lost*:

> Standing on Earth, not rapt above the Pole,
> More safe I Sing with mortal voice, unchang'd
> To hoarce or mute, though fall'n on evil dayes,
> *On evil dayes though fall'n, and evil tongues;*
> *In darkness, and with dangers compast round,*
> *And solitude;* yet not alone, while thou
> Visit'st my slumbers Nightly, or when Morn
> Purples the East: still govern thou my Song,
> *Urania*, and fit audience find, though few.
>   (*PL* 7.23–31; emphasis mine)

It must be mentioned of course that *A Witness Tree* was published in 1941–42, when World War II was in its darkest phase, so that no one was likely to take Frost's "circumstanced with dark and doubt" to refer to merely personal or purely poetic circumstances—and surely Frost made his book witness to the darkness around his nation as well as his own person and life as he neared the age of 70.

Milton and Frost: Before and After the Fall

Frost, then, with the first two poems of *A Witness Tree*, lets astute readers know what he will be doing in the book. Three other poems in the volume, like his title poem, make use of Milton: "The Most of It," "Never Again Would Birds' Song Be the Same," and "The Subverted Flower." Each of these reflects on human social identity, first in relation to the nonhuman animal world (with a subtext involving male companionship), then in relation to the Edenic and post-Edenic marriage of Adam and Eve, and finally in relation to heterosexual relations in the fallen world. Each of the poems is set in a biblical context—that with which Milton reframes Genesis in books 7 and 8 of *Paradise Lost*.

"The Most of It" is about Adam's crying out for human company before Eve was created; "Never Again Would Birds' Song Be the Same" is a report (by a child or grandchild) of what Adam said about how Eve's presence changed and humanized the whole world; and "The Subverted Flower" is about the painful twisting and knotting of sexual relations after the Fall. Frost's personal crisis, and his long-term grappling with questions of human boundaries, divine presence, suffering and its meaning, are all dealt with elsewhere in *A Witness Tree*, but in these poems they are examined darkly in biblical terms, as through a Miltonic glass.

One clue that Frost is playing these three poems off *Paradise Lost* is their being placed sequentially together in *A Witness Tree*. "The Most of It" takes its cue—if I am right—from the dialogue between Raphael, Adam, and God in *Paradise Lost* 8.338 and following, a look at which shows how Frost's poem is a response to, indeed a dramatic rendering of, Adam's desire for human companionship, which God answers by creating Eve.

In *Paradise Lost*, Adam tells Raphael how as a newly created being he was taken in a dream by his Creator up to the top of the paradisal mount, where he waked and found before his eyes "all real, as the dream / Had lively shadowed." The Creator then gives to Adam and his race "all the earth...and all things that therein live," and brings all of these before Adam to receive from him their names. As he names them, says Adam, he "understood their nature"—but, he says, "in these / I found not what methought I wanted still." He then daringly asks God how "all this good" can be enjoyed without companionship: "In solitude / What happiness?"

God smiles at this naïve question, then tests Adam—asking what he means by "solitude," since the earth and air are full of living creatures at Adam's command to "come and play before" him, and Adam knows "their language and their ways, they also know, / And reason not contemptibly"—so, God suggests, Adam should "with these / Find pastime, and bear rule." Adam passes the test, by pointing out that God has made these creatures "inferior, far beneath," and asks,

> Among unequals what societie
> Can sort, what harmonie or true delight?
> Which must be mutual, in proportion due
> Giv'n and receiv'd.
> ....
>
> Of fellowship I speak
> Such as I seek, fit to participate
> All rational delight, wherein the brute
> Cannot be human consort; they rejoyce
> Each with thir kinde, Lion with Lioness;
> So fitly them in pairs thou hast combin'd;
> Much less can Bird with Beast, or Fish with Fowle
> So well converse, nor with the Ox the Ape;
> Worse then can Man with Beast, and least of all.   (*PL* 8.383–97)

In reply, God, "not displeased," compliments Adam on his discriminating taste in rejecting solitude and subhuman companionship in favor of "rational fellowship," but he then wonders what Adam thinks of God himself, who is "alone / From all eternity, for none I know / Second to me or like, equal much less" (405–07). God (as Adam points out) does not need to propagate, being already infinite; and whenever he wishes can raise one of his created beings "to what height thou wilt / Of union or communion, deified," but Adam cannot "erect / From prone" (431–33) the animals to speak with them. In response to Adam's reasoned plea, God then creates Eve: and by Adam's account, she (as he rhapsodizes to Raphael) is not only "so lovely fair / That what seemed fair in all the world, seemed now / Mean, or in her summed up, in her contained" (471–73), but "Greatness of mind and nobleness their seat / Build in her loveliest, and create an awe / About her, as a guard angelic placed" (557–59).

If we turn now to look at Frost's poem, "The Most of It," I propose that it is Frost's dramatic rendering of Adam's state of mind while wandering about Eden, seeking companionship, before God appeared to him in a dream, took him up to Eden, held the conversations we have just been listening to, and created Eve in response to Adam's lonely yearning for a human companion. Here is the poem:

THE MOST OF IT

He thought he kept the universe alone;
For all the voice in answer he could wake
Was but the mocking echo of his own
From some tree-hidden cliff across the lake.
Some morning from the boulder-broken beach
He would cry out on life, that what it wants
Is not its own love back in copy speech,
But counter-love, original response.
And nothing ever came of what he cried
Unless it was the embodiment that crashed
In the cliff's talus on the other side,
And then in the far-distant water splashed,
But after a time allowed for it to swim,
Instead of proving human when it neared
And someone else additional to him,
As a great buck it powerfully appeared,
Pushing the crumpled water up ahead,
And landed pouring like a waterfall,

And stumbled through the rocks with horny tread,
And forced the underbrush—and that was all.

One unsettling thing about this poem is its title, "The Most of It." It is, perhaps, a weary comment by Frost on the usual experience, for Adam and for us, of seeking some kind of rational fellowship in the world. His poem, so the title suggests, is a commentary both on Adam's situation before the creation of Eve, and that of human beings in a post-Edenic world: *for the most part*, the search for a companionship of equals ends in disappointment. I think we, as readers, must see the man's search as not reducible to a sexual, or intellectual, or merely human-sized seeking, because (as it seems to me) Frost here as always raises the stakes to the spiritual; even in a "purely human" encounter like that which Frost focuses upon in "Two Tramps in Mud Time," the stakes are equally high:

> Only where love and need are one,
> And the work is play for mortal stakes,
> Is the deed ever really done
> For Heaven and the future's sakes.   (67–70)

In the world of Frost's poetry, human always neighbors heavenly, though both may be wearing homespun or guised as animal, and they may keep stone walls and witness trees between them.

Nevertheless, in *A Witness Tree* the poem that follows "The Most of It" celebrates an achieved Edenic companionship, that of Adam and Eve. Frost, however, characteristically distances this, making the poem a half-mocking report by one of Adam's children of what Adam used to say, perhaps after Eve had died. It is a miraculous sonnet, as exquisitely casual and conversational as Chaucer at his best, and it celebrates not only the "counter-love, original response" that Adam and Eve found with each other, but the musical echo of that companionship which humans still hear in the song of birds:

NEVER AGAIN WOULD BIRDS' SONG BE THE SAME

He would declare, and could himself believe,
That the birds there in all the garden round
From having heard the daylong voice of Eve

> Had added to their own an oversound,
> Her tone of meaning but without the words.
> Admittedly an eloquence so soft
> Could only have had an influence on birds
> When call or laughter carried it aloft.
> Be that as may be, she was in their song.
> Moreover her voice upon their voices crossed
> Had now persisted in the woods so long
> That probably it never would be lost.
> Never again would birds' song be the same.
> And to do that to birds was why she came.

This poem's speaker reports to us what Adam used to say—and not only reports it with raised eyebrow, but tells us that Adam himself said it in a way that suggested bemused and uncertain belief in what he was saying. Adam "could himself believe" what he would declare. We can all but hear Adam, on one day of many when he was reminiscing to their children about their mother: "I declare, and I can believe it too, that..." But once he has declared that the birds, from having heard Eve's constant talking and singing, had picked up "an oversound, / Her tone of meaning but without the words,"[25] he qualifies this as if he's conceding to common sense that the declaration sounds peculiar: "I admit that her voice was ever soft and low, so the only way the birds could have picked up her tone was from her calling out, or laughing—not when she was just speaking to me or the animals down among us, but when she raised her voice in calling me, or laughing." What the birds picked up from Eve, and added to their songs as an oversound, was therefore Eve's companionable call to Adam or the children or the animals, or her laughter: nothing but happy sounds ever went from Eve into the song of birds.

But Adam goes on to dismiss this doubt, and to state firmly his belief: "Be that as may be, *she was in their song.*" And he adds with what at first seems equal certainty, "*Moreover,* her voice upon their voices crossed / Had now persisted in the woods so long / That" (10–12)—but here, his common sense pulls him up. He was about to affirm that this "oversound" in the song of birds would never be lost, but he does not want to make absolute statements about what the future may hold, so (I imagine him here as responding to the expression of his amused and quizzical listener—his child or grandchild) he throws in a word of caution: "That *probably* it never would be lost." And yet, now that it is time for him to sum up his "declaration" (and time for Frost to finish the sonnet with a couplet), he roundly declares, "Never again would birds' song be the same. *And to do that to birds was why she came.*" For me, this is both an amusing and a heartbreaking declaration of love, a recognition of loss beyond compare, one of the great tragicomic moments of literature in the English language. It is also a wonderful "Miltonic answer" to the frustrated Adamic longing in the preceding poem, "The Most of It."

What follows this rosy Edenic sonnet, though, is a dramatic lyric full of weeds and thorns, a sexual encounter set in a fallen world, ending in misery, as vivid as a D. H. Lawrence story, indeed almost a contrarian response to Lawrence, a comical tragedy. It begins with a woman and man standing near each other in (as we learn) a field. He has picked a flower and must have just said something that has made her draw back from him in alarm; he remains calm and tries to explain, but so roughly that she grows fearful.

THE SUBVERTED FLOWER

She drew back; he was calm:
"It is this that had the power."
And he lashed his open palm
With the tender-headed flower.

We are not told what he had just said, but from what he now says about "the power," illustrated by lashing his open palm with "the tender-headed flower," we infer he was talking of the power of sexual attraction; and from the woman's drawing back in alarm, it seems—to put it very crudely—he was using a kind of "Darwinian" argument to suggest that he and the woman are feeling just such natural attraction to each other and perhaps therefore might...? Unluckily for him, he illustrates this too roughly, by lashing his palm with the flower, and then tries to make up for it by smiling, inviting her to smile along with him.

> He smiled for her to smile,
> But she was either blind
> Or willfully unkind.
> He eyed her for a while
> For a woman and a puzzle.
> He flicked and flung the flower,
> And another sort of smile
> Caught up like fingertips
> The corners of his lips
> And cracked his ragged muzzle.

When she stands off, "either blind / Or willfully unkind," the man, baffled, retreats into an abrupt misogyny, then makes it worse by angrily tossing the flower and by smiling "another sort of smile"—which now frightens the woman, and for a moment Frost lets us look through her eyes at the man as a wolfish threat with a smile that "cracked his ragged muzzle." Then we see the two of them in sunlight, she beautiful and aloof, he aching to touch her:

> She was standing to the waist
> In goldenrod and brake,
> Her shining hair displaced.
> He stretched her either arm
> As if she made it ache
> To clasp her—not to harm;
> As if he could not spare
> To touch her neck and hair.

But his words only make things worse, pleading for her to recognize that their attraction is mutual, when she is appalled by his passion—and once again Frost lets us see the man through the woman's frightened eyes even as he pleads for understanding:

> "If this has come to us
> And not to me alone—"
> So she thought she heard him say;
> Though with every word he spoke
> His lips were sucked and blown
> And the effort made him choke
> Like a tiger at a bone.
> She had to lean away.

> She dared not stir a foot,
> Lest movement should provoke
> The demon of pursuit
> That slumbers in a brute.

Now, suddenly, Frost drops into the scene a shadow of Eden, the bright voice of Eve calling to her daughter:

> It was then her mother's call
> From inside the garden wall
> Made her steal a look of fear
> To see if he could hear
> And would pounce to end it all
> Before her mother came.

Frost gives us here the fallen world's spectacle of human loneliness and isolation: the corruption of Edenic love, companionship, and communion between humans, transformed to fear and violence that border on, and may become, the bestial. Yet Frost gives us, in the final lines of the poem, the clear understanding that this is "all in the mind," that (as D. H. Lawrence used whole novels to argue) this is not how things need to be, though only too often it is how things are. The woman "sees" a kind of reality, the man's rough and beastly passion, how "a flower had marred a man," but the poem shows us what she fails to see, that "the flower" need not be "base and fetid," and that some of what is wrong is in her own heart.

> She looked and saw the shame:
> A hand hung like a paw,
> An arm worked like a saw
> As if to be persuasive,
> An ingratiating laugh
> That cut the snout in half,
> An eye become evasive.
> A girl could only see
> That a flower had marred a man,
> But what she could not see
> Was that the flower might be
> Other than base and fetid:
> That the flower had done but part,

> And what the flower began
> Her own too meager heart
> Had terribly completed.

But the story in this poem has no happy ending: the man flees the scene, the mother retrieves her daughter, and (as in the final line of "The Most of It") "that was all":

> She looked and saw the worst.
> And the dog or what it was,
> Obeying bestial laws,
> A coward save at night,
> Turned from the place and ran.
> She heard him stumble first
> And use his hands in flight.
> She heard him bark outright.
> And oh, for one so young
> The bitter words she spit
> Like some tenacious bit
> That will not leave the tongue.
> She plucked her lips for it,
> And still the horror clung.
> Her mother wiped the foam
> From her chin, picked up her comb,
> And drew her backward home.

In "The Most of It" Adam in solitude longed for a companionship beyond the animal; in "Never Again Would Birds' Song Be the Same" he remembered the "Edenic" companionship with Eve, still echoing in the song of birds; in "The Subverted Flower" the man and woman are caught in a post-Edenic misery of solitude, a wretched alienation of male from female human. Humans may be, or be seen as, bestial, unfit for human company. The woman is frightened for her life, although it would seem that the man, at least as he thinks of it, is only declaring a frank sensuality and hoping "to clasp her—not to harm." In solitude, hoping for a lover, he uses the flower to suggest what he thinks is natural (both Edenic and Darwinian) sexual attraction, but his gesture has a kind of violence and roughness that frighten her; and she is not capable of seeing "that the flower might be / Other than base and fetid," and that her own responsiveness was part of what frightened her so much: "what the flower began / Her own too meager heart / Had terribly completed."

Why, though, do I think Frost's language in the poem suggests that he is setting this poem with the others as a trio of Miltonic/Edenic pieces? Because it contains lines that, I believe, evoke Eve as this young woman's mother:

> It was then her mother's call
> From inside the garden wall
> Made her steal a look of fear
> To see if he could hear
> And would pounce to end it all
> Before her mother came.

Frost does not capitalize "garden wall," so we might take this to be an ordinary nineteenth century encounter of an amorous young man and a prudish young woman, in a field just outside her mother's walled garden. But placed as the third in this trio of poems, with the first evoking Adam in the garden of Eden before Eve was created, and the second evoking Adam and Eve in the garden (though set, it would seem, after the death of Eve), surely "The Subverted Flower" is best seen as evoking a daughter of Eve, outside a garden created by Eve in the fallen world, and wooed by an all too plain-speaking and rough-acting lover—"raising Cain," as it were.

Milton as Muse for *A Witness Tree*

Frost's *A Witness Tree* looks to me as if he had been reading and meditating on biblical stories (Laban and Jacob, the Gospel account of Jesus entering Jerusalem, the Fall as narrated in Genesis), and on Milton's versions of these in *Paradise Lost*. And if we trace Frost's biography over the years 1938–42, when he was gathering and perhaps composing some of the poems in that book, I think we can see that he was taking Milton as a kind of muse for his own poetry. He would have known that Milton (1608–74) died not long before his sixty-sixth birthday,[26] and we may note that in 1941, when *A Witness Tree* was about to go to press, Frost (1874–1963) would have been 66 or 67 years old. That Frost knew Milton's poetry very well is clear: *Lycidas,* for instance, he knew by heart. He might not even have needed to reread *Paradise Lost,* which most likely was alive and echoing in his mind, an "oversound," of the blind poet "On evil days though fall'n and evil tongues; / In darkness, and with dangers compassed round, / And solitude" (*PL* 7.26–27). For my part, I find it deeply satisfying that in 1942, Frost won a fourth Pulitzer Prize for *A Witness Tree,* and that during the 21 years from then until his death in 1963, Frost not only found a fit audience, but one that grew and widened year by year—much as Milton's fame and audience grew in the years from 1667 (when *Paradise Lost* was published) until his death in 1674. I think their audiences will continue to read them as long as the English language is understood. The small fact that Frost was never given the Nobel Prize is as much a shame as the petty fact that Milton was never named poet laureate of England—but I suspect that Frost will be recognized, ultimately, with Walt Whitman and Emily Dickinson, as one of the three great poets who up to now have written within the United States.

Washington University, St. Louis

Is There Freedom Afterwards?
A Dialogue between *Paradise Lost* and DeLillo's *Falling Man*

Rachel Falconer

The terrorist attacks of 2001 cast their shadow not only over contemporary literature, but also over the ways we read literature of the past. In Milton studies, for example, a major critical controversy erupted over the question of whether or not *Samson Agonistes* could be read as a work in favour of terrorism.[1] In this essay, I would like to read Milton's other masterpiece, *Paradise Lost* (1667), in the presence of Don DeLillo's *Falling Man* (2007), and vice versa, to read DeLillo's novel in the presence of Milton's epic. When read in the twenty-first century, both texts are transfigured by the events of September 11, 2001.[2] But read alongside each other, they also illuminate a countertheme: that no historical event, however apocalyptic, can determine our response to it. The activity of reading, in both texts, is dramatized as a discipline by which we come to know how fundamentally we are free, free to choose for ourselves what events can mean, or when they fail to mean. Coming to John Milton's epic post-DeLillo, and DeLillo's novel post-9/11, one discovers remarkable affinities between the two texts, as well as passages that richly interilluminate each other even when they diverge in argument or tone. Where they do converge, and with particular force, is in their unfolding of this countertheme: that by working carefully through (reflecting, writing, or reading) a moment of historical catastrophe one may unravel the sense of inevitability that accrues to it retrospectively. Or, to put it in seventeenth century theological terms, one may achieve that ultimate goal: to recover freedom, after having freely chosen not to be free.

In *Falling Man*, three characters stand looking at a still life painting, by Giorgio Morandi (1890–1964). Himself a painter of second and third glances, Morandi produced a number of still lifes on the same theme, depicting the same cluster of objects, but it seems to be the 1956 *Natura morta* (fig. 1) which is described in the novel.[3] There were: "seven or eight objects, the taller ones set against a brushy slate background. The other items were huddled boxes and biscuit tins, grouped before a darker background.... Two of the taller items were dark and somber, with smoky marks and smudges, and one of them was partly concealed by a long-necked bottle. The bottle was a bottle, white."[4]

The three characters are in an apartment in New York City, and the time is shortly after the attacks of September 11, 2001. One of them is an art collector named Martin Ridnour, and he says to the other two, "I keep seeing the towers in this still life." Another character looks at the painting (she is Lianne Neudecker, who together with her husband Keith are the two main protagonists of the novel), and she agrees. Looking at "the two dark objects," what she sees are the Twin Towers (49). Similarly, when I show a pre-2001 photograph of the World Trade Center to my students, they tell me they already imagine an image of the towers being destroyed. This is a problem of perception in the aftermath of a historical catastrophe. Not only is the past irrevocably final, as offended Nietzsche's Zarathustra, but also, its complexity and depth collapse so that all we can see are premonitions of disaster.[5]

The problem of how we see things naturally also affects how we respond to the disaster. Many public commentators in Britain now agree that the war in Iraq was driven by a national thirst for

Fig. 1. Giorgio Morandi, *Natura morta* (1956). Musée Morandi, Bologna. By permission of Artists Rights Society (ARS), © 2011, New York / SIAE, Rome.

revenge in the aftermath of 9/11. "In times of crisis, people need a scapegoat"; so a BBC Radio 4 presenter commented in December 2009, which shows the on-going relevance of René Girard's ideas about the function of the scapegoat, or *le bouc émissaire*, in modern as well as archaic societies.[6] According to Girard, the scapegoat is sacrificed in order to break the cycle of mimetic desire that leads to rivalry and violence. In *Falling Man*, Martin argues that the two towers expressed "fantasies of wealth and power," which in their very construction produced an opposing "fantas[y] of destruction."

As he says, "You build a thing like that, so you can see it come down. The provocation is obvious" (116).[7] Killing the scapegoat, or in this case, launching a war, initiates a new cycle of violence. According to the cultural critic W. T. J. Mitchell, the Twin Towers provided a precise emblem of the way terror operates by "cloning itself"; it produces an instantaneous, mimetic response that escalates like a virus.[8]

Read in the shadow of 9/11, *Paradise Lost* and *Falling Man* emerge as texts twinned in their determination to resist the fatalistic response to catastrophe. Both Milton and DeLillo were writing in the aftermath of a historical disaster. For DeLillo, the old New York City, the *lost,* pre-9/11, city had been unique in its commingling of rituals and beliefs from many diverse cultures. Milton thought the collapse of the commonwealth, and the return to monarchy in 1660, represented a backslide from a condition of freedom to one of enslavement.[9] "Reason is but choosing," he asserted in *Areopagitica,* but if one's sanity is lost, how does one recover the capacity for free choice?[10] For all their substantial differences—in religious faith, in attitude to military violence, in their understanding of the public function of the writer—both Milton and DeLillo dramatize how the way out of hell lies in developing new modes of perception (without this, one's sense of having escaped hell turns out to be a delusion, as happens to Satan). For example, later in *Falling Man,* Lianne's mother Nina looks again at the Morandi still life. She says, "these shapes are not translatable to modern towers, twin towers. It's a work that rejects that kind of extension or projection. It takes you inward, down and in." A still life in Italian is called a *natura morta.* Nina thinks this is what the painting is about: "It's all about mortality...being mortal, being human" (111). Whether or not you agree with her insight, what is important is that her inward looking frees her from an automatic, overdetermined form of response. One might compare this to that passage at the opening of *Paradise Lost,* book 3, in which the narrator (like the author) regrets the loss of his sight: "Seasons return, but not to me returns / Day" (3.41–42).[11] By way of compensation he invokes celestial light to "shine inward, and the mind through all her powers / Irradiate, there *plant eyes*" (3.52–53; emphasis mine).

Morandi spent years (all the years of World War II, in fact) staring very intently at his bizarre collection of objects; he never seemed to tire of looking at them because he painted them many times, and each still life records a fresh discovery. Since the cure for responding automatically to disaster lies in rereading the detail, we are going to approach Milton and DeLillo's grand theme, the Fall, from a very literal and microscopic perspective. Perhaps rashly, we will set aside the larger ramifications of the Fall for the moment, to concentrate simply on how the body falls through space, and how it is observed to fall. It is in the minutest of such details, I suggest, that the two texts begin to unwind the fatalistic mindset that pervades in the aftermath of disaster.

What is the value of adopting this Janus-faced, comparative approach? Besides bridging two academic communities, it is especially apposite for these two texts, since they demonstrate paradoxically how the best close-up view is obtained by first stepping outside the frame. Such an approach may not produce an orthodox reading, but Milton and DeLillo are not orthodox thinkers. On the contrary, I would describe each text as deliberately imaginative, in the strong sense described by Edward Casey, where he characterizes the imagination as a distinctively autonomous mental activity, where the mind moves, unimpeded by ethical demands of the immediate present, "projecting and freely contemplating a proliferation of possibilities."[12] This can, of course, be taken as a criticism, and both texts have been accused of failing to address their contemporary political moment directly enough. In my argument, this imaginative detachment is rather to be understood as a strength, and a deliberate strategy that derives its impulse from a profound commitment to history and politics. *Paradise Lost* and *Falling Man* both use techniques of imaginative suspension in order to recast the story of the Fall into a narrative of *descent:* that is, a willed journey downward, and a conscious embrace of human finitude. The following discussion will attempt to illuminate that theme in both texts, by reading one against the other.

William Blake famously insisted that Milton was of the devil's party, but for me, still more arresting and persuasive is his recognition that Milton's imaginative vision is nearly always exercised downward: from heaven to hell, from heaven to earth, and from the earthly paradise down into the real world.[13] Samuel Johnson wrote of Milton as having a "lofty and elevated" mind.[14] Blake, however, imagined Milton thus: "as a wintry globe descends precipitant, thro' Beulah bursting, / With thunders loud and terrible, so Milton's Shadow fell / Precipitant, loud thund'ring, into the Sea of Time and Space."[15] This poem collapses the author of *Paradise Lost* with the text itself and imagines a fate for Milton that evokes his depiction of the Son of God's, as well as Adam and Eve's, fall into the "sea of time and space." Because they were tempted by Satan, Adam and Eve's fall is reversible, while Satan's is not — or so God tells the assembled angels in book 3,

> The first sort by their own suggestion fell,
> Self-tempted, self-depraved: man falls deceived
> By the other first: man therefore shall find grace,
> The other none.   (*PL* 3.129–32)

At first glance, the decision of England's political leaders to recrown a monarch in 1660 looks more like a satanic fall than an Adamic one: "Self-tempted, self-depraved." In *Paradise Lost*, we never get a close-up view of *how* Satan tempted himself, perhaps because by the time we meet Satan it is already too late: he has always already fallen. But at what point does it become *too late* to exercise free choice? This point comes later than one might suppose, particularly for a reader who experiences the poem after September 2001, and perhaps, even more so, after reading *Falling Man*.

Satan's physical fall from heaven is narrated at length three times in the course of the epic: twice directly, 1.44–54 and 6.856–66, and a third time, by analogy, in the fall of Mulciber, 1.742–46. The iteration of this image, of a body falling physically through space, seems to me to underline the belatedness of Satan's existential condition. Once you're falling, all the important decisions have been made; *les jeux sont faits*, as Sartre reminds us.[16] Or perhaps not. Each time Milton describes Satan's fall, or Mulciber's, he presents the scene from a different vantage point. As I hope to show, each time the fatality of the event becomes a little less fixed. Whether or not the eventual outcome is changed, the reader is invited to enter the imagination's *pays du possible*.[17]

In addition to these three major descriptions, there are a number of briefer allusions to, or reports of, the satanic fall. In line with his description in book 1, there is the narrator's reference to the satanic fall in the Argument to book 1 ("was by the command of God driven out of heaven").[18] In book 2, Sin's recollection of the event is likewise that they were "driven" down by overmastering force: "down they fell / Driven headlong from the pitch of heaven, down / Into this deep" (2.771–73). Earlier in book 2, Belial has also vividly imagined the possibility of a repetition of the fall in the future: not only that "this firmanent / Of hell" should fall upon their heads, but that the fallen angels might sink still further, "Under yon boiling ocean" (2.175–83); this, too, would be a case of being physically overpowered. In contrast to these, there is the narrator's mention of Satan's fall in the Argument to book 6, where he adopts a markedly different perspective, seemingly in anticipation of Raphael's own description later in book 6. In the following discussion, I will focus on the three long descriptions of the satanic fall, both for the sake of clarity and because (in my view) the briefer allusions repeat and amplify the overall trajectory of the major descriptions, rather than introducing any countercurrent of their own.

Repetitions in epic poetry, perhaps especially in the work of a blind poet, are apprehended aurally; one hears and remembers hearing sounds one has heard before. But *Paradise Lost* is no less concerned with developing new modes of seeing, as the narrator's admiration for Galileo, "the Tuscan artist" with his extraordinary "optic glass," shows us from the start (1.288).[19] Both he and his protagonists are engaged in an analogous process of seeing better, both farther and more inwardly. The Argument to book 10 describes Adam "more and more perceiving," thus signaling that the process of seeing anew has already begun. My argument here is that for the reader of *Paradise Lost*, the repeated sight (and sound) of Satan falling through space helps us to see farther, or more inwardly, into the meaning of historical disaster (this being, for Milton's readers, the failure of the republic, and the return to monarchy).

The first extensive description of Satan's fall occurs just 40 lines into book 1. The narrator relates how God crushes the rebellion of Satan and his followers:

> Him the almighty power
> Hurled headlong flaming from the ethereal sky
> With hideous ruin and combustion down
> To bottomless perdition, there to dwell
> In adamantine chains and penal fire,
> Who durst defy the omnipotent to arms.
> Nine times the space that measures day and night
> To mortal men, he with his horrid crew
> Lay vanquished, rolling in the fiery gulf
> Confounded though immortal. (*PL* 1.44–53)

Milton writes in English blank verse: that is, unrhymed iambic pentameter. He chose *not* to write in rhyme, against the fashion of the day, because he wanted to restore to English verse what he called the "ancient liberty" of classical epic.[20] There's not much sense of liberty being expressed here, though. The trochaic inversions (him, hurled, headlong, flaming) beat downwards, on a figure who is remorselessly viewed from a vantage point high *above* the action. The narrator assumes the perspective of an omnipotent god, in that Satan is not only morally condemned by his description (the defier with his "horrid crew"), but also his anticipatory "there to dwell" presumes to know Satan's eternal future. In fact, although we may think we're reading about Satan falling, it turns out to be a description of his already *having fallen:* "Nine times the space that measures day and night" sounds like the description of distance being traveled, until we get to the main verb, "Lay vanquished." So for nine days, he has been lying there already. This is the most overdetermined account of Satan's physical fall.[21]

Later in the same book, the narrator recounts a similar scene, but with opposite effect. The analogy with Satan is implicit, but here the falling figure is Hephaestus, the Greek god of architecture. Milton calls him by his less familiar, Roman name, Mulciber. In Homer's *Iliad*, Hephaestus himself recalls how he had once been thrown out of heaven by Zeus, when he tried to defend his mother, Hera, from Zeus's jealous rage. This is how Milton retells the Homeric lines:[22]

> how he fell
> From heaven, they fabled, thrown by angry Jove
> Sheer o'er the crystal battlements: from morn
> To noon he fell, from noon to dewy eve,
> A summer's day; and with the setting sun
> Dropped from the zenith like a falling star,
> On Lemnos the Ægæan isle.   (*PL* 1.740–46)

In contrast to the previous description of the falling angels, here the fall is cast in slow motion, with the beautifully symmetrical phrases "from morn to noon he fell," "from noon to dewy eve," echoing each other, across a midline caesura. The buoyancy of the rhythm contributes to the sense of the body being lightly suspended in the summer sky.

Unlike the earlier passage, this time the fall seems to be totally silent and painless. Looking *up* at the figure dropping toward him, the narrator seems entranced by the beauty of the image. He neither judges nor empathizes with it. And then he continues,

> thus they relate,
> Erring; for he with this rebellious rout
> Fell long before...
>   nor did he scape
> By all his engines, but was headlong sent
> With his industrious crew to build in hell.   (1.746–51)

Among Milton scholars, it has become obligatory to respond to Stanley Fish's reading of these lines, which he takes as emblematic of Milton's strategy in *Paradise Lost* to lure the reader's judgment to sleep, and then pounce, with a sudden revelation of the sin into which he or she has drifted.[23] Against this reading, it should be noted that the narrator begins with a disclaimer, "they fabled," so it cannot come as a complete surprise to the reader to discover that the following lines are not entirely true.

But, without wishing to rehearse the whole debate over Fish's proposed pattern of corrective reading, we could address the crux of the matter in brief: that is, how one interprets the placement of "erring" in the return of the line. If we concede that, having drifted away from his argument, the narrator sharply recollects himself, does it follow that this pattern of thinking is to be rejected by the reader as dangerous? My view is that, on the contrary, erring opens up the space for reflection, the value of which is repeatedly demonstrated in the poem as a whole.[24] For example, by eating the forbidden fruit, Adam and Eve sentence themselves to death, which they assume will be instantaneous, but it turns out they have plenty of time before the sentence falls. In the last two books of the poem, we see the whole of human history unfolding and the moment of absolute finality still hasn't arrived.

To "err" can mean to make a mistake, or to wander from the path, or to wonder, as in to "speculate freely." Erring, in all three senses, generally produces the most gripping drama and the most nuanced poetry in *Paradise Lost*. The last we see of Adam and Eve, they are leaving Eden "with wandering steps and slow." In any case, there is no theologically correct way to read the narrator's account of Mulciber's fall. The god—or is he an angel?—falls out of a Greco-Roman sky into a Christian hell. Why is this composite angel damned, and by whom? Was Mulciber really an angel tempted by Satan? Or, on the contrary, is Zeus's vengefulness being imputed to God? We don't know. But the aesthetic suspension allows us the space to reflect on various interpretations of the fall.

Turning to the third passage, we find Raphael narrating the fall of Satan to Adam in the garden of Eden. This description occurs in book 6, in the midst of Raphael's account of the angels' rebellion in heaven:

> The overthrown he raised, and
> ....
> Drove them before him thunderstruck, pursued
> With terrors and with furies to the bounds

>   And crystal wall of heav'n, which op'ning wide,
>   Rolled inward, and a spacious gap disclosed
>   Into the wastful deep; the monstrous sight
>   Strook them with horror backward, but far worse
>   Urged them behind; headlong themselves they threw
>   Down from the verge of heav'n, eternal wrath
>   Burnt after them to the bottomless pit.   (6.856, 858–66)

Several verbal echoes link this passage to the fall of Mulciber, and behind that, the earlier description of Satan falling: in all three passages, the angel falls "headlong," and the "crystal wall" of heaven recalls the "crystal battlements" of Jove.

In this passage, though, the punisher is not God or Zeus, but the Son of God, and Milton's Son is that aspect of divinity that turns itself toward humanity. Another sign of the more human scale of this account is that Raphael imagines how the angels *felt* as they hesitated on the threshold: he tells Adam, "the monstrous sight / Strook them with horror." Raphael is of the same order of being as the rebels, and he was there at the time, unlike the epic narrator. He places the listener on the same plane as the action, rather than above or below. Theologically, this is a risky strategy, because as John Carey has argued, once you give a devil human interiority, he becomes much harder to condemn.[25]

Here is where reading Milton in a post-DeLillo context can make a crucial difference for how one understands the lines: "the monstrous sight / Strook them with horror backward, but far worse / Urged them behind." This is no longer merely verbal thunder, but the precise description of an actual, unbearable choice. The angels hesitate, and then they throw *themselves* into space. Why is this different than saying that they fell, as the narrator did before? Theologically, it helps Milton to absolve God from the charge of being vengeful if the devils themselves chose their own fate. As God tells the remaining angels, "Freely they stood who stood, and fell who fell" (3.102). Milton thus stakes out his position in the great debate of seventeenth century religions: does God's omniscience imply that all our actions are predestined? With the Arminians, Milton replies, no, we are always free to choose.[26]

Well, we already knew that Satan chose to rebel. But it is one thing to succumb to temptation when you're in heaven, and God is bizarrely disguising his omnipotence. It is quite different to know you have a choice, even when divine vengeance is crashing down on your head. It may not seem like much, but it is the very extremity of their position that makes the angels' choice—or, the fact they *have* a choice—important. Indeed, this is one of the rare passages in the poem in which the fallen angels are given a fully *human* dignity. For as Viktor Frankl wrote in another context, "the ability to choose one's attitude to a given set of circumstances" is "the last of human freedoms."[27]

Even in the context of a poem about the Fall from paradise, Milton's attention to the concrete motif of a body falling through space is, at first glance, strangely obsessive. The repeated return to this image suggests to me that it becomes, for Milton, a symbol of the human imagination's potential to transform tragedy. In this sense, the passages we have considered above demonstrate the "logic of the imaginary" understood by Lévi-Strauss in *Tristes tropiques* as "the fantasy production of a society seeking passionately to give symbolic expression to the institutions it *might* have had in reality."[28] The "meaning" of the motif lies not in the image itself, but in the poet's repeated working over and working through the image so that with each recurrence we hear an increasing number of resonances, or better, dissonances, resisting closure at the very moment when the tragic outcome of historical reality appears most inevitable.

Don DeLillo's novel also asks us to imagine this Miltonic motif of the falling body, but with a post-9/11 awareness that things like this happen to human beings, in the actual, historical world. *Falling Man* was published in 2007, after quite a number of novels, films, and documentaries had already been made about 9/11. But given his previous fiction's preoccupation with terrorist violence, expectations were high that DeLillo's novel would deliver *the* definitive representation of 9/11.[29] *Falling Man* is a richly allusive work; among its literary ancestors are Bellow's *Dangling Man* (1944), Camus's *La chute* (1956), and Golding's *Free Fall* (1959).[30]

But given DeLillo's title, none of these intertexts was as likely to be as immediately present in the reader's mind, in 2007, as the by-then famous photograph taken by Richard Drew of an unidentified man falling from one of the towers.[31] While other novels, such as Jonathan Safran Foer's *Extremely Loud and Incredibly Close* (2005) made a feature of this photograph, incorporating it into the fictional narrative, DeLillo excludes the representation itself and instead describes characters in the novel *thinking* about the image. For the problem that DeLillo sets out to address, and *re*dress, is that 9/11 is an overdetermined subject, for which we already possess a mental library of abject images, and a narrative master plot of debilitating, collective trauma.[32] However real these may be, they actually prevent us from thinking about the subject imaginatively; that is, in an autonomous frame of mind that resists the most obvious response to such images.

The first chapter of *Falling Man* describes the day of the attacks, from the point of view of Keith Neudecker, who was in one of the towers when it was struck. The narrative follows the lives of Keith; his estranged wife, Lianne; her mother, Nina; and Nina's lover, Martin, and various others such as a group of Alzheimer patients with whom Lianne works. This rather meandering narrative is cut through, at various points, by a subplot concerning Hammad and the terrorist group planning the attacks on the towers. While Keith and Lianne's story starts on the day of the attacks and moves forward in time, the terrorist subplot starts some years before and moves up to the day of the attacks. In the final chapter, the subplot catches up with the beginning of the main plot, and the novel ends on the day it began, with a repeat account of the catastrophe.

Despite the dramatic opening description, many of the novel's first reviewers found the rest of the novel disappointing. Adam Mars-Jones's review is indicative, when he writes that *Falling Man* "gives the...impression of having no kernel inside its various shells."[33] In its defense, some critics have argued that its hollow core constitutes an authentic representation of trauma. Linda Kauffman elucidates the features of clinical trauma that appear in the novel, such as repetition, mirroring, and doubling.[34] Thus, one could argue that the thin, unindividuated portrayal of the characters is deliberate because they have become incoherent to *themselves*. This is certainly a reading that fits with many other narratives about the destruction of the towers, so many, in fact, that they have been rechristened the "World Trauma Center."[35] But *Falling Man* is a work of imaginative speculation rather than mimesis—note the subtitle: *A Novel*. The narrator never refers to 9/11, or the World Trade Center; he refers instead to "the attacks" and "the towers," and the dates are not specified. Whereas the ground of the novel is indeed collective trauma, its real subject is the problem of perception in the aftermath of catastrophe.[36]

DeLillo begins, "It was not a *street* anymore but a *world*, a time and space of falling ash and near night" (3). In the shift from street to world, the city seems to have dropped out of history into an afterlife as final and mythic as Milton's hell.[37] The wreckage of human existence rains down from the sky. Shoes, handbags, shirts, and office paper, emptied of human presence, have become "otherworldly things" (3). Despite the mayhem of flying objects, there is a flat finality to the whole scene: "the noise *lay* everywhere they ran, stratified sound collecting around them" (4). In an undeniably traumatized state, Keith Neudecker is wandering, concussed and confused, *back* toward the tower from which he has just emerged. In passing, he barely registers seeing "figures...a thousand feet up, dropping into space." In other words, he *fails* to see them.[38]

In the chapters that follow, DeLillo shows us a range of characters, all struggling to overcome a certain vagueness of perception. The Alzheimer's group provides one notable example. The narrator himself is groping for new ways of seeing; hence, the drifting, cobwebby surrealism of the middle chapters, which reveal him in the act of imagining, rather than presenting imagined objects in a finalized state. Edward Casey usefully distinguishes two phases of imagining: the "act phase," which refers to the mental process of imaging, and the "object phase," which refers to the image conjured by the mental effort.[39] DeLillo's novel gives us markedly more of the former than the latter. The hazy narration and characterization of *Falling Man* might also be usefully compared to Gilles Deleuze's notion of a "thinking image" (*image pensée et pensante*) in cinema, which would oppose itself to the traditional "action image" of traditional Hollywood film.⁴⁰

The title of DeLillo's novel refers to a performance artist who stages falls from various buildings around the city. While he never explains his intentions, the effect of his performances is to sharpen the perception of those who see him fall. We see his performance three times in the novel, each time focalized through Lianne, who is the Eve of this text. The first performance causes outrage and offense in the onlookers, because he appears to be imitating the pose in the photograph by Richard Drew. Lianne catches sight of him when he has already fallen. He is "dangling upside down," hanging by a safety harness from a rope. Wearing a business suit, he is holding "one leg bent up, arms at his sides" (33). Lianne is shocked, as she says, by the "awful openness of it, something we'd not seen, the single falling figure that trails a collective dread" (33). She recoils from the sight.

The second time, Lianne finds herself trapped at a much closer viewing point. Janiak has positioned himself over a train tunnel, so that the people inside the train will catch sight of him at the instant he falls (the UK cover refers to this episode, with the photograph of a train strikingly pictured inverted onto a vertical axis, so that it rushes downwards). Lianne understands that Janiak wants his audience to be unprepared, but it isn't until the train arrives that we learn of another reason for his adopting this position: "The train comes slamming through and he turns his head and looks into it (into his death by fire) and then brings his head back around and jumps" (167–68). Beyond wishing to imitate the surface gesture of falling, as a photograph might, Janiak positions himself so that he can inwardly reexperience the choice on the threshold. Since, as we later learn, he will actually die of injuries sustained during these falls, this may be an instance of acting out, rather than working through, trauma. But in this instance, his performance has a further effect on his audience. Lianne catches sight of a threadbare old man whose "face showed an intense narrowing of thought and possibility. He was seeing something elaborately different from what he encountered step by step in the ordinary run of hours. He had to learn how to see it fit correctly, find a crack in the world where it might fit" (168). There is the sense of the insertion of an enigma into the daily routine, which requires an adjustment in the gaze itself. Or, in Milton's terms, one could say the spectacle *plants eyes* in the observer. It irradiates inward, instigating a new way of seeing.

The third time, the falling man is no longer actually present. Lianne comes across his obituary in a newspaper. The journalist is speculating whether Janiak had been imitating a particular photograph when he fell in a particular pose:

> She did not read further but knew at once which photograph the account referred to. It hit her hard when she first saw it, the day after, in the newspaper. The man headlong, the towers behind him. The mass of the towers filled the frame of the picture. The man falling, the towers contiguous, she thought, behind him. The enormous soaring lines, the vertical column stripes. The man with blood on his shirt, she thought, or burn marks, and the effect of the columns behind him, the composition, she thought, darker stripes for the nearer tower, the north, lighter for the other, and the mass, the immensity of it, and the man set almost precisely between the rows of darker and lighter stripes. Headlong, free fall, she thought, and this picture burned a hole in her mind and heart, dear God, he was a falling angel and his beauty was horrific. (221–22)

It is important to recognize that what Lianne is recalling is unmistakably a *composition,* an imaginary reconstruction, prompted by the *written* account of an artist imitating a photograph imitating reality. This distance from reality is underlined by the insistence on the act of reflection: *she thought, she thought.* The falling figure appears to her to be set "almost precisely" within a frame of light and dark: so like the abstraction of Morandi's painting, the frame within a frame provides her with the mental space necessary to think through what she has seen.

Reading DeLillo post–*Paradise Lost,* one can hardly fail to hear an echo of Satan's fall in the poetic word "headlong" (elsewhere DeLillo uses the more prosaic "headfirst"). And then there is the unmistakably Miltonic, "he was a falling angel." Why an "angel"?

In colloquial parlance, "angel" is often used to signify innocence (an innocent cherub, for example), and for some viewers, perhaps Drew's photograph did predominantly convey a sense of pathos for an innocent victim. In *The Wake of the Imagination,* Richard Kearney suggests that images of actual, political atrocity (he cites the example of photographs of child victims of Hiroshima) are a means of escape from the sterile circulation of depthless images of postmodern art, in that they demand an ethical response from the viewer toward the subject of the image, regardless of its medium or frame: "it demands moral outrage. It demands that we sit up and say, 'this must end.'"[41] Maybe because the tiny figure set against its enormous frame implies a resistance to being finalized, like Satan's rebellion and fall from heaven.

Whatever the nature of the viewer's insight, it is achieved by dwelling on the image in the mind's eye, where it assumes the shape of an autonomous composition. Though one should also stress that the aesthetic suspension contains within it a movement toward abjection: angelic beauty strikes Lianne as *horrific.* So this is not a transcendent, modernist epiphany. Quite the reverse, it drives the observer downwards into a confrontation with the real. The composer Karlheinz Stockhausen notoriously described the attacks of September 11 as "Lucifer's greatest work of art."[42] Even if his remarks were misinterpreted as expressing admiration for the terrorists, it is easy to understand why people were offended by the very idea that terrorism could *be* art. And yet it is undeniably true that destructive acts do generate new realities and are in that sense creative. But DeLillo's falling angel is the victim of a terrorist act, not its architect, and in any case, his novel is not making the claim that horror *is* art. Rather, it shows how art *contains* the horror, both in the sense of being constituted by it, and in the sense of limiting and framing its effects.

Even though Janiak is no longer alive, his art "succeeds" with Lianne in the sense that her hazy memory is driven into sharp focus, and the thought of the falling man "pierces" her mind and heart. Later in the novel, *in contrast to* the terrorist who renounces the world for his god, Lianne concludes that "it's the *world itself* that brings you to God...Beauty, grief, terror, the empty desert, the

Bach cantatas" (234; emphasis mine). For Lianne, the body in free fall thus becomes an image *both* of human mortality, *and* of our freedom to decide what this condition means to us. One might also consider this repeated motif of the falling body through space in the light of the "logic of the imaginary" described by Lévi-Strauss in *Tristes tropiques* as "the fantasy production of a society seeking passionately to give symbolic expression to the institutions it *might* have had in reality" (emphasis in original).[43] So in our case, the "meaning" of the motif of falling lies not wholly in the image itself, but in the writer's repeated working over and working through the image so that with each recurrence we hear an increasing number of resonances, or better, dissonances, resisting closure at the very moment when the tragic outcome of historical reality appears most inevitable.

Lianne's husband, Keith, is quite literally pierced by the eruption of the subplot concerning Hammad, into his own narrative in the final chapter of the novel. Thus far we have been following Keith and Lianne's lives after the attacks. If Lianne reaches some kind of understanding, Keith seems to be burying himself in a robotic, obscurely vengeful existence playing poker and causing other people to lose money. The narrative then shifts back in time to recount the terrorist Hammad's preparations for the day of the attack. We follow Hammad's thoughts through to his final moment of consciousness, inside the plane, where it explodes into Keith's office in the north tower. The arc of one extraordinary sentence takes us from Hammad's viewpoint to Keith's, as two separate timeframes collapse into one: "A bottle fell off the counter in the galley, on the other side of the aisle, and he watched it roll this way and that, a water bottle, empty, making an arc one way and rolling back the other, and he watched it spin more quickly and then skitter across the floor an instant before the aircraft struck the tower, heat, then fuel, then fire, and a blast wave passed through the structure that sent Keith Neudecker out of his chair and into a wall. He found himself walking into a wall" (239). The "he" of "he found himself" is now Keith. And there is a sense in which this piercing of one plot by another "finds" Keith, in a way that he has not yet been able to do in his own life thus far. As I said earlier, this chapter returns us to the first scene. But there, we met Keith witnessing the aftermath of the destruction from *outside*. Inexplicably, he was carrying a briefcase which turned out not to be his. In the final scene, we see him *inside* the towers, several minutes *before* that opening scene took place. He tries to save his close friend's life but is forced to leave the body and descend the stairs himself. As he descends, he listens to the conversations on the stairwell:

There were voices up behind him, back on the stairs, one and then another in near echo, fugue voices, song voices in the rhythms of natural speech.

> This goes down.
> This goes down.
> Pass it down. (245)

Here we are being invited to revisit the spectacular scene of destruction with which we began, in order to discover an *interior* scene if not of salvation, then of *salvaging* the human. Inside the traumatic scene of the already doubling, virally escalating fall, there is also unfolding the story of a willed *descent*. If the first chapter presented a violently dismembered world, through which Keith is wandering dazedly and alone, here objects are being handed downstairs, from one person to another. That Keith joins in this human chain is indicated by the presence of the unknown briefcase in his hand. Rather than stratified noise filling the air, there are human voices, blending into this Bach-like fugue.[11]

This last chapter is also highly reminiscent of the final scene in Milton's *Paradise Lost*. The last two books of the epic have recounted at accelerated speed the cycle of human history from Genesis to the present, and each chapter, it seems, has ended heavily with a scene of apocalyptic destruction. At the end of time, there is the promise of final reckoning, but meanwhile Adam is strangely rejuvenated by the thought of the immediate task before him: to find Eve and descend from the garden of Eden into history. With a look back at paradise, over which flamed the brandished swords of the angelic guard, they begin their descent:

> The world was all before them, where to choose
> Their place of rest, and providence their guide.
> They hand in hand with wandering steps and slow,
> Through Eden took their solitary way. (12.646–49)

By way of conclusion, we could turn back to the beginning of *Falling Man*, where Keith catches sight of something unexpected in the chaos. The novel ends, with Keith seeing this image, returning to this point in time. So is what he sees a sign of traumatic repetition, a demonstration of history as the eternal recurrence of the same? "There was something else..., outside all this, not belonging to this, aloft. He watched it coming down. A shirt came down out of the high smoke, a shirt lifting and drifting, in the scant light and then falling again, down toward the river" (4). This *could* be read as a deathly image, in the way it uncannily doubles for the human body, yet fragments and empties it of substance. But this isn't all there is to be seen. There is also the echo of a Miltonic suspension: "from morn / To noon he fell, from noon to dewy eve, / A summer's day; and with the setting sun / Dropped from the zenith like a falling star." The rhythm of DeLillo's sentence similarly holds the image, aloft. I take this to be an image of consciousness, whether of the writer, or the reader: a mental act that indicates our freedom to stand "outside" catastrophe, so that our response is not wholly determined by it. One might compare the British sculptor Andrew Gormley's exhibition, entitled "Event Horizon," which consisted of figures poised on the precarious edges of various tall buildings around London, looking down at humanity below, like the human Jesus of Milton's *Paradise Regained*. In the latter poem, heroism consists of standing and thinking, rather than precipitately taking action, which is likely to be vengeful even (or especially) if driven by pathos, as in the famous case of Virgil's Aeneas, who is stirred by the memory of a boy soldier's death to murder his own defeated and suppliant enemy.[45]

The bodily fall of a man, or an angel, or a god, through space, appears at first glance to be a motif that signifies the inescapable *belatedness* of the human condition, for both Milton and DeLillo. Paradise is already lost, and there is no recovery from the trauma of the fall. But as has been emphasized here, both *Paradise Lost* and *Falling Man* are works about the importance of the second and third glance, where a new mode of perception develops out of the very awareness of human finitude. The autonomy that we possess is constrained by historical circumstance, but it is the very sense of limit and constraint that gives value to our freedom. And if the past is irrevocably past, still the perception of events can be imaginatively altered, and from that alteration flows the possibility of an unscripted future.

University of Lausanne

NOTES

Note to Preface

1. Sonnet 12, line 11, from *John Milton: Complete Shorter Poems*, ed. Stella P. Revard (Oxford, 2009). Further Milton quotations are from this edition.

Notes to Hale and Cullington, "*Universis Christi Ecclesiis*"

1. *De doctrina Christiana*, ed. John K. Hale and J. Donald Cullington, vol. 8 (2012), in *The Complete Works of John Milton*, gen. ed. Thomas N. Corns and Gordon Campbell, 11 vols. (Oxford, 2008–); hereafter cited as OM followed by volume and page.

2. *Ioannis Miltoni angli De doctrina Christiana libri duo posthumi*, ed. Carolus Ricardus Sumner (Cambridge, 1825).

3. *The Works of John Milton*, gen. ed. Frank Allen Patterson, 18 vols (New York, 1931–38). Vols. 14–17 comprise *De doctrina Christiana*. Subsequent references to Patterson's volumes are hereafter cited as CM and followed by volume and page number.

4. John Milton, *De doctrina Christiana*, in *The Complete Prose Works of John Milton*, 8 vols., ed. Don M. Wolfe et al. (New Haven: Yale University Press, 1953–82), vol. 6, ed. Maurice Kelley; hereafter cited as YP, followed by volume and page number.

5. The manuscript is transcribed from Public Record Office (now National Archives), SP (state papers) 9/61. The opening epistle is found on pp. 1–5, referred to here as MS.

6. Some points are treated in a different way in "Notes on the Style of the Epistle to All the Churches: Observations and Implications," chap. 17 of John K. Hale, *Milton as Multilingual: Selected Essays, 1982–2004* (Dunedin, 2005), 265–78.

7. The two are named by Edward Phillips, Milton's nephew, pupil, then friend, in his biography; see *Early Lives of Milton*, ed. Helen Darbishire (London, 1932), 61. The comment is very interesting, in that (1) Ames was a dissident and exiled fellow of Milton's own college, and (2) you would not guess from Milton's explicit references that either theologian was important: Ames is mentioned once, and not much cited incognito, while Wollebius is very often absorbed or summarized without being named at all. This adds up to a confirmation that Milton wants *De doctrina* to be seen and known as all his own work. And so it is, in the same way that Shakespeare appropriates many others' materials, yet no one in their right wits questions his originality, the personal voice and stamp. It is the appropriation and new advance (the "wading further") that counts.

8. Equivalent references for the manuscript pages cited here are: MS 386 = OM 8:798, YP 6:577, CM 16.254; MS 7 = OM 8:16–18, YP 6:127, CM 14.18; MS 63 = OM 8:154, YP 6:227, CM 14.224–26.

9. Both points are made more fully in Hale, "Notes on the Style of the Epistle," 266–68.

10. The punctuation inclines one to read the four injunctions as a single linked entity, in which case the middle pair, "judge" and "use," which certainly are linked, might need to be linked in the mind with the surrounding two, "cultivate" and "live and thrive." It is easier to connect the first with the middle pair as concerning how the reader should now read ahead, than to relate the final one, which relaxes his grip and opens out into a concluding generalized benevolence, like any letter and like most of the scriptural ones.

11. G. B. Caird, *The Language and Imagery of the Bible* (Philadelphia, 1980), 33.

12. Luke's Paul, but neither Milton nor his opponents would distinguish. He might have done so, in that Acts is as late as the Gospels are, but now this is not his point.

13. On the Jacobean habit of settling doctrinal disputes by etymology, in this learned and cantankerous milieu, see Adam Nicholson, *When God Spoke English: The Making of the King James Bible* (London, 2011), 91, regarding the difference between a schism and a sect.

Notes to Rutherford, "The Experimental Form of *Lycidas*"

I would like to thank Lee Johnson, Jeff Dolven, Nigel Smith, Vance Smith, Stephen Fallon, Sean Keilen, and the late Marshall Grossman for their comments on this essay.

1. *The Milton Reading Room*, June 2011, www.dartmouth.edu/~milton. John Carey reviews much of the best scholarship on the structure of *Lycidas* in *Milton: Complete Shorter Poems*, rev. ed. (New York, 2007), 237–43. Quotations from *Lycidas* are from this edition. See C. A. Patrides, ed., *Milton's "Lycidas": The Tradition and the Poem*, rev. ed. (Columbia, Mo., 1983), for additional fundamental bibliography.

2. See Edward Weismiller, "Studies of Style and Verse Form in *Paradise Regained*," in *A Variorum Commentary on the Poems of John Milton*, vol. 4, ed. Walter MacKellar (New York, 1975), 253–82. A series of essays by John Creaser, "'Service Is Perfect Freedom': Paradox and Prosodic Style in *Paradise Lost*," *Review of English Studies* 58, no. 235 (2007): 268–315, places Miltonic scansion on a new footing. Creaser rejects classical approaches to verse form in favor of the method of Derek Attridge, providing particularly persuasive evidence of the latter's superiority in dealing with problem lines. I do not engage recent controversies about beats and feet here, since it is my principal intention to indicate how it can be problematic to approach *Lycidas* with *any* theory of metrical prosody.

3. Edward Weismiller, "Studies of Verse Form in the Minor English Poems," in *A Variorum Commentary on the Poems of John Milton*, vol. 2, part 3, ed. A. S. P. Woodhouse and Douglas Bush (New York, 1972), 1070.

4. Ibid., 1072.

5. For an analysis of Pindaric characteristics of *Lycidas*, see Stella Revard, "Alpheus, Arethusa, and the Pindaric Pursuit in *Lycidas*," in *Poetry and Politics: New Essays on Pindar and His World*, ed. P. G. Stanwood (Binghamton, N.Y., 1995). David Norbrook, *Poetry and Politics in the English Renaissance*, rev. ed. (Oxford, 2002), 252–69, situates *Lycidas* in a neo-Spenserian context. I owe particular debts to scholars who have located Italian poetic and musical precedents for Milton's formal techniques. See F. T. Prince, *The Italian Element in Milton's Verse* (Oxford, 1954); Ants Oras, "Milton's Early Rhyme Schemes and the Structure of *Lycidas*," *Modern Philology* 52, no. 1 (1954): 12–22; Clay Hunt, *Lycidas and the Italian Critics* (New Haven, 1979).

6. Simon Daines, *Orthoepia Anglicana* (Menston, 1967), A4–A5.

7. John Milton, *Accedence Commenc'd Grammar*, in *Complete Prose Works of John Milton*, 8 vols., ed. Don M. Wolfe et al. (New Haven, 1953–82), 8:86, hereafter cited as YP. There is a similar comment in *Of Education* about how "the prosody of a verse...could not but have hit on...among the rudiments of grammar" (YP 2:404).

8. Gill's concluding remark, in his chapter on accented rhymed verse, is telling: "To sum up, our poets indulge in such license with types of poems and rhythms, and combinations of both that almost

nothing can be devised which you will not find exemplified in them." *Alexander Gill's Logonomia Anglica*, part 2, ed. and trans. Bror Danielsson and Arvid Gabrielson (Stockholm, 1972), 185.

9. George Saintsbury, *A History of Criticism and Literary Taste in Europe*, vol. 2 (London, 1902), observes that in the second book of Scaliger's *Poetices libri septem*, entitled "Qui et Hyle," "this hyle—this 'material' of poetry—is frankly acknowledged to be verse," adding in a footnote that "the decision of this is all the more remarkable in that Scaliger does not, as unwary moderns might expect, make verse the *form* of Poetry, but the *matter*" (72).

10. *The Genesis of Tasso's Narrative Theory: English Translations of the Early Poetics and a Study of their Comparative Significance*, ed. and trans. Lawrence F. Rhu (Detroit, 1993), 116. Milton extols Tasso as a critical model in *Of Education*, 403–05.

11. Laura Lunger Knoppers, *The 1671 Poems: Paradise Regain'd and Samson Agonistes*, in *The Complete Works of John Milton*, vol. 2 (Oxford, 2008), instances the practice of Samuel Say as an example (lxviii). For more on metrical transformations of Milton's poetry, see Raymond Dexter Havens, *The Influence of Milton on English Poetry* (Cambridge, Mass., 1922); and Dustin Griffin, *Regaining Paradise: Milton and the Eighteenth Century* (Cambridge, 1986).

12. Thomas Fuller, *The Church History of Britain: From the Birth of Jesus Christ until the Year 1648* (1655), ed. James Nichols (Oxford, 1868), 31.

13. Although there is a dearth of explicit metrical analyses like Fuller's, there is extensive implicit evidence that poets expected their readers to understand the significance of deliberate metrical irregularities. John Creaser, "Prosody and Liberty in Milton and Marvell," in *Milton and the Terms of Liberty*, ed. Graham Parry and Joad Raymond (Rochester, N.Y., 2002), is correct to declare that "seventeenth-century poets were as aware as any that verse-form is embodied meaning, not just an envelope" (37). For further information on engagements with Milton's prosody in early editions of *Paradise Lost*, see John Leonard, "'Doing What He Describes': Enactment in Milton's Poetry," *Cithara* 49, no. 1 (2009): 7–25, accessed June 22, 2011, www.ProQuest.com.

14. Henry Cotterill, *Milton's "Lycidas"* (London, 1902), 97. Although many critics acknowledge the unusual metrical structure of this (arguably) eight-stress line, it has not engendered the kind of lengthy and notoriously acrimonious prosodic debate that surrounds the line 621 in book 2 of *Paradise Lost*. Donald Hall, *To Read Poetry* (New York, 1981), provides a conventional discussion of this problematic line, which captures the different effect of the first line of *Lycidas*: "If you were asked to scan the single line—'Rocks, caves, lakes, fens, bogs, dens, and shades

of death'—you would be right to refuse. But if you came upon this line deep in Milton's *Paradise Lost*, when you had learned to step to the tune of iambic pentameter, you would sort it by twos, giving a sharp beat like a foot tap to the even-numbered syllables" (77). Perhaps in consequence, one could say that critics have been right, by and large, to refuse to scan the opening of Milton's most metrically inventive shorter poem.

15. There are salient exceptions to this rule, especially within the sonnet tradition. Poets including Donne and Shakespeare frequently open their poems with metrically deviant lines, such as "Batter my heart, three personed God," or "When to the sessions of sweet summer's thought." Spenser's *The Shepheardes Calender*, an important source for both the content and form of *Lycidas*, provides even more radical metrical experimentation. For an analysis of the "contest" between different metrical forms throughout the *Calender*, see Jeff Dolven, "Spenser's Metrics," in *The Oxford Handbook of Edmund Spenser*, ed. Richard A. McCabe (Oxford, 2010), 385–402.

16. Edward Le Comte, ed., *Justa Edovardo King: A Facsimile Edition of the Memorial Volume in which Milton's "Lycidas" First Appeared* (Norwood, Pa., 1978). Only William More's contribution to the volume, "I do not come like one affrighted," has prosodic irregularities at the start, beginning as it does with a series of partial end-rhymes and irregularly placed caesuras. Unlike in *Lycida*s, however, every line is clearly iambic, and the couplet rhyme scheme is immediately clear.

17. Derek Attridge, *Poetic Rhythms: An Introduction* (Cambridge, 1995), 120–22; George T. Wright, *Hearing the Measures: Shakespeare and Other Inflections* (Madison, Wis., 2001), 172–79.

18. For discussion of the "concent of words and music," and of Milton's knowledge of music theory, see Diane Kelsey McColley, *Poetry and Music in Seventeenth-Century England* (Cambridge, 1997).

19. See Neil Forsyth, "*Lycidas:* A Wolf in Saints' Clothing," *Critical Inquiry* 35 (2009): 695. The clergy's bad music "grates" against the ottava rima form at the close of the ninth paragraph.

20. My argument, in the end, is meant to complicate previous arguments about meter by theorists as different as Derek Attridge, Edward Weismiller, and John Hollander. It is common among metrists to discuss the prosody of a line in terms of rhythm and meter. In *Vision and Resonance* (Oxford, 1975), Hollander explains, "The word of flow, 'rhythm,' characterizes the series of actual effects upon our consciousness of a line or passage of verse: it is the road along which we travel. The meter, then would apply to whatever it was that might constitute the framing, the isolating; its presence we infer from our scanning" (135–36). My argument, in effect, conflates the distinction, since the reader of *Lycidas*, at the beginning of the poem, is not given a

sufficiently regular rhythmic pattern from which to make definitive judgments about the metrical frame.

21. Edward Weismiller, "Rhymes and Reasons," in *Classical, Renaissance, and Postmodernist Acts of the Imagination*, ed. Arthur F. Kinney (Newark, Del., 1996), 239. Milton's own uses of the word "rhyme" usually connote poetry in general, as it does in the first paragraph of *Paradise Lost*.

22. A. E. Barker, "The Pattern of the *Nativity Ode*," *University of Toronto Quarterly* 10, no. 2 (1941): 171–72. For an equally compelling, though much less influential, analysis of the bipartite design of the poem, including an impressive list of imagistic correspondences in the first and second parts, see J. Martin Evans, *The Road from Horton: Looking Backwards in Lycidas* (Victoria, B.C., 1983), 62–63.

23. Tasso, qtd. in Rhu, *The Genesis of Tasso's Narrative Theory*, 116.

24. See Paolo Luparia, ed., *Il mondo creato* (Alessandria, 2006), 1.1–77; 6.1051–1127. There has been a great deal of examination of numerological patterns in Milton's poetry and the contemporary cultural significance of numerology. See Alastair Fowler, ed., *Paradise Lost*, rev. 2nd ed. (New York, 2007), 25–33; all quotations to the poem are from this edition. For more on the "numerological onslaught" and discussion of the methodological problems of numerological analysis, see John K. Hale, "*Paradise Lost*, A Poem in Twelve Books—or Is It Ten?" *Philological Quarterly* 74 (1995): 131–49. In any case, I focus on structural, as opposed to numerological, correspondences in *Lycidas*.

25. This fact about Milton's epic has not, to my knowledge, been noticed. If my argument that Milton creates patterns of allusion between paragraphs by giving them similar structures is correct, it may be worthwhile to look for evidence of this technique in *Paradise Lost* (although discriminating accidental from intentional structural correspondences in paragraphs within an epic poem would require a great deal of tact on the part of the critic).

26. Keith Rinehart, "A Note on the First Fourteen Lines of Milton's *Lycidas*," *Notes and Queries* 198 (1953): 103.

27. Punctuation that is crucial to my argument is stable across the various texts of *Lycidas*. See Creaser's "Editing *Lycidas:* The Authority of Minutiae," *Milton Quarterly* 44, no. 2 (2010): 73–103, for a sophisticated exploration of textual issues and an eclectic text of the poem.

28. Harris Francis Fletcher, ed., *John Milton's Complete Poetical Works, Reproduced in Photographic Facsimile*, vol. 1 (Urbana, Ill., 1943).

29. These paragraphs do not possess a conventional form like sonnet structure, but it is possible that Milton attributed symbolic sig-

nificance to numbers taken from the Fibonacci sequence. See Lee M. Johnson, "Milton's Mathematical Symbol of Theodicy," in *Symmetry: Unifying Human Understanding*, vol. 2, ed. István Hargittai (New York, 1986).

30. Jon S. Lawry, "'Eager Thought': Dialectic in *Lycidas*," PMLA 77, no. 1 (1962): 30.

31. For more on the cyclical rhyme patterns in *Lycidas*, see Joseph Wittreich, "Milton's 'Destined Urn': The Art of *Lycidas*," PMLA 84, no. 1 (1969): 60–70.

32. Forsyth, "*Lycidas*: A Wolf in Saints' Clothing," 691.

33. G. Wilson Knight, *The Burning Oracle: Studies in the Poetry of Action* (Oxford, 1939), 70; Stanley Fish, "*Lycidas*: A Poem Finally Anonymous," in Patrides, *Milton's "Lycidas,"* 319–40.

34. Qtd. in Stephen Dobranski, *Milton, Authorship, and the Book Trade* (Cambridge, 1999), 4.

35. Richardson qtd. in Helen Darbishire, *The Early Lives of John Milton* (1932; reissued Ann Arbor, 1972), 291; Gordon Campbell, "Milton and the Lives of the Ancients," *Journal of the Warburg and Courtauld Institutes* 47 (1984): 237.

36. Franciscus Junius, *The Literature of Classical Art*, ed. Keith Aldrich, Philipp Fehl, and Raina Fehl (Berkeley, 1991), 181, 227. Junius intersperses such commonplaces throughout his work; see, in particular, the second chapter of the third book (225–38), which concerns proportion.

37. Marvin Trachtenberg, "Building Outside Time in Alberti's 'De re aedificatoria,'" *RES: Anthropology and Aesthetics* 48 (2005): 125, accessed June 22, 2011, www.jstor.org/stable/20167681.

38. See Henry Wotton, *The Elements of Architecture: Its Record in Early Printed Books Published in Facsimile* (New York, 1970), 11–12. Milton sought the retired diplomat out in Eton, only a few miles away from his residence at Horton, prior to undertaking his journey to the Continent; for more on this meeting, see Thomas Corns and Gordon Campbell, *John Milton: Life, World, and Thought* (Oxford, 2008), 104.

39. For alternative analyses of the meaning of Milton's temple-building imagery, see David Loewenstein, *Milton and the Drama of History: Historical Vision, Iconoclasm, and the Literary Imagination* (Cambridge, 1990), 35–50; and Noam Reisner, "Spiritual Architectonics: Destroying and Rebuilding the Temple in *Paradise Regained*," *Milton Quarterly* 43, no. 3 (2009): 166–82.

40. Milton refers to the revolt in Ulster that began on October 23, 1641, which he thought constituted evidence of the inefficacy of Charles I and episcopal governance. Corns and Campbell observe that

Milton's sympathy for Protestants in Ireland was "deep-felt and long-standing" (*John Milton*, 214).

41. John Rumrich, "Milton's God and the Matter of Chaos," *PMLA* 110, no. 5 (1995): 1041.

42. John Rumrich, *Matter of Glory: A New Preface to "Paradise Lost"* (Pittsburgh, 1987), 126.

43. Samuel Butler, *Hudibras, Parts I and II and Selected Other Writings*, ed. John Wilders and Hugh de Quehen (Oxford, 1973), 1.1.203–04.

44. Simon Jarvis, "For a Poetics of Verse," *PMLA* 125, no. 4 (2010): 933.

45. For a detailed analysis of the monistic implications of Milton's prosody in *Paradise Lost*, see Beverley Sherry, "Milton, Materialism, and the Sound of *Paradise Lost*," *Essays in Criticism* 60 (2010): 220–41.

Notes to Liebert, "Domestic Adam"

1. John Milton, *Paradise Lost*, ed. Alastair Fowler, 2nd ed. (London, 1998), 9.1155–61. All subsequent references to *Paradise Lost* are to this edition and will be cited parenthetically in the text.

2. Joseph Addison, *Criticisms on John Milton* (London, 1905), 151.

3. For a review of earlier scholarship on the book 9 debate, see Diane McColley, "Free Will and Obedience in the Separation Scene of *Paradise Lost*," *SEL* 12, no. 1 (1972): 104–05.

4. Joan S. Bennett, *Reviving Liberty: Radical Christian Humanism in Milton's Great Poems* (Cambridge, Mass., 1989), 115. Bennett sees Adam's capitulation at the end of the conversation as a failure not so much to command obedience but to persist until Eve truly understood his right reasoning and was able to make her own free choice of good with unclouded mind.

5. Claudia M. Champagne, "Adam and His 'Other Self' in *Paradise Lost:* A Lacanian Study in Psychic Development," *Milton Quarterly* 25, no. 2 (1991): 56.

6. Fredson Bowers, "Adam, Eve, and the Fall in *Paradise Lost*," *PMLA* 84, no. 2 (1969): 270.

7. That Adam should have categorically demanded Eve's obedience is the suggestion of G. K. Hunter, *Paradise Lost* (London, 1980), 196. Robert Erickson claims that Adam "virtually challenged her to leave" in *The Language of the Heart 1660–1750* (Philadelphia, 1997), 129. Ricki Heller, "Opposites of Wifehood: Eve and Dalila," in *Milton Studies*, vol. 24, ed. Albert C. Labriola (Pittsburgh, 1998), 192, condemns Adam's final decision as an abrogation of husbandly authority.

8. Deborah A. Interdonato, "'Render Me More Equal': Gender Inequality and the Fall in *Paradise Lost*, 9," *Milton Quarterly* 29, no. 4 (1995): 98.

9. William Gouge, *Of Domesticall Duties* (London, 1622), 371; hereafter cited parenthetically in the text by page number.

10. William Haller and Malleville Haller, "The Puritan Art of Love," *Huntington Library Quarterly* 5, no. 2 (1942): 256.

11. Alexander Niccholes, *A Treatise of Marriage and Wiving* (London, 1615), 2. See also Henrie Smith, *A Preparative to Mariage* (London, 1591), 8–9; Thomas Carter, *Carters Christian Common Wealth* (London, 1627), 6. Carter, a layman who dedicated his work on matrimony to the Company of Goldsmiths, offers some delightfully homely advice based on the mode of woman's creation: "I see no...fitter place to keepe her in, then that from whence shee came, neere thy heart man, I mean, I know shee came from thence, lay her there again, lay her there again" (7–8). The use of u/v and i/j in early modern quotations has been silently regularized throughout this essay.

12. Niccholes, *A Treatise of Marriage and Wiving*, 1, 6.

13. Smith, *A Preparative to Mariage*, 52, 26.

14. Even at its best, conduct literature for youths is little better than a list with brief explanations of why one should walk or sit or talk in such and such a way. Examples include Erasmus's *De civilitate morum puerilium*, translated by Robert Whittington and reprinted through the sixteenth and seventeenth centuries, and Francis Hawkins's hugely popular *Youths Behavior*, which appeared in ten impressions before 1672. Transposed to verse for mnemonic purposes, such treatises quickly become offensive to modern sensibilities; Robert Crowley's versified *The Schoole of Vertue*, 2nd ed. (London, 1621) is perhaps one of the most nauseating examples.

15. See Gouge, *Of Domesticall Duties*, 280–81, 315–17; Smith, *A Preparative to Mariage*, 59–60.

16. John Heydon, *Advice to a Daughter, in Opposition to the Advice to a Son* (London, 1659), 57.

17. In *A Bride-Bush; or, A Wedding Sermon* (London, 1617), William Whately recommends that the wife learn submission by rote, reminding herself that *"Mine husband is my superiour, my better"* until she has "the lesson perfectly...without booke, even at her fingers ends" (36).

18. Carter, *Christian Common Wealth*, 20.

19. Smith, *A Preparative to Mariage*, 53. Compare also Carter, *Christian Common Wealth*, 42.

20. John Milton, *The Reason of Church-Government*, in *The Complete Prose Works of John Milton*, ed. Don M. Wolfe et al. (New Haven, 1953–82), 1:823. Further references to Milton's prose are to

this edition and will be cited in the text as YP. On Milton's familiarity with Puritan ideas of marriage, see Haller and Haller, "The Puritan Art of Love," 235–37; Chilton Latham Powell, *English Domestic Relations 1487–1653: A Study of Matrimony and Family Life in Theory and Practice as Revealed by the Literature, Law, and History of the Period* (New York, 1917); Catherine Gimelli Martin, ed., *Milton and Gender* (Cambridge, 2004).

21. Smith, *A Preparative to Mariage*, 23.

22. Niccholes, *A Treatise of Marriage and Wiving*, 4, 14.

23. Discussing this initial description of Adam and Eve, John Rogers, "Transported Touch: The Fruit of Marriage in *Paradise Lost*," in Martin, *Milton and Gender*, 115–32, suggests that gender hierarchy in *Paradise Lost* is both arbitrarily imposed by God and essentially frangible because it coexists in paradoxical tension with natural equality. He suggests that although this passage appears to direct the reader toward natural inequality, the only concrete detail it adduces is the first couple's respective hairstyles and dismisses this as "exceedingly fragile evidence," for social convention, not nature, associates women with long hair (123). However, he does not address the simile that compares Eve's hair to the curling vine, a simile that not only suggests by parallel a natural (i.e., created) inequality but also participates in contemporary attempts to explain metaphorically the close inequality of marriage and, most significantly, leads to Milton's most direct engagement with the solution to that paradox: the need to require gently and yield willingly female submission.

24. Haller and Haller, "The Puritan Art of Love," 235.

25. Addison, *Criticisms on Milton*, 96.

26. Roberta C. Martin, "'How Came I Thus?': Adam and Eve in the Mirror of the Other," *College Literature* 27, no. 2 (2000): 66; Leonard Mustazza, *Such Prompt Eloquence: Language as Agency and Character in Milton's Epics* (Lewisburg, Pa., 1988), 74.

27. Martin, "How Came I Thus?" 67.

28. Diane McColley, *Milton's Eve* (Urbana, 1983), 170.

29. In *Terms of Address: Problems of Patterns and Usage in Various Languages and Cultures* (Berlin, 1988), a study of comparative address behavior in English, Portuguese, Norwegian, and Arabic, Friederike Braun examines politeness as a social construct and observes that, when several terms of address are available and equally appropriate in a given situation, the speaker's exercise of choice reveals a great deal about how he or she views the relationship in which he or she stands vis-à-vis the addressee. See particularly 295–96.

30. John Dod and Robert Cleaver, *A Godly Forme of Houshold Government* (London, 1650), N4r [8].

31. Desiderius Erasmus, [*De civilitate morum puerilium*] *A lytell booke of good maners for children*, 2nd ed., trans. Robert Whytyngton (London, 1532), C8v–D1r.

32. Dod and Cleaver, *Houshold Government*, N4r [9]. A similar insistence on the importance of "dutiful titles" underscores Smith's advice to wives: "Likewise the woman may learne her dutie of her names. They are called goodwives, as goodwife *A.* and goodwife *B.* Everie wife is called goodwife; therefore if they be not good wives, their names do belie them, and they are not worth their titles, but answere to a wrong name, as Players doe upon the stage" (*A Preparative to Mariage*, 58).

33. Whately, *A Bride-Bush*, 41. Sarah was a conduct literature favorite: see, for example, Gouge, *Of Domesticall Duties*, 283, and, in *The Colloquies of Erasmus*, trans. Craig R. Thompson (Chicago, 1965), 117, Eulalia, Erasmus's model wife and spokesperson for the duties of women in his colloquy on marriage. Sarah's behavior had, of course, been established as a model for all Christian women by Saint Peter: "For after this manner in the old time the holy women also, who trusted in God, adorned themselves, being in subjection unto their own husbands: Even as Sara obeyed Abraham, calling him lord: whose daughters ye are, as long as ye do well" (1 Pet. 3:5–6).

34. Compare the description of "*a Mistresse, or rather what a Mistresse ought to be,*" in *The Mirrour of Complements*, 2nd ed. (London, 1634): "She never arrived with so much familiarity with man, as to know the Diminutive of his Name, and to call him by it" (179). Clearly, the idea that a virtuous woman would not challenge hierarchy by addressing a man by a pet name was widespread.

35. Thomas Dekker's tongue-in-cheek advice in *Guls Horn Booke* (London, 1609) similarly references the power of names to subvert hierarchy and so corrode hierarchical identity. In this anticonduct manual, the Jacobean gallant is instructed to greet a knight or squire *not* with the title "Sir such a one, or so, but [to] call him Ned or Jack" (19). In other words, he is advised to practice the discursive behaviors specifically advised against in serious conduct literature.

36. Philip Stubbes, *A Christal Glasse for Christian Women* (London, 1623), A4v.

37. The allusion is noted by both Fowler (282–83) and Merritt Y. Hughes, ed., *John Milton: Complete Poems and Major Prose* (New York, 1957), 302–03. Compare also Howard Schultz, "Satan's Serenade," *Philological Quarterly* 22, no. 1 (1948): 25.

38. See Smith, *A Preparative to Mariage*, 49–50; also Gouge, *Of Domesticall Duties*, 117–23, which explores the parallel relationship between man and wife and Christ and the church in some detail.

39. Fowler cites Newton: "The only one of the joys which is a *part* of me" (245). Seventeenth century readers may also have heard in Adam's opening words echoes of the faculty psychology that saw Adam and Eve as higher and lower faculties, respectively, within the psyche. Although discussion of faculty psychology lies outside the scope of this essay, I would direct the reader to two valuable studies: Kenneth Borris, "'Union of Mind, or in Both One Soul': Allegories of Adam and Eve in *Paradise Lost*," in *Milton Studies*, vol. 31, ed. Albert C. Labriola (Pittsburgh, 1995), 45–72, and Kent A. Hieatt, "Eve as Reason in a Tradition of Allegorical Interpretations of the Fall," *Journal of the Warburg and Courtauld Institutes* 43 (1980): 221–26.

40. Smith, *A Preparative to Mariage*, 9.

41. Although the primary focus of Deborah Tannen's discourse analysis is familiar discourse, not literary dialogue, I find her examination of repetition as an "involvement strategy" in *Talking Voices: Repetition, Dialogue, and Imagery in Conversational Discourse* (Cambridge, 1989), particularly interesting in the context of Milton's Eden. Repetition, Tannen writes, "not only ties parts of discourse to other parts, but it bonds participants to the discourse and to each other, linking individual speakers in a conversation in relationships" (52). Repetition is "the level at which messages about relationships are communicated" (96). This certainly seems true of Milton's Adam and Eve.

42. The question with which Eve concludes her second speech has been characterized as abrupt (Hugh MacCallum, *Milton and the Sons of God* [Toronto, 1986], 139) or involving "faulty assumptions" (Barbara Lewalski, "Innocence and Experience in Milton's Eden," in *New Essays on "Paradise Lost,"* ed. Thomas Kranidas [Berkeley and Los Angeles, 1971], 101–02). However, the question emerges naturally from the content of the speech: Eve only enjoys the beauties of Eden as they are mediated through her relationship with Adam; if beauty is enjoyed through relationships and yet all creatures are sleeping, for whom does the beauty of night exist? Thus, the question serves, as Marshall Grossman, *Authors to Themselves: Milton and the Revelation of History* (Cambridge, 1987), maintains, as "a request for discursive understanding of the harmony she has just invoked" (89).

43. *Francis Bacon: A Critical Edition of the Major Works*, ed. Brian Vickers (Oxford, 1996), 443. Rogers maintains that Eve's retrospective characterization of subordination as entailing a lack of freedom in *PL* 9.820–25 "makes clear that the arbitrary marriage commandment helped produce the conditions that made her disobedience possible" ("Transported Touch," 125). However, reading Eve's vocatives as *laudando praecipere* suggests that prelapsarian Eve views marital hierarchy not as a repressive, inflexible restraint but as a flexible, enabling

reality that allows her to participate in and even direct Adam's developing identity while he is reciprocally involved in her growth.

44. Kristin Pruitt, *Gender and the Power of Relationship: "United as one individual Soul" in "Paradise Lost"* (Pittsburgh, 2003), notes a further echo in Adam's description of the effect Eve has on him in 8.521–59 and observes that "both Adam and Eve are saying the same thing: the other is the embodiment of the human bliss represented in the paradisal state" (52).

45. In an article on discursive difference in Eden, Mary Jo Kietzman, "The Fall into Conversation with Eve: Discursive Difference in *Paradise Lost*," *Criticism* 31, no. 1 (1997): 55–88, goes so far as to contend that in their unfallen state Adam and Eve "do not converse." The fault is largely Adam's, for, failing to appreciate and adopt Eve's open, emotionally oriented speech, he consistently deploys a repressed and repressively authoritarian discursive style. Again, this late-twentieth-century response could not be more different from Addison's: "The posture in which he regards her is described with a tenderness not to be expressed, as the whisper with which he awakens her is the softest that ever was conveyed to a lover's ear" (*Criticisms on Milton*, 104).

46. MacCallum writes of that experience: "For both ...it brings home the fact of their separateness. Adam was absent in Eve's dream and their conversation and kisses now are an attempt to effect their reunion" (*Milton and the Sons of God*, 139). Compare also Pruitt's excellent analysis of the impact of the dream on Eve in *Gender and the Power of Relationship*, 92–101.

47. Critics are divided on whether or not Adam's analysis adequately and accurately accounts for the phenomenon Eve experienced; nevertheless, it achieves its end by reassuring her that she has not offended. As Kathleen Swaim observes in *Before and After the Fall: Contrasting Modes in "Paradise Lost"* (Amherst, 1986), "Adam's reasoned estimation of the operations of the 'misjoining' and 'ill-matching' faculty allays Eve's anxieties and clears her mind totally of the event. There is no residue of troublesome memory to burden her future or, as we see in retrospect, to aid her judgment at the moment of crisis: 'So all was clear'd'" (229). While Swaim may well be correct, another possibility exists: that the apparent experiential differences between the two temptations fail to trigger the appropriate response. In the book 5 dream, Eve watches an angel wittingly, willingly disobeying and reveling in its disobedience; in book 9, she is approached by a serpent who ate (it claims) without knowledge, driven only by innocent, natural desire. Had Satan approached Eve a second time as an angel, would a "residue of troublesome memory" have come to her aid? The reader can only speculate. See also Dan Collins, "The Buoyant Mind

in Milton's Eden," in *Milton Studies*, vol. 5, ed. James D. Simmonds (Pittsburgh, 1973), 235–37.

48. Of that final vocative, "O woman," Fowler claims that it is "Not coldly formal, but referring to the ontological relationship between man and wo-man" (488n343). So also John Leonard, *Naming in Paradise: Milton and the Language of Adam and Eve* (Oxford, 1990): "The tone of this is still gentle, and 'Woman' is still a tribute to Eve's nature, but it is significant that Adam shifts from Eve's uniquely individual name to that which declares her origin in him" (41).

49. Heller, "Opposites of Wifehood," 192; Bowers, "Adam, Eve, and the Fall," 270.

50. Smith, *A Preparative to Mariage*, 54–55. Carter's unpolished rhetoric carries all the persuasive power of common sense: "why brother, doest thou thinke to make thy Wife love thee by beating of her, alas silly man, how art thou deceived?" (*Christian Common Wealth*, 20).

51. Smith, *A Preparative to Mariage*, 61.

52. Whately, *A Bride-Bush*, 25. In *Matrimoniall Honour* (London, 1642), Daniel Rogers, who was not a Puritan but a clergyman in the Church of England, also advocates patience with a striking simile: just as coal miners watch the candle that warns of "dampe," hurrying from their work if it should go out and returning when the "dampe is over," so should husbands "give place to this dampe and distemper of discord and contention, and when its over, then returne to thy wonted course" (192).

53. Whately, *A Bride-Bush*, 28.

54. Ibid., 28.

55. Compare also Rogers: "If thou canst posesse thine owne spirit, thou shalt conquer hers. The best victories are by yeelding in this kind. Strange is the nature of a quiet spirit: it must prevaile at last, because it will wayt, till it have no nay" (*Matrimoniall Honour*, 196).

56. Smith, *A Preparative to Mariage*, 49–50.

57. Whately, *A Bride-Bush*, 29–30.

58. Bennett, *Reviving Liberty*, 113–15.

59. Whately, *A Bride-Bush*, 29–30.

60. Lewalski, "Innocence and Experience," 96.

Notes to Komorowski, "Milton's Natural Law"

I am grateful for the perceptive and very generous criticism of David Scott Kastan, Catherine Nicholson, John Rogers, David Quint, and an anonymous reader for *Milton Studies*. I would also like to thank the members of the Pomerium Working Group at Yale University for their comments and encouragement while I was writing this essay.

1. All citations from Milton's prose are taken from *Complete Prose Works of John Milton*, 8 vols., ed. Don M. Wolfe et al. (New Haven, 1953–82), hereafter cited as YP.

2. Citations from *Paradise Lost* are taken from John Milton, *Complete Poems and Major Prose*, ed. Merritt Y. Hughes (New York, 1957), hereafter cited in the text.

3. Stephen M. Fallon, *Milton's Peculiar Grace: Self-Representation and Authority* (Ithaca, N.Y., 2007), 110–45. The quotation is taken from the second edition of *The Doctrine and Discipline of Divorce* (YP 2:226).

4. For the biographical context of Milton's writing of the divorce tracts, see Barbara Kiefer Lewalski, *The Life of John Milton: A Critical Biography*, rev. ed. (Oxford, 2003), 154–97; and Gordon Campbell and Thomas N. Corns, *John Milton: Life, Work, and Thought* (Oxford, 2008), 152–85.

5. On the development of natural law arguments in the constitutional debates of the 1640s, see Ernest Sirluck, vol. ed., YP 2:21–51, 130–35; Richard Tuck, *Natural Rights Theories: Their Origin and Development* (Cambridge, 1979), 101–18; Victoria Kahn, *Wayward Contracts: The Crisis of Political Obligation in England, 1640–1674* (Princeton, N.J., 2004), 95–111; and Perez Zagorin, *Hobbes and the Law of Nature* (Princeton, N.J., 2009).

6. In the second edition of *Doctrine and Discipline* (YP 2:350–51), Milton's final chapter asserts that the civil prohibition of divorce violated the law of nature and of nations. He cites John Selden's *De iure naturali & gentium, iuxta disciplinam Ebræorum* (London, 1640) in support of his position, but does not strongly integrate the claim in this work.

7. All scriptural citations are taken from the Authorized Version (1611). In *Tetrachordon* and, later, in *De doctrina*, Milton specifies that "fornication" is to be understood extremely liberally, including "a constant alienation and disaffection of mind" (YP 2:673) or, in fact, "anything which is found to be persistently at variance with love, fidelity, help and society" (YP 6:378).

8. On the idealism of Milton's claim that ending a sinful marriage represents true Christian charity and his at times contradictory impulses to lash out at intellectual and personal foes in *Doctrine and Discipline*, see James Grantham Turner, *One Flesh: Paradisal Marriage and Sexual Relations in the Age of Milton* (Oxford, 1987), 188–229.

9. Anonymous, *An Answer to a Book, Intituled, The Doctrine and Discipline of Divorce* (London, 1644), 29.

10. This refrain echoes throughout *Tetrachordon*. For similar sentiments, see YP 2:618 and 2:653. See also *Doctrine and Discipline* (YP 2:272, 309–10).

11. Milton articulates the germ of these sentiments in the second edition of *Doctrine and Discipline* (YP 2:228–29).

12. For a body of scholarship so attentive to the intricacies of the development of Milton's thought, the critical literature has been curiously less willing to discuss *Tetrachordon* as substantively as *Doctrine and Discipline*. *Tetrachordon* is most often engaged as Milton's restatement of *Doctrine and Discipline* with greater attention to Scripture, which has the effect of flattening differences between the two texts and of shifting the critical discussion to *Doctrine and Discipline* as if *Tetrachordon* were a bastardized version of the early, uncorrupt form of the argument. I suspect that the vibrant rhetoric and imagery of *Doctrine and Discipline* with its unforgettable carcasses chained together and its invocation of Eros and Anteros are largely responsible for this critical preference, but *Tetrachordon* presents Milton's argument refined to an exceptional degree, thoroughly incorporating his thinking on natural law and on the harmony of Mosaic law and Gospel. Substantive treatments of *Tetrachordon* can be found in Reuben Sánchez Jr., *Persona and Decorum in Milton's Prose* (Madison, N.J., 1997), 77–96; and Fallon, *Milton's Peculiar Grace*, 122–32.

13. Turner, *One Flesh*, 191.

14. What Milton calls "the *secondary law of nature and of nations*" was most often understood in the period as the *ius gentium*, or the law of nations, a set of positive laws common to many nations. God permits these laws because humans have fallen and regulations governing social hierarchies and property ownership have become necessary. The lawyer Sir John Davies (1569–1626), arguing for royal prerogative, describes the origins of the law of nations: "By the Law of Nature all things were cōmon, and all persons equal, there was neither *Meum* nor *Tuum*, there was neither King nor Subject; then came in the Law of Nations, which did limit the Law of Nature, and brought in property, which tooke awaye communitye of thinges, which brought in Kings and Rulers, which took away equality of persons, for property caused Contracts, Trade, and Traffique, which could not be ministred without a King or Magistrate; so as the first and principal cause of making Kings, was to maintain property and Contracts, and Traffique, and Commerce amongst men." See John Davies, *The Question concerning Impositions, Tonnage, Poundage, Prizage, Customs, &c.* (London, 1656), 29. This work circulated in manuscript from the mid-1620s. I have emended a clause in the printed work, "which brought in community of things," with the manuscript reading "wch tooke awaye Cōmunitye of thinges." See *Whether the Kinge of England by His Prerogative May Sett Impositions, Loanes or Privy Seales without Assent of Parliament*, Osborn MS b166, Beinecke Library, Yale

University, f. 18v. On the early modern understanding of the relationship of the *ius gentium* to positive and natural law more generally, see Donald Kelley, "Civil Science in the Renaissance: The Problem of Interpretation," in *The Languages of Political Theory in Early-Modern Europe*, ed. Anthony Pagden (Cambridge, 1987), esp. 72–76.

15. Jason P. Rosenblatt, *Torah and Law in "Paradise Lost"* (Princeton, N.J., 1994), 51–52, draws a sharper distinction than I do between the "privilege and exclusivity of private property" in Edenic marriage and the possibility of alienating that property which the Deuteronomic law permits. But the fact that marriage is property for Milton necessarily extends the relevance of the Deuteronomic law to Eden.

16. Milton hints at this distinction in the second edition of *Doctrine and Discipline*, calling marriage "a civil, an indifferent, a sometime diswaded Law" (YP 2:228–29), while "divorce is not a matter of Law but of Charity" (345), and "to forbid divorce compulsively, is not only against nature, but against law" (346).

17. John Rogers, "Transported Touch: The Fruit of Marriage in *Paradise Lost*," in *Milton and Gender*, ed. Catherine Gimelli Martin (Cambridge, 2004), 115–32, makes this observation, although he finds this chapter less theologically coherent than I argue here. He argues that Milton's difficulty in explaining the theological necessity of the prohibition governing the tree of knowledge in *De doctrina* affects his representation of Eve in *Paradise Lost* as Milton must account for her fall by means of an inherently fragile gender hierarchy.

18. See also *Christian Doctrine* (YP 6:383–84).

19. YP 6:388; *De doctrina Christiana*, in *The Works of John Milton*, 20 vols., gen. ed. Frank Allen Patterson (New York, 1931–40), 15:190, hereafter cited as CM. I have emended the somewhat misleading translation of "civil rights" for *civitatem* in YP to "citizenship." Milton follows Ames on this point, although it is Milton's innovation to link the Fall with the loss of land and citizenship. Compare with Ames's position that Adam fell not only as an individual, "but also as a publique person," in *The Marrow of Sacred Divinity, Drawne out of the Holy Scriptures, and the Interpreters Thereof, and Brought into Method* (London, 1642), 54–55.

20. See Steve Pincus, "Neither Machiavellian Moment nor Possessive Individualism: Commercial Society and the Defenders of the English Commonwealth," *American Historical Review* 103 (1998): 705–36.

21. For helpful background on Grotius's intellectual development, see Richard Tuck, "Grotius and Selden," in *The Cambridge History of Political Thought, 1450–1700*, ed. J. H. Burns and Mark Goldie (Cambridge, 1991), 499–529; and Richard Tuck, *Philosophy and Government, 1572–1651* (Cambridge, 1993), 154–201.

22. Hugo Grotius, *The Rights of War and Peace* [*De jure belli ac pacis*], 3 vols., ed. Jean Barbeyrac and Richard Tuck (Indianapolis, 2005 [1625]), 1:xx (Pro., 11).

23. Ibid., 1:xiv. Grotius assigns this position to the ancient skeptic Carneades. Carneades' position has survived only secondhand in Lactantius, *Divine Institutes*, 5.17. See the translation by William Fletcher in *The Ante-Nicene Fathers: Translations of the Writings of the Fathers down to A. D. 325*, 10 vols., ed. Alexander Roberts and James Donaldson (Grand Rapids, Mich., 1979–82), 7:151–52.

24. Grotius, *The Rights of War and Peace*, 2:145–46 (2.2.2.2–5).

25. Ibid., 2:185–215 (2.5). In his manuscript work *De iure praedae*, written nearly 20 years earlier, he had been even more explicit: "liberty in regard to actions is equivalent to ownership in regard to property" (*quod libertas in actionibus idem est dominium in rebus*). See Hugo Grotius, *Commentary on the Law of Prize and Booty*, ed. Martine Julia van Ittersum, trans. Gwladys L. Williams (Indianapolis, 2006), 34; Grotius, *De jure praedae commentarius*, ed. H. G. Hamaker (The Hague, 1868), 18. See also Tuck's discussion of this idea and Grotius's development of international maritime law in *Natural Rights Theories*, 59–62.

26. This was especially true of Henry Parker, an important figure in the development of natural law arguments for Parliamentarians, who rejected Grotius's theory of voluntary servitude. See Michael Mendle, *Henry Parker and the English Civil War: The Political Thought of the Public's "Privado"* (Cambridge, 1995), 131–32.

27. Anthony Ascham, *Of the Confusions and Revolutions of Government*, 2nd ed. (London, 1649), 18.

28. Ibid., 21.

29. Ibid., 22. The scriptural reference is 1 Samuel 21:1–6. Jesus cites this episode as an instance of obedience to the spirit if not the letter of the law in Matthew 12:3–4.

30. See William Ames, *Marrow of Sacred Divinity*, 55, and, for example, Henry Vane, *The Retired Mans Meditations, or the Mysterie and Power of Godliness* (London, 1655), 60, who goes further than Ames and assimilates the command to abstain from the fruit with the natural law.

31. *Christian Doctrine* (YP 6:353). On the arbitrariness of the command and the indifference of the fruit, see Michael Lieb, *Poetics of the Holy: A Reading of "Paradise Lost"* (Chapel Hill, N.C., 1981), 89–118. On Milton's thoughts on things indifferent more generally, see Victoria Kahn, *Machiavellian Rhetoric: From the Counter-Reformation to Milton* (Princeton, N.J., 1994), 171–84.

32. John Selden, *De iure naturali & gentium*, 1.9, esp. 109–13. For this account of Selden's thought, I have relied on J. P. Sommerville,

"John Selden, the Law of Nature, and the Origins of Government," *Historical Journal* 27 (1984): 437–47, which builds on Tuck's discussion of Selden in *Natural Rights Theories*, but takes issue with him on this point. Tuck has subsequently incorporated Sommerville's critique into a more expansive view of Selden's contributions to natural law theory in his *Philosophy and Government*, 214–18. See also the learned work of G. J. Toomer, who finds Selden's thoughts on the transmission of natural law more equivocal in *John Selden: A Life in Scholarship*, 2 vols. (Oxford, 2009), 2:502–04. For Milton's relationship with Selden's thoughts on natural law, see Rosenblatt, *Torah and Law*, 126–29, whose account I modify slightly.

33. Whether this formulation of natural law was revolutionary or merely revamped has been debated widely. For the argument of novelty, see Tuck, *Natural Rights Theories*; Ian Shapiro, *The Evolution of Rights in Liberal Theory: An Essay in Critical Anthropology* (Cambridge, 1986); Michael P. Zuckert, *Natural Rights and the New Republicanism* (Princeton, N.J., 1994), 119–49; Knud Haakonssen, *Natural Law and Moral Philosophy: From Grotius to the Scottish Enlightenment* (Cambridge, 1996); and most of the essays in *Rhetoric and Law in Early Modern Europe*, ed. Victoria Kahn and Lorna Hutson (New Haven, 2001). For an opposing position, see Johann Sommerville's essay in *Rhetoric and Law*, which argues that the natural law formulations of Grotius and Selden represent no substantial rhetorical or conceptual change over earlier Thomist models: "Selden, Grotius, and the Seventeenth-Century Intellectual Revolution in Moral and Political Theory," 318–44.

34. On Milton's intellectual debts to Grotius and Selden on this issue, see especially Jason P. Rosenblatt, *Renaissance England's Chief Rabbi: John Selden* (Oxford, 2006), 135–57. For a contrasting picture of Hobbes's and Milton's conceptions of natural law, see Catherine Gimelli Martin, "The Phoenix and the Crocodile: Milton's Natural Law Debate with Hobbes Retried in the Tragic Forum of *Samson Agonistes*," in *The English Civil Wars in the Literary Imagination*, ed. Claude J. Summers and Ted-Larry Pebworth (Columbia, Mo., 1999), 242–70. On Milton's engagement with Hobbes's conception of liberty, especially toleration, see Christopher N. Warren, "When Self-Preservation Bids: Approaching Milton, Hobbes, and Dissent," *English Literary Renaissance* 37 (2007): 118–50.

35. See, for instance, *Areopagitica* (YP 2:515–16, 527).

36. Lieb stresses the importance of the literal meaning of "reasonless" as without reason, that is, inapprehensible by means of the faculty of reason (*Poetics of the Holy*, 96).

37. Contemporary legal definitions of divorce always list its two types: *a mensa et thoro* (separation) and *a vinculo matrimonii*

(dissolution). See, for instance, Thomas Blount, *NOMO-ΛΕΞΙΚΟΝ: A Law-Dictionary* (London, 1670), s.v. "divorce."

38. On Adam's joint role with God in Eve's creation and the subsequent complication of prelapsarian communication and poetic accommodation, see Jeffrey S. Shoulson, *Milton and the Rabbis: Hebraism, Hellenism, and Christianity* (New York, 2001), 185–88. See also Shoulson's account of the rabbinical understanding of Moses' efforts to save his people from divine destruction (113–17).

39. Rosenblatt, *Torah and Law*, 200.

40. Adam has been insecure in his sense of self since meeting Eve. On this and his abandonment of discursive reason in Eve's company, see David Quint, *Epic and Empire: Politics and Generic Form from Virgil to Milton* (Princeton, N.J., 1993), 288–92.

41. On this manner of framing theological problems in the poem more generally, see Dennis H. Burden, *The Logical Epic: A Study of the Argument of "Paradise Lost"* (Cambridge, Mass., 1967), esp. 157–62, on the logic of Adam remaining undeceived.

42. Milton proposes the titles *Samson marriing* and *Salomon Gynæcocratumenus*, that is, "women-governed," in the Trinity manuscript among his numerous ideas for biblical tragedy (YP 8:556). For descriptions of these figures as "uxorious," see *Samson Agonistes*, 945, and *Paradise Lost*, 1.444.

43. This acute attention to himself just before the Fall evokes Eve's love of her own reflection in the pool in book 4. See John Guillory, "Milton, Narcissism, Gender: On the Genealogy of Male Self-Esteem," in *Critical Essays on John Milton*, ed. Christopher Kendrick (New York, 1995), 194–233. On the implications for gender, see Mary Nyquist's classic essay, "The Genesis of Gendered Subjectivity in the Divorce Tracts and in *Paradise Lost*," in *Re-membering Milton: New Essays on the Texts and the Traditions*, ed. Mary Nyquist and Margaret W. Ferguson (New York, 1987), 99–127.

44. For reasons that I explain below, I cannot endorse Burden's claim that Adam ought to have sued for divorce (*Logical Epic*, 163–77). Dennis Danielson's much subtler argument contends that by the logic of typology, Adam could have fulfilled Christ's redemptive function by offering to sacrifice himself for Eve's sin. See his "Through the Telescope of Typology: What Adam Should Have Done," *Milton Quarterly* 23 (1989): 121–27. This argument is much closer to the poetics of marriage in *Paradise Lost* by which Adam's love for Eve necessarily informs, but does not erase, his view of himself. The ideal version of that marriage would have Adam distinguish himself from Eve in some meaningful way.

45. In *De doctrina*, Milton specifies that the description of marriage in Genesis 2:23–24 ("one flesh") has nothing to do with monogamy since the example of patriarchs such as Abraham reveals marriage as both polygamous and godly (YP 6:355–56).

46. John Rogers, *The Matter of Revolution: Science, Poetry, and Politics in the Age of Milton* (Ithaca, N.Y., 1996), 144–76, draws attention to the conflicting and contradictory accounts that the Father provides for the expulsion of Adam and Eve from the garden. One is naturalistic (11.48–57), the other interventive (11.93–111), and the contrast between these explanations highlights the change in Adam and Eve's subjectivity as they move from "shadowy Types to truth" in their interaction with the divine. Their rational obedience will be based not on fear or custom but free choice. Rogers locates this momentous shift only in the final lines of the poem, but I argue that such a change begins much earlier.

47. Stanley Fish, *Surprised by Sin: The Reader in "Paradise Lost,"* 2nd ed. (Cambridge, Mass., 1997), 154–55, argues that the curse is simply a ratification of what has already taken place in nature. God formalizes the serpent's corruption because the serpent has become "polluted" (*PL* 10.167). The question of fairness is beside the point in this reading.

48. Milton had begun to work out this symbolism in *De doctrina* as he read the episode of the brazen serpent of Numbers 21:4–9 as evidence of Christ's spiritual presence among the Israelites (YP 6:282). For the importance of this imagery in *Paradise Lost* and *Paradise Regained*, see Neil Forsyth, "At the Sign of the Dove and Serpent," *Milton Quarterly* 34 (2000): 57–65.

Notes to Wallace, "Miltonic Proportions"

1. John Milton, *Paradise Lost*, 2nd ed., ed. Alastair Fowler (New York, 2007), 9.689–90. All quotations of the poem are from this edition and will be cited parenthetically in the text by book and line number.

2. The classic study of the lot in Athenian society is James Wycliffe Headlam, *Election by Lot at Athens* (Cambridge, 1891). Headlam's study notes the tension between the religious function of lots as an appeal to the gods and their purely political function as a mechanism for selection. Later scholarship has seen more continuity between religion and politics in the ancient world, notably E. R. Dodds, *The Greeks and the Irrational* (Berkeley and Los Angeles, 1951), 42. See also Richard G. Mulgan, "Lot as a Democratic Device of

Selection," *Review of Politics* 46 (1984): 539–60; William A. Beardslee, "The Casting of Lots at Qumran and in the Book of Acts," *Novum Testamentum* 4 (1960): 245–52; and Neal M. Soss, "Old Testament Law and Economic Society," *Journal of the History of Ideas* 34 (1973): 325–28.

3. See Numbers 26:55–56: "Notwithstanding the land shall be divided by lot: according to the names of the tribes of their fathers they shall inherit. / According to the lot shall the possession thereof be divided between many and few." I cite the Bible from the Authorized Version of 1611.

4. Sixteenth century scholars often acknowledged the value of lots in maintaining equality and fairness in civil society. Jean Bodin and Louis Le Roy noted the widespread use of lots in Israelite, Athenian, Persian, and even contemporary Venetian society; see Bodin, *The Six Bookes of a Common-Weale* (1576), trans. Richard Knolles (London, 1606), 734; and Le Roy's commentary in *Aristotles Politiques; or, Discourses of Government*, trans. I. D. (London, 1598), 88. During the English Interregnum, some wove the use of lots into their vision of a reformed commonwealth; see James Harrington, *The Political Works of James Harrington*, ed. J. G. A. Pocock (Cambridge, 1977), 212–22, 363–65; and *Chaos; or, A Discourse wherein is Presented... a Frame of Government by Way of a Republique* (London, 1659), 41.

5. Stephen M. Fallon, *Milton among the Philosophers: Poetry and Materialism in Seventeenth-Century England* (Ithaca, N.Y., 1991), 79–110; and John P. Rumrich, "Milton's Arianism: Why It Matters," in *Milton and Heresy*, ed. Stephen B. Dobranski and John P. Rumrich (Cambridge, 1998), 75–92.

6. See John T. Shawcross, *John Milton: The Self and the World* (Lexington, Ky., 1993), 243; Victoria Silver, "'A Taken Scandal Not a Given': Milton's Equitable Grounds of Toleration," in *Milton and Toleration*, ed. Sharon Achinstein and Elizabeth Sauer (Oxford, 2007), 166–67; and Stephen M. Fallon, "'Elect above the rest': Theology as Self-Representation in Milton," in Dobranski and Rumrich, *Milton and Heresy*, 105–06.

7. Victoria Kahn, *Wayward Contracts: The Crisis of Political Obligation in England, 1640–1674* (Princeton, N.J., 2004), 220–21.

8. Milton's epic thus acknowledges, but revises, the seventeenth century debate about rights-based versus duty-based natural law that occupied Grotius, Hobbes, and Pufendorf; for a discussion of which, see Knud Haaksonssen, *Natural Law and Moral Philosophy: From Grotius to the Scottish Enlightenment* (Cambridge, 1996), 26–42.

9. See Diane Kelsey McColley, "'All in all': The Individuality of Creatures in *Paradise Lost*," in *All in All: Unity, Diversity, and the*

Miltonic Perspective, ed. Charles W. Durham and Kristin A. Pruitt (Selinsgrove, Pa., 1999), 25.

10. J. M. Evans, *"Paradise Lost" and the Genesis Tradition* (Oxford, 1968), 14.

11. For the argument that Milton's view of inequality is relatively inflexible, see Mary Nyquist, "The Genesis of Gendered Subjectivity in the Divorce Tracts and in *Paradise Lost,*" in *Re-Membering Milton: Essays on the Texts and Traditions,* ed. Nyquist and Margaret W. Ferguson (New York, 1987), 99–127. But Jason P. Rosenblatt, *Torah and the Law in "Paradise Lost,"* (Princeton, N.J., 1994), 201, argues for a more "monistic" view of Genesis 2, wherein the priority of Adam matters less for Milton than the material unity of the first humans. See also Rosenblatt's edition of Milton's poetry, *Milton's Selected Poetry and Prose* (New York, 2011), 233, where he disagrees with the "overwhelmingly negative" readings of Milton's gender politics in the 1980s.

12. See especially Diane Kelsey McColley, *Milton's Eve* (Urbana, Ill., 1983), 22–61; Joan S. Bennett, *Reviving Liberty: Radical Christian Humanism in Milton's Great Poems* (Cambridge, Mass., 1989), 94–118; Deborah A. Interdonato, "'Render Me More Equal': Gender Inequality and the Fall in *Paradise Lost,* 9," *Milton Quarterly* 29 (1995): 95–106; Elisabeth Liebert, "Rendering 'More Equal': Eve's Changing Discourse in *Paradise Lost,*" *Milton Quarterly* 37 (2003): 152–65; Alice M. Mathews, "'Among Unequals What Society': The Dynamics of Punishment in *Paradise Lost,*" in *Arenas of Conflict: Milton and the Unfettered Mind,* ed. Kristin Pruitt McColgan and Charles W. Durham (Selinsgrove, Pa., 1997), 129–39; Joshua Scodel, *Excess and the Mean in Early Modern English Literature* (Princeton, N.J., 2002), 275–79; and John Rogers, "Transported Touch: The Fruit of Marriage in *Paradise Lost,*" in *Milton and Gender,* ed. Catherine Gimelli Martin (Cambridge, 2004), 115–32.

13. For Satan's introduction of dualistic, Pauline notions of spiritual mobility into the garden, see Rosenblatt, *Torah and the Law,* 164–203.

14. *Decretum gratiani emendatum et notationibus illustratum,* vol. 1, *Corpus iuris canonici* (Rome, 1582), cols. 119–20; consulted through UCLA's Canon Law archive, available at digital.library.ucla.edu/canonlaw; the translation is my own. For an etymology and history of the terms "lot" and "cleric" from one of Milton's contemporaries, see Joseph Mede, *The Works of the Pious and Profoundly-Learned Joseph Mede, B.D., Sometimes Fellow of Christ's Colledge in Cambridge,* ed. John Worthington (London, 1672), 182; see also C. T. Onions, *The Oxford Dictionary of English Etymology* (Oxford, 1966), s.v. "cleric."

Thanks to Paul Harvey and Laura Lunger Knoppers for significantly increasing my knowledge of the etymological history of these terms.

15. Gillespie, *An Assertion of the Government of the Church of Scotland in the Points of Ruling-Elders* (Edinburgh, 1641), 4–5.

16. *The Complete Prose Works of John Milton*, 8 vols., ed. Don M. Wolfe et al. (New Haven, 1953–82), 1:540. All references to Milton's prose are from this edition, hereafter cited as YP.

17. For a reading of Satan and his angels as parodies of the original 12 disciples, see Lee Erickson, "Satan's Apostles and the Nature of Faith in *Paradise Lost* Book 1," *Studies in Philology* 94 (1997): 382–94.

18. Thomas Gataker, *Of the Nature and Use of Lots: A Treatise Historicall and Theologicall*, 2nd rev. ed. (London, 1627), 332.

19. Ibid., 188–89; "ordinary providence" from Lorraine Daston, *Classical Probability in the Enlightenment* (Princeton, N.J., 1988), 155.

20. For the argument that Milton's theology allows partial knowledge of God by means of his representation in Scripture, see Neil D. Graves, "Milton and the Theory of Accommodation," *Studies in Philology* 98 (2001): 251–72.

21. Vincent Alsop, *Melius Inquirendum; or, A Sober Inquirie into the Reasonings of the Serious Inquirie* (London, 1678), 243.

22. See Reid Barbour, *Literature and Religious Culture in Seventeenth-Century England* (Cambridge, 2002), 215–16.

23. See Nicholas Tyacke, *Anti-Calvinists: The Rise of English Arminianism, c. 1590–1640* (Oxford, 1987), 7, 53.

24. Thomas Jackson, *The Works of Thomas Jackson*, 12 vols. (Oxford, 1844), 1:lxiii.

25. Robert Shelford, *Five Pious and Learned Discourses* (Cambridge, 1635), 193.

26. John Owen, *A Display of Arminianisme* (London, 1643), 29.

27. For the difference between the democratic "lot" and the aristocratic "vote," see Bernard Manin, *The Principles of Representative Government* (Cambridge, 1997), 70–71.

28. See Dennis Danielson, *Milton's Good God: A Study in Literary Theodicy* (Cambridge, 1982), 49, 158; Benjamin Myers, *Milton's Theology of Freedom* (New York, 2006), 112–25; Stephen Jablonski, "'Freely We Serve': *Paradise Lost* and the Paradoxes of Political Liberty," in McColgan and Durham, *Arenas of Conflict*, 109–14; and Fallon, *Milton among the Philosophers*, 214–15.

29. See Marshall Grossman, *"Authors to Themselves": Milton and the Revelation of History* (Cambridge, 1987), 34.

30. Critics of the poem have remarked on the way that Chaos itself functions as a generative force, which means that "unpredictability and complexity are not synonymous with randomness nor antithetical

to a monist conception of the world"; see Mary F. Norton, "'The rising world of waters dark and deep': Chaos Theory and *Paradise Lost*," in McColgan and Durham, *Arenas of Conflict*, 141. See also John Rumrich, "Milton's God and the Matter of Chaos," *PMLA* 110 (1995): 1035–46; Yaakov Mascetti, "Satan and the 'Incomposed' Visage of Chaos: Milton's Hermeneutic Indeterminacy," in *Milton Studies*, vol. 50, ed. Albert C. Labriola (Pittsburgh, 2009), 35–63; and David Quint, "Fear of Falling: Icarus, Phaethon, and Lucretius in *Paradise Lost*," *Renaissance Quarterly* 57 (2004): 859–61.

31. For an influential critical formulation of this conflict between fortune and art, see Martha C. Nussbaum, *The Fragility of Goodness: Luck and Ethics in Greek Tragedy and Philosophy* (Cambridge, 1986), 89–121, 298–306.

32. See Johann Heinrich Alsted, *Templum musicum*, trans. John Birchensha (London, 1664): "after a proportion of Equality, a proportion of inequality followeth" (7). And, "As in numbers there is one proportion of Equality, and another of Inequality: So also in Sounds, one is equal, and another is unequal. And again as in numbers, the Proportion of quality is the *Radix* of all the rest: So in Sounds, the Simple Unison is the principal and *Radix* of all Musical *Intervals*. For the Simple Unison doth consist of a proportion of Equality" (16).

33. Servius Grammaticus, *Servii Grammatici qui feruntur in Vergilii Bucolica et Georgica commentarii*, vol. 3, fasc. 1, ed. Georgius Thilo (Leipzig, 1887), 105; my translation.

34. See Liebert, "Rendering 'More Equal,'" 155.

35. See Karen Edwards, "Ant," *Milton Quarterly* 39 (2005): 192–94.

36. Selden, *De synedriis et praefecturis juridicis veterum ebraeorum*, in *Johannis Seldeni jurisconsulti opera omnia*, 3 vols., ed. David Wilkins (London, 1726), 1:1258; my translation.

37. Hobbes, *Leviathan*, ed. Richard Tuck (Cambridge, 1991), 296–97.

38. Hobbes, *Elements of Law, Natural and Politic*, ed. Ferdinand Tönnies (Cambridge, 1928), 70.

39. Bodin, *Six Bookes of a Common-Weale*, 757; see Euripides, *Phoenissae*, ed. Donald J. Mastronarde (Cambridge, 1994), line 538.

40. See Jason P. Rosenblatt, *Renaissance England's Chief Rabbi: John Selden* (Oxford, 2006), 229–30; Richard Tuck, *Philosophy and Government, 1572–1651* (Cambridge, 1993), 217–19; and Tuck, *Natural Rights Theories: Their Origin and Development* (Cambridge, 1979), 126–30.

41. Theobald, *Discourse concerning the Basis and Original of Government... wherein the Excellency of Monarchy above any other Kind is Evidently Demonstrated* (London, 1667), 12.

42. See Bodin, *Six Bookes of a Common-Weale*, 757.

43. Plato, *Laws*, 2 vols., ed. and trans. R. G. Bury (1926; repr., Cambridge, Mass., 1967), 1:415 (757d–e).

44. Alexander, *God's Covenant Displayed by John Alexander, a Converted Jew* (London, 1689), 13–14; see also Shawcross, *The Self and the World*, 134–35.

45. Alexander, *God's Covenant*, 15–16.

46. Jackson, *A Treatise of the Divine Essence and Attributes*, in Jackson, *Works*, 5:207.

Notes to Groves, "Pilgrimage in *Paradise Lost*"

I would like to express my thanks to John Barton and Melanie Marshall, who helped me with aspects of this essay.

1. William Blake, *Milton a Poem and the Final Illuminated Works: The Ghost of Abel, on Homer's Poetry [and] on Virgil, Laocoön*, ed. Robert N. Essick and Joseph Viscomi (London, 1993), 213 (see notes to lines 27–28); Nancy M. Goslee, "'In Englands Green & Pleasant Land': The Building of Vision in Blake's Stanzas from *Milton*," *Studies in Romanticism* 13 (1974): 109. The allusion to the myth is generally accepted by editors despite the lack of documentary evidence of the myth prior to the 1890s: A. W. Smith, "'And Did Those Feet...?': The 'Legend' of Christ's Visit to Britain," *Folklore* 100, no. 1 (1989): 63–83.

2. For the importance of feet in Blake's *Milton*, see Blake, *Milton: A Poem*, 20–21, 27–28. For feet in pilgrim narratives, see Adamnan, *Adamnan's De locis sanctis*, ed. Denis Meehan, *Scriptores Latini Hiberniae V*.3 (Dublin, 1958), 64–65; *The Pylgrymage of Sir Richard Guylforde to the Holy Land, A.D. 1506*, ed. Henry Ellis (London, 1851), 51, 49, 32–33; M. C. Seymour, ed., *The Defective Version of Mandeville's Travels*, (Oxford, 2002): 47. Both Blake and pilgrim narratives are also influenced by Isaiah: "How beautiful upon the mountains are the feet of him that bringeth good tidings" (52:7). All biblical references are to the King James translation, as this is the version Milton predominantly uses in *Paradise Lost:* James H. Sims, *The Bible in Milton's Epics* (Gainesville, Fla., 1962), 4–5; Harris Francis Fletcher, *The Use of the Bible in Milton's Prose* ...(Urbana, 1929), 94.

3. For more on the widespread tradition of the sacred footprint, see Alexandra Walsham, "Footprints and Faith: Religion and the Landscape in Early Modern Britain and Ireland," in *God's Bounty? The Churches and the Natural World*, ed. Peter Clarke and Tony Claydon (Woodbridge, 2010), 169–83.

4. Goslee, "'In Englands Green & Pleasant Land,'" 108n5.

5. Seymour, *Defective Version of Mandeville's Travels*, 3. The proverbial nature of this belief is shown by its presence over 200 years later in Shakespeare's *1 Henry IV:* "those holy fields / Over whose acres walked those blessed feet" (1.1.24–25). The usage of u/v and i/j has been silently modernized throughout this essay.

6. *The Ynformacion* (ca. 1480–1526), published in Josephie Brefeld, "An Account of a Pilgrimage to Jerusalem," *Zeitschrift des Deutschen Palästina-Vereins* 101, no. 2 (1985): 139. This stone had been presented by the Dominicans to Henry III and was one of the most precious relics of Edward the Confessor's shrine in Westminster Abbey; see D. J. Hall, *English Mediaeval Pilgrimage* (London, 1965), 178.

7. John Milton, *Paradise Lost*, ed. Alastair Fowler, 2nd ed. (London, 2007), 11.329; hereafter cited in the text.

8. Fowler's note to 11.307–10. See the notes to 11.315–33, 429–47, 450–52, 504–06, 553–54, 599–602, 632–36, 770–73. For an exploration of Adam's growth under Michael's tutelage, see Ann W. Astell, "The Medieval *Consolatio* and the Conclusion of *Paradise Lost*," *Studies in Philology* 82 (1985): 477–92.

9. Hebrews 11:13. All biblical quotations are from *The Holy Bible, Conteyning the Old Testament and the New,* King James version (London, 1612). "Civitatem vero Dei peregrinantem in hoc saeculo," in Augustine, *De civitate Dei, corpus Christianorum, series Latina* 48, book 15, chap. 20, lines 13–14. Translation from *Concerning the City of God against the Pagans*, ed. G. R. Evans, trans. Henry Bettenson (London, 2003), 630.

10. For the classic statement of the "pilgrim theme" in *Paradise Lost*, see Mary Christopher Pecheux, "Abraham, Adam, and the Theme of Exile in *Paradise Lost*," *PMLA* 80, no. 4 (1965): 365–71. See also N. H. Keeble, "Wilderness Exercises: Adversity, Temptation, and Trial in *Paradise Regained*," in *Milton Studies*, vol. 42, ed. Albert C. Labriola (Pittsburgh, 2002), 86–105.

11. John Milton, *The Complete Prose Works of John Milton*, 8 vols., ed. Don M. Wolfe et al. (New Haven, 1953–82), 2:515n102. "Wayfaring" has been changed "warfaring" in all four presentation copies and "F." All references to Milton's prose are to this edition, cited parenthetically in the text as YP.

12. Another example, although at one remove, comes in Milton's reference to Spenser's Palmer (*PL* 2:516) in an episode in which he is not, in fact, present in *The Faerie Queene*. For more, see Ernest Sirluck, "Milton Revises *The Faerie Queene*," *Modern Philology* 48 (1950): 90–96.

13. Dee Dyas, *Pilgrimage in Medieval English Literature, 700–1500* (Cambridge, 2001), 6. See also 65, 141–44, and passim.

14. Hugh Latimer, *Sermons*, ed. George Elwes Corrie (Cambridge, 1844), 490. Dent's *Plaine Mans Path-way to Heaven* was republished at least 30 times between 1601 and 1684. For more on Protestant pilgrimage imagery, see N. H. Keeble, "'To Be a Pilgrim': Constructing the Protestant Life in Early Modern England," in *Pilgrimage: The English Experience from Becket to Bunyan*, ed. Colin Morris and Peter Roberts (Cambridge, 2002), 238–56.

15. For the parallel flowering of pilgrimage metaphors in secular Protestant literature, see Beatrice Groves, "Pilgrimage in post-Reformation Literature," in *Pilgrims and Pilgrimage: Journey, Spirituality and Daily Life through the Centuries* (York, 2007), CD-ROM.

16. *Pylgrymage of Sir Richard Guylforde*, 32; see also 19.

17. *Egeria's Travels to the Holy Land*, ed. and trans. John Wilkinson (Warminster, 1981), 96.

18. For these altars, see *Pylgrymage of Sir Richard Guylforde*, 39; William Lithgow, *The Totall Discourse...*(London, 1640), 261; Eugene Hoade, ed., *Western Pilgrims* (1952; repr., Jerusalem, 1970), 43; *Theoderich's Description of the Holy Places*, trans. Aubrey Stewart (London: Palestine Pilgrims' Text Society, 1891), 44; Martin Biddle, *The Tomb of Christ* (Stroud, 1999), 88. For the piles of stones, see *Pylgrymage of Sir Richard Guylforde*, 19, 34; Hoade, *Western Pilgrims*, 68.

19. *Pylgrymage of Sir Richard Guylforde*, 36–37.

20. Brefeld, "An Account," 144. See also *Pylgrymage of Sir Richard Guylforde*, 24–25.

21. Jonathan Z. Smith, *To Take Place: Toward Theory in Ritual* (Chicago, 1987), 89 and passim.

22. "It was always our practice when we managed to reach one of the places we wanted to see to have first a prayer, then a reading from the book, then to say an appropriate psalm and another prayer" (*Egeria's Travels*, 105–06; see also 95).

23. See, for example, Josephie Brefeld, *A Guidebook for the Jerusalem Pilgrimage in the Late Middle Ages: A Case for Computer-Aided Criticism* (Verloren, 1994), 200–01, 204–05.

24. Brefeld, *Guidebook*, 210–11. See also *Pylgrymage of Sir Richard Guylforde*, 34, 43, 46.

25. *Egeria's Travels*, 159, 160, 155.

26. Brefeld, *Guidebook*, 210–11; *Felix Fabri (circa 1480–1483)*, 4 vols., trans. Aubrey Stewart (London, 1892), 4:421; *Egeria's Travel*, 6.

27. See R. A. Markus, *The End of Ancient Christianity* (Cambridge, 1990), 139 and passim; Dorothea R. French, "Journeys to the Center of the Earth: Medieval and Renaissance Pilgrimages to Mount Calvary," in *Journeys toward God: Pilgrimage and Crusade*, ed. Barbara N. Sargent-Baur (Kalamazoo, Mich., 1992), 74; Mircea Eliade, *Images and Symbols:*

Studies in Religious Symbolism, trans. Philip Mairet (London, 1961), 39–40; E. Relph, *Place and Placelessness* (London, 1976), 15, 65.

28. Dyas, *Pilgrimage*, 234–35. See also Joan E. Taylor, *Christians and the Holy Places: The Myth of Jewish-Christian Origins* (Oxford, 1993), 308.

29. Taylor, *Christians and the Holy Places*, 307–09. Henry Maundrell's skeptical account of his 1697 journey to the Holy Land, *A Journey from Aleppo to Jerusalem in 1697*, ed. David Howell (Beirut, 1963), contends that the reason so many Holy Land sites were held to have taken place in grottos was because "grottos were anciently held in great esteem" (154).

30. Fowler's note to 11.335–54.

31. Jerome, *Letters and Select Works*, ed. Henry Wace and Philip Schaff (Oxford, 1893), 120 (letter 58, section 3). At other times, as one would expect, Jerome writes in praise of geographical pilgrimage; his attitude in this letter is probably inflected by his desire to placate Paulinus as he withdraws his offer for the latter to come and visit him in the Holy Land. For more on the circumstances of this letter's composition, see Dennis E. Trout, *Paulinus of Nola: Life, Letters, and Poems* (Berkeley and Los Angeles, 1999), 96–98.

32. Adam's desire is strikingly similar to the "idle traditions" of the early church in which, according to Milton in *Of Prelatical Episcopacy* (1641), "with lesse fervency was studied what Saint *Paul*, or Saint *John* had written then was listen'd to one that could say here hee taught, here he stood … that cold stone whereon he rested … and that pavement bedew'd with the warme effusion of his last blood, that sprouted up into eternall Roses to crowne his Martyrdome" (YP 1:641–42). Even in the cut and thrust of pamphlet debate Milton cannot resist the rhetorical flight in which literal effusions bloom again as roses of the correct liturgical color for a martyr's crown.

33. Jason P. Rosenblatt, *Torah and Law in "Paradise Lost"* (Princeton, N.J., 1994), 5, 228; Sims, *Bible*, 202–03. See also Pecheux, "Abraham"; John E. Parish, "Milton and the Anthropomorphic God," *Studies in Philology* 56, no. 4 (1959): 624.

34. The Bishops' Bible headnote to Genesis 18; Abbot Daniel, *The Pilgrimage of the Russian Abbot Daniel in the Holy Land*, ed. and trans. C. W. Wilson (London, 1895), 44.

35. Vaughan's "Religion," lines 13–16, in *The Works of Henry Vaughan*, ed. L. C. Martin (Oxford, 1957), 404.

36. Both Vaughan's "Religion" and Adam (11.320–22) allude to the fountain by which the angel of the Lord speaks comfort to Hagar (Gen. 16:7) and to the trees out of or near which God spoke to Moses, Gideon, and Abraham (Exod. 3:2–4, Judg. 6:11, Gen 18:4).

37. Hoade, *Western Pilgrims*, 71.

38. *Anonymous Pilgrims, I–VIII*, ed. Aubrey Stewart (London, 1894), 32. See also Daniel, *Pilgrimage*, 1; *Felix Fabri*, 1:283. For the evidence that earth was taken from these spots in particular, see E. D. Hunt, *Holy Land Pilgrimage in the Later Roman Empire* (Oxford, 1982), 130.

39. *Felix Fabri*, 1:283. For more on Christ's footsteps in this narrative, see 1:282, 285; 2:484–87. For Jerusalem as a contact relic, see Suzanne M. Yeager, *Jerusalem in Medieval Narrative* (Cambridge, 2008), 2.

40. *Letters of Paulinus of Nola*, 2 vols., ed. and trans. P. G. Walsh (London, 1967), 2:273 (letter 49, section 14).

41. Brefeld, *Guidebook*, 26, 30; J. G. Davies, *Pilgrimage Yesterday and Today: Why? Where? How?* (London, 1988), 68.

42. Henry Timberlake, *A True and Strange Discourse of the Travailes of Two English Pilgrimes* (London, 1603), 9. (Timberlake's work was reprinted 13 times before the end of the century.) A parodic account of pilgrimage, published two years prior to *Paradise Lost*, expresses the pilgrim's desire to visit Jerusalem with exactly the same phrase "to see the sanctified places which our Saviours feet have trod": Symon Patrick, *The Parable of the Pilgrim: Written to a Friend* (London, 1665), 429.

43. For the Incarnational stress on the physical in late medieval devotion, see Michael O'Connell, *The Idolatrous Eye: Iconoclasm and Theater in Early Modern England* (Oxford, 2000), 47, 64–65; Gail McMurray Gibson, *The Theatre of Devotion: East Anglian Drama and Society in the Late Middle Ages* (London, 1989), 6–8 and passim; Eamon Duffy, *The Stripping of the Altars: Traditional Religion in England c.1400–c. 1580* (London, 1992), 22–37, 183–86.

44. For other examples of these tropes in New Testament Epistles (which were all believed to be by Paul in the seventeenth century), see Heb. 11:13, Gal. 5:7, Phil. 2:16, 2 Tim. 4:7–8. In *Areopagitica* Milton brings together the Pauline metaphors of journey and race for the Christian life: "He that can apprehend and consider vice with all her baits and seeming pleasures, and yet abstain, and yet distinguish, and yet prefer that which / is truly better, he is the true wayfaring [this edition "warfaring"] Christian. I cannot praise a fugitive and cloister'd vertue, unexercis'd & unbreath'd, that never sallies out and sees her adversary, but slinks out of the race, where that immortall garland is to be run for, not without dust and heat" (YP 2:514–15). For more on this trope in Puritan and Miltonic writing, see Keeble, "'To Be a Pilgrim,'" 255; Keeble, "Wilderness Exercises," 90, 100.

45. Gregory of Nyssa, *The Life of Moses*, ed. and trans. Abraham J. Malherbe and Everett Ferguson (New York, 1978), 119 (section 251).

46. Rowan Williams, *The Wound of Knowledge: Christian Spirituality from the New Testament to St. John of the Cross* (London, 1990), 63.

47. Nyssa, *Life of Moses*, 118 (section 245–46).

48. *The Oxford English Dictionary*, s.v. "trace."

49. This idea is also literalized in the "least erected" (*PL* 1.679) Mammon who spends his time gazing at the golden pavement even while he is in heaven. For an expression of the classical idea, see Ovid's *Metamorphoses*, trans. George Sandys (London, 1626), 3: "And whereas others see with downe-cast eyes, / He with a loftie looke did Man indue, / And bade him Heavens transcendent glories view" (lines 84–86).

50. Fowler's note to 12.648. The note in Fowler's first edition (1968) is noticeably more negative about the meaning of "wandering," perhaps influenced by Isabel Gamble MacCaffrey's claim in *Paradise Lost as "Myth"* (Cambridge, Mass., 1959), that "the word *wander* has almost always pejorative, or melancholy, connotation in *Paradise Lost*" (188; see 188–206 for her full discussion). MacCaffrey's view, however, appears skewed by her concern with Satan's wandering as the "ultimate analogue" for that of Adam and Eve rather than, as Fish argues, a contrast: Stanley Fish, *Surprised by Sin: The Reader in "Paradise Lost"* (London, 1967), 130–41. See also the excellent discussion of wandering in Edward W. Tayler, *Milton's Poetry: Its Development in Time* (Pittsburgh, 1979), 9–104. As suggested by Fowler's revision of his note, critics seem to have become more open to the positive theological possibilities of wandering in Milton's poem.

51. *OED*, s.v. "wander."

52. See, for example, Edmund Spenser, *The Faerie Queene*, ed. A. C. Hamilton with Hiroshi Yamashita and Toshiyuki Suzuki (London, 2001), 1.i.10.5, 1.i.13.6, 1.ii.12.2, 1.x.34.1. Redcrosse's Protestant quest is rendered particularly difficult by the fact that Spenser's epic embraces the Catholic symbolism of medieval romances in which quests were inflected by the culture of pilgrimage; see Beatrice Groves, "The Redcrosse Knight and the George," *Spenser Studies* 25 (2010): 371–76; Helen Cooper, *The English Romance in Time: Transforming Motifs from Geoffrey of Monmouth to the Death of Shakespeare* (Oxford, 2004), 45–105, esp. 96.

53. The potential of this power for evil, as well as good, is suggested by Belial's celebration of "thoughts that wander through eternity" (2.148). See David Quint, "Ulysses and the Devils: The Unity of Book Two of *Paradise Lost*," in *Milton Studies*, vol. 49, ed. Albert C. Labriola (Pittsburgh, 2009), 29.

54. Christopher Ricks, *Milton's Grand Style* (Oxford, 1963), 111. See also Arnold Stein, *Answerable Style: Essays on "Paradise Lost"*

(Minneapolis, 1953), 66–67; John Leonard, *Naming in Paradise: Milton and the Language of Adam and Eve* (Oxford, 1990), 233–92. Leonard is excellent on the balance of joy and grief in this device, one aspect of a poem which, as he argues, "admits the darker notes of the fallen world into that voice which strives ever for the unfallen" (292).

55. Fish writes, "By confronting the reader with a vocabulary bearing the taint of sin in a situation that could not possibly harbor it, Milton leaves him no choice but to acknowledge himself as the source, and to lament," in *Surprised by Sin*, 136. (Like Leonard, *Naming in Paradise*, 234, I find Fish overly despondent about the effect of this device). For Milton's view of conative virtue, see YP 1:363; Dennis Richard Danielson, *Milton's Good God: A Study in Literary Theodicy* (Cambridge, 1982), 172–77; William Poole, *Milton and the Idea of the Fall* (Cambridge, 2005), 138–40.

56. John Foxe, *The Gospels of the Fower Evangelistes Translated in the Olde Saxons Tyme out of the Latin into the Vulgare Toung* (London, 1571), ¶2r.

57. John Foxe, *A Sermon Preached at the Christening of a Certaine Jew, at London, by John Foxe*, trans. James Bell (London, 1578), M8r.

58. Thomas Brightman, *A Revelation of the Revelation* (Amsterdam, 1615), 140; Thomas Adams, *The Happines of the Church* (London, 1619), 57. See also Josias Nicholls, *Abrahams Faith; That is, the Olde Religion* (London, 1602); John S. Coolidge, *The Pauline Renaissance in England: Puritanism and the Bible* (Oxford, 1970), 102.

59. Leonard, *Naming in Paradise*, 245–46.

60. *Select English Works of John Wyclif*, 3 vols., ed. Thomas Arnold (Oxford, 1869), 2:348.

61. The idea of exile as pilgrimage had inspired the "peregrini" who did not travel to a known shrine but remained in perpetual exile, an exile that they believed nourished their commitment to the spiritual life: Philip Edwards, *Pilgrimage and Literary Tradition* (Cambridge, 2005), 18–19. Other pilgrims likewise attempted to reclaim the holy possibilities of "wandering," insisting that pilgrimage lies not simply in a physical journey to Jerusalem but in a wandering of the spirit: "Id circo decrevi, hunc librum non Peregrinatorium, nec Itinerarium, nec Viagium, nec alio quovis nomine intitulare, sed EVAGATORIUM": Felix Fabri, *Fratris Felicis Fabri Evagatorium in Terrae Sanctae, Arabiae Et Egypti Peregrinationem*, 2 vols., ed. Cunradus Dietericus Hassler (Stuttgart, 1843), 1:3.

62. John Milton, *Complete Shorter Poems*, 2nd ed., ed. John Carey (London, 1997), 1.8–9. Milton is following Luke 4:1: "And Jesus being full of the Holy Ghost returned from Jordan, and was led by the Spirit into the wilderness."

63. Edwards, *Pilgrimage and Literary Tradition*, 7.
64. The Bishops' Bible headnote to Genesis 18; Daniel, *Pilgrimage*, 44.
65. Fish, *Surprised by Sin*, 141.
66. For Eve's repentance, see 10.863–65, 914–36.
67. Ruth 1:16; Barbara K. Lewalski, "Milton on Women—Yet Again," in *Problems for Feminist Criticism*, ed. Sally Minogue (London, 1990), 59.
68. Keeble, "'To Be a Pilgrim,'" 245.
69. For more on this idea, see Keeble, "Wilderness Exercises," 96.
70. Brightman, *Revelation of the Revelation*, 51.
71. John Bunyan, *The Heavenly Foot-man* (1698), in *The Miscellaneous Works of John Bunyan*, 13 vols., ed. Roger Sharrock (Oxford, 1980–94), 5:150, quoted in reference to *Paradise Regained* in Keeble, "Wilderness Exercises," 101.
72. Andrew Fichter, *Poets Historical: Dynastic Epic in the Renaissance* (New Haven, 1982), 24.
73. Ibid., 51.
74. Augustine, *Errationes in Psalmos, Corpus Christianorum*, series Latina 39 (Ps. 62:6).
75. Psalm 107:4–7. As Fowler writes: "Those who heard this echo would remember the continuation" (note to 12.649).

Notes to Crouch, "Fighting for Saint Michael"

1. *Paradise Lost*, 2nd ed., ed. Alastair Fowler (New York, 1998), hereafter cited parenthetically in the text.
2. All biblical quotations are from the Geneva edition. Usage of u/v and i/j has been silently regularized in early modern quotations and titles throughout this essay.
3. *The Complete Prose Works of John Milton*, 8 vols., ed. Don M. Wolfe et al. (New Haven, 1953–82), 6:347; hereafter cited as YP in the text.
4. On artistic concerns, see John Peter, *A Critique of "Paradise Lost"* (Hamden, Conn., 1970), 79; on battle tactics, see Robert Thomas Fallon, *Captain or Colonel: The Soldier in Milton's Life and Art* (Columbia, Mo., 1984), 213; as parody of warfare, see Arnold Stein, *Answerable Style: Essays on "Paradise Lost"* (Seattle, 1953), 26; on militant church, see Austin C. Dobbins, *Milton and the Book of Revelation: The Heavenly Cycles* (Tuscaloosa, Ala., 1975), 31; Stella Revard, *The War in Heaven: "Paradise Lost" and the Tradition of Satan's Rebellion* (Ithaca, N.Y., 1980), 112; on Restoration poet's

disillusionment, see Revard, *War in Heaven*, 126; Jason P. Rosenblatt, "Structural Unity and Temporal Concordance: The War in Heaven in *Paradise Lost*," *PMLA* 87 (Jan. 1972): 38; William G. Madsen, *From Shadowy Types to Truth: Studies in Milton's Symbolism* (New Haven, 1968), 110–11; Bob Hodge, "Satan and the Revolution of the Saints," in *Literature, Language and Society in England, 1580–1680*, ed. David Aers, Bob Hodge, and Gunther Kress (Totowa, N.J., 1981), 192–99; Michael Lieb, *Poetics of the Holy: A Reading of "Paradise Lost"* (Chapel Hill, N.C., 1981), 302, 312.

5. Stanley Fish, *Surprised by Sin: The Reader in "Paradise Lost,"* 2nd ed. (Cambridge, Mass., 1998), 4.

6. It was commonly believed, as the parliamentarian Henry Lawrence argues in *An History of Angells* (London, 1649), that "the Church being now confirmed by God, needs not those visible, and sensible confirmations, as formerly, which is the reason also of the ceasing of miracles." In modern times, people "have faith enableing us to converse with the Angells in a way more spirituall" (16–17).

7. John, of Damascus, Saint, *Three Treatises on the Divine Images*, trans. and ed. Andrew Louth (Crestwood, N.Y., 2003), 3:115–16.

8. John Bale, *The Image of both churches after the moste wonderful and heavenly Revelacion of Saint John...* (London, ca. 1550), sig. e. vi^r.

9. *Testament of Dan* 6:2, qtd. in Leo R. Percer, *The War in Heaven: Michael and Messiah in Revelation 12* (Ph.D. diss., Baylor University, 1999), 97. *The Testament of Dan* is part of the Old Testament pseudepigrapha, specifically, the Testaments of the Twelve Patriarchs.

10. The language of 1 Timothy 2:5 is strikingly similar: "For there is one God, and one Mediatour betweene God and men, the man Christ Iesus." For Michael's role as protector of and intercessor for the Israelites, see Milton's *De doctrina Christiana* (YP 6:347); Daniel 10:13–14, 10:21, 12:1; Richard F. Johnson, *Saint Michael the Archangel in Medieval English Legend* (New York, 2005), 15; Percer, *The War in Heaven*, 98–99.

11. On Michael as the leader of the heavenly host in the Bible, see Revelation 12:7; in the apocrypha, see Darryl D. Hannah, *Michael and Christ: Michael Traditions and Angel Christology in Early Christianity* (Tübingen, 1999), 39–40, 64. On Christ's claim to this role, see Matthew 16:27 and 2 Thessalonians 1:7. On Christ more generally as a conqueror or victor, see Hannah, *Michael and Christ*, 148–49; Revelation 3:21, 5:5, 17:14, 19:14–15.

12. The risen Christ of Revelation 1:12–18 who appears amid "seven candlestickes" (13), for example, has eyes like a "flame of fire" (14) and

wears a "golden girdle" (13), just like the Old Testament vision of the angel usually identified as Michael that appears before Daniel in 10:5–9. For a detailed analysis of resemblances between the imagery of Christ and Michael, see C. Rowland, "A Man Clothed in Linen: Daniel 10.6ff and Jewish Angelology," in *Journal for the Study of the New Testament* 24 (1985): 99–110.

13. While modern scholars largely reject the hypothesis that the depiction of Christ in the New Testament represents a direct subsumption of ancient Judaic literature about Michael, there is no question that Christian theologians from the earliest centuries recognized the dangerously protomessianic aspects of Michael's representations. For a survey of research and debates about the interrelationships of the Michael and Christ traditions, see Hannah, *Michael and Christ*, 1–11.

14. *Paradise Lost*, of course, neutralizes this threat by unequivocally establishing the Son's presence both before and during the war in heaven. Nevertheless, God's ambiguity in pronouncing that "This day I have begot whom I declare / My only Son" seems to allow for the possibility that the Son's creation as an entity postdates that of the other angels (5.603–05). Satan suggests precisely this in his speech in 5.853–66. I agree with Fowler that Milton's discussion of this question in *De doctrina Christiana* (206) should be interpreted to mean that the poet takes "begot" as referring to the Son's exaltation rather than his creation.

The question of Milton's views on the Son's "creation," particularly as expressed in *De doctrina*, is a notoriously vexed one. For a review of the major arguments on both sides of the debate, see, for example, Richard S. Ide, "On the Begetting of the Son in *Paradise Lost*," in *SEL* 24 (Winter 1984): 141–55. For a review of seventeenth century theological views on this question and Milton's relation to these views, see Dobbins, *Milton and the Book of Revelation*, 1–25.

15. Satan, in insisting upon his equivalence to Christ, and in denying his own creation and Christ's preexistence relative to the other angels (5.853–61), identifies the Son as a being no different from himself (5.864–66). He denies the Son his rightful godhead by claiming godhead for himself and, by implication, on behalf of all the angels.

16. Church of England, *The Booke of Common Prayer* (London, 1635), sig. B6v.

17. Lewes Hughes, *Certaine greevances... for the satisfying of those that doe clamour, and maliciously revile them that labour to have the errors of the Booke of common prayer reformed* (London, 1640), 21.

18. Ibid., 21.

19. Hannah, *Michael and Christ*, 218. On the messianic appropriation of roles traditionally assigned to Michael, see also Percer, *The War in Heaven*, 218.

20. Bale, *The Image of both churches*, sig. e. vi^r. Intriguingly, passages referring to Michael that were not perceived as a challenge to Christ's authority sometimes were taken to signify the literal archangel, even when "Michael" was taken in the same book as a signifier of Christ. Compare, for example, the Geneva Bible's glosses on Daniel 10:21 (where Michael retains his independent identity as one "appointed for the defence of the Church under Christ") and Daniel 10:13 (where "Michael" is glossed, "that is, Christ Jesus the head of angels").

21. Thomas Taylor, *Christs Victorie over the Dragon; or, Satans Downfall* (London, 1633), 329.

22. David Pareus, *A Commentary upon the Divine Revelation of the Apostle and Evangelist John*, trans. Elias Arnold (Amsterdam, 1644), 266, professor of theology at the University of Heidelberg, attempts to reconcile the manifest absurdity of a celestial war by arguing that the vision itself must have appeared in the heavens above, rather than having heaven as its setting. The Somersetshire preacher Richard Bernard, *A Key of Knowledge for the opening of the secret mysteries of St Johns Mysticall Revelation* (London, 1617), is so adamant that "there could bee no such fighting" there that he proclaims the witness John a liar: "Neither was the divell and his angels seene of *John* in heaven" (213). The prolific English polemicist John Bale, while relocating the celestial war to "this world," offers a rare Protestant defense of Michael's involvement in the battle: "But why may not one angell bee chiefe amongst the good Angels, as well as one Devill is chiefe amongst the evill Angels? And if so, it is no whit absurd to say that he is like God, being so eminent an image of his maiesty and excellency" (*The Image of both churches*, 393–94).

23. The English clergyman Arthur Dent, *The Ruine of Rome; or, An Exposition upon the whole Revelation* (London, 1603), 159 (reprinted nine times through 1656); the English preterist Hezekiah Holland, *An exposition…upon the Revelation of Saint John* (London, 1650), 91; and the French Protestant Pierre Du Moulin, *The Accomplishment of the Prophecies* (Oxford, 1613), 202–04, interpret the celestial war as an allegorical representation of Christ's defeat of Satan through his Crucifixion and Resurrection. Pareus, in *A Commentary*, agrees with this reading but adds that it also signifies Christ's overcoming of Satan in the temptation (266) and, in a secondary sense, Constantine's victories in the primitive church (267–68). Bernard (*A Key of Knowledge*, 213); Bale (*The Image of both churches*, sigs. [e.vi.^{r}]–e.vii.^{v}); Patrick

Forbes, bishop of Aberdeen, Scotland, *An Exquisite Commentarie upon the Revelation of Saint John* (London, 1613), 108; the Genevan commentator Augustin Marlorat, *A Catholike exposition upon the Revelation of Sainct John. Collected by M. Augustine Marlorate out of divers notable Writers* ([London] 1574), 174; and the radical English Puritan Thomas Cartwright, *A plaine explanation of the whole Revelation of Saint John* (London, 1622), 74–75, read the war as an allegory of the militant church's battle on earth.

24. Gesturing at specific scriptural passages, Milton also writes, "And Jude says of Michael *when disputing about Moses' body he did not dare...*, whereas it would be quite improper to say this about Christ" (*DDC,* YP 6:347).

25. *Robert Bellarmine: Spiritual Writings,* trans. and ed. John Patrick Donnelly and Roland J. Teske (New York, 1989), 151–52.

26. Urban VIII, pope from 1623 to 1644, formally adopted Michael as his de facto patron saint. Not only did he schedule his coronation for the feast of Saint Michael, but he also orchestrated an elaborate iconographic campaign to "dramatise his sacred alliance with the archangel." See Louis Rice, "Urban VIII, the Archangel Michael, and a Forgotten Project for the Apse Altar of St Peter's," *Burlington Magazine* 134 (July 1992): 429.

27. On the May 1644 ordinance adding angels to Parliament's list of prohibited images, see Julie Spraggon, *Puritan Iconoclasm during the English Civil War* (Rochester, N.Y., 2003), 78–80.

28. A sixteenth century example is provided by Peter Gottland's engraving, *Allegory of the Triumph of the New Faith over the Old* (1552), which depicts the infant Christ on horseback piercing a prostrate dragon with a spear, reproduced in Samantha Riches, *St. George: Hero, Martyr and Myth* (Phoenix Mill, England, 2000), 153, fig. 5.6.

29. Spraggon, *Puritan Iconoclasm,* 22. On the iconoclastic debates over the concepts of *dulia* and *latria,* see also John Phillips, *The Reformation of Images: Destruction of Art in England, 1535–1660* (Berkeley and Los Angeles, 1973), chap. 1.

30. John Calvin, *Commentary on Epistle to the Ephesians,* trans. Arthur Golding (London, 1577), fol. 53r.

31. As Robert H. West, *Milton and the Angels* (Athens, Ga., 1955), remarks with some understatement, Milton's depiction of the archangel must have "come as a mild shock to the perhaps considerable proportion of his readers who thought... that to suppose Michael a prince of angels was one of the marks of a papist" (125).

32. See Stella Revard, "Milton and Millenarianism: From the Nativity Ode to *Paradise Regained,*" in *Milton and the Ends of Time,* ed. Juliet Cummins (Cambridge, 2003), 42–81. For early modern commentaries

published in England that treat the Revelation reference to Michael as a title solely signifying Christ, see, for example, Bernard, *A Key of Knowledge*, 213; Dent, *The Ruine of Rome*, 158; Forbes, *An Exquisite Commentarie*, 108; Holland, *An exposition*, 90–91; and Du Moulin, *Accomplishment of the Prophecies*, 201–02.

33. Most, but not all, scholars now accept Milton's millenarianism as fact, even if they disagree about its specific character. For a selection of relatively recent scholarship on the issue, see Cummins, *Milton and the Ends of Time*. For a summary of debates about the poet's millenarianism, see especially William B. Hunter, "The Millennial Moment: Milton vs. 'Milton,'" and John T. Shawcross, "Confusion: The Apocalypse, the Millennium," both in Cummins. On Milton's beliefs in the activities of angels on earth, see *De doctrina Christiana*, book 1, chap. 9, "On the Special Government of Angels," especially (YP 6:345–46), which describes the angels as ministering to believers, "patrol[ling] the earth" and executing divine vengeance. On the publication of Brightman's and Mede's works, see Revard, "Milton and Millenarianism."

34. As Christopher Hill, *The English Bible and the Seventeenth-Century Revolution* (New York, 1993), points out, the religious revolutionaries of the period interpreted the term "saints" in Revelation 13:7 as prophetically referring to themselves as the "chosen people within the inadequately protestantized English state church" (264–65). Despite the nationalist rhetoric that often surrounded the use of the term, it was not taken normally to exclude members of other nations, any more than it was intended to signify the universal body of English men and women.

35. Isaac Penington, qtd. in Hill, *The English Bible*, 268n18. Note that the publication year is 1659, not 1650, as in Hill.

36. John Blenkow, *Michaels Combat with the Divel; or, Moses his Funerall* (London, 1640), sig. [B4]^v.

37. On Michael's perceived military role in the apocalypse, see Percer, *The War in Heaven*, 113–14; Johnson, *Saint Michael*, 100; Hannah, *Michael and Christ*, 102–03. For a seventeenth century discussion, see John Eachard, who claims that "Michael and his angels will fight for you," and that "the civil war begun shall last till Rome be burnt and the Jews called" (qtd. in Hill, *The English Bible*, 103).

38. Joseph Mede, *The Key of the Revelation* (London, 1650), 38.

39. Thomas Brightman, *A Revelation of the Apocalyps* (Amsterdam, 1611), 333–34.

40. For the relationship between Milton and Mede, see William Kerrigan, *The Prophetic Milton* (Charlottesville, Va., 1974), 118; Sarah

Hutton, "Mede, Milton, and More: Christ's College Millenarians," in *Milton and the Ends of Time*, 29–41; and John Peter Rumrich, "Mead and Milton," in *Milton Quarterly* 20, no. 4 (1986): 136–41.

41. Mede, *The Key of the Revelation*, 36, 39–40.

42. Among the members of the New Model Army, Milton writes, no one "think[s] it more glorious to smite the foe than to instruct himself and others in the knowledge of heavenly things, or think[s] it more noble to practice warlike rather than evangelical combat. And indeed, if we consider the proper function of war, what other conduct would be more fitting for soldiers who have been organized and enrolled to be defenders of the laws, uniformed guardians of justice, champions of the church?" (YP 4:648–49).

43. See, for example, Revard, *War in Heaven*, 108–09.

44. Such transfers of angelic authority, it is important to note, did not undermine the dissenters' revolutionary narrative. The historical identification of Michael with a human agent was based upon a perceived correspondence in military and spiritual roles, rather than on some criterion demanding a fixed identity. In addition, the typological hermeneutic recognized a whole host of types of Christ, emphasizing the multiplicity of types against the singularity of the antitype.

45. Alan R. Young, ed., *The English Emblem Tradition*, vol. 3 (Toronto, 1988), 171, plate 0315.0. The red and white feathers on the figure's helmet are also suggestive of Saint George, the patron saint of England whose hagiography and iconography were closely modeled on the archangel's. The archetypal image of Michael, as leader of the militant church and prototype of Christ, underwrote the vitae of a vast array of national saints, including George's. As Riches notes, "From very early times the Greek Church represented St. George trampling the dragon of the Apocalypse, representing the Devil, accompanied by a crowned virgin, representing the Church." This legend "began as a stylised way of representing the saint overcoming evil, in almost exactly the same way as St Michael with the Devil/dragon, but gradually came to be treated as a legend in its own right" (Riches, *St. George*, 27). Raphael's *Saint Michael* (fig. 2) is part of a diptych that also depicts, in a parallel stance, Saint George.

46. John Taylor, *The Conversion, Confession, Contrition* (Oxford, 1643), title page, 2–3. An even earlier, though less unequivocal, example is provided by a military banner apparently carried by Lionel Copley, a member of Essex's Regiment of Horse, beginning in 1642. The flag depicts an armed man with an upraised sword seated on a rearing bay horse. Its motto reads: "Nay, but as a captaine of the hoste of the Lord am I now come" (Young, *English Emblem Tradition*, 119, fig. 0219.0).

This quote from Joshua 5:14 repeats the words of an angel who has arrived to preside over the chosen people, described here as the Lord's host or army. Given Michael's established role as protector of the Israelites, the identity of this angel is unambiguous. While not specifically invoking the celestial war, the banner provides further evidence of the typological association of Michael's unique angelic roles with the preeminent military leader who stood in opposition to the king.

47. John Cleveland, *The character of a London diurnall* (London, 1644), 67–68. Although I have not found any documentation to support the conjecture, "Burroughs" undoubtedly refers to the Quaker activist Edward Burroughs (1633–63).

48. See, for example, the title pages to *Flagellum; or, The Life and Death, Birth and Burial of O. Cromwell The late Usurper* (London, 1669); *The History of Oliver Cromwel: Being an Impartial Account* (London, 1693); and *The History of the Life and Death of his most Serene Highness, Oliver, Late Lord Protector* (London 1659).

49. Fox, *To Thee Oliver Cromwell*, (London, 1655), sig. [A^r].

50. "Cromwell, Our Cheif of Men," in *The Complete Poetry of John Milton*, rev. ed., ed. John T. Shawcross (New York, 1990), 6.

51. It must be admitted, though, that Milton's remark that the regularity of Cromwell's pay operated as a factor motivating the troops to flock to him ironically brings the general's almost supernatural virtue somewhat down to size.

52. Laura Lunger Knoppers, *Constructing Cromwell: Ceremony, Portrait, and Print, 1645–1661* (Cambridge, 2000), I think importantly, shifts responsibility for the fashioning of Cromwell's image away from the Protector, arguing that his "self-effacement and reluctance to shape his own image paradoxically enabled a wide range of image-makers and image-breakers, including those who wished to remake him in the image of a king" (6). Moreover, she notes, "Although the protectoral court has been widely viewed as monarchical, manuscript evidence and a late protectoral portrait indicate that Cromwell's own style remained plain and non-regal" (7).

53. *A Further narrative of the passages of these times in the Common-Wealth of England* ([London?], 1658), 28.

54. Lucy Hutchinson, *Memoirs of the Life of Colonel Hutchinson*, ed. N. H. Keeble (London, 1995), 214.

55. Ibid., 256.

56. This engraving has been often discussed, though only Knoppers considers the iconography of Michael. See, for example, J. C. Davis, *Oliver Cromwell* (New York, 2001), 116–118; Laura Lunger Knoppers, "The Antichrist, the Babilon, the Great Dragon: Oliver Cromwell, Andrew Marvell, and the Apocalyptic Monstrous," in *Monstrous Bodies/Political*

Monstrosities in Early Modern Europe, ed. Laura Lunger Knoppers and Joan B. Landes (Cornell, 2004), 93–95, where the illustration is reproduced; Bruce Lawson, "The Body as a Political Construct: Oliver Cromwell's Image in William Faithorne's 1658 Emblematic Engraving," in *Deviceful Settings: The English Renaissance Emblem and its Contexts*, ed. M. Bath and D. Russell (New York, 1999), 113–38.

57. Bale, *The Image of both churches*, sig.e.vi^r.

58. David Loewenstein, *Representing Revolution in Milton and His Contemporaries: Religion, Politics, and Polemics in Radical Puritanism* (Cambridge, 2001), 209.

59. *The Souldiers Pocket Bible* [1643], in *The Christian Soldier: Religious Tracts Published for Soldiers on Both Sides during and after the English Civil Wars, 1642–1648*, ed. Robert Thomas Fallon (Tempe, Ariz., 2003), 14.

Notes to Yu, "From Judgment to Interpretation"

I would like to thank Blair Hoxby for the guidance that allowed this article to take shape.

1. John Milton, *Paradise Lost*, ed. Barbara Lewalski (Oxford, 2007), 9.214–25; cited hereafter by book and line number in text.

2. Christopher Ricks, *Milton's Grand Style* (Oxford, 1963), 146.

3. John Guillory, *Literary Study in the Age of Professionalism*, forthcoming. I am grateful for access to an early version of Guillory's manuscript; the chapter entitled "The Origins of Close Reading: I. A. Richards and William Empson" provides a fuller account of the brief outline I attempt here. See also Terry Eagleton, *Literary Theory: An Introduction* (Minneapolis, 1996), 37.

4. W. K. Wimsatt and Monroe Beardsley, *The Verbal Icon: Studies in the Meaning of Poetry* (Lexington, Ky., 1954), 18, 339.

5. Guillory, *Literary Study in the Age of Professionalism*, forthcoming.

6. I. A. Richards, *Practical Criticism* (London, 1929). From his review of a series of undergraduate responses to poetry, Richards concludes that "a large proportion of average-to-good...readers of poetry frequently and repeatedly *fail to understand it*, both as a statement and as an expression.... [Readers of poetry consistently] misapprehend its feeling, its tone, and its intention" (12).

7. The specificities of the historical context ensured the success of New Criticism in American universities: as Eagleton points out, it provided a sensible method for teaching the growing number

of undergraduates who were arriving with different levels of literary knowledge. Moreover, the academic community found the seeming silence of close reading on political matters appropriate to the cold war climate (*Literary Theory*, 43).

8. Eagleton argues that the New Critics' exclusion of historical context and political concerns from textual analysis effectively reduced criticism into "a recipe for political inertia, and thus for submission to the political status quo" (*Literary Theory*, 43).

9. William Empson, *Some Versions of Pastoral* (New York, 1935), 149–92. Empson insists that the strange ambiguities Bentley attempts to amend are not errors but telling signs of Milton's ambivalence toward the appeals of the Christian paradise.

10. Empson's most commendatory line comes upon reading Pearce's interpretation of the construction of Pandemonium. Where Satan and the fallen angels "op'nd into the Hill a spacious wound / And dig'd out ribs of Gold," Pearce sees an allusion to the creation of Eve (1.689–90). "I call this a profound piece of criticism," Empson writes (*Some Versions of Pastoral*, 176).

11. David Marshall, "Shaftesbury and Addison: Criticism and the Public Taste," in *The Cambridge History of Literary Criticism*, 9 vols., ed. H. B. Nisbet and Claude Rawson (Cambridge, 1997), 4:633.

12. René Le Bossu, *Treatise of the Epick Poem…Made English from the French…by W. J.* (London, 1719), 2. The original treatise in French was published in 1675.

13. Though *On the Sublime* was first translated into English in 1652, Longinus's influence is mainly felt later in the eighteenth century. Addison may have been familiar with Nicholas Boileau-Despréaux's French translation (1674). For the distinctively English assimilation of classical principles, see Colin Burrow, "Combative Criticism: Jonson, Milton, and Classical Literary Criticism in England," in *The Cambridge History of Literary Criticism*, 9 vols., ed. Glyn P. Norton (Cambridge, 1999), 3:487–99.

14. René Rapin, *Reflections on Aristotle's Treatise of Poesie* (London, 1674), 31. "Admirable" can be understood in the sense of marvelous or wonderful. It is difficult to define exactly what can be considered "probable" according to Aristotle's *Poetics*, but this idea of "probable" should not be confused with the realism of the novel. Stephen Halliwell, "Aristotle's Poetics," in *The Cambridge History of Literary Criticism*, 9 vols., ed. George A. Kennedy (Cambridge, 1989), believes that Aristotle likely meant that "the denouements of plots should issue from the plot as such, and not from a deus ex machina.…The deus ex machina should be employed for events

outside the drama—preceding events beyond human knowledge, or subsequent events requiring prediction and announcement ...there should be nothing irrational in the events; if there is, it should lie outside the play" (1:15).

15. Rapin, *Reflections*, 15, 32.

16. Joseph Addison, no. 315 (Mar. 1, 1712), *The Spectator*, 5 vols., ed. Donald F. Bond (Oxford, 1965), 3:145–46.

17. Ibid., 3:145–46.

18. Rapin, *Reflections*, 34.

19. A contested division dating back to the sixteenth century, when Italian epic theorists attempted to define the proper bounds of epic as a genre in the wake of the popular success of such romances as Ariosto's *Orlando Furioso* and Tasso's *Gerusalemme liberata*.

20. Aristotle, *Poetics*, trans. S. H. Butcher, *The Internet Classics Archive*, available at classics.mit.edu/Aristotle/poetics.1.1.html. See also George Whalley's translation of *Poetics* (Montreal, 1997), 1462a1–7.

21. Addison, *The Spectator*, no. 297 (Feb. 9, 1712), 3:61.

22. Empson, *Some Versions of Pastoral*, 22. Compare with Leopold Damrosch Jr., "The Significance of Addison's Criticism," *SEL* 19, no. 3 (1979): 421–30. Damrosch places a stronger emphasis upon Addison's independence from the classical critics.

23. Addison, *The Spectator*, no. 345 (Apr. 5, 1712), 3:284.

24. Irving Howe, "Modern Criticism: Privileges and Perils," in *Modern Literary Criticism: An Anthology*, ed. Irving Howe (Boston, 1958), 8–9. Though New Criticism in general privileges interpretation over judgment, the latter component, as Howe recognizes, is never altogether absent. New Criticism implicitly generates new standards of judgment. T. S. Eliot and F. R. Leavis, for example, frowned upon what they took to be Milton's imprecise grandiloquence on the grounds that it could not withstand the scrutiny of close reading.

25. A. E. Housman, *Introductory Lecture* (1892), in *Selected Prose*, ed. John Carter (Cambridge, 1961), 12.

26. Samuel Johnson, preface to *The Plays of William Shakespeare*, in *The Major Works*, ed. Donald Greene (Oxford, 1984), 443.

27. Margaret Kean, *John Milton's "Paradise Lost": A Sourcebook* (New York, 2005), 45.

28. Aristotle, *Poetics*, trans. Butcher; cf. Whalley translation, 1461b25.

29. Richard Bentley, *Milton's Paradise Lost: A New Edition* (London, 1732), IV.303. I have drawn from this edition throughout for Bentley's emendations; subsequent citations will be found in the text with reference to book and line number. The book number is printed

as a roman numeral in keeping with Bentley's own practice to distinguish his comments from Milton's text.

30. Aristotle, *Poetics,* trans. Whalley, 1461b23–26.

31. For other early commentators, see Ants Oras, *Milton's Editors and Commentators from Patrick Hume to Henry John Todd (1695–1801): A Study in Critical Views and Methods* (Tartu, Estonia, 1929) and John T. Shawcross, ed., *Milton: The Critical Heritage* (New York, 1970).

32. I have omitted Patrick Hume, Milton's earliest annotator, from this discussion; see Patrick Hume, *Annotations on Milton's "Paradise Lost"* (London, 1695). It is sufficient to recognize that Pearce and the Richardsons returned to and developed a form of exegetical criticism for reading *Paradise Lost* first used by Hume but subsequently displaced by the authority of neoclassical perspectives in the early eighteenth century.

33. Zachary Pearce, *A Review of the Text of Milton's "Paradise Lost," in which the Chief of Dr. Bentley's Emendations are Consider'd* (London, 1732), 5.638; hereafter cited in the text.

34. His commentary was published posthumously in 1777. See Zachary Pearce, *A Commentary with Notes on the Four Evangelists and the Acts* (London, 1777). For further reading, see Marcus Walsh, *Shakespeare, Milton, and Eighteenth-Century Literary Editing* (Cambridge, 1997), 78. Walsh lays the groundwork for this argument much more thoroughly than I have been able to do. He offers extensive support for the view that the relationship of biblical scholars to Holy Scripture was eventually transposed to critics of secular scriptures.

35. Arnold Williams, preface to *Tetrachordon,* in *The Complete Prose Works of John Milton,* 8 vols., ed. Don M. Wolfe et al. (New Haven, 1953–82), 2:572; hereafter cited as YP.

36. This distinction between English homiletic commentaries and other forms is worth drawing, even after taking into account the similarities among medieval and Latin continental commentaries. The English Protestant commentaries, either written in or translated into English, were done so for those of what one commentary calls "vulgar capacities." Thus, the annotations provided include neither the concatenation of patristic viewpoints from Catholic exegetical works nor the lengthy textual and philological passages of more technically inclined commentaries. For a different view regarding the uniqueness of these commentaries, see Richard A. Muller's introduction in *Biblical Interpretation in the Era of the Reformation* (Grand Rapids, Mich., 1996), 1–16. Muller, with an eye toward the text-critical approaches of modern biblical interpretation, emphasizes the continuity of Renaissance with medieval exegesis.

37. Henry Ainsworth, *Annotations upon the Five Bookes of Moses; the Book of the Psalmes, and the Song of Songs, or Canticles* (London, 1627), v.

38. Martin Luther, *The Creation: A Commentary on the First Five Chapters of the Book of Genesis*, trans. Henry Cole (Edinburgh, 1858), 25. Luther, of course, is more specifically speaking against the practice of layering more creative, allegorical interpretations upon the text to expand its meaning; such interpretations effectively constitute auxiliary narratives that make preceptors out of interpreters.

39. Matthew Poole, *Annotations upon the Holy Bible*, 2 vols. (London, 1683–96), 1, Gen. 3:1; italics mine.

40. Scholars from Balachandra Rajan and Stanley Fish onward have been fascinated with Milton's relationship to reading and the reader, and many have approached the topic through close readings of his poetry and prose. Dayton Haskin, *Milton's Burden of Interpretation* (Philadelphia, 2004) chronicles Milton's personal history of biblical interpretation, and Sharon Achinstein, *Milton and the Revolutionary Reader* (Princeton, N.J., 1994) argues that Milton attempts to shape a politically literate citizenry.

41. Jonathan Richardson, father and son, *Explanatory Notes and Remarks on Milton's "Paradise Lost"* (London, 1734), 3.474.

42. Cleanth Brooks, *The Well Wrought Urn: Studies in the Structure of Poetry* (San Diego, 1975), 76.

43. Luther, *The Creation*, 156.

44. Milton himself would insist in *Areopagitica* upon the centrality of the individual in uncovering truth: "A man may be a heretick in the truth; and if he believe things only because his Pastor says so...without knowing other reason, though his belief be true, yet the very truth he holds, becomes his heresie" (YP 2:543).

45. Wimsatt and Beardsley, *The Verbal Icon*, 34.

46. Poole, *Annotations upon the Holy Bible*, 2, Ps. 19:5.

47. There is some basis for this usage according to classical thought as well. Aristotle in the *Poetics* advocated the use of "language...[that] is elevated and remote from the vulgar idiom which employs unusual words. By unusual I mean foreign, metaphorical, extended—all, in short that are not common words.... These will raise the language above the vulgar idiom." See the translation by Richard Janko (Indianapolis, 1987), 1458a22–24, 32–33; cf. also Twining's translation (London, 1947).

48. Ricks, *Milton's Grand Style*, 109.

49. Kevin Sharpe, "Reading Revelations: Prophecy, Hermeneutics and Politics in Early Modern Britain," in *Reading, Society and Politics in Early Modern England*, ed. Kevin Sharpe and Steven N. Zwicker (Cambridge, 2003), 123.

50. Henry Hammond, *A Paraphrase, and Annotations upon all the Books of the New Testament* (London, 1653), 194.
51. Brooks, *The Well Wrought Urn*, 74.
52. Richardsons, *Explanatory Notes*, clxxxi.

Notes to Revard, "Milton as Muse for Keats, Shelley, and Frost"

1. "Amplify" is hardly an adequate word for what John Keats, Percy Bysshe Shelley, and Robert Frost gained by making use of a Miltonic "music" in some of their poems. Briefly, it helped them to speak not only personally but also heroically. Milton, to write a great epic poem, had to find "answerable style," and in *Paradise Lost* he tells us how desperate a struggle it was to find it. Keats, Shelley, and Frost use certain passages in which Milton tells of this struggle to lift their lyric voices up into the heroic range, and by "amplify" I refer to this lifting. Earlier uses of Milton in mock-heroic poetry, as by John Dryden (Satan /Achitophel) and Alexander Pope (Lord Hervey/Satan), work to bring down false heroes.

2. Steven Zwicker, "Milton, Dryden, and the Politics of Literary Controversy," in *Heirs of Fame, Milton and Writers of the English Renaissance*, ed. Margo Swiss and David A. Kent (Lewisburg, Pa., 1995), 270–89, esp. 283–87, elegantly exposes the political and personal agenda of Dryden in appropriating *Paradise Lost* and turning it into his opera *The State of Innocence:* far from merely "tagging Milton's verses," Dryden turned them into a piece of royalist propaganda, for which he wrote a preface even more flattering than usual, rhapsodizing about James, Duke of York, and his new bride Mary of Modena. Surprisingly, after showing how Dryden mutated Milton's work to serve precisely those views and political groups opposed by Milton, Zwicker describes this "contest" between Dryden and Milton as, on Dryden's part, "adaptation and admiration," and Milton's response as "envy and denial" (270). For a different view of the Milton/Dryden rivalry, see Nicholas von Maltzahn, "Dryden's Milton and the Theatre of Imagination," in *John Dryden: Tercentenary Essays*, ed. Paul Hammond and David Hopkins (Oxford, 2000), 32–56.

3. In the 1688 edition of *Paradise Lost*, beneath the portrait of Milton that served as frontispiece, Dryden's well-known epigram on Milton by Dryden was printed (without his name on it: his authorship was first acknowledged in a 1716 edition of the *Sixth Part of Miscellany Poems*):

Three poets, in three distant ages born,
Greece, Italy, and England did adorn.
The first in loftiness of thought surpass'd,
The next in majesty, in both the last:
The force of Nature could no farther go;
To make a third, she join'd the former two.

Quoted here from George R. Noyes, *The Poetical Works of Dryden* (Boston, 1950), 253.

4. For the growth of Milton's reputation, see John Shawcross, *John Milton, The Critical Heritage*, vol. 1, *1628–1731* (London, 1970); see also Kay Gilliland Stevenson, "Reading Milton, 1674–1800," in *A Companion to Milton*, ed. Thomas Corns (Oxford, 2001), 447–62. Already in 1685 we can see through Dryden's reluctant praise that Milton was idolized: "It is as much commendation as a man can bear, to own him excellent; all beyond it is idolatry." Others, more generous, evidently agreed with the 1694 judgment of Milton's nephew Edward Phillips that *Paradise Lost* was "the Noblest ['Heroick Poem'] in the general esteem of Learned and Judicious Persons, of any yet written by an other Ancient or Modern." Daniel Defoe could remark in 1711 that the poem "passes with a general Reputation for the greatest, best, and most sublime work now in the English tongue." Voltaire, in 1727, refers to it as "the noblest work, which human Imagination hath ever attempted" (Shawcross, 94, 103–04, 146, 249). Nothing by Dryden received that kind of praise, and by the time he died in 1700, even Dryden knew how far short he fell of deserving it.

5. See David Hopkins, "Milton and the Classics," in *John Milton, Life, Writing, Reputation*, ed. Paul Hammond and Blair Worden (Oxford, 2010), 23–42, particularly his discussion (32–41) of "critical insights that can be inferred from the Miltonic echoes in the classical translations of...John Dryden and Alexander Pope."

6. Alexander Pope, *Epistle to Dr. Arbuthnot*, 317–31, in *The Norton Anthology of English Literature: Major Authors*, 3rd ed., ed. M. H. Abrams (New York, 1975), 1195.

7. John Milton, *Paradise Lost*, ed. Barbara K. Lewalski (Oxford, 2007), book 4, lines 797–809; hereafter cited in the text.

8. See Nicholas von Maltzahn, "Milton: Nation and Reception," in *Early Modern Nationalism and Milton's England*, ed. David Loewenstein and Paul Stevens (Toronto, 2008), 401–42, esp. 430–42.

9. See Peter Kitson, "Milton: The Romantics and After," in Corns, *A Companion to Milton*, 463–80; and David Fairer, "Milton and the Romantics," in Hammond and Worden, *John Milton*, 147–65. Meg Harris Williams, *Inspiration in Milton and Keats* (London, 1982),

devotes a chapter (143–52) to a comparative discussion of "Ode to a Nightingale" and *Paradise Lost* 3.1–156, noting that in both Milton and Keats, "The poet who listens 'darkling' is...identified with the nightingale who sings 'darkling'" (147–48). She mentions also Milton's use of the word "unpremeditated" (chapter 4, 96–102; see esp. 86–90); but of course—since her concern is with Milton and Keats—she does not mention Shelley's use of that word. See also Lucy Newlyn, *"Paradise Lost" and the Romantic Reader* (Oxford, 1992); and Joseph Crawford, *Raising Milton's Ghost: John Milton and the Sublime of Terror in the Early Romantic Period* (London, 2011).

10. For outward dangers Milton faced in 1660–61, see Barbara Lewalski, *The Life of John Milton*, rev. ed. (Oxford, 2003), chap. 12, esp. 398–415.

11. In a wider context the later poets, like Milton, were indeed elbowing other poets. Certainly they are constructing their ancestry, choosing their father, naming their brother. And the Milton constructed as father or brother by Frost, or Shelley, or Keats, need not be the father or brother whom others—Wordsworth, Byron, or Pope—would have hologrammed. Nor, for that matter, is the Milton of Keats's lyric "Ode to a Nightingale" quite the same as the Milton of Keats's epic *Hyperion*—to whom critics have given most attention—or the simple Milton of Keats's saccharine early sonnet, "To One Who Has Been Long in City Pent."

12. See Williams, *Inspiration in Milton and Keats*, 143–52. In May 1819 Keats had lately been reading closely both Milton and Shakespeare, and since "darkling" occurs not only in *Paradise Lost* but (as Williams discusses) in *Midsummer Night's Dream* 2.02.86, *King Lear* 1.04.217, and *Antony and Cleopatra* 4.15.10, its Shakespearean contexts are worth exploring; but I focus here on the Miltonic and not the Shakespearean dimension of Keats.

13. Keats dropped *Hyperion* with the remark that what was life to Milton was death to him—but he could have said the same of Shakespeare, considering that his try at Shakespearean tragedy was much less impressive than his attempt at Miltonic epic: *Hyperion* is one hell of a "failure." And see Fairer, "Milton and the Romantics," 163–64, for commentary that makes use of Keats's annotations to his edition of *Paradise Lost* to discuss the shift from *Hyperion* to *The Fall of Hyperion*.

14. For the Greek text and a prose English translation of the *Hymn to Hermes*, see the Loeb Classical Library edition: *Homeric Hymns, Homeric Apocrypha, Lives of Homer*, ed. and trans. Martin L. West (Cambridge, Mass., 2003), 112–59. For Shelley's fluent (almost

Byronic) ottava rima translation of the *Hymn to Hermes* (which—as usual in Shelley's time—he called *Hymn to Mercury*), see *The Poems of Shelley*, vol. 3, *1819–1820*, ed. Jack Donovan, Cian Duffy, Kelvin Everest, and Michael Rossington with the assistance of Laura Barlow (Harlow, 2011), 508–43; poems by Shelley are from this edition and hereafter cited in the text.

15. Apposite here is the view of Zwicker, "Milton, Dryden," that Milton wrote *Paradise Regained* (1671) as a "challenge to the form, style, and ethos of the heroic drama, to its theoretical defense of the form, and to Dryden's astonishing career as the central protagonist of a new literary culture, its laureate, a commercial and critical success beyond anything that Milton had experienced or could now hope to achieve" (272). As we see in *Paradise Lost* 9.13–33, Milton in 1667 was already addressing the question of what a truly "heroic argument" must be, thinking forward (I believe) to *Paradise Regained*. As for Dryden's challenge, by the time of Joseph Addison and the early Pope, Milton was esteemed as much the greater writer, though Zwicker's phrasing points to what many royalist coffeehouse critics perhaps thought (or what royalists hoped they would think) as of 1671 or so. Milton no doubt recognized Dryden's ambition to outdo him, and fought his literary corner accordingly, in the last few years of his life: "You may tag my verses," his reputed answer to Dryden's request for license to appropriate *Paradise Lost* for his opera *The State of Innocence*, sounds faintly amused—Muhammad Ali to Norman Mailer, as it were.

16. Shelley used "unpremeditated" only three times: once in "To a Skylark" (line 5), and twice in his translation of the Homeric *Hymn to Mercury*, line 69 (stanza 9, line 6) and line 590 (stanza 75, line 2). All three uses of "unpremeditated" are noted by the editors of *The Poems of Shelley*, who comment: "Milton's *Paradise Lost* ix 20–4 had attached to the word the sense of authentic inspiration as spontaneously given"; they note that "S. seems also to be recalling the morning worship of Adam and Eve in *Paradise Lost* v 146–50," and add, "Cp. also *Hymn to Mercury*...69–70...and 590" (3:470–71). They cite also discussion of the *Hymn* by Timothy Webb in *The Violet in the Crucible: Shelley and Translation* (Oxford, 1976), 70–79, 112.

17. See *The Poems of Shelley*, 3:508–10. Richard Holmes, *Shelley: The Pursuit* (New York, 1974), 598–601, notes that Shelley was translating the *Hymn to Mercury* in the summer of 1820, in the same period he was writing "To a Skylark" and "The Cloud." Near the time he wrote "To a Skylark," he obtained and read Keats's 1820 *Lamia, Isabella, The Eve of St. Agnes, and Other Poems*, which included the "Ode to a Nightingale"—of whose twilight singer Shelley's skylark

seems a conscious counterpart; a copy of Keats's 1820 poems was recovered from Shelley's jacket pocket when his drowned body washed ashore (Holmes, *Shelley*, 730).

18. In 1814–18 Shelley had been fighting to obtain his own inheritance, which his father Sir Timothy was trying hard keep him from getting: for details, see Holmes, *Shelley*. Did Shelley identify with Hermes, not only as inspired singer but also as trickster/robber who used all his wiles to get some of the family wealth that Father Zeus had given to Apollo, half–brother of Hermes?

19. Robert Frost, "Beech," "Sycamore," "The Subverted Flower," "The Most of It," and "Never Again Would Birds' Song Be the Same," in *The Poetry of Robert Frost*, ed. Edward Connery Lathem (New York: Henry Holt, 1975). All quotations of Frost's poems in this essay are from this volume, hereafter cited in the text by line number and reprinted with permission.

20. For Frost's afflictions in 1935–42, see Jay Parini, *Robert Frost: A Life* (London, 1998), chapters 16 and 17, esp. 293–310, 328–32, 334–43.

21. See Richard Poirier, *Robert Frost: The Work of Knowing* (Stanford, 1990), 159–72; W. H. Pritchard, *Robert Frost: A Literary Life Reconsidered*, 2nd ed. (Oxford, 1993), 227–39; and Robert Faggen, *The Cambridge Introduction to Robert Frost* (Cambridge, 2008), 128–33.

22. Parini, *Robert Frost*, says of "Beech": "The poem is founded, literally, on the tree that marked the boundaries of the Homer Noble farm, an old sugar maple marred by a spike, situated near a rock cairn that delineated the poet's property" (340). This fails to recognize that Frost's poem specifies both a witness tree (as in Luke 19:1–4, the sycamore or fig tree that Zaccheus climbed, "our Lord to see") and (as in Gen. 31:43–54) a pile of stones placed as a witness.

23. By this time no reader should be startled to notice that Dante's *selva selvaggia* is just around the corner, and that Frost's poem, like the opening lines of Dante's *Inferno*, marks his own midlife crisis.

24. For a succinct account of these years in Frost's life, see Pritchard, *Frost*, 213–34; for detailed study, Donald Sheehy, "(Re)Figuring Love: Robert Frost in Crisis, 1938–1942," *New England Quarterly* (1990): 179–231.

25. A key belief of Frost's was that human speech does have such a tone, and the true poet is able to catch and word his poems to carry this: the sonnet's Adamic speaker tells us that the birds have done precisely what every true poet's task is to do. Frost gave a clear, succinct account of his "theory of versification" in a July 4, 1913, letter to his friend John T. Bartlett (Poirier and Richardson, *Frost*, 664–66). Rachel Buxton, *Robert Frost and Irish Poets* (Oxford, 2004), shows

that Seamus Heaney, Paul Muldoon, Mebh McGuckian, Eavan Boland, and Ciaran Carson, among others, knew and were influenced by this sound/sense theoretic of Frost's, valued his poems and made frequent allusive use of them, and drew far more on Frost than on T. S. Eliot, Ezra Pound, Wallace Stevens, or other "modernist" American poets.

26. Gordon Campbell and Thomas Corns, *John Milton: Life, Work, and Thought* (Oxford, 2008), 374–75.

Notes to Falconer, "Is There Freedom Afterwards?"

1. See John Carey, "A Work in Praise of Terrorism? September 11 and *Samson Agonistes*," *Times Literary Supplement*, Sept. 6, 2002, 15–16; Stanley Fish, "Condemnation without Absolutes," *New York Times*, Oct. 15, 2001, A19; and "Postmodern Warfare: The Ignorance of Our Warrior Intellectuals," *Harper's* (July 2002): 33–40. My thanks to Lukas Erne for this reference.

2. I first compared Milton and DeLillo in "Heterochronic Representations of the Fall: Bakhtin, Milton, DeLillo," in *Bakhtin's Theory of the Literary Chronotope: Reflections, Applications, Perspectives*, ed. Nele Bemong, Pieter Borghart, Michel De Dobbeleer, Kristoffel Demoen, and Koen De Temmerman (Gent, Belgium, 2010). While some points of comparison are repeated here, the earlier essay draws on Bakhtin's theory of "heterochrony" (mixed chronotopes) to compare the novelistic and epic aspects of both works, while the present essay finds affinities between the two authors' ideas of freedom and insight in the context of historical belatedness.

3. In private correspondence with the author, via his literary agent, DeLillo confirmed that the painting he had in mind was the *Natura morta* (1956), housed in the Museo Morandi, Bologna (fax/e-mail, June 1, 2011).

4. Don DeLillo, *Falling Man: A Novel* (New York, 2007), 49; hereafter cited in the text.

5. Friedrich Nietzsche, *Thus Spoke Zarathustra*, trans. R. J. Hollingdale (Harmondsworth, 1969), 159–63.

6. BBC Radio Four, News and Papers, Dec. 6, 2009. René Girard, *The Scapegoat* (*Le bouc émissaire*), trans. Y. Freccero (Baltimore, 1986). See also Girard, *Violence and the Sacred* (*La violence et le sacré*), trans. P. Gregory (Baltimore, 1977); *"To double business bound": Essays on Literature, Mimesis and Anthropology* (Baltimore, 1978); *A Theatre of Envy: William Shakespeare* (New York, 1991).

7. Many New Yorkers also remembered W. H. Auden's poem, "September 1, 1939" (*Selected Poems*, ed. Edward Mendelson [London,

2009]), which was written in New York, at the outbreak of World War I, especially these lines:
> Into this neutral air
> Where blind skyscrapers use
> Their full height to proclaim
> The strength of Collective Man,
> Each language pours its vain
> Competitive excuse:
> But who can live for long
> In an euphoric dream;
> Out of the mirror they stare,
> Imperialism's face
> And the international wrong.   (34–44)

8. W. J. T. Mitchell, "Vital Signs / Cloning Terror," in *What Do Pictures Want? The Lives and Loves of Images* (Chicago, 2005), 5–27.

9. See Milton, *The Readie and Easie Way to Establish a Free Commonwealth* (1660), ed. Robert Ayers, in *The Complete Prose Works of John Milton*, 8 vols., ed. Don M. Wolfe et al. (London, 1953–82), 7:340–88 (hereafter cited as YP), and Rachel Falconer, *Orpheus Dis(re)membered: Milton and the Myth of a Poet-hero* (Sheffield, 1996).

10. "When God gave him reason, he gave him freedom to choose, for reason is but choosing; he had bin else a meer artificiall *Adam*, such an *Adam* as he is in the motions" (Milton, *Areopagitica* [1644], YP 2:527).

11. John Milton, *Paradise Lost* (1667), ed. Alastair Fowler (London, 1998); hereafter cited in the text. See also Neil Forsyth's discussion of "therefore" in this passage, in *The Satanic Epic* (Princeton, 2003), 12–17.

12. Edward Casey, *Imagining: A Phenomenological Study* (Bloomington, Ind., 2000), 233. Casey's emphasis on the autonomy of the mental act of imagining bears some resemblance to Immanuel Kant's transcendental imagination, which also involves the mind in "free play." For Kant, too, imagining is understood as a form of thinking; hence his description of art as the embodiment of "the harmonious interplay between imagination and understanding." See Kant, *Critique of Judgment*, trans. J. C. Meredith (Oxford, 1952), 244. Kearney analyzes this passage in *The Wake of Imagination: Ideas of Creativity in Western Culture* (London, 1988), 171–77.

13. For readings of Milton sympathetic to Blake's idea that the earlier poet was "of the Devil's party," see especially William Empson, *Milton's God* (London, 1961), and more recently, Forsyth, *Satanic Epic*. For a judicious and comprehensive appraisal of Milton's antihero in the

context of mid-seventeenth-century politics, see Sharon Achinstein, *Milton and the Revolutionary Reader* (Princeton, N.J., 1994).

14. Samuel Johnson, "Milton," *Lives of the Poets* (1779), in *Norton Anthology*, 8th ed., vol. C, *The Restoration and the Eighteenth Century*, ed. Lawrence Lipking and James Noggle (New York, 2006).

15. William Blake, "Milton a Poem" (object 14, lines 9–11), copy A c. 1811 (British Museum), accessed Dec. 3, 2009, www.blakearchive.org.

16. Jean-Paul Sartre, *Les jeux sont faits* (1947), ed. M. Storer (London, 1956).

17. Casey, *Imagining*, 232.

18. There is a case to be made for the narrator of the prose Arguments being distinct from the epic narrator; some critics refer to the prose narrator as "Milton" or "the authorial voice" to emphasize his distance from the dramatized epic narrator. But I prefer to regard them both as dramatized narrators, and perhaps the same narratorial voice, since the narrator of the Arguments is not self-consistent, but rather shifts his position to reflect the perspective of the epic narrator which, as has been often noted, changes and develops over the course of the epic.

19. On Milton and Galileo, see Angus Fletcher, *Time, Space and Motion in the Age of Shakespeare* (Cambridge, Mass., 2007), 130–51. On Adam developing inward vision, see Joanna Picciotto, *Labors of Innocence in Early Modern England* (Cambridge, Mass., 2010), 400–19. I am grateful to the learned *Milton Studies* reader who reviewed my manuscript for these references, as well as the reference to the Argument of book 10.

20. Milton, "A Note on the Verse," added to the fourth issue of the first edition, in 1668. See *Paradise Lost*, ed. Fowler, 54–55.

21. Milton's account of the fall of the rebel angels derives largely from Hesiod's *Theogony* 664–735 since, as Fowler comments, "there was scant biblical authority" (ibid., 62). Fowler cites P. J. Gallagher, *English Literary History* 9 (1979): 121–28.

22. Homer, *Iliad*, trans. Richmond Lattimore (Chicago, 1951), 1:591–95.

23. Stanley Fish, *Surprised by Sin: The Reader in "Paradise Lost"* (Berkeley and Los Angeles, 1971), 37.

24. Forsyth, *Satanic Epic*, 105–07, interestingly reads these lines as a sign of the unreliability of the epic narrator. He thus sides with Fish, insofar as he believes a rebuke to the implied reader is intended, but in Forsyth's reading it is not Milton who corrects us, merely the limited narrator.

25. John Carey, *Milton* (London, 1969). Fowler (384) notes the echoes of Job 6:4 and Isaiah 51:20 in this passage. Both passages are about

human beings (not Satan or devils) suffering punishments inflicted by God.

26. For an in-depth discussion of this passage, and the theological controversy behind it, see Dennis Danielson, *Milton's Good God: A Study in Literary Theodicy* (Cambridge, 2009). For Milton's relation to other religious dissenters in the mid-seventeenth century, see Sharon Achinstein, *Literature and Dissent in Milton's England* (Cambridge, 2003).

27. Viktor E. Frankl, *Man's Search for Meaning: An Introduction to Logotherapy* (New York, 1962), 86.

28. Claude Lévi-Strauss, *Tristes tropiques* (New York, 1971). This passage is cited by Kearney, *Wake of Imagination*, 441n42. Kearney later paraphrases Lévi-Strauss on the "cathartic power of play to make what is impossible at the empirical level of existence possible at a symbolic level" (367–68).

29. In *Players* (1977), DeLillo creates a character who works in the north tower of the World Trade Center for a firm called the Grief Management Council, located there, as she says, because "where else would you stack all this grief?" This novel begins with characters in an airplane, watching the film of a terrorist massacre. In *White Noise* (New York, 1985), DeLillo imagines an apocalypse following what he obliquely refers to as an "airborne toxic event." And in *Mao II* (New York, 1991), he transports his readers from a mass cult wedding in Yankee Stadium, New York, to terrorist atrocities in Beirut.

30. Erik Martiny, "'A Darker Longing': Shades of Nihilism in Contemporary Terrorist Fiction," in *Ian McEwan: Art and Politics*, ed. Pascal Nicklas (Heidelberg, 2009), 159–72.

31. Richard Drew, "Falling Man," photograph taken for Associated Press, Sept. 11, 2001. The journalist Tom Junod later made his search for the identity of the man in Drew's photograph into a TV documentary (he was unsuccessful in identifying the victim). In his review of DeLillo's novel, Junod was sharply critical of what he regarded as the effacement of the real person in the photograph; see Tom Junod, "Falling Man," *Esquire* (Sept. 2003), accessed March 28, 2012, www.esquire.com/features/esq0903-sep_fallingman.

32. W. J. T. Mitchell was reported to comment that "after the initial reception of the images of 9/11, I think there was a kind of revulsion against recycling them endlessly, especially the images of falling bodies. It is as if the visual horror of the event was so overwhelming that its exploitation became a kind of pornography." Mitchell, interview with Margriet Schavemaker, *Metropolis M*, Oct. 23, 2008, accessed March 28, 2012, metropolism.com/features/interview-with-w.j.t.mitchell.

33. Adam Mars-Jones, "As His World Came Tumbling Down," *Observer*, May 13, 2007, accessed March 28, 2012, www.guardian.co.uk/books/2007/may/13/fiction.dondelillo.

34. Linda S. Kauffman, "World Trauma Center," *American Literary History* 21, no. 3 (2009): 652.

35. David Simpson, *9/11: The Culture of Commemoration* (Chicago, 2006). See also Cathy Caruth, *Unclaimed Experience: Trauma, Narrative and History* (Baltimore, 1996); and E. Ann Kaplan, *Trauma Culture: The Politics of Terror and Loss in Media and Literature* (Piscataway, N.J., 2005). Simpson and Kaplan are cited by Kauffman in "World Trauma Center," 652. Other examples of 9/11 fiction include Martin Amis, "The Last Days of Muhammad Atta," a fiction essay published in the *Observer*, Sept. 3, 2006; Frederic Beigbeder, *Windows on the World* (London, 2003); Paul Greengrass, dir., *United 93* (film, 2006); Jay McInerney, *The Good Life* (New York, 2006); Jonathan Safran Foer, *Extremely Loud and Incredibly Close* (Boston, 2005); and Art Spiegelman's graphic novel, *In The Shadow of No Towers* (New York, 2004). DeLillo's novel has also been compared to J. M. Coetzee's *Slow Man* (London, 2005) (see Martiny, "A Darker Longing").

36. Frederic Jameson articulates much stronger objections to trauma theory in "The Dialectics of Disaster," in *Dissent from the Homeland: Essays after September 11*, ed. S. Hauerwas and F. Lentricchia, special issue of *South Atlantic Quarterly* 101 (Spring 2002): 297–304.

37. Like other hells, DeLillo's here appears to be governed by a chronotope of arrested time and verticalized space. See Mikhail Bakhtin, "Forms of Time and of the Chronotope," in *The Dialogic Imagination: Four Essays*, ed. Michael Holquist, trans. Caryl Emerson and Michael Holquist (Austin, 1981), 157. See Rachel Falconer, "Chronotopes of Hell," in Falconer, *Hell in Contemporary Literature* (Edinburgh, 2005), 42–62.

38. Just as, in a contrastingly tranquil scene, the villagers fail to notice the fall of Icarus in Pieter Brueghel's *Landscape with the Fall of Icarus*. Cf. also Brueghel's *The Fall of the Rebel Angels*; and as a commentary on the former painting, W. H. Auden's brilliant poem, "Musée des Beaux Arts" (1940), in *Selected Poems*.

39. For Casey (*Imagining*, 59), imagination includes an "act phase" (imaging, imagining-that, and imagining-how), and an "object phase" (content of the image, imaginal margin, and its mode of givenness).

40. Gilles Deleuze, *Cinéma I: L'image-movement* (Paris, 1983), 284. Richard Kearney discusses Deleuze's "thinking image" in *Wake of Imagination*, 329–32.

41. Kearney, *Wake of Imagination*, 389.

42. A journalist asked Stockhausen how he related the events of September 11 to his own opera cycle, "Light: The Seven Days of the Week," which features three archetypal characters: Michael, Lucifer, and Eve. He replied, "what happened there is, of course—now all of you must adjust your brains—the biggest work of art there has ever been. The fact that spirits achieve with one act something which we in music could never dream of, that people practice ten years madly, fanatically for a concert. And then die. [Hesitantly.] And that is the greatest work of art that exists for the whole Cosmos.... Compared to that, we are nothing, as composers.... It is a crime, you know of course, because the people did not agree to it." "'Huuuh!' Das Pressegespräch am 16. September 2001 im Senatszimmer des Hotel Atlantic in Hamburg," *MusikTexte* 91 (2001): 76–77. See Stockhausen's response to the publication of his remarks, which he insisted were seriously misinterpreted: www.stockhausen.org/message_from_karlheinz.html, accessed Dec. 6, 2009.

43. Claude Lévi-Strauss, *Tristes tropiques* (New York, 1971). This passage is cited by Kearney, *Wake of Imagination*, 441n42. Kearney later paraphrases Lévi-Strauss on the "cathartic power of play to make what is impossible at the empirical level of existence possible at a symbolic level" (367–68).

44. Paul Celan, "Death Fugue," in *Poems of Paul Celan*, trans. M. Hamburger (London, 1988).

45. Andrew Gormley, "Event Horizon," sculpture installations (London, 2007).

INDEX

Abdiel, 154–57
Abraham, 50, 134–35, 143–45
ac, 5–6
active intellect, 85
Adam: blame for, 41–42; companionship for, 225–29, 232; description of, 189–90, 191; divorce and natural law and, 70–71; gender hierarchy and, 44, 104–05; imagined pilgrimage of, 128–34; lot of, 101–02; marriage and, 42–43, 46–48, 59–67, 72–79; positive law and, 79–99; proportionality and, 113–17, 121–23; titles and, 48–59; wandering of, 138–46
Addison, Joseph, 41–42, 48, 185, 186–88, 269n45
address, terms of, 48–59, 266n29, 267nn32–35
Aeneid (Virgil), 33
agency, 89–90, 92, 95, 109, 245–46
Ainsworth, Henry, 195
Alberti, Leon Battisti, 33
Alexander, John, 121
allusion: in *Lycidas*, 30; to Scripture in *De doctrina Christiana*, 10–13
Alsop, Vincent, 108
Alsted, Johann Heinrich, 281n32
altars, 131
Ames, William, 7, 85, 258n7, 273n19
architectural design, 32–37
Areopagitica (Milton), 129, 169, 301n44
Aristotle, 185–87, 189, 191, 298n14, 301n47
arithmetical proportion, 120–21, 123
Arnold, Elias, 292n22
art, horror and, 251
Ascham, Anthony, 82–83
Attridge, Derek, 22, 259n2
Auden, W. H., 307n7
Augustine, 146
authority, of husbands, 45, 62–65
autonomy, 89–90, 95

Bale, John, 292n22
banner, 165, 170, 295n46

Banners of the Parliamentary Army, in the time of Charles I, with the Arms of the Captains, 171
Barker, A. E., 24
Beardsley, Monroe, 183
"Beech" (Frost), 220–22, 223, 306n22
Belial, 111, 241
Bellarmine, Robert, 160–61, 162
Bennett, Joan, 64, 264n4
Bentley, Richard, 184, 185, 188–93, 199
Bernard, Richard, 292n22
Bible: English commentaries on, 300n36; scholars of, 194–96, 199–200, 201; understanding, 197; *A Witness Tree* and, 220–22
biblical hermeneutics, 185
Blake, William, 127, 128, 240
blank verse, 242
Bodin, Jean, 119
Book of Common Prayer, 153, 161
Book of Sir John Mandeville, The, 127
Bordeaux pilgrim, 132
boundaries, 221–22
Braun, Friederike, 266n29
Brightman, Thomas, 167, 168
Brooks, Cleanth, 196–97
building, 32–37
Bunyan, John, 130, 145
Burroughs, Edward, 296n47
Butler, Samuel, 37

Caird, George, 10
Campbell, Gordon, 32–33
canonization of Milton, 205–06
Carey, John, 3, 245
Carter, Thomas, 45, 265n11, 270n50
Casey, Edward, 239, 248, 308n12, 311n39
catastrophes: Kearney on images of, 251; perception and responses to, 236–39
Catholic Church, 160–62, 176
celestial war. *See* war in heaven
chance, 112
Chaos, 280n30
Charles I, 173, 178, 263n40
Charles II, 174

Christ Militant, 163
citizens' rights and citizenship, 80–81, 273n19
classical literary criticism, 186–93
classicization of Milton, 205–06
Cleaver, Robert, 49
clergymen, lot and inheritance of, 105–09
clerus, 105
Cleveland, John, 170
close reading, 182–85
commands, in positive law, 86–87, 91
commutative justice, 121
companionship, 225–29, 232
composition, Miltonic, 32–37
conduct literature, 265n14
conscience, liberty of, 65–66
Constantine, 132–33, 168
construction, 32–37
contingency, 108–09, 111–13
Copley, Lionel, 295n46
Cotterill, Henry, 21
Cranmer, Thomas, 168
Creaser, John, 259n2, 260n13
Cromwell, Oliver, 170–79, 296nn51–52
Cromwell, Thomas, 168
Crowley, Robert, 265n14

Daines, Simon, 19
Danielson, Dennis, 276n44
Dante, 306n23
"darkling," 209–11, 213
Davies, Sir John, 272n14
De civilitate morum puerilium (Erasmus), 49, 265n14
De doctrina Christiana (Milton): allusion to Scripture in, 10–13; celestial and sublunary wars in, 149, 169, 178; editions of, 3–4; epistolary approach to, 7–9; etymological proof in, 13–15; linguistic or philological approach to, 4–7; lots in, 107–08; marriage and divorce in, 74; positive law and, 79–80
Defoe, Daniel, 303n4
Dekker, Thomas, 267n35
Deleuze, Gilles, 248–49
DeLillo, Don. See *Falling Man* (DeLillo)
Dent, Arthur, 130, 292n23
Devereux, Robert, third Earl of Essex, 170
discipleship, 135–38
divorce: Milton on, 45–46, 60; natural law and, 70–79; positive law and, 79–99
Doctrine and Discipline of Divorce, The (Milton), 74–77, 271n12, 273n16
Dod, John, 49
Donne, John, 261n15
Drew, Richard, 247, 310n31

Dryden, John, 205, 302n1, 302n2, 302n3, 303n4, 305n15
dulia, 162, 166
Du Moulin, Pierre, 292n23

Eagleton, Terry, 297n7, 298n8
Edwards, Philip, 143
Egeria, 131–32
Elements of Architecture (Wotton), 34
Eliot, T. S., 182, 299n24
Elizabeth I, 168
Embleme of Englands Distractions, The (Faithorne), 174–77
Empson, William, 183, 184, 187, 298nn9–10
English civil wars, 151, 167–79
epistles: pastoral, 10; of Paul, 7–9, 11–13
Epistle to Dr. Arbuthnot (Pope), 206–08
equality and inequality: lots and, 102–04, 113–17; of men and women, 43–45, 54–55, 65, 104–05; pre- and postlapsarian, 117–19; in social relationships, 119–23
Erasmus, Desiderius, 49, 265n14
erring, 244
Essex, Robert Devereux, third Earl of, 170
et, 5–6
Eve: blame for, 41–42; as companion, 225–29, 232; description of, 190–91; divorce and natural law and, 70–71; gender hierarchy and, 44, 104–05; lot of, 101–02; marriage and, 42–43, 46–48, 59–67, 72–79, 268n43; positive law and, 79–99; proportionality and, 119–23; temptation of, 113–14; titles and, 48–59; wandering of, 138–46
"Event Horizon" (Gormley), 254
exile, 143, 288n61
Explanatory Notes and Remarks on "Paradise Lost" (Richardson), 193
extraordinary lots, 109–10

Fabri, Felix, 136
Faithorne, William, 174–77
Fall: blame for, 41–42; effect of, on marriage, 77–78; gender hierarchy and, 104–05; justice preceding, 121; as narrative of descent, 239–46; positive law and, 90–99; as sin of theft, 80, 83–85
Falling Man (DeLillo): and Fall as narrative of descent, 239–46; intertextuality of, 246–47; narrative of, 247–53; *Paradise Lost* and, 235–36, 253–55; and responding to disaster, 236–39
Fall of the Rebel Angels, The (Rubens), 155–57

Index   315

Fallon, Stephen, 72
fate, contingency and, 108–09, 111–12
feet, 127
Fish, Stanley, 31, 144, 150, 243–44, 277n47, 288n55
food, sharing, 134–35
footprints, 127, 135–36
fornication, 271n7
Forsyth, Neil, 23, 31, 309n24
fountains, as holy sites, 132
Fowler, Alastair, 134, 140, 146, 270n48, 287n50
Fox, George, 172
Foxe, John, 141
Franciscus Junius, 33
Frankl, Viktor, 246
freedom, recovering, 235–36, 238
free will, 89–90, 92, 95, 109, 245–46
Frost, Robert, 209, 220–34, 302n1, 306n25
Fuller, Thomas, 20–21
Further narrative of the passages of these times in the Common-wealth of England, A, 173

Gabriel, lots and, 109–11
Gataker, Thomas, 106–07, 108
gender hierarchy: lots and, 104–05; marriage and, 43–45, 54–65; Rogers on, 266n23; terms of address and, 266n23, 267nn33–35. *See also* hierarchies, lots and
geometrical proportion, 120–21
George, Saint, 295n45
Gill, Alexander, 19, 259n8
Gillespie, George, 106
Girard, René, 237
God: lots as will of, 102–03, 105–09, 117–19; property of, 80, 83–85; speeches of, in celestial war, 162–64; vision of, 135–37
Gormley, Andrew, 254
Gouge, William: on husbandly authority, 63, 64–65; on marital hierarchy, 61, 62; on marriage, 43; on subjection, 45; on submission of wives, 64; on terms of address in marriage, 50–52
Gregory of Nyssa, 137–38
Grossman, Marshall, 238n42
Grotius, Hugo, 81–82
Guillory, John, 183
Guylforde, Sir Richard, 131

hairesis, 13, 14–15
Hall, Donald, 260n14
Haller, Malleville, 43, 47
Haller, William, 43, 47
Hammond, Henry, 201
Hawkins, Francis, 265n14
Headlam, James Wycliffe, 277n2

Heavenly Foot-Man (Bunyan), 145
Hephaestus, 243–45
heresy, 14–15
hierarchies, lots and, 103–04. *See also* gender hierarchy
Hill, Christopher, 294n34
Hobbes, Thomas, 118–19
Holland, Hezekiah, 292n23
Hollander, John, 261n20
Holy Land, 127–28, 131–32, 135–36
holy sites, 131, 132
Homer, 187
Horace, 185–86
horror, art and, 251
Housman, A. E., 188
Howe, Irving, 188, 299n24
Hughes, Lewes, 153, 157
Hume, Patrick, 300n32
Hutchinson, Lucy, 173–74
Hymn to Mercury, 217–18

Il mondo creato (Tasso), 25
imagination, transcendental, 308n12
imagining, Casey on, 248, 311n39
imperfections, reformation and, 35–36
inequality. *See* equality and inequality
influence of Milton: on Frost, 220–34; introduction to, 205–06; on Keats, 209–14; on Pope, 206–09; on Shelley, 214–20
intellectus agens, 85
invention, Miltonic, 32–37
Israel, 145
Israelite tribes, 117–19
ius gentium, 272n14

Jackson, Thomas, 108–09, 121
Jacob, 220–21, 222
Jarvis, Simon, 37
Jerome, Saint, 133, 285n31
Jesus Christ: exaltation of, 164–67; footprints of, 135–36; Michael and, 152–53, 157–59, 178, 290n12, 291n13; in war in heaven, 153–55, 291n14
Johnson, Samuel, 17, 240
Junius, Franciscus, 33
Junod, Tom, 310n31

Kahn, Victoria, 103
Kant, Immanuel, 308n12
Kauffman, Linda, 247
Kearney, Richard, 251, 310n28, 312n43
Keats, John, 209–14, 302n1, 304n9, 304nn11–13
Keeble, N. H., 145
Keightley, Thomas, 18
Kelley, Maurice, 3–4, 7–8
Kennedy, George, 298n14
Key of the Revelation, The (Mede), 168
Kietzman, Mary Jo, 269n45

Knight, G. Wilson, 31
Knoppers, Laura Lunger, 20, 170–72, 296nn51–52

Laban, 220–21, 222
labor, 87–89
Lamb, Charles, 32
language, 301n47
latria, 162, 166
law of nations, 272n14
Lawrence, Henry, 290n6
Lawry, Jon S., 27–28
Leavis, F. R., 182, 299n24
Le Bossu, René, 185–86
Leonard, John, 270n48, 288n54
Lévi-Strauss, Claude, 246, 252, 310n28, 312n43
Lewalski, Barbara, 65, 144
liberty vs. equality, 103, 116
Lieb, Michael, 275n36
literary appreciation, 6–7
literary criticism, *Paradise Lost* and: conclusions on, 202; interpretation in, 193–202; introduction to, 181–85; judgment in, 185–93. *See also Paradise Lost* (Milton)
Loewenstein, David, 178
logic, in literary criticism, 191–92
Longinus, 186, 298n13
lots: gender hierarchy and, 104–05; overview of, 101–04; in *Paradise Lost*, 109–13; pre- and postlapsarian equality and, 117–19; proportionality and, 113–17, 119–23; sixteenth century views on, 278n4; as will of God, 105–09
love, marital, 99
Lucan, 187
Luther, Martin, 195, 197, 301n38
Luxon, Thomas H., 17
Lycidas (Milton): composition of, 32–37; meter of, 19–23; structure of, 17–19; verse paragraph in, 23–32

MacCaffrey, Isabel Gamble, 287n50
MacCallum, Hugh, 269n46
Manchester, Edward Montague, second Earl of, 170
marriage: of Adam and Eve, 268n43; gender hierarchy and, 43–45, 56–59; Milton's ideal for, 60–65; in *Paradise Lost*, 46–48; positive law and, 79–99; as property, 69–79; Rogers on, 266n23; terms of address in, 48–56, 267n32. *See also* divorce
Marshall, David, 185
Mars-Jones, Adam, 247
Matthias, 105–06
McColley, Diane, 42
meal sharing, 134–35

Mede, Joseph, 167, 168–69
meter, 19–24, 261n20
Michael: characterization of, 151–54; Cromwell and, 170–79; English civil wars and, 167–70; introduction to war in heaven and, 147–51; Jesus Christ and, 157–67, 290n12, 291n13; juxtaposition with Abdiel, 154–57; Saint George and, 295n45; Urban VIII and, 293n26
military banner, 165, 170, 295n46
millenarianism, 151, 167–70, 174–78, 294n33
Milton: A Poem (Blake), 127, 128
Mitchell, W. J. T., 238, 310n32
mixed metaphors, 199–200
Il mondo creato (Tasso), 25
Montague, Edward, second Earl of Manchester, 170
morality, in system of hierarchies, 103
Morandi, Giorgio, 236, 237, 238, 239
More, William, 261n16
Mosaic law: divorce under, 73–75, 77; positive law and, 86
Moses, 117–19, 136–37
"Most of It, The" (Frost), 220, 224–27, 232
mountains, as holy sites, 132
Mulciber, 243–45
Muller, Richard A., 300n36

names, as terms of address, 49, 50, 57, 267nn34–35
Naomi, 144
nations, law of, 272n14
natural law: Ascham on, 82–84; divorce and, 70–79; Grotius on, 81–82; positive law and, 79, 86–92, 96–98, 99; Selden on, 85–86
Natura morta (Morandi), 236, 237, 238
nec non, 4–5
"Never Again Would Birds' Song Be the Same" (Frost), 220, 224, 227–29
New Criticism, 182–83, 196, 198, 297n7, 298n8, 299n24
Niccholes, Alexander, 44, 46

obedience, 86–88, 90–91, 92, 123
"Ode to a Nightingale" (Keats), 209–14
"Ode to Liberty" (Shelley), 218–20
On the Sublime (Longinus), 298n13
ordinary lots, 109–10
original sin, 80
overinterpretation, 6–7
Owen, John, 109
ownership. *See* property and possession

Paradise Lost (Milton): Adam's imagined pilgrimage in, 128–29; architectural images in, 36; blame in,

41–42; characterization of Michael in, 151–54; divorce and natural law and, 70–71; English civil wars and, 167–79; equality and proportionality in, 113–17; exaltation of Christ in, 164–67; and Fall as narrative of descent, 239–46; *Falling Man* and, 235–36, 253–55; gender hierarchy and lots in, 104–05; ideal marital behavior in, 46–48; introduction to war in heaven in, 147–51; juxtaposition of Abdiel and Michael in, 154–57; Keats and, 209–10; lots in, 101–04, 109–13; marriage and, 42–43, 59–67, 69–70; Michael and Jesus Christ in, 157–64; natural law and, 86–88; pilgrimage in, 127–28; place pilgrimage in, 130–35; Pope and, 206–08; pre- and postlapsarian equality and, 117–19; proportionality and, 119–23; propriety in marriage and, 72–79; and responding to disaster, 236–39; and rights of spouses and citizens, 81; seventeenth century views on lots and, 105–09; Shelley and, 214–20; titles in, 48–59; vision of God and, 135–38; wandering in, 138–46; *A Witness Tree* and, 223, 224–34. *See also* literary criticism, *Paradise Lost* and
Pareus, David, 292n23
Parini, Jay, 306n22
Parker, Henry, 274n26
Paul, epistles of, 7–9, 11–13
Paulinus of Nola, 133, 136
Pearce, Zachary, 184, 185, 193–94, 195, 202, 298n10
perception, 236–38
peregrini, 288n61
Perkins, William, 45, 46
Phillips, Edward, 258n7, 303n4
pilgrimage: Adam's imagined, 128–29; antagonism toward, 129–30; exile as, 288n61; in *Paradise Lost*, 127–28; place, in *Paradise Lost*, 130–35; vision of God and, 135–38; wandering and, 138–46
Pilgrim's Progress (Bunyan), 130
place, attachment to, 128–29
place pilgrimage, 130–35
Plaine Mans Path-Way to Heaven (Dent), 130
Plato, 121
Poole, Matthew, 195, 199–200
pope, 160–61
Pope, Alexander, 206–09, 302n1
positive law, 70, 71, 79–99
Powell, Mary, 60
Presbyterianism, priestly lot in, 106, 107, 108

primary matter, 25
prohibition, positive law and, 86–87
property and possession: Asham on, 82–84; Fall as sin against, 80; Grotius on, 81–82; marriage as, 69–79, 94, 96; Milton on, 84–85; Selden on, 85–86
proportionality, 113–17, 119–23
Protestantism, 141–42, 145, 159–61, 263n40
Pruitt, Kristin, 269n44
Puritanism, 45–46
purity, 141–42

-*que*, 5–6

Raphael, 157, 158
Rapin, René, 186
raw material, 25
reason, 91–92, 94, 99, 191–92
Reason for Church-Government (Milton), 106
"redress," 182
reformation, Milton on, 35–36
"Religions" (Vaughan), 134–35
repetition, 241–42, 268n41
reproduction, 115
Review of the Text of the Twelve Books of Milton's "Paradise Lost" (Pearce), 193
rhyme: in *Lycidas*, 24, 29–30; in *Paradise Lost*, 242
rhythm: meter and, 19–23, 261n20; verse and, 23–24, 31
Richards, I. A., 183, 297n6
Richardson, Jonathan, 32, 185, 193, 194, 196–202
Riches, Samantha, 295n45
Ricks, Christopher, 141, 182, 201
Rogers, Daniel, 270n52, 270n55
Rogers, John, 266n23, 268n43, 273n17, 277n46
Romans, 7–9, 11–13
Rosenblatt, Jason P., 93, 273n15, 279n11
Rubens, Peter Paul, 155–57
Rumrich, John, 36
Ruth, 144

Sabbath, marriage and, 79–80
saints, 294n34
Saintsbury, George, 260n9
St. Michael Confounding the Devil (Raphael), 158
Sanhedrin, 117–18
Sarah (wife of Abraham), 50, 267n33
Satan: combats with Michael and Abdiel, 154–57; depicted as cleric, 106; description of, 192; fall of, 240–46; as god, 157–59; lots and, 101–02, 110–13; proportionality and, 116–17; tempts Eve, 90–91, 122–23

318 Index

Scaliger, Julius Caesar, 20
scapegoat, 237–38
Schoole of Vertue, The (Crowley), 265n14
Scripture: allusion to, in *De doctrina Christiana*, 10–13; arguments for divorce in, 73–76, 77; reading and understanding, 196–98
secondary law of nature, 77–78, 272n14
Second Defence, The (Milton), 169
Selden, John, 85–86, 118, 274n32
separation, natural law and, 88–90, 91
"September 1, 1939" (Auden), 307n7
September 11, 2001 terrorist attacks. *See Falling Man* (DeLillo)
serpent, 97–98, 277n47
Shakespeare, William, 261n15, 304n12
Shelford, Robert, 109
Shelley, Percy Bysshe, 209, 214–20, 302n1, 305n16, 305n17, 306n18
Sidney, Philip, 33
silence, 6
Smith, Henrie, 44, 45, 60, 61–62
social hierarchy, 81–82
solitude, 225–27, 232
Sommerville, J. P., 274n32
Stephen, Saint (martyr), 222
Stockhausen, Karlheinz, 251, 312n42
stones: as boundaries, 221–22; marking holy sites, 131
Stubbs, Katherine, 51
Stubbs, Philip, 51
subjection, of wives, 44–45, 60–65
"Subverted Flower, The" (Frost), 220, 224, 229–33
Swaim, Kathleen, 269n47
sword of Michael, 154
"Sycamore" (Frost), 220, 221–22

Tannen, Deborah, 268n41
Tasso, Torquato, 20, 24–25
Taylor, John, 170
Tenure of Kings and Magistrates, The (Milton), 81
terms of address, 48–59, 266n29, 267nn32–35
terrorist attacks. *See Falling Man* (DeLillo)
Tetrachordon (Milton): *Doctrine and Discipline of Divorce* and, 271n12; marriage in, 69, 70; natural law and divorce in, 73–76, 77, 96; and rights of spouses and citizens, 81
theft, Fall as sin of, 80, 83–85
Theobald, Francis, 120

Timberlake, Henry, 136, 286n42
titles, 48–59, 266n29, 267nn32–35
"To a Skylark" (Shelley), 216–17
Trachtenburg, Marvin, 33
transcendental imagination, 308n12
"Triple Bronze" (Frost), 223
True and Strange Discourse of the Travailes of Two English Pilgrimes, The (Timberlake), 286n42
true marriage, 76
truth, Milton on uncovering, 301n44
Tuck, Richard, 275n32
Turner, James, 75
Twin Towers. *See* World Trade Center
typological resemblances, 151–52

Ulster, 263n40
"unpremeditated," 214–20, 305n16
Urania, 215
Urban VIII (pope), 293n26

variatio, 5
Vaughan, Henry, 134–35
Virgil, 33
Voltaire, 303n4

Walsh, Marcus, 300n34
wandering, 140–46, 287n50
war, 295n42
war in heaven: arguments against, 292n22; characterization of Michael in, 151–54; English civil wars and, 151, 167–79, 292n23; exaltation of Christ in, 164–67; introduction to, 147–51; Jesus Christ in, 291n14; juxtaposition of Abdiel and Michael in, 154–57; Michael and Jesus Christ in, 157–64
Weismiller, Edward, 17–18
West, Robert H., 293n31
Whately, William, 50, 63–64, 265n17
Williams, Meg Harris, 303n9
Wimsatt, William, 183, 198
Witness Tree, A (Frost), 220–34
Wollebius, Johann, 7, 258n7
World Trade Center, 236–38. *See also Falling Man* (DeLillo)
woman, 59
work, 87–89
Wotton, Henry, 34
Wright, George T., 22

youth, 265n14
Youths Behavior (Hawkins), 265n14

Zwicker, Steven, 302n1, 305n15